SIDDHAS
MASTERS OF NATURE

SIDDHAS
MASTERS OF NATURE

*A journey through the more unknown dimensions
of the Ancient Siddha Path.*

by

Palpandian

Publisher: Palpandian

Siddhas - Masters of Nature
Palpandian

All rights reserved
First Edition, 2008
Second Edition, 2019
© Palpandian, 2019
Cover image © Palpandian
Cover and Interior Design by White Falcon Publishing

No part of this book may be reproduced or transmitted in any form or by any means, electronic or mechanical including photocopying, recording, or by any information storage or retrieval system, without permission. All poems in the book are translations of original Tamil poems written by the ancient Siddhas.

Disclaimer

This book is designed to provide information in regard to the subject matter covered. The purpose of this book is to educate. The author shall have neither liability nor responsibility to any person or entity with respect to any perceived loss or damage caused, directly or indirectly, by the information contained in this book.

Requests for permission should be addressed to
aswatha2008@gmail.com

ISBN - 978-93-5351-093-0

Dedicated

To my parents
Whose love and care reflects as the surrender to my

Guru

*"Realisation is, seeing the Guru's Holy form,
Realisation is, chanting the Guru's Holy name,
Realisation is, hearing the Guru's Holy words,
Realisation is, musing on the Guru's Holy being"*
Thirumanthiram-3000, verse 139,
By Siddha Thirumoolar

ACKNOWLEDGEMENTS

"Siddhas - Masters of Nature" is a journey through the more unknown dimensions of the Ancient Siddha Path. Born from the blessings and guidance of my Masters, it poses a beginning for the world to step into; a first of its kind.

The wisdom put together in the form of this book is a sacred treasure belonging to the ancient divine Sages. To Them, I am profoundly grateful for using me in the divine work of bringing it to the world as a first, in form of this book.

It is always inspiring to see how wisdom breaks all boundaries and attracts seekers from different corners of the world toward it. I have had the pleasure of teaching and sharing my insights with such people who have had the passion and drive to cross boundaries set by culture, society and even language. I am referring to my students hailing from countries other than India. They have opened themselves to the 'different' in the Siddha path and made it their new normal. I appreciate the act of Stephen Grissom (USA) for documenting his personal journey in the Siddha path as "Rivulets of the Absolute". This has, in its own way, widened the spread of this system. Samer Sayyed (Lebanon) has persevered in his contemplation and insight into this tradition and its secrets alongside his Siddha Varma healing practice across two countries. Caroline Jenson (Denmark) has arrived at a clarity and grounding in her field of healing through Siddha Varma and has been sharing this in her own country as well as India. Borbala (Hungary) has been admirably sincere in her Varma applications and continues her practice. She has accomplished the huge task of translating into Hungarian the first edition, Siddhas - Masters of the Basics, which was appreciated and celebrated by the Hungarian embassy. Each of them approached me for their spiritual search and along their inner journey, they learnt from me the healing dimension of the Siddhas. And I am proud of how they are manifesting their Dharma. I appreciate Mr. Volker (Germany) who is actively sharing awareness of the Siddha tradition amongst his group.

My Indian students, over the years, have been doing very well in both, their healing as well as personal journey. I am thankful to Vaidya Sarvanan, Vaidya Rajasekaran, Vaidya Raghuram, Vaidya Shanmugam, Vaidya Ganesan, Dr. and Prof. Joseph and my nephew Rajkumar, who along with their personal journeys have been a tremendous support in organising Siddha workshops, lectures, within India.

I would like to appreciate a few academicians of the Siddha system whose assistance I have been privileged to have through the past few years and I am grateful for their contribution in the spread of the Siddha system. Dr. Jothikumar, Dr. and Prof. Siddhque, Dr. and Prof. Damodaran, Dr. and Prof. Sashikumar, Dr. Bala Subranaian, Dr. Balamurugan, Dr. Mahendran, Dr. Srinivasan, Dr. Sankarbabu, Dr. Panneer, Dr. Gopal, Dr. and Prof. Shanmugapriya, and Dr. and Prof. Baskar. There are several others who continue to participate in the spreading of awareness of the Siddhas in a pivotal way. I extend my gratitude to all of them.

I thank the National Institute of Siddha, Tamil Nadu, and the Siddha College, Chennai, and the Vaidya Sangams of Traditional Siddha practitioners, Tamil Nadu for their support.

Salutations to the Siddhas!!

Stephen Grissom siddhavasihealing.com	USA
Samer Sayyed vasitherapy.com	Lebanon
Caroline Jenson caroline-jenson.com	Denmark
Borbala Kasza kasza.borbala@yahoo.com	Hungary

SECOND EDITION, 2019

When people came asking guidance for their difficulties and health consultations, I was repeatedly asked about the Siddha system and who were the Siddhas. This pushed me, apart from answering the individual, to write. This was around the year 2003. My first book publication came out in the name of "Siddhas - Masters of the Basics" in 2008. The book wasn't sold in bookshops. It has largely been shared by word of mouth and personal circulation until now. After Stephen Grissom's book "Rivulets of the Absolute" was published, I began to receive several more enquiries for Masters of the Basics. This is what has urged a re-edition. This time it has been made available on the global platform under the title of "Siddhas - Masters of Nature". I am thankful to White Falcon Publishing, Chandigarh, for being our Service Provider, and offering their valuable service and guidance.

A NOTE FROM THE AUTHOR

My teacher once said, *"You cannot differentiate if a Siddha is working or playing."*

This book assumes the nature of the Siddhas themselves. It demands and shakes your conditioning, as the Siddhas are the cyclonic storms that shake and uproot trees! It is not meant for passive readers.

Texts of most ancient Traditions are in forms of verse, compositions, poems, stories or even incidents, and sacred insights and teachings are by and large metaphorical. The wisdom, although recorded, stays concealed within metaphors, legendary characters and cryptic notes and without proper decoding, the priceless essence remains beyond common understanding. Time and again, Sages have illustrated messages using legendary characters and verse, composed in a cryptic or symbolist language. Significant events and ways of life are depicted through mythological epics. Myths aren't mere tales. They are to be deeply understood for the answers they carry, for generations to come.

Ancient traditions such as the Hermetic, Taoist, Cabbalistic, Vedic and Siddha, having flourished through the ages, served humanity by way of its teachings. The ever-present Immortal Masters of the Ancient Siddha Tradition speak through the sacred cryptic verses of their palm-scripts, and their tradition thrives hidden away from the eyes of the world. This book wishes to rekindle, revitalise and share the wisdom emanating from this unique age-old sacred Tradition with today's post-modern world.

I began penning down a few words in response to frequently asked questions if the cryptic verses of the Siddhas shed any guiding light for the world we live in today. Is the oldest Tradition still suitable to address today's lifestyle, a world glaringly different from ancient days? Those already intrigued by this grand Tradition eagerly asked if the ancient Sages have revealed remedies for present-day problems like personality disorders, stress, incurable diseases, etc. I have included some of these responses under *Section Two*, *Tree of Life*. All the same, I did hold the wish to share the life-nourishing learnings bestowed upon me by these revered Saints. And this I have included as the final section, *Reluctant Masters*. Through the course of this book, I have included some unbelievable or incomprehensible aspects and from time to time have authenticated these with either verses from their Works or a few words quoted by my teachers and a few personal life incidents and experiences as well.

A Siddha Master's approach of *'Salvation in the Wilderness'* replaces the mathematical attitude of today with an organic one. I would like to believe this book urges to rekindle and imbibe such legendary values into present-day life, to unfold and realise our intrinsic potential. Now and then, it is possible my reader may choose to interpret in terms of hard facts; this would only be a hindrance. So all I do is to offer a gentle hint - to start from wherever you stand.

Under the First Section, the *'Tales from the Immortals'* are not only Salutations to the Siddhas but an Invocation of Their everlasting spirit.

As a gesture of gratitude toward my Masters, I have included the Yogic dimension of the Siddha system as a part of the book. I must explain that I received oral teachings only after initiation from the wandering Siddha clan of the Kancha Mountains.

A NOTE FROM THE AUTHOR

Some areas of the book that may appear contradictory are in all actuality, complementary to each other. And even though from time to time, I have used specific terminology while describing a Siddha, such as Tantric Siddha, or Yogic Siddha or a wandering Siddha, in truth no such single classification stands applicable to a Siddha. All classifications are multifarious aspects that flourish within Him.

It gives me great happiness to say this book has come about as a 'happening' entirely orchestrated by the ever-present boundless grace of the Sat Guru, for which I am very gracious. As for myself, this revered ancient Tradition has brought me 'Home'! It has reminded me of my uncompromising, rebellious spirit without which spontaneity cannot be and, nor can there be the knowingness of the spirit of spontaneity to be uncompromising, rebellious and ever free.

The great saint Ramakrishna Paramahamsa once said *'I will give up twenty thousand such bodies to help one man. It is glorious to help even one man.'*

If this book inspires even a single reader toward a genuine journey into the world of the Siddhas, I will consider the purpose of this book fulfilled.

Pal Pandian

PREFACE

With a deeply revered approach, we begin our journey into "Siddhas - Masters of Nature", to reacquaint ourselves with the ancient Siddha Tradition rising from the southern part of India, present-day state of Tamil Nadu.

I would like to initiate with an interesting fact -

Each one of us, is always in a deeply continued connectivity with our roots.

Let us first establish a simple and precise understanding of these roots, its deep connectedness and the constant influence it has upon us as individuals and on humanity as a whole, at any given moment.

The roots I speak of are termed *'Samskaras'* in Indian terminology, which literally means 'refining'. *Samskaras* can be defined as life-shaping forces, inherited individually as well as collectively. Our *Samskaras* or inherent patterns work to influence our psyche internally as well as externally which forms our psychic attitude. In this way, we can call ourselves a continuation of our ancestors. Each moment holds an ongoing reverberation, emitting the calls of our Ancients, through the genetic map of our psyche.

Moving to the Western front for a moment, the famous psychiatrist C. G. Jung, of the last century expounded this very elementary psychic attitude as 'Archetypes'. He defines it as:

> 'The factors and motives that arrange the psychic elements into certain images, characterised as archetypal, but in such a way that they can only be recognised by the effects they produce. They exist unconsciously and presumably, thus forming the structural dominance of the psyche in general. As priori conditioning factors they represent a special psychological instance of the biological pattern of behaviour, which gives all things their specific qualities.'

He says an archetypal content expresses itself, first and foremost, in metaphors.

By this, we can somewhat fathom that our personal archetypes are ever rooted and arising from the collective archetypes of primitive tradition. Whether we are consciously aware of it or not, it evidently holds ancient history. Undoubtedly, one and all are connected to their ancient roots. But this subterranean connectedness or bond does undergo change based on present day living conditions, and accordingly expresses itself.

One cannot help but notice an undeniable oneness among all Ancient Traditions. Their surging inspiration, deep insights and blazing quests divulge an in-depth understanding of the hidden dimensions of the dynamic mystery called Life. Traditions speak of rituals or practices, techniques devoted toward an inner journey aimed at the betterment of humanity as a whole, through dimensions such as Healing, Medicine, Alchemy, Astrology, etc. Most mythological cults touch upon at least a few if not all these dimensions. Interestingly, traditional epics and mythical tales illustrate legendary characters with inherent extended faculties of flying, clairvoyance, psycho-kinesis, etc. It has been said that people living in the Lemuria continent had all these faculties and would even naturally utilise their third eye! But the strong underlying message emanating through the livingness of all these characters is an ever-prevalent flow of humility and a deep harmony shared with Mother Nature. With our archetypes rooted to primitive archetypes, one might expect each of us to have inherited those extended faculties, but we don't seem to be able to fly. But this is not to say that these faculties have been destroyed. They remain latent within us; I have explained how through a simple elucidation.

> As time went by and Man evolved, unfortunately he gradually lost all humility toward Mother Nature and in its place grew dominant over Her. This altered approach from humility to dominance was joined by a strong change in social order. Together, this caused the faculties inherent to Man to gradually project outward. Today, they express as an 'Object-Oriented Lifestyle'. In other words, inner faculties got projected as object-oriented technological knowledge. We see it everywhere as our inventions - airplanes, cameras, TV, locomotives, robots, and cybernetic revolutions, etc. Somewhere along passing times Man tried to gain happiness by projecting his 'inherency' into an object-oriented, materialistic approach and soon enough, found himself entangled in his own web of created objects. Once Man started to invest his nature into man-made objects, he had already begun losing his livingness. Till today, these objects continue to demand an excessive indulgence that keeps Man obsessively identified with the object itself.

Man continues to live in this effort. Today sees us in the Utopian place of 'Automation in everything'. Artificial intelligence, cloning, stem cell research and one crop harvests, etc. are fresh evidence.

Our recent generation clearly reveals how much change our archetypes have undergone. Barely familiar with the Ramayana, Mahabharatha and other ancient mythological epics of our land, instead their value system is invested in technology, movies, television programmes, cartoons, modern music, etc. through which an unnatural amount of violence is constantly displayed. Lives are verily disconnected from root values and we now function in a mentally-oriented fashion. Wedged into the conditioning of our current period, we can only obsessively push to interpret and function using a mentally-dominated approach. It's a shameful truth. Humanity has been moving in a direction, which now screams for the revival of lost values and roots. We may have wondered as to how our lifestyle turned so mechanical and why we lead life based on conceptual and mathematical approaches. It is so because Man seeks what he needs, outside of himself.

The life described in our epics and myths isn't a concept but *'Life Based'*. And for us to entirely receive the divine message, it is essential to understand all legendary and mythological characters as energy-evoking symbols that hit one beyond conditioned thinking patterns. The inner significance of these legends can deeply impact our lives under the guidance of mythological or mysterious cults, as they urge us to follow a visionary quest like the spirit of a warrior setting off on an adventure and bringing back a message. And giving life and vitality to it *all by the way of his life.* Walking the quest with spirited openness of risking how life chooses to open along the lines of adventure awakens the potential to meet challenges as well as attunes inherent responses toward it, leading to an amplification of life and awareness by *'abidance as consciousness'*. The one who guides another through this sort of a visionary quest is called the 'Master'. Siddhas are Masters abiding as *'consciousness that illumines'*. The word Siddha comes from a Tamil term derived from the root word *'Chit'* (pure consciousness). One that abides as consciousness is called *'Chittar'*, or *Siddhar*.

The Tamil Saints or Siddhas are *Immortal Masters; Masters of Nature*. The Eternal Masters may no longer appear to be present in the physical realm, but being beyond all limitation and having attained Mastery over the very basis of Existence, are Immortal and thus ever present. The very essence of Siddhahood is this unique vastness of being 'all pervasive' in all dimensions, even the physical. The words 'Masters of Nature' expound Their mastery of play at the Essence of Existence. They live eternally free, spontaneous, in peace and happiness, engaged in the river flow of existence.

A Siddha is beyond time and is ever living.

The encoded sacred teachings gradually folded it into a precious tradition, spread by way of divine poetry. The historical verses pertain to obstacles faced by humans, big and small, disease, and on a more profound note, impart the sacred knowledge of the grace-lit path 'Home'. The several thousand documented works of these compassionate sages speak on medicine, yoga, inner and external alchemy, vastu sastra, astrology, occult science, martial art, lifestyle and ethics, tantric knowledge, *gnana* (path of wisdom), etc. I have attempted touching upon most of these throughout the course of the book. We also see that what makes these sages and this ancient sacred art and science of living so unique from others, is the fact that everything rises from the nature of ever-existent prevalent co-relation between divinity and ongoing human conditions. Therefore, one is to start from wherever he stands. Initially, occurrences in the lives of the Siddhas may appear unbelievable, leaving the reader bewildered or even shocked. Some of the teachings, might push one to question one's own possibilities, leaving him feeling sore and confronted by limitation, which at first may shut him off from realising the ubiquity of spirit. But, the underlying factors in these stories and teachings are purposed to transcend the limitation one is bound by and the message behind unconventional and seemingly harsh teachings of the Siddhas is *'don't give up, but transcend'*.

Since four decades, alternative healing systems and Eastern spiritual practices have gained popularity. Along with an abundance of books, articles, we also find teachers, organisations and institutes flooding the market today. In which case, this book stands to be a bit different because insights, unique to the Siddha system, so far imparted solely by way of oral teachings and have never been seen in print before, have been included here. This ancient system holds numerous dimensions of which only a part of the medicinal aspect is more known and remembered. The medicinal aspect is a very small part of this oceanic tradition. So, a person practicing merely Siddha medicine cannot proclaim the name Siddha. A profession is not a persona. Along with the medicinal aspects, I have also touched upon the other dimensions to the best of the possibilities held by this book. Now and then, followers from and beyond the native land of this tradition tried to utilise it to gain *Siddhis* (Psychic powers). They failed. They also entirely missed the inherent essence and profound wisdom emanating from the sacred teachings. We can say that the tradition remains untouched, uncontaminated - shining purity, glowing wisdom and truth. One is sure to stumble upon its many colours along the way, but these are encounters or by-products that must not deviate one. An attitude of absolute humility and devotional reverence for Truth is the only doorway to receive and imbibe the true essence of these sacred teachings. It is hard to concise this immense and multidimensional science into one work. Even after several palm scripts, works and books, this tradition remains as elusive and mysterious as the Masters themselves, largely because they are beyond conceptualisation.

This book is to inspire a reader toward himself rather than a study of ancient science. It offers an invitation; indicates where you stand and reminds you of Home.

Section One, touches upon the significance and history of this Tradition and some of the contributions made by the Siddhas. It also includes select captivating incidents from the lives of the Sages. Some I read and others I came to learn of while living in close vicinity of my compassionate teachers.

Section Two, has *Tattwas,* the fundamental life-organising units within the micro as well as macrocosm after which comes *Man – The Five Elements*. After the hallmarks of Siddha Tradition, come the *Doshams*, three bio-regulating forces; one's inborn constitution; and the effect of the balance and imbalance of these forces on one's health, temperament and lifestyle. Following which are the tradition's salient principles – the *Thathus* (seven tissues) and *Suvai* (the six fundamental tastes). This leads into some forgotten wisdom relating to modern day problems such as fatal and feared diseases like AIDS and Stress, caused by obsessive hasty lifestyle, personality disorders caused by hemispherical imbalance, etc. The concluding part of section two speaks of Siddha *Kaya Kalpa* and the remarkable significance of ancient art of *Varma*, bearing the twin face - Healing and Martial Art.

Section Three carries the Yogic and Tantric dimensions of the Siddha System. Teachings hailing specifically from my Guru lineage have been carried on solely by Oral Lineage - from Master to disciple. The underlying ground of these teachings has remained unique and protected by way of secrecy and cryptic poetry. This chapter highlights how the Siddha Yogic system differs from other schools of Yoga. The practices commonly undertaken under the name of Siddha Path in Tamil Nadu nowadays are not entirely original, and techniques of different Yogic schools are being followed under its tag. Even within Tamil Nadu, it is now hard to find a genuine Yogic Siddha Master making himself available to the social world. An authentic initiation is imperative to pursue the Siddha Yogic or Tantric path. Coming from the ancient lineage, initiation is not taken casually as done today in the form of collective mantras, rituals or techniques. A genuine initiation is the Master sharing with his disciple the very sap of his living experience and surging inspiration that he abides as. The Master shares no conceptualised theories, but shares Himself. This holds exclusivity of true knowledge and is significant of the rebirth of the disciple.

The third section concludes speaking of the Tantric world of the Siddhas. Describing the true essence of Ancient Siddha Tantra, it also highlights how practitioners today bend and miss the relevant attitude imperative to receive the gracious Truth.

Section Four, describes the delightful spirit of Siddhas Masters. It explains why They remain hidden and un-revealed to ordinary eyes, and yet how one is able to dwell on the free spirit of these hidden Saints through their divine poetry. Reading the truth-emanating poems serves as great sacred teaching and revelation. The mysterious divine poems are not merely appealing but awakenings. They invoke joy, awe and delightful wonder. The short stories bring smiles or open-eyed wonder. The poems have been translated into English so the reader may sense the meaningful life-shaping experience hidden in them.

ಶ್ರೀ ಇ

CONTENTS

SECTION ONE:	**History of Siddhas**	**1**
Chapter One:	The Critic-eye of the Siddhas	3
Chapter Two:	History of Siddha Tradition	11
SECTION TWO:	**Tree of Life**	**83**
Chapter Three:	Tattwas	85
Chapter Four:	Man - The Five Elements	94
Chapter Five:	Medicine of the Sages	104
Chapter Six:	Varma - Vital Spots	205
Chapter Seven:	Stress	237
Chapter Eight:	Ardhanareeswara – Dancing Lore of Feminine and Masculine	250
SECTION THREE:	**BEING AND SHARING – Yogic and Tantric System of the Siddhas**	**277**
Chapter Nine:	Introduction to the Yogic System	279
Chapter Ten:	The Inner Map	316
Chapter Eleven:	Chakras - The Wheels of Life	324

Chapter Twelve:	Kundalini - Rivering the Fire	346
Chapter Thirteen:	Alchemy - Internal and External	359
Chapter Fourteen:	Tantra	415

SECTION FOUR: Reluctant Masters — 455

Chapter Fifteen:	Reluctant Masters – Spirit of the Siddhas	457
	Annexure 1	549
	Glossary	554
	Appendix	564

SECTION ONE
HISTORY OF SIDDHAS

The Holy feet of Siddha Bogar

(Mundanthurai Tiger Forest of Mahendragiri Mountain Range)

CHAPTER ONE

THE CRITIC-EYE OF THE SIDDHAS

Ancient history depicts science as a tradition. Devoted to freeing the human race from obstacles, fundamental difficulties, disease, the discomfort of inhospitable environment, drastic weather conditions and so on, science has always sought answers for the well-being of humanity. Along with the extension of lifespan and the prediction of catastrophic changes, science served the spiritual advancement of humanity. Science and spirituality were not separate activities. Science intended the human race to live in harmony with each other and the environment, both natural and supernatural. Science brought relief to human problems. Is science still doing the same? Little faith in ancient science survives today and what remains has been altered beyond recognition by the idea that Man is the most important creature of creation and the purpose of Nature is to serve him. Technology and mathematical modelling have turned the attention of modern science to things that have little or nothing to do with day-to-day concerns of the human race. What do scientists have to say when yet another mass murder occurs or what is their contribution to ending warfare, poverty or hunger? On the other hand, we have seen major scientific contribution toward powerful weaponry and poisonous chemicals that produce mass saleable crops which, while destroying the environment benefit a few at the expense of many! Human suffering has not diminished despite these great advances which have proven profitable for the food and drug industries. This reductionist approach coming from an exaggerated scientific mind blatantly tampers with our human connect to Mother Nature. No matter how many pieces an oak tree is divided into, the smallest piece is not an acorn. But, science continues to divide matter into smaller fragments in search of its origin, which they mistake for life, whilst entirely overlooking the transformational quality of Nature and Life. Parts of modern science negate the magnanimity of Nature. They see Her as a raw material to be recombined, consumed, blasted to bits, exploited or paved over to make way for so-called economic growth and urbanisation. Absorbed in what it believes it can know, science often ends up learning how much they do not know! But, of late, theoretical scientists on the outer fringes of physics are coming closer to views disclosed by ancient spiritual scientists of long forgotten civilisations.

THE LOST FACE OF SCIENCE

A nature-centred reading of ancient history demonstrates a time when the Gods ceased to be divine forces and became exalted men, and kings ceased to be human rulers and became living Gods. This marked the beginning of change. A new way of relating with the Divine took over, separating humanity from Nature instead of re-affirming that Divinity in Nature holds humanity as a part. Ever since Nature was demystified and re-invented as an exploitable commodity, history of mankind has been ridden with war, exploitation, conquest and slavery. Despite it, something of the ancient times survived in parts of the world; preserved and protected by ancient traditions. In some places the Oral Tradition survived, and in most the method of deciphering and decoding ancient songs and works of art and architecture have been long forgotten as people upholding this sacred art died taking the knowledge with them.

SOUTH INDIA, TAMIL NADU

Ancient spiritual scientists or the 'Yogis' of ancient Tamil Nadu encoded sacred scientific knowledge in poetic verse which passed down first orally, then in writing. These Yogis are the Tamil Siddhas. Even though a lot of their teachings live on in the twilight language of mystical poetry to this day, many works have also been rigorously persecuted. Fundamentalist Indians of religious cults, invading Muslims and Europeans made systematic attempts to eradicate ancient works. Several unprotected manuscripts were destroyed primarily because the offenders didn't wish divine revelations and its connect to human conditions be known by all. Over time, many modern scholars failed to decipher encrypted information in the palm scripts and many writings were rejected as useless. Since the British found it politically convenient to alter history and support the claim of Sanskrit as the original language of Indian culture, the tremendously rich and varied literary works of Tamil Nadu got marginalised. Some of the Siddha teachings were banned by the British because of their fear of the occult. Mandated by their religious and political goals, their basic policy toward colonial natives was to eradicate all trace of ancient or ancestral knowledge and wipe out any way-of-being that pre-existed the invasion (unless of course it served their policy). Their goal was to enforce a superior military and moral presence which required the destruction of anything that linked people to their ancient roots, their spiritual beliefs or the land itself. The British knew that a link to ancient knowledge gave a person a sense of belonging, a sense of place and purpose which is what they attempted to destroy, or else people could not be moulded to suit their economic or military needs. Siddha yogis managed to hold the confidence of the people through the downfall of ancient Indian culture, wars and invasions suffered by the subcontinent. They hid ancient treasures in shrines, caves, wells and other places and not all of it has been discovered till date.

The Siddhas are pantheons of medicinal knowledge and deciphered numerous remedies using what is naturally available - plant, animal or mineral. Their texts describe disease that fits the description of present day Cancer and HIV/AIDS for which they recorded healing methods and treatment. One of their more deeply guarded dimension is *Vasi Yoga*, which initially embraces and then transcends the primary purpose of *Swara Yoga* - freeing the aspirant from temporary planetary influence. *Vasi Yoga* is the supreme science of spiritual alchemy. It bestows nothing short of liberation from all karmic encumbrances. It is the path of attaining the "Immortal body". This alchemical journey, transforms temporal existence into immortal being-ness. The practice of *Vasi Yoga* demands high discipline, fierce determination and most of all an authentic initiation from a Master.

MODERN DAY

Our ancient sages envisioned the world and its individuals at varying stages of spiritual evolution; some close to exhausting their Karma and others weighed down by the universe's reactions to their deeds. With this in mind, the Siddhas designed arts and sciences of yoga, medicine, astrology, tantric practices, occultism, astronomy, *vastu sastra*, alchemy, etc, in relevance to the multifarious stages. They documented a higher path to eternal wisdom for more advanced aspirants. In this tradition, a direct Master-Disciple relationship is paramount. This aspect is difficult if not impossible today as this relationship demands special practice and sacrifice of certain present day lifestyle which in itself stands challenging to individuals today. Moreover, it is not easy to find a genuine Master of this system anymore. Other than that, an aspirant requires eligibility to undertake spiritual practices of native traditions unlike how one signs up for a class in present times. The Master evaluates the aspirant for sensitivity, for *satvic* body and if he holds a rebellious spirit that longs for an unconditioned mind. This is fundamentally challenging for today's individuals as these parameters are considered out of "style".

ಙ ಲ

CHAPTER ONE: THE CRITIC-EYE OF THE SIDDHAS

NAMES OF THE SIDDHAS

Here are some of the Siddhas listed by the names they were popularly known by:

Siva Vakkiyar
Punnakisar
Karuvurar
Sundaranandar
Kamalamuni
Ramadevar
Pampatti Siddhar
Gorakkar
Gnaneshwar
Kaalangi
Macchamuni
Kudambai Siddhar
Idaikattu Siddhar
Agasthiyar
Bogar
Azhukanni Siddhar
Pulasthiyar
Konganavar
Pulipani
Theraiyar
Thirumoolar
Sattaimuni Siddhar

"They lived in natural caves,
They lived in harmony,
They dined the sacred ambrosia,
They created medicated drugs and oils,
They revealed alchemy of metals,
They bound mercury into beads,
They empowered them and flew in the sky,
They are Siddhas, lived forever!"

Gnanavindham - Verse 17, Siddha Kalangi Nathar

CHAPTER TWO
HISTORY OF SIDDHA TRADITION

"What avails you now to be born?
If in a last birth, penance you denied,
The Lord made me, a good birth,
In sweetest Tamil, His glory to expound."
Thirumanthiram Verse 81, by Siddha Thirumoolar

A tradition is more of an evolution than an overnight invention. The Siddha system evolved with the development of mankind and identifies with the Tamil-speaking land as its origin. This system remains a mystery to practitioners of other native medicinal systems of India as well as to those involved in the academic study of traditional systems of medicine. It is one of the oldest systems to describe health as a holistic perfected state of the physical, psychological, social and spiritual components of a human being.

To quote saint Thirumoolar,

"That which cures physical ailments is medicine,
That which cures psychological ailments is medicine,
That which prevents ailments is medicine,
That which bestows immortality is medicine."

SECTION ONE: HISTORY OF SIDDHAS

The Tamil word Siddha comes from the root word 'Chit', meaning 'Consciousness that illumines'. An accurate way of saying 'Siddhar' is 'Chittar': the one who abides as consciousness. This tradition of the Chittars dates back beyond written history and the Dravidian race's greatest contribution is Tamil - the mother of ascetic languages.

PRE-HISTORIC TIMES

The geographical conditions of the Deccan Plateau also hold evidence that human life itself could have originated in South India. The two primary ways history is generally approached is through archaeological findings and literature. Implements from the Palaeolithic and Neolithic periods are found in abundance in South India; including the city of Chennai in Tamil Nadu. The excavation results of the Indus Valley civilisation, recently renamed as the Harappa civilisation confirm, it spread not only throughout the Indus region but elsewhere too, which helps realise the antiquity of the Dravidians. The worship of the male God and female Goddess i.e., the Siva-Uma cult is of Dravidian origin, and not of the Aryans who followed the Brahma cult. The Siddha tradition is said to have originated from Lord Siva who revealed it to Goddess Uma, His consort and was prevalent during Indus civilisation period. Even though we are unable to put an exact date to the Siddhas origin, what we do know is that the Dravidians are known to be the oldest race in India. All historians accept that. When the Aryans came to India in the first millennium B.C., the Dravidians were already there. There is a popular Tamil saying "Tamils were the race who lived with swords even during the actual formation of Earth", which also establishes the knowledge of metallurgy held by ancient Tamils.

"Thus revealed Sadasivam to Devi.
The Goddess passed it on to Nandhi.
Nandhi exposed it to Dhanvanthri.
Dhanvanthri taught it to Ashwini.
Agasthiyar received the knowledge from him,
To be passed on to Pulasthiyar.
Pulasthiyar conveyed it to Theraiyar."

Yugi Chintamani, 800 by Yugimuni Siddhar

The Siddhas recorded their teachings in the form of cryptic verse on palm-scripts. Through them we learn that the Dravidians worshiped the humped bull (Nandhi), a practice pursued even by the citizens of the Indus valley. Although detailed archaeological evidence of the medicinal practice practiced during the Indus valley era is not yet available, there is enough to believe the existence of a medicinal system identical to that of the Dravidians. The horns of the deer and antelope were used for medicinal use. Coral is extensively found around the southern coast of present day India and the worship of trees and plants such as the Pipal, Bilva and Basil also advocates correlation with the Siddha medicinal system. The medicinal use of coral and Neem tree leaves also prevailed.

THE VEDIC AGE

In the Vedic age, the oldest, Rig Veda, would have been written later than 1500 B.C, because it was during this period that Aryans, after successfully driving out the original inhabitants, settled in North of India. Atharva Veda speaks widely of occult science and treatment by mantras, gems, etc. and Ayurveda, the science of life, is said to be a sub-veda of Atharva Veda. The Siddha medicinal system has three main methods of treatment: *Mani, Mantra* and *Aushadha. Mani* means gems, mercury beads; *Mantra* means invocatory mystical words; and *Aushadha* means herbal and mineral medicines. Mystical cures and attributing the cause of disease to demons as mentioned in books of Siddha medicine lead us to understand this was earlier than the Atharva Veda period.

THE SANGAM PERIOD
(Sangam Academy)

The three Sangam periods and the number of Kings and poets forming each are already a centre of controversy. But the advanced cultural development of the Tamils leads us to believe the existence of a highly reputed academy of Tamil literature, culture and science.

ANCIENT WORKS

The first available Tamil literary classic, Tholkappiyam, authored by Tholkappiyar, possibly dates back to the first millennium B.C. Tholkappiyar's Guru is Siddha Sage Agasthiyar and in his work the author writes, "Says the poet" and "Said my teacher" implying that the literature written by Sage Agasthiyar, on instruction from Lord Siva, has been lost. Tholkappiyam elaborates on the life and habits in the five geographical divisions: Kurinji, Mullai, Marudham, Neithal and Palai which according to Tamil history are the Mediterranean, Alpine and Nordic divisions. Kurinji are the hilly regions, identical to Alpine where the first occupation of Man was hunting. Gradually as he learnt to domesticate cattle, Man came down from the hills and wandered through pastoral areas of the forest, i.e. Mullai, which can be equalled to Nordic. By witnessing forest fires due to clashing bamboos, Man learnt the use of fire and thus began the advent of cooking. Watching animals consume herbs during illness, Man realised the medicinal value hidden in Nature. The Neithal lands, near the ocean are equivalent to the Mediterranean. Marudham, land suitable for cultivation, is the last place Man moved to when he discovered how water from these lands made him prosperous and free from illness. Palai refers to sandy desert areas. Some of the Siddhas' songs describe a city by the name 'Then Madurai' ('Then' meaning south), located near present day 'Kanya Kumari' in Southern India, which could be Lemuria. It is said Lemuria may have been ruined by way of natural calamities.

Usually, a medicinal system springs up in response to disease encountered in those specific climatic conditions and its knowledge is confined to that region, such as the Arabian Unani medicinal system which predominantly speaks of heat (*Pittam*) related disease, according to the geography and climatic conditions of the desert region. But the Siddha medicinal system is expansive and covers disease born of multiple climatic conditions and variants. An ancient Sangam classical work by the name of Purananuru, written by 'Mudinagarayar, clearly describes the formation of the five elements.

> "The sandy Earth,
> The Ether that covers it,
> The Air formed by the Ether,
> The primal Fire from the Air,
> Its contradictory Water,
> From the nature."

Silappathikaram, one of the five epics of Tamil literature, is evidence of how refined the medicinal practitioners were during the later Sangam period and describes the practitioners of the science of life as highly principled. There is a mention of a poet named Maruthuvan Thamodaranar. 'Maruthuvan' in Tamil means physician, which implies that by this period medicine probably was a titled profession. The council of advisors to the King included a physician.

Titles of certain books from Sangam literature are identical to the names of medicines, such as 'Thirukadugam', 'Yelaathy' and 'Sirupanchamulam'. There is historical evidence of the existence of institutions like hospitals and smaller dispensaries during the Chola kingdom. Even the habit of appointing staff in staggered time duties is described. During the reign of the Chola kings, a hospital in the memory of Sundaram Chola at Tanjore was constructed, which held a physician, a pharmacist, an assistant and two female nurses.

In Dawson's dictionary on Hindu mythology, the Siddhas are equalled to the Magis of Europe, i.e. people who strive for spiritual perfection to attain the highest goal of life. The Siddhas are said to have been 70,000–80,000 in number. They followed the Agamas, which are Dravidian or Tamil. Even after being aware of the physical body as transient, they honoured it as the only instrument by which a person can attain the ultimate goal: to become one with the Lord. For instance, the practice of yoga, esoteric breathing practices, etc., helps one to raise the God within oneself.

'Siva Vakkiyar', one of the Siddhars says:

"It's a waste to make floral offerings;
And to chant mantras to an idol,
When God is within you;
It's like a vessel, which doesn't realise,
What is there in it?"

      Siva Vakkiyar Padalgal, Verse 521, by Siddha Siva Vakkiyar

The Ancient Seers state - service to humanity is service to the Lord of Lords, which is how they founded the system of medicine and healing. The system of Siddha medicine can be rightly called a by-product of the Siddha's practice to reach the Ultimate which explains why this science, though perfected, appears to be a mingling of art, philosophy and science.

CHAPTER TWO: HISTORY OF SIDDHA TRADITION

But it is to be remembered:

> "Science doesn't need mysticism,
> And mysticism doesn't need science.
> But man needs both."

To quote Albert Einstein, the Nobel laureate:

> "Science without religion is blind,
> And religion without science is lame."

Even though there are several Siddhas, a group of 18, referred to as the "18 Primal Siddhas", are considered significant. Different works mention various combinations of the Primal 18 because of a practice followed by each; a Siddha, in his own literary works would exclude himself from the 18. It is also possible that They were originally eighteen in number and their followers who wrote books on an identical line of thinking were also called Siddhas. Apart from the 18 Siddhas, there are also various classifications such as "Navanadha Siddhas", "Navakodi Siddhas," etc. Listed below are four different classifications:

THE FIRST SCHOOL OF THOUGHT

1. Thirumoolar
2. Ramadevar
3. Kumbamuni
4. Idaikadar
5. Dhanvanthri
6. Valmiki
7. Kamalamuni
8. Bhoganadhar

9. Macchamuni
10. Konganavar
11. Padanjali
12. Nandidevar
13. Bothaguru
14. Pampatti Siddhar
15. Sattaimuni
16. Sundaranandadevar
17. Kudhambai Siddhar
18. Gorakkar

THE SECOND SCHOOL OF THOUGHT

1. Gauthama
2. Agasthiyar
3. Sankara
4. Vairava
5. Markandeya
6. Valmiki
7. Romar
8. Busundar
9. Sattaimuni
10. Nandeesar
11. Thirumoolar
12. Kaalangi
13. Macchamuni
14. Pulasthiyar
15. Karuvoorar
16. Bogar
17. Konganavar
18. Pulippani

CHAPTER TWO: HISTORY OF SIDDHA TRADITION

According to the work Gnanakkovai, the list of Siddhas is altogether different. They are:

1. Siva Vakkiyar
2. Pattinathar
3. Patharagiriyar
4. Pampatti
5. Idaikkattu Siddhar
6. Agapai
7. Kudhambai
8. Kaduveli
9. Thiruvalluvar
10. Sattaimuni
11. Agasthiyar
12. Azhuganni
13. Nandheswarar
14. Ramadevar
15. Karuvoorar
16. Thirumoolar
17. Romarishi
18. Valmiki

NAVANATHA SIDDHAS

1. Sathyanathar
2. Sathoganathar
3. Adhinathar
4. Vegulinathar
5. Anadhinathar
6. Mathonganathar
7. Machendranathar
8. Kalendrannathar
9. Gorakkanathar

SECTION ONE: HISTORY OF SIDDHAS

The above mentioned were the more popular writers who used the Tamil script. Every Siddha hasn't contributed to the dimension of Siddha medicine, but, all Siddhas speak of the philosophical concept of life - the pillar of the Siddha system. There are differing opinions regarding the period of each Siddha. Tamil historians have their own assessment which has not yet traced them earlier than fourth century A.D. This is most likely true because the Siddha tradition was initially handed down solely through the oral lineage – the *Guru-Sishya* mode. Speaking of the Siddhas who made a significant contribution to the art of living, we find three lineages:

Bala varga: (*bala* - youth; *varga* – lineage)
> The founder of *Bala varga* is Lord Murugan; and the first Siddha is Agasthiyar.

Moola varga:
> Thirumoolar is the founder of this lineage. His foremost disciple Kaalanginathar was of Chinese origin and associated with the Taoist tradition. Later when he came to Tamil Nadu he became the disciple of Thirumoolar. Kaalanginathar went on to be known as the Guru of Bogar.

Kailaya varga:
> The founder was Sattaimuni Siddha.

Other well-known Ancient Indian Sages or Great Seers:

Kaga Busundar, Dhanvanthri, Vasishta, Kalai kottu Maharishi (the guru of King Janaka), King Janaka and Padanjali. They have written in the Tamil script expounding the multi-dimensional Siddha system and Their Tamil works are available now in book form. The Samadhi shrine of Padanjali, the founder of the Samkya system, is in Rameshwaram, southeast Tamil Nadu.

ॐ ೞ

CHAPTER TWO: HISTORY OF SIDDHA TRADITION

TALES OF THE IMMORTALS

It was never customary in ancient India to write and record history because, in Truth, one is not bound by time, so for the Timeless Ones how was birth and death to be recorded? Is he born? Did he ever die? Similar to the sacred texts of these Immortal Masters, are their tales and parables. These poetic verses written and recorded on palm-scripts carry on via oral lineage and grandma tales.

Below are inspiring anecdotes that draw you into Their world. The world of the Siddhas has always been rebellious and free of rotten rational conditioning – a paradox to today! Their world glows with the health of Life, shines with the Spirit of Existence; a world that lives on. Most Siddhas prefer seclusion. They live aloof, camouflaged by the depths of thick forests and isolated mountain peaks. They thrive in invisible realms, hidden away from society. Despite their need for solitude, the fact is that each and every verse they wrote is devoted to guide us. All their scripts about art and science are teachings. Every wisdom, insight, and divine vision stands applicable even for the modern millennium. Another powerful aspect of the Siddha tradition is its various dimensions and rewarding milestones that shine and attract many… But in a nutshell, 'by giving you what you want, they pull you over to the other side'; a kind of divine mischief or play, Their joy, and above all Their compassion for our upliftment.

SECTION ONE: HISTORY OF SIDDHAS

AGASTHIYAR

"To perceive the entire world, is full of wisdom;
To experience all objects, in essence, as infinite plains,
To have a vision of the serene space.
Understand! All these through only one means - That is Dhyanam!"

Agasthiyar Soumiya Sagaram1200, Verse 302

The father figure of Siddha medicine, literature, grammar and above all of profound wisdom is the revered Siddha Agasthiyar. The stories and mythical events of his life could fill a number of books. It has been said that he travelled to the southern tip of India to bring a balance between the North and South, as ordained by Lord Siva.

"Once, Lord Brahma was deeply involved in performing a *Yagna* (sacrificial fire ritual). Pleased by it, a radiant effulgence descended from Lord Siva and entered into the *Kumbha Kalasha* (the holy pot) placed above the *Yagna*. Soon after, a little sage holding a *yoga thandam* (holy stick) and *kamandala* emerged from the *Kumbha*. The divine beings participating in the *Yagna* saluted the little sage. The sound of sacred chants filled the air. The little sage was named Kumbha Muni or Kalasha Muni.

CHAPTER TWO: HISTORY OF SIDDHA TRADITION

This little sage, with the *yoga thandam* and the *kamandala*, was ever abiding in himself as Siva in the form of the effulgent radiance. He is Sage Agasthiyar. In Tamil, Sage Agasthiyar is known as Agathisa (Aga + isha), which means - Self as Siva.

Sage Agasthiyar performed intense penance for several years by floating on water. In Mount Kailash, arrangements began for the Holy marriage of Lord Siva and Goddess Parvathi. All devas, sages and divine beings started arriving at Mount Kailash to join the celebrations. The north of ancient India was crowded, and began sinking under the weight of the collective presence. Seeing this, as a part of His *Leela* (divine play), Lord Siva asked Siddha Nandidevar to call upon Sage Agasthiyar. Lord Siva ordained Sage Agasthiyar to immediately proceed to the Southern tip of ancient India to the Pothigai Mountain, to bring back balance!

Sage Agasthiyar was sad that he would not be present for this auspicious occasion. He was not happy to leave the side of his Lord and not participate in the wedding festivities. On seeing his dismay, Lord Siva said, 'Don't worry my son you will have the *darshan* of my marriage in the Pothigai Mountains'. Relieved, Sage Agasthiyar commenced his ordained journey to the south of India."

    (The above story appears in several ancient epics of both northern and southern spiritual traditions.)

This story shows Sage Agasthiyar's presence was equivalent to the collective presence of all the devas, sages and divine beings. Several stories describe the adventures and incidents during his journey to the southern tip. One such incident speaks of how Agasthiyar transformed the Vindhyia mountains which were towering high into the sky into small hills so as not to block anybody's way!

> "Once, while walking Agasthiyar found many sages hanging upside down on trees. He asked the reason for their strange miserable condition. They said a sage belonging to their clan hadn't married and until he didn't they had been cursed to hang upside down. The name of the sage was Agasthiyar, they said! Agasthiyar felt tremendous compassion. He introduced himself and assured them he would marry soon. The king of Vidharbha had a daughter by the name of Lobhamudra who had both divine grace and celestial beauty as her form and self. Agasthiyar married her. Lobhamudra is the accomplished Woman Siddha of the Sri Chakra Upasana; the peak knowledge of Tantra. Her Guru was Hayagreeva, the horse faced Vishnu of Kancheepuram, Tamil Nadu. As his holy complimentary, Lobhamudra served Sage Agasthiyar with all her heart, as does an ideal *Rishi Patni* (spiritual wife). Agasthiyar, who up until then was an ascetic then expressed his artful nature of the spiritual dimension by revealing several Tantric Vidyas to the world."

Lobhamudra always accompanied Agasthiyar on his journeys. There is an anecdote of one such time in relation to two *Asuras*, named Vathapy and Vilvalavan.

> "These two *Asuras* Vathapy and Vilvalavan were known to kill ascetics to ensure no one got more powerful than them. They had the ability to change their appearance. In the disguise of a Brahmin, Vilvalavan would invite wandering ascetics for a feast. Vathapy would transform into deliciously appetising food. After the innocent ascetic had eaten the meal, Vilvalavan would call out to Vathapy. On hearing his name Vathapy would tear open the ascetic's stomach and step out, thereby killing him.

> One day Agasthiyar happened to be passing through their territory. Vilvalavan as usual disguised himself as a Brahmin

and invited Agasthiyar for a meal. Agasthiyar smiled and accepted. Vathapy disguised himself as the food. Agasthiyar heartily ate his meal. After he had finished, Vilvalavan, as usual called out to Vathapy. He called out again and again but nothing happened! There was no response. Vilvalavan looked at the ascetic seated before him and realised he was no ordinary man. Agasthiyar said to him, '*Vathapy jeerno bhava*', which meant, Vathapy is digested! Vilvalavan instantly realised Agasthiyar's divine prowess and fear overtook him. He promptly asked forgiveness for all his past actions."

৪০ ৫৪

Agasthiyar wrote the work on grammar for the Tamil language by the divine grace of his Guru, Lord Murugan.

> At the time, 'Kaychina Valuthi' was the Pandya king when the first glorious Tamil Sangam was held. Agasthiyar acted as head of the first Tamil assembly and taught the divine significance and literary efficacy of the Tamil language to other poets and grammarians. 'Irayanar Agaporul', one of the Tamil classics, mentions a natural calamity to have hit the Pandya kingdom and the forty-nine nations surrounding it. Agasthiyar and a few others moving a little north of Tamil Nadu constructed a new Pandya kingdom with the available resources. Later, Agasthiyar settled in the Pothigai Mountains where he had the *darshan* of Lord Siva marrying Goddess Parvathi. He wrote many works on all the various dimensions of the Siddha Path. Agasthiyar had many disciples living around him in the mountains.

The great epic Ramayana narrates an incident that introduces Agasthiyar as a divine guest in King Dasaratha's court. Lord Rama received Siva Gita and Aditya Hridaya from Sage Agasthiyar.

SECTION ONE: HISTORY OF SIDDHAS

The first book on Tamil grammar, "Agasthiyam" (this valuable document does not exist anymore) is said to have been written by Agasthiyar during the first Sangam period. Agasthiyar lived in 'Pothigai Malai', a hillock in the Western Ghats in Tirunelveli district of southern India while writing his medicinal classics. There is a hut by the name of Agasthiyar Kudil found in the forest near Karaiar dam. From his many disciples, the Siddhas Theraiyar and Pulasthiyar have contributed significantly in the flourishing of the Siddha lineage. Amongst the medicinal works attributed to him, we find classics on ophthalmology, pharmacology, classification of diseases, etc. His works on Yoga have been highly valued for clear flowing verse and sharpness of essence.

Ancient followers of the Siddha path cleverly wove the insights and universal facts into mythological tales of the Siddhas as even a child can absorb a story through imagination and subsequently ponder its multifarious meanings in later years. For instance, let us take the story when Agasthiyar travelled from Mount Kaliash to the southern tip of India to balance the northern and southern constellations. We can identify this event by the appearance of the Agasthiyar star - called Canopus. Canopus is the brightest star in the southern hemisphere between the months of July to October and complements the northern hemisphere's polar star for those few months. The star of Agasthiyar is what guided sailors in ancient times. One other story describes how Agasthiyar collected the entire water of the river Ganges into his *kamandalu* (vessel for drinking water) and drank it. The Canopos star shines bright in September and the flow of the river is now tamed (after Agasthiyar drank it). In India, the celebration of the river festivals and holy bathing rituals happen in this month. Since ancient times the Siddha tradition, through mythological content, teaches us to harness the power of nature by harmonising with its rhythm.

"Listen to the miraculous fruits of tapas;
When He is in Siva yoga trance,
Man will find Him as man,
Woman will find Him as woman,
Yogis will find Him as Yogi,
Fiery animals will find Him as their own;
Thus entangled under His compassionate tapas."

                Agasthiyar Pari Puranam 1200, Verse 1101
                          (Tapas - intense penance)

Some of his Works are listed below.

Agasthiya paripoornam - 40	Agasthiya Vaidhiya kaviyam -1500
Agasthiya Vaidhiya rathina churukam - 360	Agasthiya Sathaganadi
Agasthiya Gunavakadam	Agasthiya Muppu Guru Nool
Agasthiya nayanavidhi	Agasthiya pancha kaviyam
Agasthiya - 21,000	Agasthiya pancha patchi
Agasthiya - 12,000	Agasthiya Vaidhiya kummi

THIRUMOOLAR

Thiru Nandhi Devar is said to have been the direct disciple of Lord Siva, and Siddha Thirumoolar is one of his eight students. The most significant event in Siddha Thirumoolar's life is the one that brought him to us. He was given the name Moolar after he entered the mortal frame of Moolan, a herdsman.

"Once, a Sage felt the desire to see Rishi Agasthiyar, then living in the Pothigai hills. Leaving Kailash, the Sage travelled south. He visited many shrines of Lord Siva on the way. Reaching Thiruvadu thurai he bathed in the river Kaveri and entered the temple for the *darshan* of his beloved Lord Siva. Later, while walking along the banks of the river Kaveri he noticed a herd of cows profusely shedding tears. Approaching them he discovered the cause. The herdsman lay there dead. The Sage's heart flowed with compassion and felt the urge to pacify the grieving cows. Using his yogic powers, the Sage hid his own body inside the trunk of a tree and entered the body of the dead herdsman. The herdsman's body instantly came to life - with the Sage within it! How were cows to know the difference? Seeing their Master alive was more than enough to make the cows rejoice in happiness.

The Sage had entered the body of Moolan, a herdsman residing in Sattanur, a village nearby. At dusk the Sage, still wearing Moolan's body, led the cows back to their village. There he noticed Moolan's wife eagerly expecting her husband's return. Seeing him she approached him happily as always. But the Sage didn't allow her to touch him. He said, "Oh lady, I am not your husband. Adore Lord Siva and attain liberation." He turned and left for a nearby Matha.

Shocked, the woman couldn't comprehend what had happened. Not knowing any other way she went and complained to the leaders of the village and described the puzzling conduct of her husband. After a brief discussion amongst themselves the leaders confronted Moolan. The words uttered by Moolan left them speechless. There was undeniable wisdom in his words and none could refute it.

CHAPTER TWO: HISTORY OF SIDDHA TRADITION

Pondering the series of events the leaders concluded that Moolan, their simple herdsman had somehow attained great spiritual evolution. They agreed he must be left alone and not troubled. Explaining this to the distraught wife they urged her to leave him alone too. Early next day the Sage followed the cows back to their fields in search of his hidden body. He searched everywhere but there was no body to be found.

Such is the Lord's Lila - a divine play!
It was the wish of Lord Siva for the Sage to encode many sacred works covering all dimensions of Truth. The moment the Sage realised his Lord's wish he returned to Thiruvadu thurai. There he stayed and worshipped the Lord, seated beneath a Pipal tree deep in meditation. He remained in *samadhi* for three thousand years. Once each year the Sage would emerge from his *samadhi* to compose a single verse, after which he would re-enter his *samadhi* state. This way, in three thousand years, the Sage wrote three thousand verses."

He has mentioned this himself in one of his own verses. This sacred work is called Thirumanthiram. The Sage is Siddha Thirumoolar.

Siddha Thirumoolar wrote other works such as Thirumoolar theetcha vithy, Thirumoolar karpam, Puvanai kakkisam, (explaining powerful occult practices) etc.

Once, Siddha Thirumoolar, Siddha Padanjali and Siddha Viyagrapathar, performed penance together at the Natarajar Temple at Chidambaram. After some years of being immersed in Yogic experience, all three simultaneously had the cosmic vision of the dance of Lord Natarajar. After this divine experience, Siddha Thirumoolar instantly disappeared into the space of Siva and mingled his existence into the sanctum of the temple at Chidambaram. After this rare occurrence Siddha Padanjali continued to wander throughout south Tamil Nadu. Later, he entered into *samadhi* in the temple at Rameshwaram, found in southeast of India. There is no literary record about what became of Siddha Viyagrapathar after this incident.

Siddha Thirumoolar's treatise on the Siddha cult, Thirumanthiram, is a pioneering work. It is empowered to assist and guide even present-day Siddha seekers. The number of written verses flows to a majestic 3000. Thirumanthiram has songs covering all dimensions of Truth, such as, the quantum nature of matter, purity of thought and action, the *Astama Siddhis* (eight occult powers), *Astanga Yoga* (eight limbs of yoga) and Tantric teachings of Siddhas and occult topics. The most treasured verses of the Thirumanthiram are Siddha Thirumoolar's teachings about both, the devotional path as well as the profound aspect of non-duality. These divine poems also speak of the importance of honouring and preserving the physical body, and the ways and means for it.

Thirumanthiram, by Siddha Thirumoolar, is an important and highly resourceful work. It has the potential to be approached in the light of modern thinking and discusses the similarities between theoretical physics (quantum theory) and mystical thought. Thirumanthiram expounds upon all the dimensions of the Siddha tradition.

> "Lord, the Prime is the atom within the atom;
> Divide an atom within the atom into a thousand parts.
> They who can thus divide and approach the Lord,
> He, indeed, is the atom within the atom."
> Thirumanthiram, Verse 2008, Siddha Thirumoolar

Siddha Thirumoolar had many disciples and his foremost disciple who became the next in lineage is Siddha Kaalanginathar.

CHAPTER TWO: HISTORY OF SIDDHA TRADITION

Some of Siddha Thirumoolar's books are:

Thirumoolar Vatham 21
Thirumoolar 608
Thirumoolar Vaidhiya
Thirumoolar Gnanam
Thirumanthira Malai

ಞ ಲ

BOGAR

"Consuming Elixir pill, I travelled eight sides,
I saw the range of mountains, and,
Saw the glittering plains of gold mines.
I saw mines abundant with copper ore,
And saw the green-mountain, and range of hills.
I saw wonders at the land of the Chinese.
I saw Mount Kailash and the reddish hills yonder.
I saw the great Meru and Siddha Roma Rishi too.
Acquainted with him, I learnt all secrets;
Then wishing to reveal the secrets of all arts,
Consuming again another Elixir, I flew to China and settled there."

Bogar Sapta Kandam-7000, Verse 1243 to 1244,
by Siddha Bogar

There are many different stories about the nativity of Siddha Bogar. One story suggests he was of Chinese origin and travelled through Tamil Nadu. Another version claims he was the disciple of Siddha Kaalanginathar (the disciple of Siddha Thirumoolar) who later travelled to China for expansion of knowledge. The incidents in Siddha Bogar's life written below have been taken from the ancient work Chathura Giri Sthala Puranam.

"In the ancient times a sage, his three disciples and a dog were walking through a deep forest in the Himalayan Mountains. Exhausted by their long journey on foot, they stopped. The sage took out an alchemical pill and handed it to one of the disciples. The disciple instantly fell unconscious. The sage gave one pill to the dog. He too dropped unconscious. Then he gave a pill each to the remaining two disciples. The two disciples having witnessed the effects of the pill were afraid. Fearing their Guru they pretended to swallow the pill but secretly threw it away. Then the sage consumed a pill himself and fell down unconscious. The two disciples were quick to assume their fellow disciple, the dog and their Guru to be dead by the pill. They decided to cremate the dead bodies after resting a while. After a few hours of rest their severe exhaustion was gone. They walked to a nearby village to arrange for the cremation. On their return, they couldn't find the bodies. The disciple, the dog and the Guru, were nowhere to be seen. The two disciples stood there shocked and perplexed. Suddenly, something far into the distance caught their eye. Looking carefully they spotted three forms climbing another mountainous terrain. It was their Guru, the dog and the third disciple! They instantly realised the grave mistake of disbelieving the Guru and his rejuvenating alchemical pill."

CHAPTER TWO: HISTORY OF SIDDHA TRADITION

"Once while walking through a village, a sage saw a woman overcome with grief, crying beside her dead husband. The sage's heart welled with compassion. From this compassion arose an intense urge to know the secret ways of resurrecting the dead. With this strong intention in his heart he went to the *samadhi* place of the Navanadha Siddhas and before their *samadhi* carried out intense *tapas*.

One day, They appeared before him and asked the reason for his *tapas*. He expressed his wish and asked for blessings. Gravely, they explained to the sage that his desire to help reduce the suffering of people by resurrecting the dead was against Divine Order. They remained unrelenting and adamant. The Navanadha Siddhas explained further, "These people who appear engulfed in grief at the death of their loved ones will not remain so for very long. They not only forget but also easily repeat the same mistake of being over indulgent in transitory things." After explaining the nature of human beings, the Navanadha Siddhas said, "As you are being highly adamant and are unable to understand you will lose all the *Siddhis* that you have attained by intense *tapas*." On hearing this, the sage replied, "Iif the desire for the well-being of fellow humans is a wrong and punishable offence then I take death in this moment!"

"No! You have already attained the knowledge of healing using valuable medicinal preparations. It must not be lost in vain. You are needed for the Siddha lineage to flourish."

Thus spoken, the Navanadha Siddhas blessed the sage with the knowledge of *KayaKalpa* Yoga and the preparation of elixir and cautioned him to share it only with a deserving few.

৪০ ൫

> "Soon after this, the sage travelled to southern India and lived in the Pothigai Hills of Tamil Nadu continuing his *tapas*. One day while walking through a village his throat felt dry and parched. He approached a hut. There he saw a group of Brahmins performing a Vedic *Yagna* outside. The sage requested for some water. Seeing his unkempt and beggar-like appearance the Brahmins instantly asked him to leave as he was interrupting a sacred ritual. In that instant, the sage turned and noticed a cat walking nearby. Picking it up, he recited some Vedic chants into the cat's right ear. Then he let it go. The cat walked up to the Brahmins, stood before them and began reciting the Vedic chants. Realising their error in recognising a true sage the Brahmins instantly asked forgiveness for their foolish and blinding arrogance."

This great Siddha, so flowing with compassion for the suffering of all people is Siddha Bogar.

> "After Siddha Bogar attained true knowledge of the *KayaKalpa* alchemical elixir, he decided to prepare it for the coming Siddhas down the lineage as well as for the benefit of suffering people. For this, he needed high quality mercury. Consuming a specially formulated bead called *'Gagan Guliga'* (Sky pill), Siddha Bogar travelled by air all the way to Rome - to the 'well of mercury'. Reaching there, he saw it was surrounded and guarded by invisible demons. He approached the well but when he tried to take some mercury it at once pulled away from him. He tried a few more times and each time the mercury would strangely slip away. Finally, Siddha Bogar offered a prayer to his Guru's Guru, Siddha Thirumoolar. He tried once again and this time he was successful in taking the mercury he needed.
>
> As He turned to leave, the invisible demons appeared and stopped him, preventing him from leaving with the mercury.

CHAPTER TWO: HISTORY OF SIDDHA TRADITION

Siddha Bogar spoke to the demons about himself. He explained that he belonged to the lineage of the great Siddha Thirumoolar and that his intention behind taking the mercury was to use it for a beneficial purpose. Even then the doubtful demons wanted Bogar to prove himself as a great Siddha. Very calmly, Siddha Bogar went to a nearby ocean and tossed in a magical pill. The pill began to drink the water of the ocean and grow in size. Fearing the ocean would go dry and they would be held answerable to their Lord, the demons pleaded to Siddha Bogar to bring the ocean water back. The great Siddha obliged."

There are innumerable incidents describing and glorifying Siddha Bogar's mystical prowess and Siddhahood.

He even had the skill of binding the *Navapashana* (nine poisonous metals) into a solid mass which shows mastery over alchemy. Siddha Pulippani is said to be Siddha Bogar's student. Siddha Bogar's contribution to pharmacology is also very great. Most of his treatises are in this branch of Siddha medicine. A few books written in the later ages have also been attributed to him. In the Southernmost part of India, nearly 250 kilometres from Madurai city, there is a tiger forest called Mundanthurai. It is situated in the Mahendragiri Mountain ranges. In the depths of this forest there is an altar called Bogar Bidam. It is where he had darshan of Lord Murugan in the form of light in his meditations. Various secret herbs are collected from this place for the preparation of the Navapashana statue. Even to this day, this place is not easily accessible to ordinary people and remains a clandestine mystical spot. On and around this spot and altar, we can find the sacred footprints of Siddhar Bogar.

I would like to share that from my own practical experience, the medicinal formulations revealed by Siddhar Bogar have been the most successful in curing ailments even to this date.

> "The pranic current through the left; the fire of moon;
> The pranic current through the right; the fire of sun;
> The current in the middle is the fire of Kundalini.
> Coalition of these three fires that is Salvation!"
>
> Bogar Gnana Sagaram -100, Verse 36

Some of His books are:

Bogar - 7000
Bogar Karpam - 30
Bogar sarakkuvaipu - 800
Bogar vasiyokam
Bogar Ponnuci
Bogar gnana Sagaram
Bogar Varma sutram
Bogar pancha patchi sastram
Bogar Vaidhiya Thirattu -700
Bogar Janana Sagaram
Bogar - 12000

The use of synthetic drugs was not unknown to Siddhars. Of these books: Bogar Sarakku Vaipu deals with the manufacture of synthetic drugs, in the absence of natural products to prepare medicine.

Bogar Karpam deals at length with means of preserving the body and the science of elixir.

Bogar Vasi Yogam deals with primordial breathing and inner alchemical practices.

Siddha Bogar has written extensively on the pharmacological and therapeutic aspects of metals and minerals. His text, Bogar 7000 contains the above stated information. In this, Siddha Bogar talks of the different methods of preparing Navapashana and mentions other various types of distillation processes in this ancient classic. This text consists of seven volumes.

CHAPTER TWO: HISTORY OF SIDDHA TRADITION

Bogar Karpam 300 discusses the rejuvenating properties of herbs and minerals. Siddha Bogar also reveals methods of producing a black-coloured variety of the desired herb from the normal variety, in the process of growing *Kalpa* plants.

Bogar Nigantu 1700 enlists a number of names attributed to the drugs of herbal plants. It lists around 570 herbal plants; animal drugs and minerals, which in different parts of Tamil Nadu are known by around 5000 different names.

Bogar Karpam is about longevity and the preparation of medicines for it (*Kaya Kalpa*).

Bogar Gnana Sagaram is about Creation.

Bogar Gnanam 100 speaks of Wisdom through Yogic practices.

Bogar Vaidhyam 700 is about Siddha medicines for diseases.

Bogar 12,000 includes all dimensions of the Siddha Tradition (This is not available in the market).

Bogar Pancha Patchi is on astrology and occultism.

Siddha Bogar's Maha Samadhi shrine is in Palani Hill, behind the Navapashana (Nava means Nine and Pashana means poison) statue of Lord Murugan.

༺ ༻

THERAIYAR

"Great Siddha, deliverer of many scripts, is Theraiyar.
A rare son of Great Sage Agasthiyar;
A 'flawless' in the clan of Brahmam,
His Attainment of Kaya Siddhi is an amazing one!"

Siddha Karuvurar Vatha Kaviyam

Siddha Theraiyar's history is also not without mythological background. He is said to have performed a craniotomy to remove a mass from the brain. Although he is not included among the 18 Siddhars, his contribution towards diagnosis and treatments in the path of Siddha medicine is much greater than many of the 18 Siddhars. A few of his books are written in high grammatical language while another set of books are written in a very simple manner. It is probable that two different persons may have composed these verses. There is reason to believe that he lived during the twelfth century A.D. because his medical classic Therar Maruthuva Bharatham is based on the great Epic Mahabharata. Therar Neekuri is a book, which deals at length with urine examination for diagnostic and prognostic purposes.

Therai (in Tamil) means toad – a small frog-like creature living among stones. There is an interesting story about how Theraiyar got this name.

> "Once, a king had an unbearable headache. Sensing the cause to be a tumour-like mass, Siddha Agasthiyar performed brain surgery. Within the king's skull he found a tiny toad – perhaps it had grown there from an egg! Completely bewildered Agasthiyar wondered what to do.
>
> Theraiyar, still a learner, much to everyone's surprise at once grasped the situation. Using his presence of mind he said, 'Sprinkle water, it will react only to water'. So, Theraiyar sprinkled water from a pot onto the tiny creature. Feeling the sensation of water the toad instantly jumped out from inside the king's brain.
>
> Siddha Agasthiyar highly appreciated Theraiyar's presence of mind and gave him the name 'Theraiyar'."

There is yet another story about how Theraiyar got his name:

> "For a long time Theraiyar meditated deep inside a cave without food and breath similar to how a toad hides between rocks or a bear hibernates in a cave. He was probably given the name Theraiyar because of his Yogic *Tapas* bearing similarity to the behaviour of a toad."

Theraiyar Neerkuri-Neikuri deals at length with urine examination for diagnostic and prognostic purposes. Theraiyar Thaila Varga Churukam is a treatise on the preparation of oil-based drugs used internally and externally.

Other books attributed to him are:

Nadakkam
Anthathi
Yamaha venba
Karisal
Sikichaikiramam
Marunthalavai (Medical logics)
Gunapada venba
Pathartha gunam
Sikkamani venba

ಲ ೧೩

GORAKKAR

Siddha Gorakkar's guru, Siddha Machendranath was a wandering Siddha and this story is about how he received the direct benediction of Lord Siva.

SECTION ONE: HISTORY OF SIDDHAS

"One day, Lord Siva seated by the seashore was imparting the sacred knowledge of *Swara Yoga* to His consort Goddess Parvathi. After some time Goddess Parvathi succumbed to sleep, but Lord Siva continued imparting the valuable teachings. At that very time in the ocean was an avid listener. A fish was listening to the Lord's sacred words. Hearing the graceful words of Lord Siva the fish transformed into human form.

In this new form, he humbly began walking towards the Lord. Seeing him, Lord Siva showered his grace on him and blessed him with the knowledge of the teachings. The Lord declared he would be a great Siddhar. He is none other than Siddha Machendranath.

As ordained, Siddha Machendranath became a wandering Siddha, begging for his food, never staying at one place for a long time. Once, passing through a village he approached a small hut to beg food. A woman emerged from the hut and promptly offered him food. Seeing the woman, Siddha Machendranath felt the grief and sorrow she carried in her heart. He asked the reason for her heavy heart. She confessed it was because she was childless. Out of compassion, Siddha Machendranath manifested *Vibhuti* (scared ash) and handed it to her, instructing her to swallow it. Blessing her with a child, he left. Fearing him to be a magic man and doubting the blessing, the woman, not finding the courage to have the *vibhuti* as instructed, threw it into a pile of ashes behind her kitchen.

Years went by. Siddha Machendranath returned to the village and stood before the same hut asking the woman to bring the child. Fearfully she confessed she hadn't consumed the *vibhuti*. When he asked what she had done with it, pointing to the place behind the house, she said she had thrown it into the ashes. To her surprise Siddha Machendranath was undisturbed. He turned and walked up to the pile and called out, "Gorakkar! Get up and come!" From amidst the ashes walked out a very young boy!"

This boy is Siddhar Gorakkar - The great Alchemist.

> I would like to share here -
> "The Siddha's Words Never Fail"

An expert in the natural medicinal system of herbs and metals, Siddha Gorakkar was the first Siddha to detoxify and use cannabis ("ganja") as medicine. Commonly called herbal "ganja" (cannabis), is originally known as "Gorakkar Mooli" and several of Gorakkar's preparations use this herb. Some of these medicines have a shelf life of many many years. These were prepared and preserved by him in a place named "Gorakkar Gundam" in the Kolli Hills, where he has been known to live in his later years. He is said to still reside there invisible to the eyes of the ordinary world. Gorakkar Gundam is concealed by an underground hill and is covered by natural protection. Only those with divine blessings can reach this place and see Siddhar Gorakkar in Yogic *Samadhi*. Even today, aspirants or devotees circumambulating the Gundam are graced by His divine blessings. Different treasures such as the many palm leaf manuscripts written by him, remain hidden in secret places in the Gundam. The number of books written by Him on the subject of medicine, yoga, alchemy, astronomical science, literature and astrology remain preserved in Gorakkar Gundam, in the Kolli Hills.

There are several *samadhi* places of Siddha Gorakkar that are worshipped. One is situated in Gorakhpur (in Madhya Pradesh) and another around 35 kilometres from Madurai, called Tirupuvannam. Siddha Gorakkar is said to have accomplished the pinnacle of alchemy in the ancient Siva temple located there, where His body transformed into gold. Close to the Siva temple is a temple called Adi Gorakkinath where Siddha Gorakkar's *samadhi* shrine is worshipped.

> "The house of our soul, the body, belongs to us;
> So, I am declaring openly to you.
> Every country has its own God;
> The world's animation is ruled, by an air-like pulsation;
> And the millions of names representing God, represent this pulsation only.
> Without this pulsation, the cosmos will just perish itself!"
>
> Gorakkar Chandra Regai

Only a few of his books have come into the world; written on palm leaves they speak of medicine, alchemy and yogic knowledge. Some of these books are:

Gorakkar Chandra Regai
Gorakkar Ravimeghalai
Gorakkar Muttharam
Gorakkar Namanasa thiravukol
Gorakkar Malai Vagaddam

Patients undergoing treatment may also pray to Siddha Gorakkar for his healing blessings. One could also chant a specific mantra to receive Siddha Gorakkar's blessings.

CHAPTER TWO: HISTORY OF SIDDHA TRADITION

SIVA VAKKIYAR

"That which is 'I'; That which is 'evil'; That which is 'in between'
That which is 'distorted'; That who is 'Guru' - O fools, tell me!
That which is 'creation'; That which 'destruction' is;
That which is the Beyond of Beyond' - The Nama that gave birth,
Is Rama! Rama! Rama!"

Poems of Siva Vakkiyar, Verse 13

"Right from his early years, Siva Vakkiyar learnt Vedantic tradition and ritualistic ceremonies from his Gurukula teacher but his inner search remained thirsty and seeking. So as soon as he was of age, he left everything and took to wandering in search of the Guru. He reached Banaras. There he heard of a cobbler with an unheard of skill. He could stitch a person's shoes by merely looking at their feet. He needed no measurements. Siva Vakkiyar wished to meet this cobbler.

On seeing the cobbler, Siva Vakkiyar felt strongly drawn to him. He sat down close by. The cobbler turned to Siva Vakkiyar and asked, 'What do you want?' Siva Vakkiyar expressed his wish, 'To know the path of *Gnana*.' The cobbler glanced at him but said nothing. Deciding to verify the fire in his quest, the cobbler removed some coins from his bag and handed them to Siva Vakkiyar. He said, 'Give these coins to my Sister Ganga.' Then he asked Siva Vakkiyar to do something strange. He gave him a bitter species of bottle gourd and said, 'Wash it enough to clean away the bitterness.' Accepting these things, Siva Vakkiyar left without a question. He first washed the bitter bottle gourd in the nearby river, Ganga. As he was washing two hands emerged from the river. He placed the coins in the outstretched palms most naturally after which Siva Vakkiyar returned to the cobbler.

This time the cobbler playfully said, 'My sister Ganga is diplomatic and won't keep the money', and handed Siva Vakkiyar a leather water flask. When Siva Vakkiyar opened the water flask two tiny hands emerged and returned the coins to him. Siva Vakkiyar in turn returned these coins to the cobbler.

All through the series of strange occurrences, Siva Vakkiyar never showed any sign of surprise or shock. Based on this nature, the cobbler agreed to share the secrets of Truth with him.

The cobbler's yogic visions had revealed that Siva Vakkiyar experienced horripilation when touched by the tiny feminine hands. So after the cobbler shared the *Upadesha* with Siva Vakkiyar, he gave him instructions. Handing him a bitter bottle gourd and a bag of sand, he asked Siva Vakkiyar to wander until he finds the woman who can cook these two things for him. She is the one he should marry. This would remove any *vasanas* that remained within him.

Siva Vakkiyar accepted and took to wandering and performed penance. Wherever he wandered, people were naturally drawn to him. Some would offer salutations. Sometimes women were attracted to him. But when he would put forward the condition that they should first cook the bitter bottle gourd and sand for him they thought him crazy and left. One day, after hours of wandering he felt hungry. He saw a group of tribals. In one of the huts was a young woman who came and asked him what he would like to have. Siva Vakkiyar expressed his hunger. He asked to see her parents. She explained that they were out in the forest cutting bamboos. She offered to give him whatever he needed. Siva Vakkiyar handed her the sand and the bitter bottle gourd and asked if she would cook it for him. Innocently she accepted. As she emptied the sand into boiling water, it miraculously turned into rice and when she added the bottle gourd to it, it turned into curry. When she offered him the food Siva Vakkiyar realised she was the one he was to marry. Just then the young woman's parents returned and seeing a Yogi in their hut respectfully offered their salutations. Siva Vakkiyar expressed his wish to marry their daughter as she was gracious and suitable to look after him during his years of penance. The parents gratefully accepted his proposal and the two were happily married.

Years passed. Siva Vakkiyar continued his penance. He would also go to the forest to cut bamboos to make cane baskets. One day when he cut open a bamboo, out flew gold dust. He reeled back in shock. He called out to Lord Siva asking why He was showing him the Lord of Yama when he had undertaken penance for eternal bliss. Hearing his loud cry four people came running and gathered around. On enquiry, they learnt when Siva Vakkiyar had been engrossed in cutting bamboo, Lord of Yama had come there. The four people turned to look to where he pointed and saw gold everywhere. They whispered amongst themselves about how Siva Vakkiyar was calling gold the Lord of Yama. Assuming him to be crazy and unfit to live in the world, the four people quickly gathered the gold dust in two bags and left. Hungry and tired after a long day of work, two friends offered to go and buy food for all four of them. Secretly, they planned to poison the food of the other two and keep the gold for themselves. The two people about to eat the poisoned food asked for a drink of water and while their two friends were drawing water from the well, they crept up behind and pushed them into the deep well. Gleefully, they returned to eat the food, but, alas, they too were dead soon! Next morning, as usual Siva Vakkiyar came walking down the path to the bamboo forest. He found two bodies in the well and two bodies on land. He proclaimed, 'For sure it is the Lord of Yama!'

༄༅

One day, Siva Vakkiyar sat outside his hut weaving a cane basket. Above, as Siddha Konganavar was flying by in the sky, he sensed powerful vibrations of devotion and penance coming from Siva Vakkiyar. Siddha Konganavar descended. Both instantly recognised each other and exchanged a few words. Secretly, Siddha Konganavar wondered why Siva Vakkiyar lived in such suffering and ordinariness even after knowing the secret of alchemy. When Siva Vakkiyar left for the forest to bring more bamboo, Konganavar approached his hut, called out to his wife and asked for an iron rod. She brought him an iron rod upon which Siddha Konganavar threw some things and it transformed into gold. After this miraculous feat he left.

Once Siva Vakkiyar returned, his wife showed him the gold, which he asked her to throw into a nearby pond. After she left to do so, it suddenly occurred to him that maybe it was his wife who may have desired for gold and asked for it from Konganavar. He decided to verify his doubt. Walking out of his hut he urinated on a stone. After his wife returned, he asked her to bring some water and pour it over the stone. She did. Fumes of smoke arose from the rock. After the smoke dispersed, she saw the stone had turned to gold. Siva Vakkiyar said that if she wanted gold she could have it. She calmly replied, 'To make something external into gold, one must first have gold within and the gold within you is your love for me which is more than enough for me'!"

Throughout his life, Siva Vakkiyar had seen people craving for material gold. He saw them suffering in their conditioned livingness not realising the futility of their pursuit. Ultimately, he resorted to writing his famous work, Siva Vakkiyar Padalgal - 1000 verses. His poems shine a rebellious spirit soaring against the limiting nature of social conditioning. He sings for people to work hard for their livelihood and abstain from falling prey to greediness. Siva Vakkiyar has expressed the secret dimensions of Yoga most divinely. His work Nadi Pariksha deals with the nature of pulse and methods of diagnosis. His poems emit a powerful call; inspiring one towards the Siddha path of Truth realisation.

"I had not known the One that was in me;
Having known the One that was in me;
Who can see the One that was in me?
By being in myself, I realised."
Siva Vakkiyar Padalgal, Verse 7

He cryptically sings of Internal Alchemy...

"In the base, Reeds grown in the pond;
If you arise early morn, cut four bundles,
The aged turn young and be Para Brahmam,
All by their gracious feet, the Blue throated One Siva, and Sakthi,
True! True! True!"
   Siva Vakkiyar Padalgal, Verse 155, by Siddha Siva Vakkiyar

Some of His available works are:

Nadi Pariksha
Siva Vakkiyar Padalgal - 1000

ಲ ಡ

YUGIMUNI

MahaMuni Bogar has furnished interesting details in his 7000 poems, 4th volume, poem 622 to 633, and Volume 6, poem no. 444.

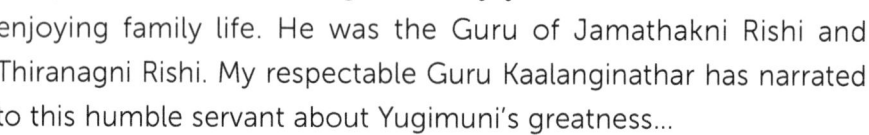

Says Bogar, "Yugimuni was one among the greatest Siddhas; living for many years enjoying family life. He was the Guru of Jamathakni Rishi and Thiranagni Rishi. My respectable Guru Kaalanginathar has narrated to this humble servant about Yugimuni's greatness...

> "Yugimuni travelled south along the 'Panri Malai' hills in search of the herbal riches of hills and mountains. Once, while walking in the thick of a stone pillar lay across his path. He chose this spot for meditation. Yugimuni remained seated there deeply immersed in trance.
>
> One day, while still in trance he was frightened by a strong tremor and thunderous sound. He sat there stunned and motionless.
>
> Before him stood a grand column of light stretching to enormous heights, surpassing the limits of the sky above. The column of light was indescribable to human eyes. The

thunderous tremor seemed to have affected the entire universe as well as the planets and stars in the cosmos. Dumbfounded at the magnanimity and overwhelming power radiating from the column, Yugimuni fell prostrate.

When he opened his eyes, he saw the great Sage Sri Sambara standing there in his light body. Yugimuni reverentially touched the holy feet of this great Siddha Yogi and prayed for the teachings of the uniqueness of *'Vasi Yoga'*. Pleased, Sage Sri Sambara revealed to him the significance and the secret dimensions of *Vasi Yoga*. He then asked Yugimuni to remain close to his *samadhi*. Saying thus, Sri Sambara entered into *samadhi* right there. Yugimuni stayed there for many years.

At last he too wished to enter into *samadhi*. On a stone, he engraved the signs that would manifest right before he re-emerged from his *samadhi*. The engraving described his return to be at a time of pre-dawn (a mixture of day and night). Yugimuni remained in the state of *samadhi* for many years.

After many years, a thundering sound was heard and Yugimuni re-emerged from *samadhi*. Even after so many years in *samadhi,* his body hadn't degenerated at all. His hair had grown long like the roots of a banyan tree. Yugimuni then lived in the world a miraculous life; giving *darshan* to many devotees. He was a supreme teacher and had accomplished all the knowledge of the ancient treatises and experienced many secret dimensions of alchemy, medicine and yoga.

Yugimuni held a great love for my Guru, Kaalanginathar..."

SECTION ONE: HISTORY OF SIDDHAS

...Thus, spoke Siddha Bogar of Siddha Yugimuni in his divine verses.

Siddha Yugimuni's classification of disease pathology is the primary one followed today by Siddha physicians. His classification of disease is extremely extensive and clear. The classification of disease in modern day medicine cannot equal it even now.

Until his time, classification of disease was based on the three *Doshams*. Siddha Yugimuni was the first to classify disease according to clinical signs and symptoms. Based on Their sound knowledge and experience, Siddha Yugimuni and Siddha Theraiyar wrote classics on clinical medicine. The insight and experience of Yugimuni is astonishing. He has even described neoplastic growth of organs such as rectum and prostate.

> "Churn the ocean and extract elixir from it;
> Mix the salt of Siva, the ruler of destiny;
> Purify and amalgamate mercury from its seven impure covers;
> If cant, you proud alchemists, will be got by the final sleep!"
> Yugimuni Madhi Venba, by Siddha Yugimuni

His work on external alchemy is highly appreciated to date.

Some of His different classics are:

Yugi Chintamani
Yugi vadakaviyam
Yugi Karisal
Yugi Vaidhiya Ula
Puranam –100
Vatha Vaidhiya vilakam
Yugimuni Tattwa Gnanam
Yugimuni Madhi Venba

CHAPTER TWO: HISTORY OF SIDDHA TRADITION

PAMPATTI

"Pampatti Siddha was a simple snake charmer. Once, while looking for snakes in a nearby forest he came upon an unusually large snake hill. Thinking there to be a large snake within it also meant finding a *'ratna'* (gem). Eagerly, he inserted his hand into the snake hole. To his surprise, he felt a strong current in his hand. He quickly withdrew his hand and retreated. Right before his eyes the snake hill vanished and there sat a holy sage.

The sage asked why he was disturbing the snakes. Pampatti explained he was a snake charmer and that snakes were his means of livelihood. The sage explained the snake species to be cursed and that he shouldn't be disturbing them. The sage asked him a question, 'Do snakes exist only outside?' He urged Pampatti to capture the snake within himself.

The words of the sage struck Pampatti at the very core of his being, making him unbearably curious about what the sage had indicated. Seeing his awakened curiosity, the sage blessed him by touch and thus began Pampatti's journey onto the path of Siddhas."

This sage was none other than Sattaimuni.

Pampatti Siddha was an expert on toxicology and mystic cures but none of his books on these topics are presently available to us. Nagamuni, yet another name for this Siddha, has also written a detailed classic on ophthalmology and diseases of the head.

"WE make a pillar appear like a small stick,
WE make a small stick appear like a huge pillar,
WE change a man into woman, and woman into man...

Throwing the eight mountains, lifting them like a ball,
Drinking and burping all the seven Oceans,
Bending skies like an archer,
Transforming the three worlds into pure Gold,
Swimming through the blazing Fire,

WE change the burning sunshine into cool moonlight,
WE ruin and destroy all, this big world,
WE create new creatures like those made by God,
WE live on equal footing to the Lord of Lords...

WE subdue the fiery tiger, elephant, Yali, to make them serve,
WE make the magnanimous God, to play with US.

O snake dance! Declaring all this, WE playfully do!"
      Poems of Pampatti Siddha, Verses 28-34

Some of His books are:

Nagamuni nayanavidhi
Siraroka vithy
Pampatti Siddhar Padalgal

DHANVANTHRI

"In ancient times when the demons and gods churned the ocean, the divine cow, Kamadhenu, came forth which the sages took possession of. Then emerged the white horse, Ucchaisrava. King Mahabali

CHAPTER TWO: HISTORY OF SIDDHA TRADITION

took possession of it. Next came the moon-white elephant Airavatha, of four tusks. Indra, the Celestial King took possession of it. Then surfaced the red Kousthubha jewel which was accepted by Lord Vishnu. After it, the wish-yielding tree of Parijatha emerged which was planted in Indra's paradise. And then the celestial nymphs, the Apsaras appeared. Now arose, Goddess Lakshmi. Indra gave her an excellent seat. The Rivers offered Her pots of their pure water. The earth offered Her herbs and flowers. She was given ablutions by the rishis. The presiding deity of the ocean presented Her with yellow silks and a garland. Lord Brahma offered a lotus flower and Goddess Saraswathi offered Her a necklace of pearls. Holding a garland of lotus flowers, Goddess Lakshmi went around, seeking a suitable husband. She saw some defect or another in all those assembled there. Some had asceticism but lacked control over anger. Some were wise but bound by attachment, while some were heroic but had not conquered concupiscence. Some had the virtue of righteousness but felt no love for fellow beings, and some had the quality of renunciation but were not conducive to final beatitude. Some held great prowess but were short-lived and some were perpetual celibates. Some had a long life but no amiability towards women. Some had a long life as well as amiability but were too inauspicious in outward conduct. Deliberating thus, Maha Lakshmi chose Lord Vishnu and placed the wreath of lotus flowers around his neck. He accepted Her even though he held no interest in Her and placed Her on His chest. After this, Goddess Vaaruni appeared. She presided over wine. The demons caught hold of her with the approval of Lord Vishnu. And then emerged a man clad in yellow robes, of broad chest that was adorned with all kinds of ornaments. Charm exuded from his every limb. In his hands, he carried a pot of nectar. He was part manifestation of Lord Vishnu or Lord Krishna. He was Siddha Dhanvanthri."

He revealed the knowledge of Ayurveda. A few books written by Dhanvanthri are available in Tamil. One among them is on pulse diagnosis, a unique specialty of Siddha medicine. His *samadhi* is found in Vaideeswararn temple near Tanjore, in Tamil Nadu.

His other works are:

Dhanvanthri Thylam – 500
Dhanvanthri Vaidhiya Kaviyam
Dhanvanthri Vaidhya - 200
Dhanvanthri Nigantu - 800
Dhanvanthri Vaidya Thirattu - 1000

ಬಿ ಲ್

THIRUVALLUVAR

Saint Thiruvalluvar has written the Tamil Veda Thirukkural. In this work we find ten couplets on disease, treatment, dietary habits and life regimen. Siddha Thiruvalluvar emphasises the necessity to understand the causative factors of any disease for cure.

He wrote:

"Noi Nadi Noi mudal nadi athu thannikum
Vai nadi vaippa cheyal"
"Find the disease, its cause and the right way to cure it."

He explains how the cooperation of the physician, the pharmacist, the patient and the drug are all vital for treatment and healing of any disease. He describes how disease is caused by an imbalance of the three humors: *Vatham*, *Pittam* and *Kapham*. (Detailed in coming chapters). He has written Gnanaveetiyan and Thiruvalluvar's Nayanar Karpa vithi: a treatise on the science of elixirs for longevity and immortality. In that book, they mention the use of one hundred and eight herbs in *KayaKalpa* as rejuvenating medicines.

> "Searching elixir for the body,
> No need to wander around forests and mountains,
> The ever-lasting elixir is within you.
> It has grown, the fools without knowing it,
> Continuously ate leaves and died.
> Oh! If you search in my works,
> The unobtainable elixir will reach you,
> So worship and understand my work Gurunool-50."
>
> Thiruvalluvar Kalpam - 300

Apart from the above, many more have contributed towards Siddha medicine. Since Their writings are still in the form of palm scripts and yet to be compiled, they lay in the form of hidden treasures. Many Siddhas have expounded oneness with God as the ultimate goal in life. It will not be wrong to say that traditional Siddha medicine is a by-product of the Siddhas seeking to reach God. They firmly believe the physical body to be an instrument to attain *Mukthi*.

Sri Bahuladevi   Kaga Busunder

CHAPTER TWO: HISTORY OF SIDDHA TRADITION

KAGA BUSUNDAR MAHARISHI

Many different stories from Vedic lore as well as the Siddha tradition talk about the life of Kaga Busundar. Here is one from the Siddha tradition.

Siddha Sri Kaga Busundar was the holy son of Saraswathi (or Sakalakala Valli, in Tamil). Goddess Saraswathi was a Guru (Master) to her son and taught him everything about the creation of the world.

> "One day, the divine assembly gathered in Mount Kailash, the capital of the mystic world. (Kailash is a holy place in the Himalayan hills). The celestial devotees of Lord Siva and Goddess Parvathi enquired about the secret of the creation of the world. Lord Siva said, 'I appoint Kaga Busundarasa Guru to this world; he is to teach the secrets of creation to all living beings and to all celestial administrators of the different worlds.' Lord Siva asked his subordinates to henceforth follow the instruction of their Guru, Kaga Busundar, who was ordained the divine Master from that day on."

From that day on, Siddhas and Maharishis sought to clarify their doubts by praying to Kaga Busundar, who continues to guide the world wisely with *dharma*. He revealed the sacred arts and yogic techniques. Kaga Busundar is the Guru of sage Vasishta Maharishi. Vasishta Maharishi is the guru of the avatar Rama. Kaga Busundar is a *'Chiranjeevi'*, (blessed with eternal life); away from the eyes of the world, he is living, blessing and guiding the world. In his classical work, Kaga Busundar Perunool Kaviyam 1000, he mentions how during *'Pralaya'* (dissolution of the world) he survived in the form of a crow and was witness to the creation of the world again. Seeing this, the Trimurti (Holy Trinity) appreciated his deathlessness and received the blessings of the wisdom of immortality.

According to the Siddha tradition, Kaga Busundar Maharishi is believed to be ever living in the form of a crow (*kagam* in Tamil). His valuable work in Tamil called 'Kaga Busundar Perunool Kaviyam-1000'k consists of ancient yogic secrets and *Kayakalpa* practices of Inner Alchemy. Another work by him is 'Kaga Busundar Pancha Patchi Sastra'. This work speaks of occult astrology. (*Pancha* means five and *patchi* means bird.) He has also written other works like 'Busundar Upanishad' and 'Busundar Kural.' In any Vedic spiritual practice while finishing a holy session, it is common to chant *'AUM SHANTHI, SHANTHI, SHANTHI'*. Likewise, Siddha Kaga Busundar revealed an important and excellent mantra to obtain the blessings of Existence. *"NAR BAVI"* - (Let good be manifested).

One can feel the presence of Kaga Busundar Maharishi in the temple of Uttar Kosa Mangai, a village 120 kilometres west of Madurai. The Uttar Kosa Mangai kovil consists of three temples: the main sanctum, the temple of Adi-Chidambaram, and a small temple containing the statue of Lord Natarajar made in emerald and a small shrine of Lord Ganesha. Behind the statue of Lord Ganesha is the sanctum of the Sahasra lingam. Built around a tree is a raised platform, containing the very ancient and holy '*paduka*' (wooden sandals) of Vyasa Maharishi. This tree, an elandai tree (with small orange-coloured fruits the size of small gooseberries, or Amlas) is said to be 3000 years old. Beneath the elandai tree is the statue of Lord Ganesha. It is believed that this is where Lord Ganesha appeared to Vyasa and wrote the great Hindu Epic Mahabharata as Vyasa narrated it. It is also said that Lord Ganesha broke one of his tusks to write with. There is also a holy tank in front of this small shrine. It has been said that Lord Natarajar shared divine secrets to the people at a holy temple in Chidambaram. Here at Uttarha Kosa Mangai, another name for Adi-Chidambaram, divine secrets were revealed only to Goddess Uma. The entire year the sanctum of Lord

Natarajar is locked after cladding the statue with sandal wood paste (*chandan*). Once a year, on the full moon of Arudra nakshatra, (mid December to mid January) the emerald-clad Lord Natarajar gives *darshan*. On this auspicious day of Arudhra, the holy sandalwood paste is washed away and offered to devotees as *prasad* and is said to have great medicinal and divine properties.

৸ Ꮓ

IDAIKATTU SIDDHA

"Blow the flute in song,
Blow the flute in song - O shepherd,
For in the music of Silence
Is Truly Freedom!"
        Poems of Idaikattu Siddha, Chapter Milking of cow,
        Verse 98

Idaikattu Siddha was born in a village called Idaikattu, 24 kilometres from Madurai. His *samadhi* is in Tiruvannamalai.

Here is an incident that took place with him.

"He was a herdsman, caring for cows. Once, he pre-cognised a famine to strike throughout the world. Taking all his cows with him he went up a nearby hill. There he called all the deities (rulers) of each of the nine planets and offered them a feast. After eating the delicious food all the planetary deities fell asleep. The deities laid down in a particular order to sleep. While they slept, Idaikattu Siddha changed their positions from a famine-causing order into a fertility-inducing order. When they woke up they realised what the wise herdsman had done. Famine didn't hit that village!"

The inner meaning to this story says: Wherever one is, if he lives according to *dharma* then the *dharma* of the universe can never fail; no disorder or disharmony will befall. The real meaning of *dharma* is: living in harmony with nature. Since Idaikattu Siddha changed the *dharma* (or nature) of time, here in Tamil Nadu he is worshipped by the followers of Siddha system at times when planetary relations can cause difficulties or bad effects on one's life.

Idaikattu Siddha Padalgal (songs) can be found in Gnana Kovai, a collection of Siddha songs edited by Aru Ramanathan.

ഇ ൕ

KONGANAVAR

"I speak all the secrets untold,
They won't tell, even if you give a million Gold,
But, my work reveals all,
That's why all Siddhas hide it from the world."

Konganavar Kalpam - 100

Siddha Konganavar undertook severe *tapas* at a very young age after which he attained many yogic *siddhis* (powers).

> "Once, as he was walking near a forest, droppings from a crane flying overhead landed upon his head. Konganavar looked up at the crane and using his third eye instantly burned it to ashes and continued walking. In those days whenever hermits came begging, householders would graciously offer food. Passing through another village Siddha Konganavar stood outside the gates of a house, with hands extended and called out: 'A Siddha has come! Offer some food!' There was

no response. He waited outside the gate and called again, 'I have come'. From inside the house, he heard the words, 'Wait'. He was kept waiting.

Inside, a woman was busy serving her husband food. She was who had called out, 'Wait'. She didn't go outside until she had finished fulfilling her *dharma*. At last she emerged from the house. Siddha Konganavar was terribly angry. Once again in anger, he used his yogic powers. To his surprise it didn't affect the woman at all. Instead she laughed and said, 'Do you think I am a crane?' 'How did she know?' he wondered. 'How is it that my *siddhi* powers had no effect?' 'How is it possible?' Siddha Konganavar's ego was shattered in that instance and he let go all his cravings for *siddhis* and yogic powers. The woman said, 'When one follows one's own inherent *dharma*, no harm can come. That is the real path to wisdom.'"

After that incident, Konganavar Siddha attained *Gnana*, self-realisation, and went on to expound all the teachings of the Siddha system with great lucidity. Siddha Konganavar's *samadhi* is at Tirupathi, in Andhra Pradesh.
Some of His works are:

Konganavar Vatha kandam has three parts.
Mudal kandam, Irandam kandam – the first and second volume are about medicinal preparations and the medicinal nature of herbs and metals. Kadai kandam (third) – clearly explains the Siddha's *Vaasi Yoga*, internal alchemical processes, the *Sri Chakra Pooja* and *Sakthi* worship. Many Siddhas appreciate and refer to the treatise of Siddha Konganavar and recommend it to seekers.

ಙ ಝ

KADUVELI

"There once lived a sage in the depths of a forest, performing penance in quiet solitude. Whenever he felt hunger he collected and ate a few dry leaves fallen from trees and continued with his penance. He lived his life peacefully.

The king of that region, wishing to verify the authenticity and true potential of the sage made an announcement throughout his kingdom. He invited anyone who could prove the true state of the sage to come forward. No one was keen to engage in this kind of endeavour, except one. A *daasi* from a small village came forward and agreed to the task. The *daasi* began living close to the hermit's hut. One day when the hermit was immersed in penance, she crept into his hut and mixed some crushed *Papad* (thin roasted bread preparation) into the collected dry leaves. She continued doing this for some time. Her plan was to gradually stimulate his taste buds for delicious foods. After a short period, she noticed a change in the sage. Gathering courage, she initiated contact and began helping him in simple household chores. This way the *daasi* gained familiarity. In due course, familiarity grew into intimacy and culminated into a strong bond. Soon she gave birth to a child. At this time, the *daasi* went to the king and declared she was ready to prove what the king had asked. Together, they conceived a plan. They invited people to the king's court where she would perform a dance. On this day, the *daasi* deliberately left home without feeding her infant child. She went to the king's court and amidst the large crowd of people began her performance.

Meantime, in the hut the infant awoke crying with hunger. During the dance, the *daasi* noticed the sage standing in one corner holding the infant in his arms. Without interrupting her performance she gave the King a knowing glance indicating the sage had arrived. Suddenly, amidst her graceful dance movements the *daasi* intentionally kicked off one of her anklets, sending it sweeping across the floor to where the sage stood. She danced towards the sage in graceful whirling movements and lifted her bare ankle out to him. The sage bent forward, lifted up the anklet and clasped it back on her raised leg. There was uproar amongst the onlookers. The court filled with laughter and mockery at the behaviour of the sage. They condemned him of having been enchanted by the *daasi* and lose his sagehood. The sage remained indifferent to the retorts of the people. Calm and unshaken he began singing...

"Let anger be dropped, victoriously,
Release the contemplating mind - until depletion,
If it were true, I sleep day and night in Grace,
May even stone split, transforming as infinite space."

Just as he finished those words, the stone sculptures in the king's court burst and shattered, leaving the people in shock. Eventually the people came forward in salutation to the sage, revering his divinity."

This is none other than Siddha Kaduveli. And this instance clearly shows one cannot judge or recognise a Siddha from mere appearance, or lifestyle as his existence prevails beyond all conditions.
His works are:

Kaduveli Siddhar Padalgal
Kaduveli Siddhar Gnanavindham

ಸಿ ಆ

AGAPAI

There is little information about Agapai Siddha. He lived the simple life of a weaver. Agapai felt a growing dispassion towards the transitory nature of the world and a calling towards the path of Truth. Whenever he observed strong attachment and heavy conditioning lurking in the people around him, out of compassion he would share his insights pointing to the transitory nature of the world so as to help them see Truth. But people lacked understanding which only made them tease him. Ultimately, he withdrew from the society and took to wandering.

One day, Agapai was walking near a forest when a Jothi Vriksha (tree of Light) appeared before him. It had a huge hole in the trunk. He felt a tremendous peace engulfing him. Agapai was pulled into the opening where he sat down in meditation. Years passed. One day, the great Vyasa Maharishi appeared before the opening and blessed him for his penance with the realisation of Truth and for him to be a great *Gnani*. The Maharishi also bestowed blessings for sharing Truth with people through his powerful divine verses. From that moment he became Siddha Agapai whose graceful and powerful songs are transformational; hitting one's core with the experience of the true essence of the Siddha path.

> "The place where I remained Summa - Agapai
> Burnt me, as I told;
> What a miracle, I do not know - Agapai,
> Then I couldn't find myself there!"
>
> Agapai Siddhar Padalgal, Verse 45

> "To whom does Saivam belong - Agapai?
> To those who have known their own Self,
> That place where Saivam is seen - Agapai,
> That is the feet of the Sat Guru."
>
> Agapai Siddhar Padalgal, Verse 55

CHAPTER TWO: HISTORY OF SIDDHA TRADITION

Some of His works are:

Agapai Siddhar Padal-90
Agapai Purna Gnanam-15

ಲಿ ಧ

PATTINATHAR

"There are rivers, groves, beautiful streets,
Encircling Temples, the sacred ash, rags to wear and loincloth;
O heart! That roars flustered, visiting daily, each house,
Begging alms; Eating sleeping and remaining poised in 'Summa',
Is, indeed 'Sugam.'"

Pattinathar Podu Padalgal, Verse 16
('Summa' means 'just being' and 'Sugam' means 'bliss')

"A child was born into a rich family of Vaisa caste (Merchant caste). He was named Swedaraniyam. Right from his early days, Swedaraniyam engaged in the family business of shipping and export of pearls to neighbouring countries. He married a woman named Sivakalai. Even after many years of marriage they hadn't conceived a child. Swedaraniyam was a pious individual so, along with his wife, he set off on a pilgrimage. One day they noticed a Brahmin couple standing under a tree holding a newborn child in their arms. Seeing Swedaraniyam they approached him, humbly requesting him to accept this child as his own. The Brahmin couple were suffering dire conditions and didn't have enough to feed themselves. Hearing this, Swedaraniyam recollected a dream he had just two nights ago. In his dream he had seen the exact same Brahmin couple coming to him and giving him a child. Recognising this as the grace of Lord Shiva, he and his wife, graciously accepted the Brahmin child. They named him Marudha Vanan. Days passed happily and Swedaraniyam's child grew up. Both parents noticed their child was disinterested in school activities and displayed steady dispassion toward worldly matters. Reaching adulthood, Marudha Vanan's father forcibly sent him on a ship to other countries to trade pearls for other gemstones. Months went by. Swedaraniyam and his wife eagerly awaited the return of their only son, wondering how he had fared on his first business trip. The ship returned. Marudha Vanan's assistants reached the house with several big bags. Swedaraniyam eagerly opened one of the bags. It was filled with cakes of cow-dung. There was no limit to Swedaraniyam's anger. He picked up a few cakes and flung them across the floor. Out spilt many many precious and valuable gemstones. Swedaraniyam was stunned. His heart filled with regret. He heard his son's calm voice first ask why he had reacted so and then say he had brought one more valuable item for him. Marudha Vanan handed over a small box to his father. Swedaraniyam refused it saying he was already overwhelmed by the gems and jewels his son had brought and didn't need anything more. But his son coaxed him to accept the small box, saying it was more precious than everything in the bags. Swedaraniyam opened the box. There was a needle with no eye for the thread to pass through and a single palm-script leaf. He lifted the palm-script. It said, 'Not even a needle without an eye will follow on your last day.' This hit Swedaraniyam hard. He felt everything around him spinning. In that instant he recognised his attachment to worldly things and its futility stared him in the face. When he looked around his son was gone. He searched everywhere, but in vain. He started calling out for his son. Hearing his cries, his wife and aged mother came rushing and enquired what had happened. Without further delay, Swedaraniyam changed into a simple loincloth and retired to a secluded spot in the town. He lived there and begged for food. He even begged alms from his own home. Swedaraniyam's sister and husband also lived in the same town. She felt ashamed of her brother and the strange turn of events. Her husband began eyeing Swedaraniyam's plentiful property. One day Swedaraniyam was walking through the street his sister lived in. Seizing the opportunity Swedaraniyam's sister called him and offered a sweet doughnut-like cake. The wicked couple had poisoned it! Holding the poisoned sweet cake in hand Swedaraniyam said to his sister, 'One's karma itself will burn oneself and this doughnut will burn the house.' At the end of these words Swedaraniyam threw the cake on the roof of the house. The roof instantly caught fire and the house began to burn. Seeing this, his sister and her husband realised their grave mistake and fell at Swedaraniyam's feet begging forgiveness."

Swedaraniyam became a wanderer and was called Pattinathar by the people. One day he travelled to the north of India for the *darshan* of Goddess Ujjaini. At the time, the King of Ujjain was BhadraHari. In later years, he became a disciple of Pattinathar and by the grace of his Guru attained realisation.

Many songs composed by Siddha Pattinathar lament for grace to reveal the transitory nature of the world. While walking by the seashore one day, Pattinathar saw young fishermen playing by hiding themselves inside a cane basket. He went up to them and asked if he could play too. The boys agreed. Pattinathar picked up the cane basket to hide in and asked the lads to come back a little later to look for him. The boys agreed. When the boys returned and upturned the cane basket, to their surprise, there was a Siva Lingam in the place where Pattinathar had sat. The name of this spot is Tiruvotriyur; a seashore in Chennai. Many flock to his *samadhi* Shrine for his divine blessings.

> "What though They do, What though They undergo,
> The Liberated are ever poised in Silence.
> With easy still, she sports a gait, flowing hands twain,
> Yet, the housemaid has an eye on the water pot,
> She carries over her head."
>
> Pattinathar Podu Padalgal, Verse 18

> "Without wrath, desire, deed, remembrance,
> Or forgetfulness, freed from intellect,
> When shall I, all alone, remain poised,
> In the blissful slumber of mystical drowse,
> O Father, O lord of Kailash?"
>
> Kailaya Darshan Padal, Siddha Pattinathar

> "There is enough clothing when the chill wind blows;
> There is something to cover when the sun's heat grows;
> There are shaded porches all over the world, for us to stretch;
> When hungry, there is Siva, the Giver;
> O heart! Nothing do we, lack."
>
> Pattinathar Podu Padalgal, Verse 17

Some of His works are:

- Arut Pulambal-116
- Koyir Tiru Agaval-4 sections
- Nenjodu Pulambal-37
- Purna Malai-102
- Gnanam-100
- Tiru Ekamba Malai
- Podu Padalgal

Iddaikattu Siddha

Siddha Thiruvalluvar

Siddha Pattinathar

Siddha Ramalingam

SECTION ONE: HISTORY OF SIDDHAS

RAMALINGAM

"It was a priest who first recognised him... A man with his five-month old child came to the Chidambaram Temple for the *darshan* of Lord Natarajar. He stood before the sanctum. The temple priest began offering *aarti* to the Lord. In the same instant, the five-month old child burst into loud laughter. The surprised priest emerged from the sanctum and walked towards the child. The priest instantly recognised him. He said to the father that his child was in Truth none other than the Lord's child. This incident took place in the year 1824.

๛ ఴ

Once, he was seated before a mirror in a dark room with only a lamp burning beside him. At that time, he was only eight years old. While looking in the mirror, the reflection of his face disappeared and instead Lord Murugan appeared in the form of a beam of light. Lord Murugan entered into the eight year old, merging into his forehead.

๛ ఴ

When he was an adult, for a few years he lived in a small house in a village called Karunguli. An old woman would come to look after him and help around in the daily housework. At nights he would write devotional poems and songs with the help of a small oil lamp. Oil lamps were lit in small mud or clay pots. To prevent the clay from absorbing too much oil, it was customary to keep the pots filled with water overnight before their first use. This would saturate the pores in the mud and prevent it from soaking in too much oil. Once, it so happened that a clay pot cracked. The old woman bought a new one. She filled it with water and left it to soak overnight. She left for the day without mentioning anything about the new clay pot. Evening came to pass and darkness began to fall. Engrossed in writing poetry, He lit the lamp and continued his divine writing."

The villagers were unaware of his divinity. It was through this incident people learned of his true nature. No one knew what his practice or *sadhana* was. They would often find him in strange paradoxical moments. At times he would be seated surrounded by a circle of fire during the hot noon sun. Some people, on entering his room unannounced, would find his body separated into nine parts. This is called '*Navakanda Yoga*', in the Siddha cult. While giving discourses, the people sitting in the last row and the people sitting in the first row would hear him the same. And many a times, he had resurrected the dead merely by his compassionate glance.

Finally, he sang in His songs

"Oh, divine Light,
You made me a great Siddha
Amongst the other Siddhas,
And all Siddhas speak in surprise of me."

He transformed His physical body into *Suddha Deha* (pure immaculate body), his subtle body into *Pranava Deha* (Omkar, or primal sound body) and his causal body into *Gnana Deha* (Body of wisdom) and attained a Light body, known as "Oli Udambu'. This is the highly revered Siddha Saint Ramalingam, also known as 'Vallalaar' by the people; the magnanimous, generous and compassionate one. He lived in society from 1823 to 1874.

SECTION ONE: HISTORY OF SIDDHAS

In the year 1874, Siddha Saint Ramalingam entered into a room and transformed into Light and disappeared before the onlookers. This room is in a town called Vadallur and many of his devotees frequent here seeking his blessings. Siddha Ramalingam's life was filled with heart-rending devotion and immense compassion towards the suffering of all living beings. This nature caused the divine phenomena of melting habitual inertia and the tamasic nature gripping the body. The transformation occurred down to the cellular level and alchemically transformed Him into a gracious eternal divine Light.

This great Siddha Saint sang of death as an ignorant habit and a careless mistake...

> "O people of the world,
> Come! Come you can live the life
> Of deathlessness,
> Speaking the truth,
> Nor exaggerate nor lie!
> But speaking the solemn truth
> Come, follow me,
> To enter the hall of Gold
> The hall of Gnosis."
>
> Verse 5876 of Thiruarutpa

This was a turning point for many Siddha followers. It brought reality to ancient belief and Truth to the myth of the immortality sung in Siddhas verses. Not long ago, this great Siddha Saint lived among people, showering his compassion and grace to one and all. And when this compassionate one did leave his physical form, he did so by merging into all living beings. This way he re-emerges as the seed, flowering into spiritual transformation. In his farewell discourse, a few moments prior to his disappearance into Light, he proclaimed to his loved devotees...

"I am in this body, henceforth, I would enter all physical bodies..."

Peru Upadesha Jan 1874

Some of His works are:

> Thiruarutpa (6000 songs)
> Manu Murai Kanda Vasagam - ethical prose work.
> Upadesha (his sacred teachings)
> Classification of Herbs
> Collection of letters to his devotees

> "He reigned supreme from my mid-point eye brow;
> In His luminosity like that of the camphor flame,
> I see no smoke, no flickering, but steady vision;
> He unleashed the closed gateway of my mid-eye,
> And liberated me from darkness to light everlasting;
> It was all His sport, glorified in the sacred lore!
>
> In the pinnacle of Light Mountain, I saw Thee,
> My eyes rejoiced in awareness serene; my eyes
> See naught but Thy light of consciousness;
> It is the light of Truth, the light of justice,
> The light of purity, the Light of righteousness;
> Such is Thy Luminosity Supreme That immersed me in bliss."
>   Verses from Mahadeva Malai By Siddha Saint Ramalingam

AVVAIYAR

The very occasion of Avvaiyar's birth is of significance. By pre-ordained karma, her parents had decided to abandon their baby on birth, but the mother could not wrench herself away. At that time baby Avvai comforted her by words, saying,

> "Lord Siva, who has intentionally brought me forth into this world and imprinted my destiny on my forehead, has not died, so, O mother even though famine stalks our land, the burden of succouring me is His. Don't be afraid to leave me alone."

A wandering minstrel, one of the lowest classes of society, brought up Avvai. Avvai remained a divine spinster all her life. In all the numerous legends and tales of her life, she is always referred as Grandma Avvai. The upbringing by a wandering minstrel gave Avvai wanderlust and groomed her into a divine singer and poet. The moment she sang of anyone, an abundance of worldly possessions would be showered upon that person. Three incidents reveal her magnanimity and deep traits of godliness, devotion and profound wisdom.

> "Once, participating in a social event held in the precincts of a temple, she sat down with legs outstretched towards the sanctum. Seeing this the priest got annoyed and said, 'How dare you sit like this. Old age doesn't entitle such liberties in the presence of God. You shall not point your legs in the direction of God.' Avvai quietly listened and then said, 'O, my friend, please excuse this old woman. Show me a direction where the Lord is not and I shall stretch my tired legs that way.'"

CHAPTER TWO: HISTORY OF SIDDHA TRADITION

There is no equal to Avvai and her spontaneous wit for satire and quick repartition. Her brilliance, genius and quick wit, all of perfect lucidity were something everyone bowed before.

Once, God wished to verify Avvai's humility...

"Avvai was winding her way along a lonely path when she saw a beautiful Jambu tree. She glanced up to check if the tree bore fruit. She saw a shepherd boy perched on some branches coolly eating fruit. In her usual audacious manner she called out, 'My little fellow, will you throw me some fruit?' The boy replied, 'Yes, grandma, but do you want hot or cold ones?' Avvai was piqued. She felt it below her dignity to ask what he meant by hot and cold fruits. She replied, 'Give me a hot one.' The boy plucked out some large ripe fruits and threw them down. They landed on the sandy earth. Avvai picked them up, blowing on each to clear the sand. Seeing this the boy taunted, 'Grandma, blow well, it's a hot fruit and will cool down only on blowing.' Startled by his retort, Avvai felt humbled. Her countenance fell. 'O, Lord am I to be humbled thus by a poor shepherd boy?' she cried. The boy jumped down from his branch. Smiling before her stood Lord Murugan with his peacock. He consoled her, 'Grandma, do not fret. We desired to hear something from you and so performed this sport. Will you answer a few questions?' Avvai was greatly relieved to see Lord Murugan. He posed four questions to her.

'What is sweet?'
Avvai said, 'Being in solitude is sweet; worshipping the Primal Lord, is sweeter. More than that is hearing divine words in the holy vicinity of the truly Divine. And the sweetest is seeing the Guru always, both in waking and dreaming...'

Next the Lord asked, 'What is hard?'
Avvai replied, 'Poverty is hard; poverty in young age is even harder. Harder still is an incurable disease. Exceedingly hard is a faithless woman and the hardest is to take food from her...'

The third question He asked was, 'What is great?'
Avvai replied, 'The world is big and Brahma, its creator, is even bigger. He was born out of the naval of Vishnu. Vishnu sleeps on the ocean of milk. All the oceans were just one sip for GuruMuni Agasthiyar. He in turn was born out of a *Kumbha* (an earthen pot); the pot is a piece of clay from the earth which hangs under the hood of the serpent Adishesha. The serpent is a ring on the little finger of Goddess Parvathi who is merged with Lord Siva. Siva is contained in the hearts of His devotees. The greatness of these devotees is indeed indescribable.'

Pleased, he asked her the last question, 'What is rare?'
Avvai spoke: 'Rare is human birth and even rarer is birth without any deformity. Even after such a birth it is rare for one to be interested in learning and wisdom. Even if one has such an interest it is rare to find one performing penance and giving charity. Even if one does penance and charity the way to liberation should unfold; that is truly most rare.'"

Delighted, Lord Murugan showered His blessings on Avvaiyar.
Avvaiyar was once asked to define the four Purusharthas (the four stages to be accomplished in human lifespan).
She replied,

"Giving is *Aram* (Dharma),
Earning in the righteous way is Porul (Artha).

Two lovers entwined in one-heartedness and an offered mutual support up to thought level, is Enbam (Kama). Relinquishing all these with your heart set on God, is Veedu (Moksha)."

On another occasion, Avvai was asked about the art of living, she said,

"That is true religion, which perceived unity in all things;
That is true valour, which has conquered the senses;
That is true learning which enables one to be kept alive forever and,
That indeed is true sustenance which does not make a slavery of another."

Avvaiyar's life on earth came to end by amazing divine grace.

"During her last days, Avvaiyar was immersed in the worship of Lord Ganesha. One day while performing her daily *Pooja*, she had the inner vision of her friend, the great Saint Sundarar, who having completed his mission on earth was being taken to Kailash, the abode of Lord Siva, at His command. Seeing this, Avvai turned anxious to leave her mortal coil and depart to Kailash along with Sundarar. Overcome by anxiety, she started doing the *Pooja* in a hurry. Lord Ganesha himself spoke, 'Grandma, do your *Pooja* as usual, without haste. We shall drop you to Kailash even before your friend arrives there.' Avvai performed her *Pooja* as usual and sang a song for Lord Ganesha. She sang beautiful praises of his infinite grace in helping all mortals. After the *Pooja*, Lord Ganesha lifted her with his trunk and placed her in Kailash! Avvai's joy knew no bounds."

SECTION ONE: HISTORY OF SIDDHAS

The song she sang on this occasion is still sung throughout Tamil Nadu during the festival of Ganesha Chaturthi. It holds symbolical significance of a yogic experience and has been added in the Yogic Section later in the book.

"Having known the One that knows him,
Then who else is there to know oneself?"
      Avvai Kural, chapter 2, Cotton on fire, Verse 5

"Having known Ajapa and gazing the awakening flame within,
No birth on earth for him."
      Avvai Kural, chapter 2, Cotton on fire, Verse 6

"Siva will not inhere in oneself,
Whose mind not be steady on any one thing."
      Avvai Kural, Gnana Veli, Verse 8

"Within the heart of the devotee who knows the self within,
Hara (Siva) resides as Love."

"At the moment of perceiving the wealth that is beyond all limits,
Illumination exists as silence there!"

"Whatever you learn and what you hear, understand
The wisdom thereof abiding in it,
Then it transforms as liberation!"

"To whom the new moon becomes the full moon,
Then life and form will be synchronised to Him!"
      Avvai Kural, chapter 10, Verse 7

Some of Her other works are:

Vinayakar Agaval
Avvai Kural (describes in depth all dimensions of yogic experience, by way of short couplets, in a Sutra form.)
Ethical works: Athi Chudi, Kondrai venthan, Moothurai...

౸ ౻

YAKOP

His original name was Ramadevar Siddha.

The miseries of the world and shallowness of ritual practice pushed Yakop to wander aimlessly. People called him crazy. Even he called himself mad. He wandered through many different places and crowds for six long years. One day, he saw a cozy and unconventional-looking man walking the street. Yakop's madness shattered before the magnanimous intoxication of divine madness that radiated from Sage Bhuthananda, who became Yakop's first Guru. After receiving his initiation into the Siddha path, from Siddha Bhuthananda, Yakop settled in a mountain cave as per his Guru's instructions. He remained in seated posture and meditative state for twelve years. The way of the mystics finally flourished! After twelve years, first Lord Subramaniam, Guru of Sage Agasthiyar appeared before Yakop. After this, Siddha Agasthiyar appeared. Yakop received teachings from them through mystical experiences of the Siddha path. In this manner, Yakop had *darshan* and meeting with all the ancient Siddhas earlier to his time. This entire information has been narrated by Yakop himself in his divine work Yakop Vakara Kandam.

౸ ౻

Once, he made a mysterious aerial visit (kagana markkam in Tamil) to Mecca. During this visit, he stood victorious in a debate on the *sastras* with some Islamic scholars. As recorded in the seventh poem of his work, Yakop Vaidhiya Chintamani, he describes how they lovingly embraced him after the debate and his victory. Perhaps, he converted to Islam influenced by his Islamic preceptor. It was his teacher who named him 'Yakopu,' the Tamilised form of Jacob. His leaning toward Islam is understood from the opening poem, as he offers prayer to both, Nabimaar (another name for the Prophet Mohammed) and to the messengers of Allah. The following poems describe worship to the Hindu Pantheon Gods, revealing his attachment to his original faith too. After narrating his autobiographical account, Siddha Yakop (or Ramadevar Siddha) directly proceeds to outline the contents of the whole text dealing with a variety of medicines.

Vaidhiya Chintamani is one of the best treatises on Siddha medicine. Books of this nature are a treasure house of native Siddha system of medicine, the secrets of which are known only to those belonging to the tradition of preceptor and pupil. Detailed instructions on the preparation of hundreds of medicines and drugs using minerals, metal dusts, nuts, roots, barks, acids, spices, herbs, and oils are elaborately presented. One medicine bears the name 'Chinese limestone' (Cheenakkara Chunnam) as recorded in poem 241 of this text. In this context, it is not wrong to note that Siddha Bogar had visited China several times and had close contact with people there, as mentioned in his medicinal treatise. Additionally, as revealed in different sources, cultural contact with foreign people is further attested through the anecdotes recorded in relation to the general Siddha tradition, and in particular of Siddha Yakop and Siddha Bogar. At present, our biggest handicap is the unavailability of some of the valued ancient Tamil Siddha literature. Due to repeated foreign invasions, most of the ancient palm-leaf manuscripts have been either destroyed or transported to other countries.

CHAPTER TWO: HISTORY OF SIDDHA TRADITION

An article written by C.S. Mohana Velu, which was included from a Hindu newspaper into Samagra Vikas, a Vivekananda Kendra Prakashan Trust Publication states:

"The Germans who came to Tamil Nadu in 1706 knew nothing about tropical herbs and diseases until they suffered from skin-rashes, boils and dysentery during their stay. Struck by nascent investigation, the Germans evinced a keen interest in the Siddha system. They collected hundreds of medicinal palm-leaf manuscripts and sent them, along with notes of German translations, to Germany "in remarkable haste, by the next available ship". Not a single native medical observation seems to have escaped their watchful eyes, nearly 300 years ago. A German diary dated February 20, 1726 said that Siddha doctors of that time (almost 300 years ago) knew and wrote about as many as 4,448 diseases and their corresponding herbal treatment. Among the hundreds of medical manuscripts which the Germans took, information is available about only a few:

>Vaguda Chuvadi deals with the origins and symptoms of diseases, their confirmation by pulse-study and treatment methods.
>Udal kooru thathuvam deals with the five elements, the five senses, diseases and related medicinal notes.
>Siddha aruda nandi chindu deals exclusively with poisonous insects and herbal treatment.
>Vaguda sasthiram (in 6 volumes and 120 chapters) deals in pathology, toxicology, surgery, as well as disease of men, women and children and its corresponding herbal treatment, as well as methods of pulse study, etc.

SECTION ONE: HISTORY OF SIDDHAS

> The Siddha system turned into a source of fascination for the Germans and through them other Western countries also came to know of the rich medicinal heritage of India. It is probable that as man started migrating, the system also spread and took on different names in different places. A treasury of Siddha source of information together with a record of observations by Germans, on the Tamil language, literature and culture, in diaries, travel accounts, station registers, personal letters, etc., numbering 200,000 manuscripts, is still available in Franken's archives of the Martin Luther University, Germany."

In Tamil Nadu, several palm scripts remain in the possession of local persons, kept undisclosed, and many have not been put to practical use. These palm scripts have not been allowed to move into the right hands. In the old days, palm scripts were passed from Master to disciple and put to use practically. It is unfortunate that the younger generations bear no understanding nor care for the palm scripts after the death of elders. Undermined or damaged, due to lack of care, palm scripts are thrown away. These palm scripts are an age-old, natural, national treasure, and hold the key for civilisation. They reveal the mysteries of life and beyond. The Government as well as people of the private sector should come forward to help in the preservation and maintenance of these valuable treasures of our country for the coming generations of the world. Native healers or vaidyas of the Siddha system, who hold in-depth valuable experience and holistic knowledge should be recognised, instead of being shunned based on so-called lack of scientific explanation. Their knowledge calls for heartfelt salutations as it is through them that the valuable healing medicinal system has carried on and survives.

෩ ෬

SECTION TWO
TREE OF LIFE

CHAPTER THREE
TATTWAS

> "Who can know the greatness of our Lord?
> Who can know His length and breadth?
> An infinite nameless flame is HE,s
> Whose unknowable roots, I venture to speak."
>
> Thirumanthiram, Verse 95, Siddha Thirumoolar

Sivam or Brahmam is pure consciousness and can be defined as the boundless plenum into which the universe is born, grows and dies; and as the continuum of experience that pervades, sustains and vitalises all Existence!

How did the world come to be?
> The Source derived an altered state, from which derived another and yet another and again and so on…until the process of evolution came to rest, at a point where no more creation was needed - here on happened only manifestation! Evolution had reached a state of perfect cosmic unrest; a state that allowed unlimited manifestation.

From the undisturbed existence of pure consciousness happens a primal alteration - a kind of distinction. Here, the first two Tattwas, the two inseparable yet distinct aspects of existence emerge; the Siva and Sakthi Tattwa (also known as MahaPrana). They are the beginning of cosmic evolution. Both aspects remain ever present, ever prevalent and cannot exist without the other. They are also known as *Purusha* (cosmic spirit) and *Prakruthi* (the cosmic substance). The entire world is nothing but a manifestation of the cosmic spirit and its substance. Every form, subtle or gross is this cosmic principle in an assumed or derived state.

> "...She assumes a million, million forms..."
> Thirumanthiram Verse 1102, Siddha Thirumoolar

Salience of this universal principle mystifies all existence - One of these two aspects is always more evident than the other.

TWENTY-FIVE TATTWAS

> "He constructs the Tattwas, twenty and five,
> To the life of me that is endless,
> Being within the egged womb, He creates;
> Knowing what I should be, He assails."
> Thirumanthiram, Verse 451, Siddha Thirumoolar

Of all the 96 Tattwas that are born, here we discuss 25. They are segregated into four distinct types.

The four types:

- That which is neither produced nor produces
- That which is not produced but produces
- Those which are produced and do produce
- Those which are produced and do not produce

> "They saw twenty five, who destroyed their birth.
> How Purusha entered the body corporeal, none else know;
> That which sought the woman's birth-pit, the bipolar,
> In form, twain rushed and fell."
> Thirumanthiram, Verse 454, Siddha Thirumoolar

Purusha or *Siva Tattwa* belongs to the first type - that which is neither produced nor produces. It is the Cosmic Spirit; the un-evolved and that which does not evolve. It is the uncaused, unborn and that which is not the cause of any new mode of being. *Purusha* is the soul of the universe and all living beings. It is the animating principle that breathes life into matter; the source of consciousness.

> "He bestowed the Truth of His
> Immanence to the world."
>
> Thirumanthiram, Verse 167, Siddha Thirumoolar

The second type - that which is not produced but produces, is the more active or evident aspect, called *Prakruthi* or the *Sakthi Tattwa*. It is also the un-evolved but it is from which evolution comes forth. *Prakruthi* is the original substance from which all things have come and to which all things will return. It is the primary nature of both the animate and inanimate - the primary nature of all existence. *Prakruthi* comprises of three constituents or forces called *Gunas*. Each *guna* is a derived aspect of existence and yet is never separate from the origin itself. A *Guna* remains distinct in its characteristics and functions.

The three *Gunas* (forces) are - *Sattwa, Rajas*, and *Tamas Guna*.
Sattwa Guna is of illumining character. It has the quality of equilibrium and manifests as light.
Rajas Guna has the quality of activity, excitement and manifests as the nature of movement.
The nature of *Tamas Guna* is inertia or darkness and has a restraining quality.

SECTION TWO: TREE OF LIFE

THE NEED FOR COSMIC UNREST

As long as the three *Gunas* or cosmic properties are in a state of perfect balance, no further evolution is possible. A state of imbalance irks their inherent functions and characteristics to come into play which, combined with interplay, turns them into causative factors and something new is born, evolution moves on. *Rajas Guna* activates with the intention of making *Sattwa Guna* or light manifest as the true nature of everything but the restraining nature of *Tamas Guna* intends to solidify consciousness into distinctive form. The process, where un-manifested energy manifests into subtle and then distinctive gross form, happens after further evolution of tattwas. As a total, the Siddhas have described 96 tattwas.

> "In two kinds of body thus God shaped;
> If I speak the subtlety of one that is subtle;
> Sound, touch, form, taste and smell,
> Buddhi, Mana, and Ahamkara are!"
>   Thirumanthiram, Verse 2123, Siddha Thirumoolar

The state of *Chittam*, the third type of tattwa emerges from within the inherent movement of *Rajas Guna*. *Chittam* is the 'whole' carrying the states of *Mahat*, *Ahamkara* and *Manas*. *Mahat* is Cosmic Intelligence born from the disturbance caused in the equilibrium of the *Gunas* and gives evolution a distinct direction. *Ahamkara* is the Cosmic 'I' sense and *Manas* is Cosmic Mind.

> "...of the organs stated eight,
> First five are Indriyas, three are Karanas"
>   Thirumanthiram, Verse 2124, Siddha Thirumoolar

Derived from the consciousness of *Manas* are the Indriyas, ten in number. These are the ten forces or capacities - five of Knowing and Cognition and the other five of Action, called Gnanendriyas and Karmendriyas, respectively. These have been tabulated below for easy reading.

	GNANENDRIYAS - senses of knowing	KARMENDRIYAS - senses of working
1	Power to hear	Power to express
2	Power to feel	Power to procreate
3	Power to see	Power to excrete
4	Power to taste	Power to grasp
5	Power to smell	Power to move

The *Tanmatras* simultaneously come into existence at this stage as they are the essence of all objects in their subtle un-manifest form. Without the *Tanmatras* or subtle elements of *Prakruthi*, the ten Indriyas would have no function to perform.

The *Tanmatras* are:

> The essence of sound
> The essence of touch
> The essence of form
> The essence of flavour
> The essence of odour

"Indriyas ten, ten too their Tanmatras;
Secretly working Vayus ten,
The Anthakarnas four, and Purusha, the experient Jiva;
All these again and again entangle,
In waking consciousness."
　　　　　Thirumanthiram, Verse 2144, Siddha Thirumoolar

All tattwas until now belong to the un-manifest realm of existence. An increase in *Tamas Guna*'s restraining nature causes the un-manifest essence to manifest as the *Mahabhutas*, the five elements which are the acting vehicles for all *Tanmatras* to manifest and express.

ॐ ☙

EVOLUTION COMES TO A REST

The subtle realm of evolution comes to rest at the *Mahabhutas*, the five elements of nature. Each *Mahabhuta* evolutes and emerges, one from the other successively. According to the cosmic order of creation, each and every *Mahabhuta* is born with a specific distinctive characteristic. It also inherits the specific nature of the previous *Mahabhuta*. In other words, each one is born denser or grosser than the previous.

Ether (Akash, Akayam): Ether exhibits the principle of vacuity, a vast emptiness.
> It has the special property of sound, so it can be heard but not felt, seen, tasted or smelt i.e. a clear sound has no touch, no form, no flavour, nor odour. Sound is beyond the array of the other four senses.

Air or wind (Vayu, Vali): Air exhibits the principle of motion.
> It functions as pressure or impact. Air's own property of touch is joined by the general quality of sound that it inherits from Ether. Therefore, Air can be felt and heard i.e. a gust of wind has touch and sound but is still beyond form, flavour and odour i.e. it cannot be seen, tasted or smelt.

Fire (Tejas, Thee): Fire bears the principle of luminosity.
The special property of Fire is Form. It also carries the inherited quality of touch and sound from Air and Ether. Fire can be seen, felt and heard. A pure blue flame has form, touch and sound but is beyond flavour and odour.

Water (Appu, Neer): Water has the principle of liquidity.
The Water element exhibits contraction. Its own special property is flavour. Water also inherits the quality of form, touch and sound from its ascendants. Water can be tasted, seen, felt and heard. But a glass of water is beyond the quality of odour and cannot be smelt.

Earth (Prithvi, Nilam): Earth has the principle of solidity.
Its function is cohesion and its special property is odour. This is in addition to the quality of flavour, form, touch and sound. Therefore, the Earth element can be smelt, tasted, seen, felt and heard. A rose has odour, flavor, form, touch and sound. Earth is the only element that can be known by all five senses.

The five *Mahabhutas* and their individual modalities:

Akayam	Ether	has sound
Vali	Air	has sound and touch
Thee	Fire	has sound, touch and form
Neer	Water	has sound, touch, form and flavour
Nilam	Earth	has sound, touch, form, flavour & odour

All manifestation is a derived state of these five elements.
Every manifestation undergoes this entire cosmic phenomenon of evolution until it comes to rest in its own modified state of the inseparable, yet distinctive ratio of *Mahabhuta Tattwas*. And to fall

back into its origin, the Source, all manifestation must undergo the cosmic phenomenon of involution. The process of creation and dissolution of the macro cosmos is individualised as the micro cosmos or Human Being. The creation of a micro cosmos is no different from the macro.

> "What takes place in the macrocosm,
> Holds good in the microcosm."
> Avvai Kural, chapter 10, Verse 9

Humans come to realise their true nature by undertaking the quest of transcending every evolutionary stage until ultimately 'falling-back' into the origin, the Source.

> "Where Tattwas are, the Lord of Tattwas is,
> Where Tattwas are not, the Lord of Tattwa is not.
> Having realised the nature of Tattwa Gnana,
> The Lord of Tattwas would there emerge!"
> Thirumanthiram, Verse 2818, Siddha Thirumoolar

THE PHENOMENA

We end this chapter illustrating the vital participation of Tattwas even in the simplest of occurrences.

The mind's first function is to be a receptacle; to receive and register an image. Let us for a moment imagine a truck speeding along the road. The form of the truck enters our mind through the eyes. The same mind then functions as the intellect when it grows aware of the image and cognises it as a 'truck' from the light of its already held knowledge. The intellect has nothing to do with the external object - the truck. It interacts only with the image registered in the receptacle mind. Then, the intellect by its inherent quality of *Raga* (attachment) and *Dwesha* (aversion) interprets this image as either good or bad. This is done for the sake of the Ego: 'something is happening in the external world. I am directly concerned with it. I must do something about it.' This feeling of 'I-ness' is called Ego. 'If the truck is speeding towards me, I will perform the action of running to safety. If the truck is speeding away then I will do no action.' The Ego sense of 'I am directly concerned with the speeding of the lorry towards me as my life is in danger' will prompt me to act.

The mind, the intellect and the ego are colours of different *Vasanas*. The intellect determines what to do: run to the safe side of the road. The mind gives the order to the Karmendriyas, the organs of action, the legs. The muscles of the leg expand and contract and the legs do the running.

CHAPTER FOUR

MAN - THE FIVE ELEMENTS

"Andathil Ulladhu Pindam
Pindathil Ulladhu Andam
Andamum Pindamum Ondre
Arinthu Than Paarkkum Pothu"

The translation:

"Whatever is in the macrocosm is in the microcosm;
Whatever is in the microcosm is in the macrocosm.
Macrocosm and microcosm are one
When you look in right understanding."

Siddha Sattaimuni

Cosmic manifestation begins once cosmic evolution comes to rest after the *Pancha MahaBhuta tattwas* (the five cosmic elements) emerge. The *Sakthi Tattwa* or *MahaPrana* weaves the *Mahabhutas* into multifarious subtle and gross forms bringing the subtle and gross world into form. The *Mahabhutas* or five cosmic elements remain eternally inter-related, inter-connected and inseparable, providing inter-proportional flexibility. An element is never non-existent and cannot be taken into account individually and/or apart from the others. The elements are classified into two halves, namely physical and subtle. The subtle ones are further subdivided into two equal parts of which one is retained and the other is once again subdivided into four equal parts. This is the phenomenon of *'Panchi*

Karna Vidya', based on which the Science of Siddha Medicine, Siddha Alchemy and *Swara Yoga* applications came into existence.

Siddhas declare man a microcosm. There are two avenues to it. One is about the creation of new life in the womb and the other is the sustenance of life outside the womb. Before we read the chapter 'Genetic wisdom of the Siddhas' which describes the role of *MahaPrana* in the creation of new life in the stages of the embryo, let's first understand the presence of five elements in man and its close-knit relationship with the external world. In the womb, from conception to birth, the dynamic design of the human body gets woven into place. The physical form, the inner physiology and its functionality are a combination of the five elements. Once the child is born and leaves the womb, a new relationship begins - with its surroundings. The faculty of 'experiencing' is also based on the five elements and is what connects the child to its new environment by way of the five senses. According to Siddha *Tantra*, the universe consists of subtle atoms that contribute to the formation of the five cosmic elements: Earth, Water, Fire, Air, and Ether. Each element corresponds to one of the five senses of the human body and is fundamental to all corporeal things in the world. Within the human body, earth is the obvious element. It gives the human body its shape through bones, tissues, muscles, skin, hair, etc. Water is the second element and is represented by blood, gland secretions, vital fluids, etc within the body. Fire, the third element facilitates digestion of physical food, mental impressions and experiences. It also imparts emotion, vigour, vitality and intelligence to the human system. Air aids absorption of digestion energy and is responsible for circulation, stimulation and respiratory and nervous systems. Ether characterises man's mental and spiritual faculties. An overall suitable inter-proportion of five elements, working harmoniously, produces a healthy organic dynamic organism, making life possible.

SECTION TWO: TREE OF LIFE

THE MUTATIVE ELEMENTS

ELEMENTS	COLOURS	RATIO	SENSES	ACTION
ETHER	Spadigam (crystal white)	½	Ears	Sound
AIR	Black	¾	Nose	Smell
FIRE	Red	1	Eyes	Sight
WATER	White	1-1/4	Tongue	Taste
EARTH	Golden & Light green	1-1/2	Skin	Touch

ೞ ಞ

Panch Bhuta (Five Elements)

To envision the details of the Tattwas
Listen! I tell you lovingly with compassion.
Follow the five elements that I speak.
Earth, Water, Fire,
The connecting Wind and Ether,
Cohesively entwined as elements, five.
Finding well by your mind's eye,
Adhere well, the obvious element!

25

Ganendriyam (Organs of Knowing)
Preserving the five elements itself,
If you envision with mind's eye, by converged eyes
You can sight the growing Mount.
The way to Chathura Giri would appear
Then assuring, no one is equal to you.
If you surrender and experience the elements,
The upright Kailash would appear.
Listen! The real Gnanendriyam!

26

CHAPTER FOUR: MAN - THE FIVE ELEMENTS

Listen to the Gnanendriyam
Graciously telling you, listen.
Surotra is ear itself.
What is meant by Thokku, is the body itself.
The sword like Satchu is eye itself.
The great Singu is mouth itself.
Agirana, the foot like, is nose itself.
These are the compassionate Gnanendriyam!

27

Thus, such five Gnanendriyam, itself,
Look at them with the gracious mind's eye,
Experience the five stages satisfactorily.
If you establish in the abode of the Guru,
Without over-lapping, then Vaasi would self-exist
And abide in the wisdom of light.
Finding refuge in those five stages
Then listen to the Karmendriyam!

28

Karmendriyam (Organs of action)

Listen, the Tongue, Feet, Hand,
Excretory and Generative organs,
All of these five are Karmendriyam.
If they became pure,
The path of wisdom never be in vain
If you find clarity in these five.
No more evil, and Vasi would raise.
So focus upon the five organs intensely!

29

Aaimpulam (Five senses)

Listen now to see the Aaimpulam.
Along with the Sabda, the Sparsa, the Roopa,
The Rasam and the Skanda, these five
The pleased Aaimpulam, as called.
Coherently sensing the Aaimpulam
If you find clarity mindfully,
It would reveal to you the Siddha in the path.
Oh Son! Listen to the analysis of Aaimpulam!

30

SECTION TWO: TREE OF LIFE

    Analysing each Aaimpulam,
    Reaching their root-core,
    Visualising the aspect of Vasi,
    Climbing in that Vasi with clarity,
    Reaching the oracle of the cosmos to engulf it,
    And if abide there with immaculate awareness,
    To sustain in it further the need of Anthakarnas.
    Telling openly, listen!
                                              31

Anthakarnas (inner instruments)

    Oh the Maharishi Pulasthiya, listen.
    The gracious faculty of Anthakarnas,
    The Manas without falseness is one,
    The sharp Buddhi is another one.
    Listen, the Ahamkaram is the next one,
    Chittam, the purity of Sivahood, is another.
    Rule these four faculties then
    They would function consciously!
                                              32

    Understand the Atma-tattwa.
    What I spoke till now is of twenty-four.
    Keeping intent, if you find the merits
    Of Atma-tattwa, then the Vasi would climb.
    Incubate this Vasi after finding its essence.
    If sighted the core of Atma-tattwa
    Who is equal to you, my son.
    Now you listen to the Vidya-tattwa!
                                              33

Vidya Tattwam

    Speaking the Vidya-tattwa, Listen!
    Nothing but the Kala, the Niyathi,
    The covering Kalai, the Vidya,
    The pleasant Ragam, the Purusha,
    And the Maya, all these are seven.
    Being aware of Vidya-tattwa for the goodness,
    Obtain the body of space,
    Then listen to the aspect of Siva-tattwa!
                                              34

CHAPTER FOUR: MAN – THE FIVE ELEMENTS

Listen to the nature of Siva-tattwa
Oh my gracious Pulasthiya, carefully.
Oh son! The ruling Suddha-Vidya, Iswara,
Then the Sadakya, Sakti and Siva.
All these five are called Siva-tattwas.
This order of thirty-six Tattwas
Know as the instruments for body-consciousness.
Realising this, oh my son, start to see yourself!

35

Focusing on oneself,
Observing the source of body-consciousness,
Standing without waver, then the glory
Of Tattwas would reveal, be mindful.
If you keep mindfulness in it,
The other dependant Tattwas would appear.
Who would know in the five elements,
All those ninety-six Tattwas came into being!

36

Aspect of Earth

The derived forms of five elements, listen!
Oh son, the aspects of Earth element become
The Hair, the Bone, the Skin,
The Tendons of nerves, the Flesh, five total.
The magnificent aspect of Earth, as told,
Understand it and abide in it consciously.
After this, the aspect of Water element.
Oh! My good Pulasthiya, focus in it!

37

Aspect of Water

Speaking the aspect of Water, to see
The softest Plasma, Blood,
The coherent Sperm, Brain and Marrow,
All these five are the aspects of Water.
The significance of these Water aspects
You see with clarity. By sensing yourself,
If you sense them as self-awareness,
Then I would proceed to the aspect of Fire!

38

SECTION TWO: TREE OF LIFE

Aspect of Fire

Listen to the aspect of the Fire element.
Nothing but Hunger, the Sleep,
Overwhelming Copulation, Fear and Laziness.
All these total five are aspects of Fire.
Realising this razor edge Fire aspects,
Be mindful of the inner nature of yourself.
If your mindfulness becomes established,
Then it leads to the aspect of Air!

39

Aspect of Air

Oh! Listen to the aspect of Air itself,
My Pulasthiya! The Walk, the Run,
The Sitting, along with the Lying down, and
The Getting up, all become totally five.
Understanding the expansive aspects of the air element,
Focus on the unfoldment of your inner self further.
If you focus with the grace of the glorious Guru,
Listen to the aspect of Ether!

40

Aspect of Ether

Exclusivity of the aspect of Ether itself.
Telling you significantly its nature, Listen!
The enmity, the possessiveness, the greed,
The envy and the pride, all these five,
See them, how they emerge in the base.
If you establish as Self itself,
The waning Vasi gets augmented.
These are the twenty-five functions of the sacred five!

41

CHAPTER FOUR: MAN - THE FIVE ELEMENTS

Ten Nadis

The five pairs of Nadis, are ten,
Will now tell you, listen keenly!
Ever-functioning Ida, Pingala, Sulinai,
Lustrous Gandhari, Atthi,
Interiorising Aswini, Alampu, Purudan,
Forcible Gudham and the Singuvu.
All these self-portrayed ten positions,
Are the airy aspect of the Earth element itself!

42

Regarding the course of the airy aspect of Air,
Listen mindfully, will speak its flow.
The straight Prana, and the Apana,
The realistic Udana, and the Samana, Oh Son,
The non-pouring Vyana, all are five,
Have become the fiery Air itself.
If you find the whirling fiery Air,
Then listen to the next elemental Airs!

43

Listen to the Nagan, Koormam, my son,
Girigaram, Devadattam, Dananjeyen.
All these are known as the five elemental Airs.
Amazing! Experience the directional Air.
Understanding the base of directional Air,
If you abide compassionately in Sivayoga,
No more evil, all can be accomplished.
Now listen to the airy aspect of Ether with intent!

44

Oh son! Listen to the airiness of Ether itself.
Compassionately speaking, listen attentively!
The razor-edged Arthaedeana is one,
The assorted Yukthiedeana is one,
The engulfed Ulagaedeana is third,
Experiencing the airiness of Ether with clarity,
Stand in the secret inner whirl,
Then understand the source of sound!

45

SECTION TWO: TREE OF LIFE

Envision the source of the sound,
The intrinsic Vaasanam and Kemanam,
The straight Visargam, Anandam, all five.
Seeing these rooted five, arising from Vaasanam,
Seeing the core of the rooted support.
To follow further the course of other instruments,
Listen to the matter, now heart-fully uttered
...!

46

Listen son, the Rajas, the Tamas
And the gracious Satvic characters are three.
Understanding these three characteristics,
Listen to the order of the airy aspect of Vindu,
The engulfing Sandhi, Madhimai, Vaikari,
And Sukuma, all these four are sound.
Seeing this strata of sound, four itself,
Devotionally look at the base itself!

47

Find in this base itself
The internal thirty-six physical instruments,
Combined with external sixty instruments.
If you see clearly the internal and the external,
Those appearing ninety-six tattwas
Can be experienced in your heart itself.
They are nothing at all, just the garbage of tattwas.
The divine game of Pathi, Pasu and Pasa, between themselves!

48

-Verses 25 to 48 from Saumiya Sagaram 1200,
by Siddha Sage Agasthiyar

Tree of Life

CHAPTER FIVE

MEDICINE OF THE SAGES

The Siddha and Ayurveda systems stand for the antiquity of the medicinal tradition prevalent in the Indian subcontinent. The Indian government and researchers of ancient South India recognise Ayurveda to be approximately 6000 years old and the Siddha system as nearly 10,000 years old. The Siddha tradition began as an oral lineage where Masters entrusted their erudite and enlightened disciples with the sacred teachings that unfolded through yogic visions. Much later, the practice of recording teachings on palm scripts, by way of direct commentary began. Over time, the lineage grew and gathered into an in-depth healing and spiritual system. The Siddha system is reverentially described as a *'Karpaga Vriksha'*; a Desire Tree that holds in its imperial vastness all things knowable and experiential to Man. It deals with all of existence. In human terms, it deals with mundane essentials as well as the spiritual path. However, the medicinal dimension is considered a vital door to this mystic tradition and shines as its hallmark.

The ancient healing system fell out of use relatively recently - in the century dominated by the British rule. Over and above the Siddha and Ayurveda systems, South Asia has seen the presence of the Unani system of medicine which also contributed to its recent decline. Scholars of Arabia and other parts of the near east brought a prominent rise in the Unani system during the period of the Mogul Empire. There was a time in history when the Siddha, Ayurveda and the Unani system were in use simultaneously, without conflict, due to their common fundamentals. After the turn of the century, western medicine was introduced into India, by the British. Improved sanitation together with gaining control of infectious and childhood diseases, western medicine or Allopathy, grew increasingly popular. Those years of India also witnessed a changeover to the British educational system alongside other social changes. The West saw parallel advances in technology, understanding of human physiology and the cellular metabolic pathways surfaced as a dimension under the allopathic approach of treating acute diseases. Allopathic medicine was compact, presentable and most importantly fast-acting. The introduction of capsules and sterile injectables changed the perception of people and their fascination and trust fast swayed towards it. But little did we, as a human race know that by investing in the miracle of technology, we would de-invest in the infinite miracle of humanness. Believing modern technology to be a miracle of another kind, people quickly lost trust, faith and forgot the extraordinary healing power inherent within the human body-mind-spirit. People began to depend upon technology which is devoid of any kind of trust in Nature. The native vaidyas of Ayurveda, the native maruthuvars of the Siddha system, the hakims of the Unani system and the 'healing Grandmas' of the village, who were once seen as divine, were now termed 'primitive'. Since then doctors of modern medicine have grown in number and traditional healers dwindled. Even so, over thousands of years the ancient medicinal treasure trove of the Siddhas continues to act as the bedrock of all medicine and survives in the hands of Native Healers living in rural regions. Just as certain people are born with a green thumb, these people are born healers. They hail from generations of vaidyas, passing on the sacred art, the expert eye and a finely attuned sensitivity, making healing a natural response instead of gadget-dependant analytical science. These custodians keep the tradition alive by honouring the faith of millions even in today's age where man doubts first, listens later and then if at all, believes. The democratic system of curing and healing of Nature (man) by Nature (herbs and plants) and for Nature, (the balance of body-mind) continues to serve. The new age echoes a question... 'Do we need God?' In response I rephrase, 'Do we need parents?'

The root meaning of the word Siddha is *'Chit'* or Consciousness. The ultimate aim of the Siddhas medicinal dimension is to 'dissolve the veil of ignorance that shadows the illumination of pure consciousness'. These veils are physical ailments, disease, mental blocks, various abnormalities, pranic disorders and the Primal Ignorance of our existence. While most other medical theories are confined to reducing suffering in the human body, the Siddha system addresses the body-mind-spirit continuum. It is the Medicine of the Sages. Food plays a vital role in determining our daily health and state of mind. Being an external factor, it allows conscious choice. Food is composed of the five elements, carries its qualities and can be classified into *Satvic, Rajasic* and *Tamasic*. By the intake of food, we imbibe these qualities into our body, mind and consciousness. Our physical body and mental constitution are under the influence of the three *Gunas* (*Satva, Rajas*, and *Tamas*) through the food we eat.

> *Satvic* food keeps the body light and gives mental clarity.
> *Rajasic* food provokes excessive activity in the body and makes the mind state agitated.
> *Tamasic* food generates heaviness in the body and dullness of mind.

Through a consciously-designed diet, one could neutralise abnormal states of mind or attend to discomforting bodily signals.

CHAPTER FIVE: MEDICINE OF THE SAGES

The diet should be appropriate to the individual's state of mind, constitution and must resonate with the changing climate, season and environment. Dietary change should be gradual. A periodical revaluation aiming to enhance natural healing within the body and mind is paramount. For instance, chronic depression, dullness and lethargy could be due to an excess intake of *Tamasic* food. After examining the present diet, the imbalance can be neutralised by introducing *Rajasic* food to remove the restraining tendency of *tamas*. The individual should experience freedom from chronic dullness and begin to enjoy newly-acquired briskness generated by *Rajasic* food. This change should be stabilised, balanced and most importantly sustained by introducing *Satvic* food. A prolonged intake of *Satvic* food evokes freshness, enthusiasm, lightness, calmness, and clarity in one's being. *Satva* is the harmonious and integrated blend of *Rajas* and *Tamas*.

> One of the core teachings of ancient Siddhas says,
> 'Immaculate primordial energy wanes when temporal energy waxes.'

On birth, breastfeeding is the first form of acquired temporal energy. Food is the new doorway to various influences. An adult acquires energy majorly through food and his relationship with it makes him either healthy or ill. The unique and distinctive hallmark of the medicinal aspect of Siddha Tradition rises from this fundamental understanding. Even today Native Healers apply the same eternal underlying principles. The Siddhas have taught the influence of food and shown us how to employ this external factor to heal instead of harm. Their revelations take us right up to unveiling the ignorance withholding an individual's true nature from himself.

ಸಾ ಡಾ

SECTION TWO: TREE OF LIFE

HALLMARK OF THE SIDDHA SYSTEM OF MEDICINE

First, I would like to briefly discuss Ayurveda. Popularly known as the science of Life, the preliminary founders of Ayurvedic Science were Sage Charaka and Susrutha. Their works have abundant information on the nature of the human body, disease, healing, herbal preparation and of course, lifestyle regime but none of their early texts mention the medicinal use of minerals and metals. This implies the medicinal use of metals and minerals was not present in the preliminary period of Ayurveda. Siddha Nagarjuna, a great alchemist, from Andhra Pradesh devoutly followed the Siddha path and attained Siddha-hood. He is known to have settled in North India bringing the knowledge and mastery of alchemy to that region. The knowledge of metals and minerals, absent from early texts, is mentioned in later periods and has been flourishing as common practice ever since. But this is not the crucial distinguishing factor of Siddha Medicine.

Anupana
(Adjuvant)

The hallmark of Siddha Medicine includes utilising one medicine to heal and cure multiple diseases by altering only the *Anupana*. (*Anupana* being the carrier or medium with which the actual medicine is taken).

Muppu
(Universal Salt)

Another hallmark is the preparation and application of the 'Universal Salt'. (In other traditions, the Universal Medicine is known as the

Philosopher Stone, Elixir or Panacea.) Ancient wisdom of the Siddhas says - all manifestation inherently comprises of a dual character - a life-giving aspect and a life-destroying aspect, called as *Amritha Pakam* and *Nanju Pakam* in Tamil. In the chapter 'Creation of Tattwas', *Prakruthi* is described to obscure the *Purusha* aspect. She veils the 'single' sense; the sentient aspect, using her multi-sense forms. This is no different than the *Nanju* aspect (life-destroying). It curtains the *Amritha* (life-giving) aspect and indirectly acts as the impetus for its gain in momentum. In other words, both aspects are the same energy working within a single pathway or mode, in a complimentary fashion. The Life-giving aspect nurtures life with its balanced healing tendency while the life-destroying aspect generates imbalance to bring deterioration. This apparent contradiction is a complimentary function as both aspects arise from one Source. The Siddhas applied this cosmic law to spiritual realms and incorporated it in their illustrated panoramic view describing *Maya* or illusion as eternal, inherent and as vast as Spirit or *Purusha*. *Maya*, who obscures perception and veils one's true silent spirit or *Purusha* from oneself, is also the one to bestow blessings and grace for realising IT. Likewise, in the medicinal area, on the dissolution of the poisonous aspect (Nanju Pakam) of a substance, the *Amritha* aspect manifests as the entire whole and occupies the vacant space of *Nanju Pakkam*. From then on the traits of *Amritha* aspect flourish and express in entirety, altering the inherent state of each and every material to immaculate vitality, nourishing and nurturing it with life-giving expression.

The Sages of ancient cults created a formula to initiate and accelerate the process of activating the entire healing potential hidden in all things by using the Universal Salt as the catalyst. There are different formulae for purification and removal of the poisonous aspect which explain how it alters and transforms the split within a substance and refines it to its purest one pointed potential. This is 'Muppu', which means the Three Salts or Essence. It is used extensively in external alchemical preparations of *KayaKalpa* medicines of longevity and immortality. More of this is explained in 'External Alchemy'. In Ayurveda, these formulae are applied mostly for metallic medicinal preparations whereas the Siddha system employs this process to every preparation - herbs, spice, metals and minerals included.

Jayaneer (Victorious Water)

A highly unique purification process, indigenous to the Siddha system, uses a rather miraculous preparation called *Jayaneer*. Liquid metal and sulphur are volatile under fire. To incinerate and prepare them medicinally, they first need to lose their volatile nature. *Jayaneer* (Victorious Water) overrides the influence of fire, water and air elements and they no longer evaporate in contact with fire! The Siddhas used this magical preparation to purify many a poisonous materials right down to the atomic level, even mercury. Mercury and other volatile substances when blended with *Jayaneer* lose their volatile nature with fire. The Siddhas used this to reverse the nature of different poisons present in each metal and ready it as medicine devoid of any ill/side-effects. Another preparation hailing from the Siddhas that also uses *Jayaneer* is the forgotten yet valuable preparation of *Kattu* (binded) and *Kalangu* (looks like Tuber). These preparations have an un-imaginable shelf life of a thousand years!

CHAPTER FIVE: MEDICINE OF THE SAGES

SELF REFERRAL

According to my *Pitta* nature, I had a curious questioning mind. During the early years of my quest, I was in the company of a few native vaidyas. They would work day and night. I watched them mixing, grinding herbs and preparing medicines. They answered most of my questions, yet I found I didn't truly know the underlying principles of this ancient healing system and questions still remained. Such a question would never occur to them as their medicinal journey was inherited over generations and customary.

> During the same time, I would also visit Chandrashekhar Swami. It was a long journey to Erode, but Swami never allowed me to stay there with him. I would visit as frequently as I could. After several such visits, I recall being determined to stay longer. Surprisingly enough, Swami allowed it. That particular time, I had first visited two temples and then taken the long bus journey to Erode. Immediately on reaching, I got involved watching the activities at Swami's place. He had several assistants and a lot of people waited for medicinal consultation. Some complained of a lack of spirit for life while others of physical illnesses. I was eager to see how he sensed and helped each one. I keenly watched his assistants help him and others prepare native Siddha preparations. All in all I behaved like a perfect window shopper. I didn't want to learn anything in particular. I didn't even know what I was looking for. I spent the first two days like this.
>
> By the third day, I felt a bit under the weather. I had a runny nose and burning sensations but my curiosity didn't let up. I spent every minute observing and watching. By the fifth day a burning high fever kept me bed-ridden. Several assistants recommended herbal preparations but strangely enough no

one gave me any. Neither did Swami attend to me. I just lay there tired and weak. A day later Swami called out to me, "Go outside, there is a plant." I hobbled out. And there it was. I saw a plant that hadn't been there a few days ago. The assistants gathered around and expressed amazement at the sudden appearance of this mysterious plant. Not common to the area and nor the right season for it, how did it get there? On Swami's instructions, an assistant took a part of the plant and prepared a decoction which I was given to drink. One of the assistants asked Swami, "How did this plant suddenly grow here?" Swami's teasing retort was, "Don't you know, Pal Pandian sir has come to our place…"

Swami Chandrashekhar is a healer hailing from the lineage of Siddha Gorakkar. He is a channel of healing steam. I definitely wouldn't describe him as a popular candy-floss, all smiles teachers! He never allowed his students to cling to his personality and promptly trampled it, if at all.

Unable to stay calm, I asked, "But you didn't answer Chandra's question (assistant)." To this he said to me, "Don't you have this question within you? Nature knows you!" The sudden appearance of the plant and Swami's words, hit me hard! I gradually understood how it all came to be. As I had travelled a long distance, a lot of heat had generated in my body. On arriving, I immediately involved myself in activity. In fact, Swami said that my throat was already dry and burning by the first two days. But I had ignored my body alarms after which it set off louder alarms but I let those pass too. With no other option Nature Alarms you! Yes, nature alarms you into understanding your personal boundaries and what it means to protect yourself from influence like external demands or your own obsessive behaviours - both of which don't support growth in life.

CHAPTER FIVE: MEDICINE OF THE SAGES

Ancient Siddhas describe Nature as an endless flowing phenomena, always changing, always moving. When Her river flow of existence experiences a block, it responds by an alarm! As a planet we know how our insensitive acts hamper the flow of Mother Nature and result in frightening natural calamities. Our bodies are no different. Disease and illness are a result of insensitivity; an undeniable evidence of us persistently turning a deaf ear to what our bodies have to say. The Siddhas have a specific word for this river flow of natural existence that continually nurtures life – *'Vasi'* (living). They refer to its blocks as *'Viyadhi'* which means deviation.

> I asked Swami, "What do you mean by Nature knows you? Doesn't She know all of us?". He smiled, "Of course She does, but She responds to those who live as Nature. One can live as Nature only by loving Her. Life is a journey; the journey of a spiritual being experiencing human life. Humans forget to identify with the language of the Universe, and don't feel the abundance Nature shares. The frogs, the birds, the falling leaves, the wind… all have something to say to you. Pal, you have forgotten how to listen! From a new dimension of awareness, you can actually listen to silence and be with yourself with great ease without the itch of being always on the move or keeping up with demands. We owe it to them! By listening to them and ourselves, we create and ensure an environment that nurtures and recognises them, preventing them from being pushed into obscurity by overwhelming human aggressive misuse.
>
> When you listen to the language of Nature, you feel part of the grand Universe, of life, and inextricably connected to the physical dimensions by being in your body. The energy pervading all over the living Universe is embodied and rooted

in physical form and as it nurtures your spirit-mind-body, each moment your connection with it nurtures it in response. Yes, it is Life. Inside each of us is an oceanic rhythm that aspires to live; a rhythm whose pulse animates us; this life-pulse is *'Vasi'* revealed by the Siddhas. Any block to this life-sustaining pulse manifests as disease. Dis-ease simply indicates how we have mis-conceived our inspiration and misaligned our actions. This is what spiritual traditions are concerned with by their philosophical teachings; in other words 'being and becoming'.

Self-referral! To listen and attend to our inner call is not a far-fetched conceptualised theory. It is an attitude to be lived; a natural way of being. Modern day high-strung lives, crowded with demand make it easy to drop 'self-referral'. It gets replaced by an object-oriented mentality which brings stress, fatigue, disorder, and chronic conditions. It is possible to meet a typical desk job with something other than a workaholic approach. A stretch or two, frequent drinks of water, resting the eyes on some greenery or something refreshingly natural, can allow you to attend to mundane activities with a marked difference. An object-oriented mentality sooner than later turns into a pressure generator whereas working through self-referral grows into an extension of one's energy. If we frequently reconnect with ourself and pace out our connection with the external demands we would stay attuned. The strength of our detachment from the demanding external scenario is proportional to the strength of our sensitivity and inner-focus of our inspiration to live. Whenever exasperation and tension push you off centre, become sensitive to your inner inspiration level. The silver lining is the aspiration to express, which lurks between our inspiration and actions. That is what keeps us creative and healthy in this multifaceted fast track world. A sustained awareness of our inspiration during all activity is self-healing and transcends stressful situations that mostly demand one to live as an off-centred person.

CHAPTER FIVE: MEDICINE OF THE SAGES

Living with Chandrasekhar Swami, several experiences got me pondering the underlying principles of this ancient healing system. Resources in ancient times were very different. They had no instruments, gadgets, machines, gauges, etc. and yet the healing system flourished widely within their few resources.

With a little visualisation let's walk the ancient era...

Living in the time of B.C., if you were physically or emotionally-ill, taking the advice of friends or a physician you would have prepared to travel far to an ashram or a healing shrine on a hill or inside a cave or maybe on the banks of a river. Your decision to travel could not have been casual because back then healing was a sacred process; a communion with oneself and the sages. The travel itself would have lasted several days. Along the journey, you would have heard stories of miraculous cures from those returning home. Filled with hope and expectation, you would reach the gates of the sage's ashram. First, the process of purification by cleansing methods and fasting would begin; symbolic of shedding toxic attitudes and unhealthy conditionings due to improper habits of daily life. After this, you would enter into a dynamic healing environment. Strolling in the sage's ashram or healing shrine, you would enjoy the beautiful gardens and graceful serene statues and sculptures. Being immersed in the moisturising medicated herbal oil tub bath, spring or river would rejuvenate your body. Wandering minstrels would lift your spirit and you would participate in lively spiritual dialogue which would confront your intellectual crisis and challenge you to consider an alternate perspective to your current life situation. Devotional *bhajans* (songs) would expand your perspective of life. Chanting holy mantras would remind you of your inner centre. Each day would free you from accumulated stress of daily life. Eventually, your diet, massage, relaxation, self-examination, rejuvenation and inner grounding would experience a gradual return in energy and vitality. Finally, the day would come when you would be restored to health, filled by a sense of wholeness, balance and harmony; ready to return. Engrossed in activities for body, mind and spirit, you would have learnt about yourself and developed new attitudes and behaviours; healthy and life-supporting ones. All of this would bring an empowered meaning to live your life.

The entire cosmos was a laboratory for our ancients and the human pulse their stethoscope. Their baseline was self-referral and self-sufficient which kept them nature-centred and holistic. The sages lived one with their environment acknowledging the entire cosmos as a flow of intermingling forces of Nature. From this deeply-held cosmic view, unfolded revelations that the nature of the human body is no different from the working cosmos; an outcome of the same intermingling natural forces - constantly combining, converging and patterning. From the strength of such revelations, they never needed complex terminology or part-wise distinction of cells, bones, organs, etc. Siddhas' diagnostics are sourced from the very basis of Nature's existence - The Siddhas are the Master's of the Basics.

Self-referral is living in I-am-ness. It is not to be understood as the ego. 'I am-this or I am-that' is a fixation, a pseudo-holding centre. Egoistic attitude is an obsessive pre-occupation with our age long layers of habitual mental patterning. The influence of these encrusted layers, turn us into uptight, fearful people of poor discrimination and sensitivity. It restricts inspiration from turning into fluid aspiration for creative action. Whatever we hold onto in our consciousness gets drawn to us and before long, it begins to afflict as disease. A disease is the external manifestation of our internal imbalance. The state of our consciousness is the base for our psychological framework. Before a disease can heal, it is necessary to become aware of how we perceive and identify with it because the derangement reflects the cause and represents the time our consciousness identified stress and imbalance. Our body stands as a limited perception of our consciousness and mirrors stressful identifications our consciousness has had with life. Disease is a reminder to change perceptions, identifications and the degree to which we tend to create our own reality. The fundamental definition for medicine in the Siddha tradition has been revealed by Siddha Thirumoolar as:

> "Refusing the disease of the body,
> Refusing the disease of mind (psyche),
> Refusing further as a prevention,
> Refusing death itself ensures real medicine."

Siddha Thirumoolar's simple song has a thundering definition. The first and best medicine is your perception. He emphasises a 'self-referral approach' as the primal healing attitude. Freedom from this prison is possible by widening our livingness; by embracing actions that lead to naturalness. To be natural means to be sensitive to spontaneity; to be immersed in the unending flux of life without conceptual distortion. As integrated as I am that much healthy my body and livingness!

GENETIC WISDOM

Why is an infant born with deformities? Why do people die young? What determines our life span? What determines our emotional and intelligence quotient? The ancient songs of the Siddhas reveal answers to questions that baffle the world even today. The knowledge of creation revealed by the sages is thorough down to the last atom.

VITAL ANIMATION

The Siddhas say the Divine Creator creates a matrix of primal patterns using the principle life-shaping energy called *MahaPrana* - this forms the cosmos. Everything visible, invisible, with form and without, from the single atom to the entire universe, is formed by *MahaPrana*. It bestows an inseparable connectivity, bridging the external and the internal together as one.

> Place your left index finger on your wrist, just below your right thumb and feel your pulse. Without removing your finger hold your breath for a few seconds. Your pulse pattern will change. The rate diminishes for those moments. Another, not so apparent change also occurs during this time. Holding the breath somewhat reduces the smooth flow of incoming air making for a slight rise in body temperature. This tiny rise is capable of destroying millions of microbes. What if the vital force of the universe was retrained for a few moments? The entire cosmos would perish!
>
> Holding our breath influences the external environment as well. Even a tiny restraint of breath damages external microbes. The effect of any restraint extends beyond ourself, to all over the universe causing appropriate results or reactions, like a chain reaction or the butterfly effect. And where does this chain reaction end? It ends when it returns to us! Taking this thought a bit further - the formless vital force repeatedly acquires bodies in this world - where does this cycle end? It continues until we attain a state that acquires a liking to remain without a body; as pure vital force, the silent Spirit.

Similar to the creation of the cosmos, the divine creative principle uses *MahaPrana* to structure the formation of the human body within the womb. In the formative stages of a foetus, this principle life-shaping energy forms a three-layered structure which develops into the complete human body. In medical terminology, these three layers are known as the ectoderm, endoderm and mesoderm - the outer, inner and the middle layer. These three layers lay the path for the manifestation of the three-fold bio-regulating forces of *Vatha*, *Pitta* and *Kapha*, collectively called *Doshams* in the Siddha tradition. *Doshams* are paired combinations of the five elements. They are the three fundamental pillars of the human body. These active governing forces regulate the human form and determine the constitution of the individual. Diagnostics in the Siddha system is primarily based on the *Tridosham* theory (the three *doshams*) and the *prakruthi* (constitution) defined by it.

Songs written on the foetus by the Siddhas describe the formation of different cells. The animating *MahaPrana* by its own flow forms a basic route of invisible channels called *Nadis*. Depending on the region, the *nadis* assume different names. The central channel, *Sushumna Nadi* is said to be the *Kapha Nadi* as it nourishes the organs and enkindles both, the *Ida* and *Pingala Nadis*, while keeping the body temperature in check. It is the *nadi* for homeostasis. The *Pingala Nadi* is said to be the *Pitta Nadi* as it works on the solar principle of giving vitality, growth, metabolism, etc to the embryo. The *Ida Nadi* is the *Vatha Nadi*, as it acts as the governing animating principle.

Creation within the womb begins at the subtle level and gradually evolves down to the physical form. *MahaPrana* connects our formless state with our formed state. *Prana* creates and maintains this holistic genetic structure and is in turn maintained by it. Scientists are astounded at the complexity of the human genetic structure and the multifarious functions performed within and by each cell. The Genetic Wisdom of the Siddhas flourishes from a holistic understanding of the ever-active Cosmic Vital Animation. Just as the presiding influence of *MahaPranic* animation determines Cosmic happenings, it takes equal lead at individual level, in the formation of the microcosm - our human body, by determining the design of the three life-shaping forces of a human - the *doshams* - *Vatha, Pitta* and *Kapha*.

The Siddhas have described in their mystic songs the secrets of -
> How the foetus is formed,
> How the foetus acquires diseases,
> How congenital defects are formed, so on and so forth.

> "After emission, if the fluid hits five-finger speed,
> The infant born lives hundred years;
> If the fluid hits four finger width speed,
> The infant born lives eighty years..."
>
> Siddha Thirumoolar, Thirumanthiram, Verse 479

At the time of sexual union, if the male sperm emits with the speed of five-finger width (ancient method of measurement), the lifespan of the baby is determined to be a 100. The speed of emission determines the strength with which the sperm and ovum are bound together as well as the strength of the life force of the baby. So, if the emission is of four-finger width, the age determined is 80. So on and so forth...

> "The Prana pushing the vital flow is short; dwarf baby.
> The Prana pushing the vital flow is feeble; handicapped baby.
> The Prana pushing the vital flow is intermittent; hunchback baby.
> All these apply not to the woman."
>
> Siddha Thirumoolar, Thirumanthiram, Verse 480

Sperm gets secreted through a progressive functioning of all the six *Thathus* (fundamental tissues) at the time of union and cannot emit by itself. In fact, according to the Siddhas, all physiological

CHAPTER FIVE: MEDICINE OF THE SAGES

function gets momentum from the subtly functioning *Prana*. At the time of union, the Pranic pulsation from the centre of the eyebrows, under the influence of lovemaking gets directed downwards and directs the sperm to emit from the sperm bag. A person highly agitated during the sexual act would lose sperm quickly whereas a person, submissive and un-agitated would sustain prolonged intercourse. A centring in the upper realm is advised by Tantric sexual yoga to realise the prime mover of all physiological function - *Prana*.

If the Pranic pulse is feeble, the baby is born short and if it is extremely feeble, the baby is born handicapped. If it is intermittent, the baby is born hunchback. Such conditions of Pranic imbalances apply only for the male partner. The state of the woman partner plays a different role in the formation of the baby. If the woman suffers chronic constipation and an excess of faeces remain stagnant in her intestines, the baby is born dull. Instead of solid faeces if there is excess water retained in her intestines, the baby is born dumb. And if both are present, mixed in equal excess, the baby born is blind. Stagnant faeces produce stale air.

> "In intercourse, if mother's bowels are heavy in stomach; dull baby.
> If the mother is holding excess water in stomach; dumb baby.
> If both exceed in mother's stomach; blind baby.
> Thus, baby being determined according to mother."
>
> Siddha Thirumoolar, Thirumanthiram, Verse 481

The Siddhas' songs describe a host of subtle forces created on conception and are responsible for the formation of the human body. After birth, these forces continue to preside over the functioning of the individual until death.

The concept of *Tridosham*

The three *doshams* or *Tridoshams* are three bio-regulating forces formed during the formative stages of the embryo. They are derived from a pairing-off of the five elements into combinations and proportions unique to each individual. The *tridoshams* are open to influence from the external world through the intake of food and therefore, vulnerable to deviations that bring ill health. Health can be called - maintaining a balance of the three *doshams*. The *doshams* reflect the quality and condition of individual health. A Siddha Vaidya depends upon the reading of these forces for diagnosis. In fact, the Siddhas pathology and pharmacology is based on information gathered from a collective reading of these forces.

The concept of Ten Vital Airs

We live by inhaling oxygen from our surrounding air, however, a dead body does not come alive even with all the healthy air around him. Something outside of us, in order to be individualised is turned organic by a team of primal inner forces. They help the selfless energy to internalise as self energy. These are the *'Dasa Vayus'*; *Dasa* means ten and *Vayu* means air. The *Dasa Vayus* are primal forces in our body and all future forces generated within our body are a combination of these. The Siddha yogic physiology describes these vital airs to be a crucial part of the human organism. They are primary in the science of Siddha *varmam* and play a major role in the formation of the foetus as well as in the sustenance of human life. Their knowledge is greatly dependent upon the medicinal dimension as well as the spiritual path. The ten vital airs, like the *tridoshams* are subtle in nature, are subdivisions of *Vatha Dosham* and have highly specific functions. Deviation show up as debilitates corresponding to respective functions in the system.

The upward moving vital air is *Prana* (not to be confused with *MahaPrana*) and the downward moving one is called *Apana*. *Apana* is responsible for all acts of bodily elimination such as urination, bowel movements, procreation and menstruation. For instance, chronic constipation is a result of an imbalance in the downward moving vital air *Apana*. A stagnant *Apana* also imbalances the menstrual cycle causing the stale menstrual blood to turn into tiny clots that produce stale air. Conception in this condition would influence foetus formation. Siddha Thirumoolar mentions this under the section of Yoga of Lovemaking (sexual yoga) in his work Thirumanthiram and emphasises a woman should cleanse her stomach one day prior to union.

The concept of Nadis

16 circulatory channels are responsible for the formation, transportation or elimination of material within the body. Three channels are for intake, such as: respiration, digestion and the intake of fluids. The next three channels are for elimination such as: urination, defecating and sweating. The next seven channels are one each for the fundamental seven tissues of our body, and the remaining for the mind. The body of a woman has extra channels meant for menstrual flow and breast secretions. The circulatory channels within our body include the functions of mind as well as emotions and integrate this relationship as body-mind-spirit.

The concept of Thathus

Compared to *doshams* and vital airs, the *Thathus* are tangible aspects. Acting as the building blocks of the physical form, it is the realm where disease manifests in detectable form.

SECTION TWO: TREE OF LIFE

The concept of Prakruthi

The word *Prakruthi* means Nature. In very simple terms, we can say that an individual's *prakruthi* is the nature of his entire being - his body, mind and spirit - a dynamic statement of an individual's boundedness. The *prakruthi* (constitution) is derived based on the *tridosham* ratio, established at birth. Prakruthi governs throughout our lifetime and as long as this dynamic statement remains intact, health flourishes.

All of the above-mentioned forces participate at the foetal level in creating the subtle and physical form of the infant, and are presided over by the divine creative principle, which manifests and navigates the entire design, within the womb. The genetic parlance of the Siddhas describes major as well as minor milestones that determine the formation of a healthy baby. Their words can be seen as precautions to ensure the formation of a healthy child, or as guidelines/treatment protocol for genetic disorders. The Siddha's description of embryology is evidence that creation of humans and of the cosmos is no different.

Health is a reflection of all the subtle forces governing the human body. A collective reading of these forces is a diagnosis that reveals the condition of an individual. One mode of such a reading is the Pulse. Pulse reading is a systemic perspective also pointing to the root cause of imbalance. Symptoms being common to several disorders do not indicate the root cause which is why the Siddhas depend upon the subtle picture to identify and treat the deviation. A Siddha vaidya of high calibre having transcended this method, would read one's health by merely looking at an individual.

The following songs are self-explanatory...

"At union,
If the breath flows through right nostril; male baby.
If breath flows through left nostril; female baby.

If Apana opposed Prana; twins.
If breath is equal in both nostrils,
Eunuch there will be."
>> Siddha Thirumoolar, Thirumanthiram, Verse 482

"If male and female partners' breath synchronise,
The infant born will be handsome.
When in both, breath pattern is chaotic,
No conception will there be."
>> Siddha Thirumoolar, Thirumanthiram, Verse 483

Apart from these yogic insights from Siddha Thirumoolar, other Siddhas also elucidate on these organising forces as well as on the human mind-set and how it determines foetus formation. Some of them have been listed below:

- If union is on the day of New moon and conception too, then the baby will have discolouration or four or six fingers.
- If the male partner returns from a long and tiring journey and there is immediate union and conception too, the baby will be a dullard.
- If there is union and conception the next day after New moon, then the baby will have a nature of habitual lying.
- If there is union and conception on the third day after New moon then the baby will have a short life span.
- If there is union on the day of full moon and conception too then the baby will have physical deformities.
- If there is union and conception on the day after full moon then the baby will have a long life even after several threats to his life in his/her early years.
- If there is union and conception on the 15th day, the baby will suffer leucoderma (white spots), black discolouration or ailments related to *Vatha* imbalance.

- At the time of union, if both partners are engaged in perverse speech the baby will be a eunuch.
- If union and conception takes place during early afternoon on a Friday the baby born will have a squint in one eye.

The Siddha system of medicine comprises of different fundamental hypotheses or unchanging facts – that's what I thought, and due to this my initial experience was dry and lacked relevance. It was mere theory, because of which I obviously didn't experience any resultant unfolding...until I met my teacher. Post which a whole new vista of the healing aspect of the Siddha system unravelled before me.

TRIDOSHAM - THE THREE BIO-REGULATING FORCES

> "The embodied form has plasma, blood,
> Flesh, fat, bone, bone marrow, generative fluid -
> All the seven *Thathus* are formed.
> They, mixed with *Rasa*, then begin
> Entrance of *Vatha*, *Pitta* and *Kapha*.
> By the past birth karmas, first *Vatha* rules,
> Then *Pitta* rules 33 years, then the *Slethumam*,
> For 37 years rules the body.
>
> After the period of *Slethumam*,
> If the body still lives a 100 years, then *Chittam*,
> *Buddhi*, *Ahamkara* make the person
> Experience the remaining Karmic happiness and sorrow.
> After which, activity reduces; thinking falters;
> And one succumbs to dejection..."

CHAPTER FIVE: MEDICINE OF THE SAGES

> "...This body - elements five,
> Senses five, *Karmendriyas* five,
> *Gnanendriyas* five, *Karanas* four..."
>
> Pancha Ratnam, Verses 137 and 138, by woman Siddha Oorvasi

Phrases such as - boiling with rage, I am all fired up, my blood is boiling, I am burning up, etc. have one thing in common - Heat! These are not just metaphors. They accurately describe an existential experience of the element of Fire! Similarly, phrases such as, I am flying, time flew, I took off, etc. say, I am Air! A flood of relief, drowning in misery, swept away, tears pouring down, all say, I am Water! My spirit is soaring, heart feels open, larger than life, are all descriptions of the experience of Space! Descriptions of stability, firmness, consistency such as sticking to one's ground, standing firm, my feet are on ground, I feel the earth below me, I am bound by my commitment, etc. point to the Earth element. Humans are expressions of the five natural elements - Ether, Air, Fire, Water and Earth.

Each element is born from the previous one in a successive and progressive order. The evolutionary order, internally and externally looks like this: Space - Air - Fire - Water - Earth. From Space is born Air; from Air is born Fire; from Fire is born Water; and from Water is born the Earth. The evolution begins with Space and progresses when a disturbance in the spaciousness of non-resistance gives birth to something new, the birth of Air. Once the mobility of Air gets restricted, it generates heat which gives birth to the third element, Fire. A decline in the intensity of heat results in coolness, which gives birth to Water. And when water cools, it gets confined and cemented into the last element, Earth. Each element bears a distinctive quality, a specific eminence that distinguishes it from the rest. The subsequent element inherits this eminence and couples it into its own specifics. This pattern carries down to the last of the five, which carries all the four preceding eminences, coupled with its own.

Eminences:

Space or Ether expresses quality of non-resistance, yielding, a sense of soaring and feelings of expansion, openness and allowing.

The Air element expresses strong mobility, movement, coldness, roughness, subtlety, dryness, light and a fleeting nature.

Fire expresses as heat, sharpness, emits light, has odour and is liquid in nature.

The Water element is flowing, relatively mobile but heavier than its precedents. It expresses sticky-ness and smoothness. It can be static or form globules and carries the property of coolness.

Earth qualities are stability, form, hardness, binding, cementing, retaining, storing, holding, contouring, firmness, and static; it is granular in nature.

The cosmos is a consequence of the intermingling of five natural elements and so is our human body. The Siddhas define the human body as the miniature replica, a microcosm. Their songs describe the body and its functions as an expression of the five elemental qualities. How do these five tremendous forces of Nature function within the human form?

CHAPTER FIVE: MEDICINE OF THE SAGES

IN PAIRS!

According to ancient Masters, the principle that draws a man and a woman together as a couple in support of each other, is the same one that combines natural forces to blend in appropriate ratios or idyllic combinations. Under the eye of the presiding cosmic intelligence, three pairs in idyllic ratios are born in a way that enhances their respective traits and eminences and facilitates optimal functionality. Each element behaves as an underlying support, augmenting its complimentary partner. What better opportunity does activity have than a field of non-activity? Or, sound is best heard in the space of Silence.

Housed within the mansion (the human body), these three pairs are ever-functioning from conception to death and are imperative for human existence. Each element expresses a distinct quality and coupled into pairs, they animate combined and complimentary functions. The three perfectly-paired inhabitants are the *Tridoshams - Vatham, Pittam, Kapham*. The *Doshams* are not visible nor are they abstract. They can be sensed, felt, are in constant motion and in an ever-shifting dynamic balance with one another. Imperative for life to happen, they are the bio-regulating principles of the human body. Each individual is born with a unique constitution (an inter-proportional combination of the three *doshams*). Any one of the three, usually exerts a predominant influence throughout the individual's lifetime. Health can be defined as a harmonious balanced functioning of the *tridoshams*.

Vatham:

Air element coupled with the element of Space is called *Vatham*. Space being an ideal field of non-resistance provides perfect occasion for the free movement of Air. *Vatham* asserts as propulsion, quick movement, mobility and fleeting in nature that tends to leave behind a kind of emptiness; a typical energy-spending attribute. The inter-proportional ratio between Air and Space determines the qualitative aspect of Vatham, as the amount of ether (or space) affects the ability of the air (wind) to gain momentum.

Kapham and *Pittam* cannot move independently and go wherever movement (Vatham) takes them, just as clouds carried by the wind. Hence *Vatham*, the activating bio-regulating force in our body, is an enabler. A *Vatham*-depleted body is physically listless, and our sensory sharpness, perceptivity and motor organs, all depend on the proper functioning of *Vatham*. *Vatham* is seen as bodily functions like breathing, blinking of eyelids, movements of muscles and tissues, pulsation of the heart, motions of expansion, contraction, and impulse in the nerve cells. Impulses or energy-spending activities and urges such as thirst, hunger, sleep, sex, defecation, urination, sneezing, coughing, yawning, belching, tears or crying, heavy sighs, etc. are characteristics of *Vatham*. It also enables the expression of the other two *Doshams* (*Pittam* and *Kapham*). Psychologically, *Vatham* governs feelings and emotions of freshness, nervousness, fear, anxiety, pain, tremors and spasms. And its most important function is to carry the movements of body, mind and speech. *Vatham*-based expressions called *Vegams* are segregated into two categories. The Siddhas caution to not suppress or control these urges. The thirteen *vegams* mentioned above are the first of the two categories and are always to be expressed. The second category of *Vegams* like anger, envy, jealousy, evil impulses, etc. are psychosomatic in nature and as per sacred texts, are to be sublimated, i.e. not expressed or encouraged, yet not controlled nor suppressed.

CHAPTER FIVE: MEDICINE OF THE SAGES

Pittam:

Pittam is the bio-regulating force born of a dynamic interplay between the elements of water and fire. The conjunction of the water element ensures the presence of something denser and cooler than fire itself which naturally enhances its burning properties. Not changing, but modulating each other, they are vital for life processes. According to its quality, the Fire element is present wherever any nature of conversion takes place. Most obvious expressions of *Pittam* are the heat of our body, hunger, vision or eyesight, *tejas* (complexion), valour, sharp intellect, etc. *Pittam* governs digestion, conversion, assimilation, absorption, nutrition, metabolism, body temperature, skin coloration, lustre in the eyes, etc. - all of which are manipulative and balancing functions based on the faculty of discrimination. Psychologically, *Pittam* is responsible for anger, hatred, jealousy, intelligence, comprehension and the ability to digest and assimilate life-events and inner experiences. *Pittam*, takes on the name of *Agni* during the process of digestion and conversion of food. The Siddhas have described thirteen *Agnis*.

- The first five are the *Pancha Bhuta Agnis* (the fiery aspect of each of the five elements) that act as conversion catalysts between elements.
- *Anna Agni*, the sixth, is responsible for digesting food.
- The next seven *Agnis* are conversion catalysts in each of the seven *Thathus*, the seven tissues (Plasma, Blood, Flesh, Fat, Bone, Bone Marrow and Reproductive fluid) of the human body and are called the *Sapt Thathu Agnis*.

Once food is digested by *Anna Agni*, it is catalysed and converted into *Rasa Thathu* (the first tissue, Plasma) by the first *Sapt Thathu Agni*. The next *Agni* acts as a catalyst to form the second *Thathu*, *Rakta*, (Blood tissue) and so on. Plasma, blood, flesh, fat, bone, bone marrow and reproductive fluid are the *Sapt Thathus* (seven tissues) and each has an *Agni* working for its formation and nourishment.

Kapham:

The dynamic interplay between the element of water and earth creates the bio-regulating force, *Kapham*. This union increases the attribute of coolness significantly, by overriding the influence of fire which generates properties of cementing, binding, formation and form, solidity, etc. The animating qualities of *Kapham* are stability, consistency, firmness, contouring, structuring, cohesion, lubrication and support - rarely leaving a feeling of emptiness. One can visualise *Kapham* as a stirring force that keeps water and earth from separating. If we add sand to a pot half filled with water, it would sink to the bottom. The only way to keep water and sand as one is to keep stirring the mix. This is the force of *Kapham*. *Kapham* cements the elements within the body and provides material for physical structure. This Dosham *maintains* bodily resistance, stamina, fortitude, strength, resilience and grounding. The water element is the predominant constituent of *Kapham* and is physiologically responsible for biological strength, natural tissue stamina and resilience of the body. *Kapham* lubricates the joints, provides moisture to the skin, helps heal wounds and fills spaces in the body. It supports memory retention, gives energy to the heart and lungs and maintains immunity. Psychologically, *Kapham* exhibits emotions like attachment, greed and long-standing envy. It also expresses as calmness, firmness and love.

CHAPTER FIVE: MEDICINE OF THE SAGES

The three bio-regulating forces, *Vatham*, *Pittam* and *Kapham* make for the substance of the human form and govern all physical, emotional and mental aspects of human function. The cryptic verses of the accomplished Masters speak meticulously of the secret ways of Nature and reveal that none of the five elements is ever absent anywhere in the entire cosmos at anytime. All five coexist at all times by adopting different roles of catalyst, supporter, ground, base or acting field, or enabler of the other, to accentuate the most called for quality. Likewise, in the human body, none of the elements ever cease to exist. Elements at different times exhibit alternative behaviours and appear to be absent but are obscure. So even though we categorise them into three pairs, each element is ever-present, either offstage or on.

Let us understand this by way of an interesting story...

Once I was visited by a young French man. He was lean and active. He was curious and keen to learn Siddha's healing practices. He was interested in Indian healing traditions and had been learning Ayurveda from many different places in India since the past five years. In response to his wish to learn Siddha healing, I said, 'Continue your tour all over India. Visit different places teaching Indian medical systems.' He was curious to know the reason behind my words. At that time in his life, he wouldn't be able to learn any one system in depth, neither could he live in one place for long. What he needed was versatile learning because at that stage in his life, a single subject in a single dimension would not fuel his inspiration enough. He smiled, 'I understand, you mean I am a *Vatha* person.' 'Yes, maybe that is one reason,' I replied. 'If I am *Vatha*, can I never learn anything deeply enough and crystallise it? He prodded. I said, 'Please don't consider your constitution only in one obsessive way. Can I ask you something? Even though you have gone many places in these five years, what has been your one aim?' 'Ayurveda', he retorted. 'So, your aim has been a strongly grounded one, with solidity in your learning. This is your *Kapha* nature. Now tell me, are you *Vatha* or *Kapha* person?' I asked. He raised his eyebrows!

Can you imagine Nature with only one *dosham*? Man is miniature Nature! It is the western attitude of both Indian and western scholars to see things in a tailor-made way. We prefer shortcuts to acquire something which gives a feeling of control. But, a living being is dynamic - impossible to capture into illusionary static theories. The post-modern influence believes: to learn about *doshams* is all that is needed to know about Ayurveda and human beings. But Ayurveda means the science of life. It is much more than *doshams*. Moreover, the *doshams* are dynamic - not static. Even though *doshams* are vital keys in the Indian native healing systems, they actually have a much wider application. And even though everybody is governed by a predominant *dosham* defining his *Prakruthi*, the remaining two *doshams* are equally present as hidden potential, proportionate to the dominant one, taking it to more expressive levels of life.

Just think about the different roles the *doshams* play in each one's life...

- The dominant *dosham* - as the *Prakruthi*
- The *dosham* of *Vikruthi*, the *dosham* of disease (The nature of imbalance one acquires by deviating from his *Prakruthi* is *Vikruthi*.)
- Life-stage *dosham* - The *dosham* governing that particular period of life
- Daily life-cycle *dosham* - The influencing *dosham* in the daily life cycle

- The *dosham* of seasonal-cycle - *dosham* influencing the seasonal cycle
- The *dosham* of a particular disease can mutate from one to another when it turns into a chronic *dosham*/disease.

Doshams are the basic platform of human existence. What then defines an individual's unique constitution or *Prakruthi*?

Vatham	-	Movement and propulsion
Pittam	-	Heat and conversion
Kapham	-	Form and stability

This intermingling influence is continually influencing each basic to complex function within us.

Example 1: Digestion (Pittam process)

> Influence of Pittam on a Pittam-based function:
> Digestion governed by Pittam (influence of its own kind) will perform its best as it gets enhanced.
>
> Influence of Vatham on a Pittam-based function:
> Digestion governed by Vatham imbibes Vatha characteristics giving it a quality of inconsistency or unpredictability.
>
> Influence of Kapham on a Pittam-based function:
> The force of Kapham can also be described as decline in heat, resulting in a solidifying effect. Digestion governed by Kapham would mostly be weak in nature as its fiery characteristic somewhat declined under its cooling influence.

Example 2: Physical activity (Vatham function)

Influence of Vatham on a Vatham-based function:
As all physical activity is Vatham-related, under its own governance, activities are faster.

Influence of Kapham on a Vatham-based function:
Vatham qualities are airy and light whereas Kapham expresses solidity and heaviness. The nature of Kapham is opposite to Vatham which shows as slowing down of activity; lethargy.

Influence of Pittam on a Vatham-based function:
Pitta has minimal influence of the earth element and carries a predominant water and fire influence which would make the physical activity moderate in comparison to the high and airy nature of Vatha and the solid and slow nature of Kapha.

Prakruthi, or inherent constitution, is the collective expression of the *tridoshams* governing the human organism. The word *Pra* means 'first' or 'natural' and *Kirthi* means 'born' or 'form', which transliterates to, 'the first born nature or form'. *Prakruthi* doesn't change throughout the lifetime, but the influence of climate, habitual patterns, lifestyle, food, etc. make apparent alterations which the Siddhas name *Vikrithi* (deviation). *Prakruthi* is born of a combination of the parents' *Prakruthi*. The genetic patterns, the state of health, the state of mind, etc. of the two partners during union are factors that determine the constitution of the child.

CHAPTER FIVE: MEDICINE OF THE SAGES

PRAKRUTHI

What is Prakruthi?

Our human body is built and run based on the three-bio regulating forces, *Vatham, Pittam* and *Kapham*; the three natural inhabitants of the body. Our actions and mobility depend upon *Vatham*; *Pittam* governs our processes, functions and conversions; and the force of *Kapham* builds the structure and substance of our form. Collectively, they illustrate the constitution of the individual, known as *Prakruthi*. *Prakruthi* can also be described as the pattern of the three combining pairs, at conception. This imprint governs upon the individual the entire lifetime. An alteration is seen as a deviation, the dissolution of which would make the individual at once fall back into his inherent pattern, his *Prakruthi*.

Why is it that all the people on the planet do not look, walk, speak, etc the same? After all we are made of the same five elements. What causes differences in height, skin colour, hair, habits, behaviour, characters, etc.? No two human beings are alike.

The co-existence of the five elements (combined into *tridoshams*) is confirmed by the unique and complex versatile functions humans perform. Walking, running, belching, hunger, sex, sleep, etc. are done by *Vatham* confirming the presence of Space and Air. Digestion, sight, body warmth, etc. confirm the existence of *Pittam* (fire and water elements). Body shape, weight, flexibility, stability, etc. confirm the presence of *Kapham* (earth and water). One or two of the *doshams* assert an influence over the others, which is different for everyone. This is *Prakruthi*. *Prakruthi* is always active and colours everything giving a unique shade or flavour, making each one typical to his *Prakruthi*. This brings us to two questions. How many types of *Prakruthi* are there? And, what factors decide the type of constitution?

The ancient Siddhas listed ten types of *Prakruthi*:

1. Vatha
2. Pitta
3. Kapha
4. Vatha-Pitta
5. Vatha-Kapha
6. Pitta-Vatha
7. Pitta-Kapha
8. Kapha-Vatha
9. Kapha-Pitta
10. Vatha-Pitta-Kapha type is a relatively rare constitution.

Prakruthi Types

Recognising the Predominant Dosham of One's Inborn Constitution
Evaluating your own individual constitution type:

Vatha - V
Pitta - P
Kapha - K

To determine your own individual constitution, evaluate yourself as accurately and honestly as you can. Avoid temptation to see yourself as you would like to rather than as you are. If during your evaluation, you feel like you belong partly to one constitution and partly to another, please write both.

Body Frame
    V people - either unusually short or unusually tall, with slender and lanky body frame. Bone structures are either light or rather heavy and often protrude forming prominent joints.

CHAPTER FIVE: MEDICINE OF THE SAGES

P people - medium or average body frames and are proportionate in height and weight, which indicates a prudent use of developmental energy.

K people - built with a heavy or broad body frame with heavy bone structure, clearly indicative of their tendency to store energy. Their feet and toes are noticeably short and squarish.

Weight
V people - rarely gain weight due to high degree of energy spending. The dryness of their constitution promotes a dominant leanness of body. In case for some reason they do put on weight, they lose it equally easily, quickly.

P people - gain or lose weight relatively easily and are able to maintain their weight with minor fluctuations.

K people - Tendency to gain weight due to *kapham*'s trait of energy conservation and reluctance towards energy spending. Therefore, they gain weight all too easily but face difficulty losing it.

Walk
V people - A very quick gait with swift movements, always in a hurry.
P people - Moderate to normal walking pace. Walk displays intent.
K people - Walk is slow, relaxed with a steady gait.

Associated movements of body while walking
V people - Show lot of body movement e.g. shoulders, arms, hips, etc.
P people - Walk in a normal fashion with their body displaying compact alignment.
K people - Show no associated movements in their walk.

Teeth
V people - Known for crooked, uneven teeth. Their innate irregularity may show in their jaw, making it either too small to fit all the teeth or too big and protruding. Sometimes some teeth may be significantly larger than the other ones.

P people - Have a set of medium and average-sized teeth that fit well in a moderate and proportionately formed jaw, but their teeth are prone to cavities.

K people - Have a large and gleaming set of teeth, which rarely need medical attention.

SECTION TWO: TREE OF LIFE

Digestive power
- V people - Irregular appetite and their digestive power is inconsistent.
- P people - Have a powerful digestive system. Strong stomach!
- K people - Have a weak, fragile digestive system and frequently suffer digestive issues.

Ability to bear hunger
- V people - Have an innate ability to bear fluctuating hunger intervals.
- P people - Show poor ability in bearing hunger and depend on their intake of food.
- K people - Have a high degree of ability to bear hunger and can go for long periods without proper food.

Thirst
- V people - Show irregular nature of thirst.
- P people - Are often thirsty.
- K people - Are seldom thirsty.

Quantity of food
- V people - Have irregular and inconsistent appetite and consume varying quantities.
- P people - Inclined to have a large appetite and consume large quantities of food at meal times.
- K people - Display normal appetite and consume normal quantities of food.

Groups of desired tastes
- V People - Inclined toward foods of sweet, salty and sour flavours and nature.
- P people - Inclined toward food that is sweet, bitter and astringent in taste.
- K people - Prefer pungent, astringent and bitter tasting foods.

Foods desired
- V people - Like warm food.
- P people - Like cold food.
- K people - Like warm and dry food.

CHAPTER FIVE: MEDICINE OF THE SAGES

Bowel movements
- V people - Irregular bowel movements and often suffer constipation.
- P people - Are rarely constipated and enjoy regular and frequent bowel movements.
- K people - Have regular well-formed stools but they may be slow in elimination.

Perspiration
- V people - Seldom perspire implying a typical cold body and dry constitution.
- P people - Perspire heavily and easily because of their ever-fiery constitution but may suffer body odour due to excess sweating.
- K people - With their wet constitution, they perspire normally in any climate.

Sleep
- V people - Light sleepers. Often suffer interrupted and little sleep but sometimes due to severe exhaustion, they could fall into deep slumber and are impossible to rouse. Even after a long sleep, they could wake up without feeling rested as their minds continue to spend energy even in sleep.
- P people - Enjoy normal sleep patterns, fall asleep easily and wake up alert.
- K people - Display unusually deep and excessive sleep patterns as they innately enjoy saving energy.

Dreams
- V people - Mostly dream of flying, jumping, climbing hills, etc.
- P people - Dream of violence, fights and struggles.
- K people - Dream of water bodies, clouds and romance.

Personality Traits
- V people - Innately resist any sort of regularity and thereby respond easily to changes in environment. They are extremely changeable and sensitive, often high strung and restless as their mind demands continual stimulation. Although they are high in their energy levels, they burn out quickly.
- P people - Are strong and forceful in their dealings. They are dedicated to the practical side of life. When possible they turn domineering. They are inherently courageous and strongly believe in fair play.

K people - Enjoy the peace and pleasure of home and family. They are serious, steady and calm individuals with virtues like patience, fortitude and humility, which in excess could turn into passivity, attachment, possessiveness and greed. They are naturally compassionate in nature and their strong maternal instincts arise from the predominant influence of the Earth element in them.

Speech and Voice Qualities

V people - Talk very fast, often skipping or missing words in sentences, with a high-pitched voice. They often tend to stray from the subject. They are highly talkative and can speak on almost any subject for hours, as talking involves spending energy. V people show an in-ability of keeping anything solid within them. In other words, they gain satisfaction only after expulsion.

P people - talk in a sharp, provocative and clear-cut manner, typical of their fiery constitution. They are concise and always know what they want to communicate, what response they desire and what nature of energy needs to be projected to obtain it. Their tone is usually intense and often carries a note of impatience. P people are often accused of having sharp tongues.

K people - Talk slowly, cautiously without volunteering much. Their voice is pleasant, clear and resonant, much lower in pitch than V or P people. They strike up a conversation only if they have something important to say and when they do, it is a pleasure to listen to them.

Energy spending

V people - Have a tendency to overwork due to the stirring nature of the air principle within them.

P people - Show moderate energy levels indicative of their natural inclination for balance.

K people - Exude a flow of steady energy.

Performance of activities

V people - Carry out activities with high initiative and rather quickly. They are fast and nimble in their work.

CHAPTER FIVE: MEDICINE OF THE SAGES

- P people - Maintain a moderate pace in performing their activities and express a medium initiative.
- K people - Work slowly and consistently. Their pace is calm and gradual, undisturbed by anything.

Excitability
- V people - Get excited easily and quickly, lose interest equally speedily due to the natural tendency to expend high amounts of energy.
- P people - Get excited and react quickly and tend to remain in that mode for rather long.
- K people - Get excited rather slowly, show no signs of being impacted too suddenly. They take their time, which allows a calm response indicating reluctance to expend energy easily.

Grasping power
- V people - Are equipped with a naturally-fast grasping power.
- P people - Have a quick grasping power.
- K people - Are slow in grasping anything new.

Memory
- V people - Have a very short memory so although they remember easily, they tend to forget equally easily. They may burst out in a sudden spurge of anger but it is gone and forgotten equally soon.
- P people - Show a medium or average memory span. They remember easily but find it hard to forget. They may simmer in the feeling of anger or resentment for long.
- K people - Have an unusually long memory, don't forget anything easily although they need to be told something more than once before it completely sinks in. Their natural ability to store encourages the memory to retain every detail for a long time.

Nature of moods
- V people - Show traits of impulsive and erratic behaviour.
- P people - Are highly forceful and assertive by nature.
- K people - Are far more relaxed and reliable but on the other hand, show traces of eccentric behaviour.

Attitude to problems or difficulties their characteristic emotions

- V people - In difficult situations, show anxiety and severe worry. Display signs of instability or inconsistency mainly because they are unable to digest and assimilate the ongoing situation. But when they do cope, they carry out activities quite creatively and face situations with enthusiasm.
- P people - deal with most problems with reactions of anger or get provoked to levels of high irritability if they feel overwhelmed by a situation. But when they begin to cope, they grow pensive and remain with a deep pondering attitude.
- K people - are peaceful, slow and steady when faced by problems and difficulties as they innately avoid confrontations. They display a calming steadfastness in dealings, but this could assume forms of passivity or inactivity at times.

On counting the number of V, P and K's, you will find that one or two are in majority. This determines your *Prakruthi*. For e.g. if the number of V's are 9, P's are 13 and K's are 3 then your constitution is likely to be Pitta dominant with Vatha as the secondary influence.

QUALITIES EXPRESSED BY THE THREE DOSHAMS WHEN IN BALANCE AND IMBALANCE

VATHAM		PITTAM		KAPHAM	
Balance	Imbalance	Balance	Imbalance	Balance	Imbalance
Active	Anxious	Decisive	Confused	Steady	Sluggish
Creative	Dull	Ambitious	Envious	Loving	Possessive
Secure	Insecure	Knowledgeable	Complaining	Peaceful	Insensitive
Inspired	Depressed	Understanding in depth	Irritable	Caring	Attached
Flexible	Unstable	Clarity	Anger	Consistent	Stubborn/rigid

CHAPTER FIVE: MEDICINE OF THE SAGES

Ayurveda enlists seven different types of *Prakruthi* (inherent constitution) but the Siddha system declares ten. Below are the characteristics of the various *Prakruthi* permutations, with one *dosham* in the forefront and the second active in the background.

Vatham-Pittam Individual:

A person born with predominant Vatham and secondary Pittam could be of dark complexion, with skin that is both dry and sensitive, wavy hair, weak health and a mental makeup liable to be shaken up easily. Such individuals desire to be truthful yet lean on falsehood, are abnormally prone to fearful anger bouts. They desire frequent sexual indulgences, are highly indecisive in nature and crave sweet and tangy food. As air tends to fan the fire, the personality can get more irritable and impulsive as both fire and air are upward moving. These people are often seen to suffer diseases related to acid eructation, constipation, headaches and eye disorders.

Vatha-Kapha Individual:

'Coolness' is common to both Vatham and Kapham. A balanced ratio of this combination generates a composed personality, but if imbalanced, it shows an astringent nature. The individual would be flabby, slow in movement and have a rosy complexion with a skin type that is generally dry with some oily zones. The person would be drawn to yogic practice and prefer pungent, sour food. A common characteristic I found in Vatham-Kapham personalities is a rigid adherence to obsessive disciplines. Many are time-obsessive, fixated or obsessive in following routines - (a personality of heavy external-reference) and therefore more than often fail to digest the crux of the discipline. Kapham's rigidity, like the earth element, combined with the 'cool' nature of the air element increases, resulting in diseases like stiffness of joints, frozen shoulders, rheumatism, weak digestion and circulatory disorders.

Pitta-Vatha Individual:

People of this constitution have a fair complexion, are intelligent, have a pleasant voice, are appreciative of sweet aroma and incline toward initiating research in new areas. They have a typical short cough, dry skin and desire sweet and sour food. The Fire element with its ability to expand the airy nature of the personality generates more creativity when in idyllic balance. But, in imbalance makes the individual workaholic. Physical ailments typically suffered are gastritis and chronic fatigue syndrome.

Pitta-Kapha Individual:

People of this constitution have a skin complexion akin to the colour of the Champaka flower, have a pleasant voice, enjoy the company of the learned and incline toward the mysteries of meditation. They are abundantly charitable in nature and express kindness towards the whole of creation. They often show craving for spicy and bitter food. The psychological aspects of Pittam dominance and Kapham arrogance and solidity increase the eccentric nature of this personality. Many kings or rulers were of Kapham constitution or its derivatives such as Kapha-Vatha and Kapha-Pitta. Great warriors, majority of ancient day soldiers who supported their rulers were of Pittam constitution, especially the Pittam-Kapham derivative. People popular for sacrifice, giving of their life in battle, or dedicated to charity, field of research, etc. are often of Pittam-Kapham constitution.

Kapha-Pitta Individual:

Kapham-Pittam individuals are of rosy complexion, tinged slightly green, often with red hair. They typically have oily and sensitive skin, brilliant orator skills, a clear tone of voice and are capable of attracting and kindling sexual desire. They incline to the path of wisdom; stand steadfast in the path of truth and desire for sweet and spicy food. Their Pittam traits of sharp intelligence get channelised under the solidifying influence of Kapham. Ancient philosophers, assassinated for declaring insights that contradicted conventional belief, seem to be of this type. This constitution in imbalance suffers metabolic disorders, skin disease such as urticaria etc.

Kapha-Vatha Individual:

Kapham-Vatham individuals are of robust body, dark or rosy complexion with excessive sexual appetite. They harbour intentions of gaining power, yearn for occultism and desire research. They hold a special reverence for elders and love for the learned. They have a natural ability to lead, take initiative and are forward in action. They enjoy sour, pungent food. Once again, the cooling nature of both Kapham and Vatham creates circulatory issues. As for the positive aspect, the grounding nature of Kapham mingled with the creativity of Vatham, gives birth to 'leading personalities', Rulers of a Nation or corporate sectors and/or in areas of new invention of gadgets and mechanisms.

The true purpose behind understanding one's *Prakruthi* is to help recognise one's natural inclination or pre-established resonance with Nature. This inner perspective guards one from deterrences.

৸ ଓ

NATURE LIMITS YOU!

Are you confined by your *Prakruthi*?

A Vatham body, naturally cold in nature, in cold climates gets even colder which can trigger disorders that hamper lifestyle. In cold climate, a Vatham *prakruthi* needs to protect his body against the cold to deter an increase in Vatham. This is his limitation! Contrarily, Pittam people need to keep their bodies cool in summer as it is governed by the fire element. Each *prakruthi* implies a certain limitation, or one can see it as a set of parameters one should live by. Pittam, a naturally-fiery constitution easily enjoys cooler climates and faces difficulty in hot weather. Kapham *Prakruthi* prefers moderate cold and doesn't mind the heat. Even though I called *Prakruthi* a 'limitation', at no point does it turn incompatible with Nature! I would better describe *Prakruthi* as Nature's gift of possibilities to flourish by.

Living by the choices provided by Nature provides us great advantages and unfolds extraordinary options. *Prakruthi* is that perfect design, that idyllic blend that ensures the required life mission can be enacted to completion. What we learn of our deeper self not only enhances our health but also the quality of life. Understanding *Prakruthi* is learning the skill of true self-expression. Even though we can reach within to learn, it is often difficult. But it is possible that we understand our personal choices and what it means to protect ourselves from non-conducive influence. We can begin to care for our inner constitution. Recognising our *Prakruthi* teaches us the meaning behind our illness, which gives hope and empowerment to 'refuse the disease' from within our body-mind. So far, we have read about each *Prakruthi* and both its variants - in balance and/or imbalance, known as *Vikrithi*. Either way, it expresses a distinctive nature. A harmonious balance of the *doshams* positively affects the mental and emotional states of an individual, whereas imbalance manifests as negative characteristics, traits and attitudes. Let us see the causative factors.

෴

CAUSES OF DERANGEMENT OF THE THREE BIO-REGULATING FORCES

Vatham (Air-dominant principle):

Excessive activity or habitual patterns that can aggravate *Vatha Dosham*:

- Excessive manual labour
- Excessive sexual indulgences
- Excessive studying
- Speaking in a very high-pitched voice
- Excessive mental exercise
- High-level fear and/or anxiety
- Swimming against the current
- Excessive fasting
- Suppressing calls of nature, e.g. urinating, defecating, passing of wind (farting), etc.
- Excessive intake of bitter, pungent, astringent or dry food substances, and/or continuous use of particular kinds of pulses and rice
- Over-exposure to cloudy and stormy days in the early morning and in the evening

The following symptoms indicate a reduction of *Vatham* in one's physical and psychological structure:

- Shifting pain all over the body
- Fits of depression
- Low receptivity
- Difficulty in putting words together fluently
- Slowing down of all bodily activities
- Lack of creative nature
- Difficulty in adapting to new situations

Pittam (Fire-dominant principle):

Excessive activity or habitual patterns that aggravate *Pittam Dosham:*

- Grief
- Anger
- Arguments
- Physical exercises at mid-day or in very hot weather
- Unnatural sexual intercourse
- Intake of food at irregular times
- An excessive intake of bitter, sour, salty, or spicy food
- Excessive exposure to the sun during summer and autumn seasons
- Aggravation can also occur at noon and midnight since both times are ruled by *Pittam* nature

The reduction of *Pittam* shows symptoms of:

- Poor appetite
- Inability to concentrate
- Inability of logical understanding
- Difficulty in gaining orientation
- Difficulty in programming and planning

Kapham or slethumam: (Water-dominant principle)

Excessive activity or habitual patterns that aggravate *Kapham Dosham*:

- Sedentary habits
- Laziness
- Sleeping in daytime

CHAPTER FIVE: MEDICINE OF THE SAGES

- Living in the same kind of situation for a prolonged time
- Excessive intake of sweet, salty, oily and cold food
- Excessive intake of food
- Over-exposure to the chills of winter or spring in the forenoon and the evening
- Unwillingness to start any new venture in life

The reduction of *Kapham* shows symptoms of:

- Thirst
- General debility
- Insomnia
- Sinking feeling
- Impulsive psyche
- Irritation while dealing with situations
- Poor grounding nature in oneself and in life

The immortal Siddha Masters describe 'health' as the harmonious equilibrium in the three main functionalities (*Doshams, Thathus, Malas*) of the human body:

- The balanced functioning of the three *doshams* within our body.
- The healthy functioning of the seven *Thathus* or tissues that constitute the formation of the body.
- The balanced functioning of the elimination system: the *Malas*

Arogyam or health is called '*Sama Dosham*', a state in which the three *doshams* of our body co-exist in optimal equilibrium. *Sama Dosham* comes from maintaining harmony along with immunity to overcome changing influences. Ill health is a disturbance of this equilibrium. As the three *doshams* and the seven *Thathus* are composed of the five natural elements, Space, Air, Fire, Water and

Earth, we can conclude that the elemental ratios suffered change which disabled function and altered the quality. A disturbance can either be an exaggeration or decline of the elements or their complimentary half. For instance, when the idyllic ratio of Air and Space in *Vatham* is hampered, both elements get altered along with their qualities and performance. Similarly, if *Pittam* (Fire with Water) is over-exposed to the Air element, it dries up the cooling aspect and hence aggravates the Fire.

ಸಿ ಡ

Vatha

Air and Space

Pitta

Water and Fire

Kapha

Water and Earth

SECTION TWO: TREE OF LIFE

THE FLUX OF DOSHAMS

The *Tridoshams* within our body are constantly exposed to internal as well as external influences, one of which is seasonal change. They increase and decrease according to changes in season. The inner environment during these shifts is what could invite disease. Deviations instantly alter normal activity of the *dosham*, which show up as symptoms or new behavioural patterns. To avoid vulnerability, the ancient Siddhas recommend conscious changes in behaviour and life-style each changing season.

The *doshams* change even during the course of a single day under the influence of food, day-to-day situations, change in routine, events and encounters, etc. The sun is hottest in the afternoon. During the night, the moon cools the atmosphere down. In other words, *Kapham* increases during the hours of early night and early morning and during mid-day and midnight *Pittam* increases. In the late evening and late night hours, the force of *Vatham* increases. These changes influence both our body and mind. A shift in doshic equilibrium can be expected whenever an individual travels from one place to another or from one climate to another.

Like seasons, every individual goes through stages in his lifetime. According to the Siddhas, the three stages of a human lifetime are governed by a *dosham*.

VATHAM	Early years to adolescence
PITTAM	Early adulthood to beginning of old age
KAPHAM	Old age, unto death

Vatham predominates in the early years as this is the stage of growth, activity and rapid changes in physical appearance. In this stage, an individual has a relatively flexible and receptive mind. Gradually, *Pittam* takes over and introduces traits like striving, surging ambition, goal-oriented-ness and intentions of planning and establishing oneself in a chosen career, etc. This characterises one's years as an adult. As the individual matures, his perception of life gets refined and concerns about one's successor or children arise. One tends to drop competitive tendencies, grows more willing to accept whatever has already been acquired and accomplished and lives with a feeling of contentment. In this stage, *Kapham* takes over as the predominant bio-regulating force governing one's body-mind experience. The description of life stages in the science of Ayurveda is different from the Siddha Tradition. Ayurvedic hierarchy of the ruling bio-regulating forces is given below:

KAPHAM	Early years to adolescence
PITTAM	Early adulthood to beginning of old age
VATHAM	Old age, unto death

ஸ் ௳

Understanding our constitution allows us to maintain natural equilibrium and enjoy good health. Symptoms indicate a loss of sensitivity to our inner balance. A *Vatha*-dominant person's inherent sensitivity must guide him to imbibe changes according to the changing climate. In a severely cold climate, (naturally incompatible to his body type), warm clothes or being close to fire to keep his *Vatham* from imbalance are imperative. He must know a way to amplify his fire element to meet the exaggerated *Vatham* environment. If he ignores this so-called limitation, it leads to sickness. Siddhas point to Nature's ways to lead to abundance:

Food
Lifestyle
Planetary influences
Evil Spirits
Karmic diseases

SECTION TWO: TREE OF LIFE

These five aspects, woven into human existence, are either enablers or adversaries based on our ignorance or sensitivity. On the path of self-referral, diversions do not make their appearance.

- Food - daily diet, long-term eating habits, timing, quantity, combinations, etc.
- Lifestyle - daily routine, physical activities, chronic habits, sleep pattern, nature of work/profession, behaviour, attitudes, etc.
- Planetary influence - prevailing influence of planets. Diseases that do not respond to medicine/treatment are often associated with negative planetary influence. There are several remedies. A native Siddha healer always considers the planet that carries the power to cause that disease; the kinds of disease likely to occur; in which parts of the body and when. As health and longevity of an individual are of primary concern, they are often the first things examined in the natal chart.
- The dimension of evil spirits - cases of possession, personality disorders that do not respond to conventional treatment/medicine, etc.
- Karmic Diseases - acquired by one's past life deeds.

Food and lifestyle are the only two direct doorways. We can change, alter, modify, enhance, pacify, reduce our food and lifestyle. The Siddhas have spoken of food in great depth. Food is classified into six tastes - Sweet, Sour, Pungent, Bitter, Astringent and Salty, which describe the properties and quality of food. Food is composed of the five elements and carries impact on the balance of the three *doshams*, the *thathus* and the resultant *malas*. As this is an inevitable and necessary influence, awareness is vital as discussed in later chapters.

```
                  Food
    _____
Six tastes              Relation of Doshams/Thathus/Malas
```

CHAPTER FIVE: MEDICINE OF THE SAGES

Endogenous and exogenous influences, collectively affect the equilibrium of the *doshams*, the *thathus* and the *malas*. Exogenous elements are the *doshams* around us that express as time, seasonal change, etc. As these elements mingle with our endogenous functions, they become the primary reason for all medicinal preparations to be administered in consideration of them (food, lifestyle, climate, season, time of day, etc.). The ancient medicinal approach also examines dietary habits, routine and seasonal changes in lifestyle to unearth causative factors. After pursuing the above nature of treatment (food and lifestyle-based) if a native Vaidya finds the symptoms to persist, the alternative approach of examining planetary influence, evil spirits and karmic causes is pursued. Ancient palm scripts disclose how these factors interfere with the balance of the body, and healing these areas uses a different approach. *Mantras* (words of power), specific rituals (pujas and homas), other yogic and tantric methods to alter planetary forces, karmic influences, etc. are applied. These work more at the level of the mind and are particularly effective for mental disorders, psychic disorders and spirit possessions. Although the Siddhas have revealed remedies for all possibilities, they attribute great importance to the simple dimension of Food and Lifestyle, describing them as doors that can deter the adverse influence of planetary positions, evil spirits as well as karmic disease. They exemplify this by their own livingness. The oneness with which one can live in harmony, rhythm and resonance, flow with the ever-changing movement of Nature, without battle, is what they call 'refusing the disease'. The self-referral approach exhibits a natural, sensitive manoeuvrability that has the strength to carry on through the variables of Nature with simple flexibility.

ಙ ಔ

SECTION TWO: TREE OF LIFE

THATHUS - THE MATRIX OF THE BODY

The human body is composed of seven tissues or *Thathus*. *Thathu* formation is a unique process where each *Thathu* emerges from the previous. This successive formation is called *Thathu Parinamam* - evolution of the fundamental tissues. They are formed from the quintessence of the food consumed. To put it simply - our body is made up of what we eat.

Seven *Thathus* (tissues):

English	**Tamil**	**Sanskrit**
Plasma	Ninaneer	Rasa
Blood	Chenneer,	Rakta
Muscle	Mamisam,	Mamsa
Fat	Koluppu,	Medas
Bone	Enbu,	Asthi
Bone marrow	Moolai,	Majjai
Reproductive fluid	Suronita,	Sukra

The *Thathus* are formed starting from *Rasa* to *Rakta*, *Rakta* to *Mamsa*, *Mamsa* to *Medas*, *Medas* to *Asthi*, *Asthi* to *Majjai*, and lastly *Majjai* to *Sukra*.

Vatham (dosham of movement) ensures that the transformation from *Rasa Thathu* (first) to *Sukra Thathu* (seventh) happens harmoniously. But the quality of the formation depends on the food we eat and the quality of our digestion. For example, *Rasa Thathu* is formed after the first stage of digestion and *Rakta Thathu* on the second stage and so on. Poor digestion at any stage results in a weak tissue. The seven *Thathus* and the five *Bhuthas* (elements) are assimilated from the food we eat. Our food should be a combination of the necessary components. Only solids or only liquids would create imbalance. All four varieties are mandatory. To nourish and form the earth element, we need bulky or heavy food. The formation of the liquid aspect in our body demands the intake of liquid and to improve and enhance our digestive capacity, we need fiery food like the spices we add to our food.

ಬಿ ಛ

THE ARCHITECTS

Food, in the mouth, is met and worked on by the Water element - saliva; a subordinate of the *Kapha dosham* network. *Vatha* subordinates execute chewing and swallowing activities. As food travels down to the digestive region, it is loosened and softened to a liquid state. *Pittam* subordinates play the part of extracting the essential from the inessential and break it down to a nutrient fluid called *Anna Rasa*. The rest is waste that is eliminated as urine and faeces.

We will take a look at the function of each *Thathu* and follow the progressive journey of *Anna Rasa* (nutrient fluid) and see its effect on the body. In this journey we meet different processes, various subtle catalysts, results of the cooking and conversion functions and their waste emissions, the elemental nature of each and the qualitative impact on the body. *Anna Rasa* is cooked, converted, partly consolidated and partly potentiated for its next course. Its entire journey is to build, nourish and maintain the seven *Thathus* - plasma, blood, flesh, fat, bone, bone marrow and the reproductive fluid, that build the human form. From the first tissue to the last, each is born from the previous, in a sequential and successive order and all seven remain interconnected in all aspects.

RASA THATHU (Ninaneer)

Anna Rasa is met by the subtle fire, *Rasa Thathu Agni*, which facilitates the replenishment of the first *Thathu* - *Rasa* or Plasma. The fire of the *Rasa Thathu Agni* cooks the nutrient fluid and converts it to plasma, lymph, etc. until the tissue is sufficiently nourished. The *Rasa Thathu Agni* cooks another portion of *Anna Rasa* to convert it into a higher potentiate for the next *Thathu* in line. The entire cooking and conversion process generates a waste of *Kapha* quality which shows as phlegm in the body.

The elemental nature of *Rasa Thathu* is *Kapha*, Water.

Anna Rasa, being cooked and converted at its first stage, is a refreshing experience for the body as plasma formation takes place. Plasma is found all over the body and the refreshing feeling spreads to every nook and corner. The conversion is instantaneous and provides the body immediate nourishment similar to a drink of water when thirsty. The 'refreshing' experience turns into a psychological state - we enjoy a refreshing outlook toward our activities and situations. But if our food does not carry sufficient nutrition, the very first conversion fails and we suffer *Rasa* depletion. The psychological implications of this experience show as weariness.

RAKTHA THATHU (Chenneer)

A portion of *Anna Rasa* of the *Rasa Thathu* leads to the formation of *Raktha* (Blood). The *Rasa Thathu Agni* cooks this portion until it transforms into the next successive tissue - *Raktha Thathu*, Blood. This portion contains its corresponding *Agni* - the *Raktha Thathu Agni* that continues to cook it to generate and replenish the blood tissue in our body to a satisfactory mark. The waste generated in forming *Raktha* is bile which is of *Pittam* nature.

Formation of fresh blood is enlivening for the entire body. The body experiences revitalisation as red blood cells get formed. *Raktha*

Thathu, in the form of the Fire element, joined by the Water element, give the body a healthy glow. The warmth of the blood keeps the skin soft to touch. A dissatisfactory formation of this tissue shows as rough or dry and cracked skin. Psychologically, a depleted *Rakta Thathu* reflects as mental and physical dullness and poor skin texture.

MAMSA THATHU (Mamisam)

Once again, *Raktha Thathu Agni* cooks a potentiated portion and transforms it to the third tissue, *Mamsa* or Flesh. With the inherent conversion catalyst, this tissue generates flesh as required by the body. After sufficient replenishment, it sets aside the required portion for the fourth tissue. The waste formation at this stage is the water element that releases as fluid from bodily orifices. The flesh formed carries the Earth element. The psychological impact felt by the body by the formation of flesh are qualities of earth - feelings of grounding, discernment and a cemented, well-formed outlook. A lack of *Mamsa* reflects as a scattered or dispersed mind. Excessive *Mamsa* shows up as heaviness around the abdomen/midriff, thighs, etc. and depletion results is muscle reduction or pinching, stabbing pains in parts of the body.

MEDAS THATHU (Koluppu)

From the essential part of *Mamsa* is born the fourth tissue, *Medas Thathu* or Fat. As *Medas Thathu Agni* continues cooking, the necessary conversion happens and the body gets replenished with sufficient fatty tissue. The waste generated is sweat as fat burns while cooking. The elemental composition of this tissue is Water combined with Fire. In the body, this tissue shows as gain in weight. Excessive formation leads to obesity and depletion brings debility. Its subtler essence radiates an embracing feeling in the individual;

a feeling of being 'held'. It radiates unctuousness which reflects as sociability or flexibility as a part of the individual's nature. A converse of these characteristics display rigidity, anti-social behavior, etc.

ASTHI THATHU (Enbu)

The potential portion of *Medas* creates the fifth tissue of the human body - *Asthi Thathu*, Bone. Bone, in our body, is comprised of the Air element combined with the Earth element which provides precise shape and form. The waste generated at this stage of *Thathu* formation is nails, hair, etc. Just as bones give body its frame and support, its psychological reflections are no different. They give the individual psychic grounded-ness, constructive mentality and well-formed ideas, etc. A weak bone structure would show psychic instability, airy nature, frivolous behavior, etc.

MAJJA THATHU (Moolai)

As the essential portion continues its journey, the resultant conversion is the formation of the sixth tissue, *Majja* Thathu, Bone marrow. This tissue is formed by the Water element and reflects its qualities. The waste that emerges from this stage of cooking is the secretion from eyes. The role of bone marrow in our body is to 'fill'. Its psychic counterpart shows as contentment and satisfaction and imbalance reflects psychically as discontentment, dissatisfaction, etc.

SUKRA THATHU (Suronita)

From the potentiated portion of *Majja* is born the last of the seven tissues, *Sukra Thathu* or reproductive fluid and is the most essential part of *Anna Rasa*. It is formed of Water element. *Sukra Thathu* also cooks in its formation but no further tissue formation happens, instead a few resultant effects are observed. The role of reproductive fluid is to procreate. Psychically, this function reflects as an individual's wish for a successor, maternal or paternal instincts, creativity, etc. Physically, it reflects as suppleness of body. A derangement at this stage reflects as low libido, inability to achieve and a fear of death.

Anna Rasa cooked through all the seven stages reaching the intended result. Its elemental nature changed at each stage, resulting in the physical formation of each tissue. It released inessentials as waste and extracted the essence for further cooking at each stage. Through its journey, as it underwent elemental changes, it reflected those qualities and characteristics in the individual's character and personality. The Siddhas speak of another consequence of this seven-fold journey; its quintessence called Amritha. This quintessence returns itself to the voyage, giving it qualitative nourishment, which is immunity or shield of the human body. If, through the journey, the nutritional content doesn't fulfil required tissue formation, the quintessence at the end of the seventh tissue is poor in quality with drop in immunity, leaving us open to disease.

ಙ ಖ

Siddhas give importance to *Malas* (excreta) as they do to the *Thathus*. Although, all *Malas* are meant to be expelled from the body, they still play a role. For instance, our eyes and nose would turn completely dry as *Malas* provide lubrication. Faeces, urine and sweat are the three important *Malas* that carry out specific roles. The function of faeces is to support the body just as pillars support a building. Its entire expulsion weakens the body to a great extent. In a person suffering depletion in all seven *Thathus*, it is the faecal matter that acts as the last sustaining factor and provides strength. It is said that complete depletion of *Malas* can cause greater harm than its accumulation.

Urine is a carrier of all bodily exudation. So as to not deplete the moisture content of the body, sweat performs the important function of retaining the right amount. If there is no warmth within the body, the skin would get parched, dry and start peeling, turning black in colour. The retention of right amount of moisture lets the skin stay soft. Optimally functioning three *Malas* attain an ideal, balanced state.

ಸಿ ಲ

SUVAI

Ancient Sages say,
>'The body is made of food. It takes the food Earth offers. This food is made up of six tastes. Mind identifies itself with the body and through it with the world.'

Earth has been refining herself from the beginning of time; weaving and refining cosmic memory through the genetic coding of life-forms proving the presence of cosmic communion between all earth's inhabitants. Doshams embody the karmic and genetic codes that we are irrevocably linked to and affected by such as the universal code of the stars, planets, galaxies, minerals and elements. Siddhas have revealed a systemised code of human behaviour in relation to food and taste. Every food-taste, every emotion, every dream is a memory of the past and a reflection of the future. The five elements continually transmute into each other to create atoms, molecules, minerals, food and life-form. Food is the prime keeper of all five elements and through it the body of life is formed.

Man is an integrated part of the whole cosmos through his faculty of identification. Imbalance in identity demonstrates sorrow. Ayurveda speaks of three *Malas* whereas the Siddha tradition points

CHAPTER FIVE: MEDICINE OF THE SAGES

to *Malas* present even in *Tattwas* (variables of Nature). The three primordial impurities, *Aanavam*, *Kanmam* and *Maya*, could curtain the light of consciousness when imbalanced, or serve as a transparent medium to ever-shining consciousness, *Chit*. *Aanavam* is an aspect of identification that establishes its individual nature by action or function (karma) while enchanted by the delusive nature of worldly affliction, *Maya*. Just as for a healthy body, the presence of *Malas* is essential and required proportion is withheld by the body for survival, likewise, *Aanavam* in its Satvic aspect (proper functioning and right inter-connectedness) serves to integrate and ground individuality.

Life reaches symbiotic unity by resonating with the whole. Nature has provided each being with unique qualities, living or non-living and Man, through the attribute of 'taste' asserts his individuality and becomes a part of the cosmos. He identifies with 'matter' through taste and in this way, makes it a part of himself too. The process of taking-in food re-invokes cosmic memory of symbiotic nature. Internal assimilation of food in turn makes him a part of the larger cosmos. In the case of a tree, Nature offers space to grow, air in the atmosphere, heat from the sun, rain and soil to ground its roots. A tree is nurtured by Nature through all Her five dimensions - the five elements. A full-grown tree gives back to Nature and completes the cycle by replenishing and nurturing other living beings on earth. A tree makes the earth more binding, it invites rain, offers oxygen to living beings and even after its death is used as timber for our homes. My teacher would say, 'A tree is an ideal living being, one who is eligible to live on earth as it gives back whatever it has received from Mother Nature, in a better way. It takes Nature's raw energy and offers it back as more beautiful and refined so that others can benefit'.

A human is also a microcosm. The Siddha system of medicine says, 'Instead of nutrition through supplements, eating wholesome food is the most proper way to energetic living as it re-invokes the function of the cosmos in him.' Taste is all about transformation and the inner experience of cosmic reality. The democratic Siddha system of curing and healing of nature (man), by nature (herbs and plants), for nature (mind and body balance) has served generations. This is what the Siddha path explains, 'Eating is worshiping Nature and relating with food becomes yoga itself.' The tree *'Aala maram'* (Ficus Religiosa) found in Tamil Nadu belongs to a species similar to the banyan. It grows upward from the ground, branching high toward the sky. After its strong aerial growth, it sends down roots from its branches. From its aerial position, it reaches down to the ground by its roots, implanting more and more roots for new trees to grow. After several years, one cannot identify the first tree among the many, and in all actuality there is only one tree in a garden of ficus trees! The cosmos is similar. There seem to be a multitude of separate beings but everything carries the same undercurrent of cosmic memory and genetic codes, representing the mini-cosmos and return to the grand Universe.

Ancient Folklore:

> Thousands of years ago, a young woman, her husband and mother-in-law lived in a hut in a small village. One winter day, the young woman fell ill with a cold and cough. She set some water to heat to help soothe her sore throat and racking cough. Her angry-natured mother-in-law, seeing the woodpile being reduced for such a flimsy reason decided to disrupt the daughter-in law's plans. She plucked a few leaves from a nearby plant and dropped them into the water and walked away happy. Her share of 'daughter-in-law's bashing' was done for the day. The cough-racked young lady, seeing leaves floating in the water, removed them and drank the infusion. Her throat slowly stopped aching and ever since she heated water with those leaves. These fragrant leaves, used by sages during prayers and rituals are from the plant *'tulsi'* (holy basil). It is believed that the ritual of making infusions and home remedies was born thus.

CHAPTER FIVE: MEDICINE OF THE SAGES

In Tamil, taste is called *Suvai*. Ayurveda calls it *Rasa* and in English it is called Taste or Sap. Ancients categorised food into six basic tastes, each having a distinctive nature and qualitative impact. Down the ladder of evolution, from Space unto Earth there exists a set of common qualities with complimentary parts. This platform is used to assess the principles of taste as they too are formed of the five natural elements of Nature. Starting from Space, right down to Earth, the properties permute between...

Hot ....Cold
Heavy.......Light
Oily..........Dry

From the food we eat, the *Thathus* (body tissues) and *Malas* (waste) are formed showing us what a strong influence food has upon our body. '*Padaartham*' or edible substance is that which is capable of producing an action or effect. This action or effect is determined by the properties and qualities which the Siddhas call *Suvai*, or taste, flavour. *Suvai* points out the nature of the food or medicine we consume. Each flavour or *Suvai* influences our three-bio-regulating forces and our state of mind (*Sattwa*, *Rajas* and *Tamas*), with its characteristic property. Based on this principle, Siddhas use *Suvai* to regulate both, physical and mental health.

Six Suvai:
Sweet, Sour, Salt, Bitter, Pungent and Astringent
(Bitter is the taste of Neem leaves; Pungent is the taste of chilli or black pepper; and astringent is the taste of plantain flower or of Areca nut.)
Suvai can increase or decrease a dosham. This principle is used while choosing a diet and constitutes an important part of the treatment process as a Siddha healer always prescribes a dietary regime in consideration of the disease. This method also ensures that food does not interfere with the working of the medicine and/or food itself can act as medicine.

Six Suvai are divided into three groups:

Group 1   Sweet, Sour and Salty
Group 2   Bitter, Pungent and Astringent
Group 3   Astringent, Bitter and Sweet.

The table below displays the corresponding response of the bio-regulating forces to each group and how each dosham responds to each different group of flavours.

Dosham	Decrease	Increase
Vatha	Sweet, Sour, Salty	Bitter, Pungent, Astringent
Kapha	Bitter, Pungent, Astringent	Sweet, Sour, Salty
Pitta	Astringent, Bitter, Sweet	Sour, Salty, Pungent

How a response and change in the functioning of each dosham serves as a healing platform:
The first group of *Suvai*: Sweet, Sour, Salty, reduces *Vatham* dosham. These tastes can be used for a person suffering from an aggravated *Vatham* condition. Based on its pacifying influence on *Vatha*, it is called the *Vatham*-pacifying group.

The remaining three Suvai: Bitter, Pungent and Astringent increase *Vatham* and hence are termed as the *Vatham*-aggravating group and are used to stimulate a weakened *Vatham* condition.

A look at *Kapha* dosham's response shows an opposite behaviour. Group 1: Bitter, Pungent and Astringent increase *Kapham* in the body whereas *Kapha* is reduced or pacified by Sweet, Sour and Salty flavours. A person suffering from excessive phlegm, which is a condition of increased Kapham, is advised against taking any Sweet, Sour, Salty foods and instead, is prescribed a diet to pacify *Kapham*.

Pittam is pacified by Astringent, Bitter and Sweet tastes. And the remaining three tastes - Sour, Salty and Pungent aggravate it. This ancient principle is essential in treatment for jaundice. Jaundice is a condition of excess *Pittam*; an imbalance in the bile flow and its content in the body. The person is put on a completely bland diet. Flavours like Sour, Salty and Pungent that increase *Pittam* are completely withdrawn. Milk is continued, as it is of sweet taste. And medicines of Bitter and Astringent flavours are prescribed to reduce the *Pittam*.

The knowledge of specific taste substances is necessary and highly effective in keeping the bio-regulating forces in a balanced state. Moreover, if one is able to recognise the dosham affected by the disease and the nature of imbalance, i.e. increase or decrease, it is possible to bring them to normalcy using appropriate tastes as medicine. The Siddhas have revealed that one of the many types of pulse diagnosis is based on the theory of *Suvai*. Pulse diagnosis is based on readings of both hands as the pulse of each hand carries certain specifics of the three tastes based on which treatment can proceed.

ಞ ಈ

SAP OF LIFE

Each flavour or taste has a specific characteristic which corresponds to a quality of certain elements and their characteristics. In other words, the five elements prelude the formation of flavours and impart their elemental qualities to it. Consistent to their nature, earth and water promote bulk and growth whereas fire, wind and ether help reduce it, because earth and water are heavy in nature and the other three lighter. This implies, flavours to be either heavy and bulk-promoting or light and bulk-reducing which acts as a principle during treatment methods. This being the base parameter, let us venture into each of the six tastes. The Siddha Tradition reiterates - everything is inter-related and interconnected - the basic nature - Inter-being-ness. The six tastes are interrelated at different levels and in complimentary ways based on elemental properties.

Sweet

The Sweet taste is not to be misunderstood as readymade sweet-tasting food, but food that quickly satiates, fills you with satisfaction and takes away any further desire to eat. Even a small quantity of such food can do the trick. This is the quality and influence of the sweet taste and implies a heavy nature. Since it instantly nullifies the appetite for more, it evidently has to be of cold nature as against fire (heat) that is responsible for triggering an appetite. Lastly, sweetness does not localise itself; it spreads. This indicates a flowing nature implying oiliness. From this, its elemental composition is comprehensible - Earth and Water.

Foods of corresponding qualities are - Starchy foods, carbohydrates, sugar, fats and amino acids.

Sour

The elemental composition of Sour is Earth and Fire. This describes the journey 'Sweet' takes and alters itself. As we know, lemon juice is often used as an appetiser which implies the presence of the fire element and so its property is hot. Let's see how Sour gets its heavy and oily properties by a small experiment. Cook rice and potato (both sweet in nature) and leave them unrefrigerated for two days. By the third day, the food would have gone 'sour'. The 'sweet' natured food was cold, heavy and oily, but in a matter of two days it altered to Sour, making it hot, heavy and oily.

Foods of corresponding qualities are - organic acids.

Salty

Salty is the third taste and its elemental composition is Water and Fire. The sharp taste of salt implies it is hot in nature and therefore, a stimulant for appetite. Another simple experiment illustrates the properties of salty taste. We often add water to things that are sweet or sour in order to dilute them and make them palatable, for example lemon juice. How does water have the ability to dilute the strength of the original taste? The natural salts contained in water give it this quality. Sometimes, we even add a bit of extra salt to lemon juice after we have added water to make it more palatable. Additionally, we already know how vital an ingredient salt is in cooking. It enhances the taste of food. This indicates that salt (whether in water or otherwise) is a solvent by which we recognise the Water element in it.

Foods of corresponding qualities are salts.

Pungent

Coming to the centreline, we reach the fourth taste. Something pungent on our tongue feels sharp and can leave one gasping - you feel you are on fire and make you jump about frantically. This describes the presence of Air as well as Fire in it. The pungent taste stands for qualities like hot, light and dry.

Foods of corresponding qualities are essential and volatile oils and phenols.

Bitter

The fifth natural taste is Bitter. If you place something bitter on your tongue, the taste of bitterness spreads. Secondly, it is difficult to change a bitter taste as it has the tendency to stay for a while. This indicates its position on the higher end of the evolutionary ladder. Since bitterness doesn't remain localised and spreads, its elemental composition is Air and Space which give it the qualities of light, dry and cold.

Foods of corresponding qualities are alkaloids, glycosides, bitter principles.

Astringent

This is the sixth and the last taste in the natural taste lineage and unique in its own way. The astringent taste is relatively localised which is a clear indication of Earth nature. The Astringent taste is also sharp and dry making the tongue rough or dry which characterises Air. Therefore, composed of Air and Earth, the sixth taste is dry, light and cold.

Foods of corresponding qualities are Tannins.

Taste	Major Dosha Affected	Elements	Major Influence In body	Example
Inippu (Madhu) (Sweet)	↑ Kapha ↓ Pitta	Water + earth	Anabolic & increase in weight	Rice/dal/ jaggery/tuber milk/egg
Pulippu (Amla) (Sour)	↑ Pitta ↓ Vata	Earth +Fire	Stimulate agni & improves taste	Lime/tomato/ citrus/fruit
Uppu (Lavana) (Salty)	↑ Pitta ↓ Vata	Fire +Water	Imparts taste to food	Fish/Salt
Kasappu (Tikta) (bitter)	↑ Vata ↓ Kapha	Air +Space	Reduces weight	Fenugreek/ bitter gourd/ turmeric spice

| Kaarppu (Katu) (Pungent) | ↑ Pitta ↑ Vata ↓Kapha | Fire +Air | Stimulates hunger | Pepper/Red Chillies |
| Thuvarppu (Kashaya) (Astringent) | ↑ Vata ↓ Kapha | Earth + Air | Good for Skin | Honey |

After this assessment, we will now look at how each taste influences the human constitution and the Tridoshams. The six tastes balance the Tridoshams through our daily diet, but their ability to influence is put to deeper use medicinally as they have the strength to deeply and qualitatively penetrate the doshams.

ಶ್ರೀ ಇ

THE TRIDOSHAMS AND THE SIX TASTES

Let us start with the *Vatham* Dosham - the Air and Space duo and observe the impact of each taste. For reference, we can turn to the tabulated tastes for their elemental composition.

VATHAM

When a *Vatham*-dominant person experiences imbalance, the governing dosham *Vatham*, is said to have deranged from its inherent ratio. *Vatham* could be stagnant or aggravated. *Vatham* is light, airy, quick, irregular, etc. but in case of stagnation, the person experiences dullness. The stagnant *Vatham* needs stimulation to reach its original ratio which is done by introducing hot, light and airy tastes - the Air-dominant tastes. Symptoms of stagnant *Vatham* are cold hands and feet, low blood pressure, sinking pulse, fainting, stiffness of joints, etc.

For Stagnated	Air and Fire	Pungent
Vatha - Air and Space	Air and Space	Bitter
	Air and Earth	Astringent

Aggravated *Vatham* shows as hyperactivity, anxiety, hypertension, etc. and can be pacified by introducing the other three tastes. Symptoms of aggravated *Vatham* are body pain, agitation, restlessness, etc.

For Aggravated	Earth and Water	Sweet
Vatha - Air and Space	Earth and Fire	Sour
	Water and Fire	Salt

KAPHA

The elements in *Kapham* are Earth and Water, therefore tastes comprising of the Earth and Water elements will stimulate or increase *Kapham*. Tastes comprising of the Air element work conversely and decrease or pacify *Kapham* dosham. Symptoms of *Kapham* stagnation are lethargy, inflexibility of joints, phlegmatic diseases, respiratory disorders, poor digestion, etc.

For Stagnated	Earth and Water	Sweet
Kapha - Earth and Water	Earth and Fire	Sour
	Water and Fire	Salty

Symptoms of aggravated *Kapham* are obesity, rheumatism, cardiac disorders, disorders in blood circulation, etc.

For Aggravated Kapha - Earth and Water	Air and Fire	Pungent
	Air and Space	Bitter
	Air and Earth	Astringent

PITTAM

The elemental composition of *Pittam* is Fire and Water. In order to pacify an aggravated *Pittam* dosham, the following three tastes are put to medicinal use as they are converse to *Pitta* nature. Symptoms of aggravated *Pitta* dosham are giddiness, vomiting, headache, skin diseases, bilious disorders, etc.

For Aggravated Pittam - Fire and Water	Earth and Water	Sweet
	Air and Space	Bitter
	Air and Earth	Astringent

To stimulate or increase stagnated Pittam, the three fiery tastes are used. The symptoms are poor digestion, pigmentation problems, eye disorders, etc.

For Stagnated Pittam - Fire and Water	Water and Fire	Salt
	Earth and Fire	Sour
	Air and Fire	Pungent

When tastes are being introduced through medicinal preparations, the diet must alter accordingly. Inappropriate or causative tastes must be eliminated for a stipulated time until the doshams are brought back to equilibrium.

Another influential factor of Taste is its qualitative experience. Bitter, astringent or even sweet tastes are 'constrictive' to the body, whereas salty, sour and pungent are expansive or outward. At the start of the chapter, we discussed how man enjoys an integrated and grounded life if his identification aspect, (Ahamkara or Aanavam) is in balance and how it brings suffering, when not. Our feeling of balance co-relates with the sense of being satiated or content - evidently, we are speaking of the sweet taste, as by its nature it doesn't stimulate for more, but satisfies. But just as soon as 'sweetness' recedes from man's memory, a desire for it is born again. Man, anywhere on this planet, is always looking for this sweet satiating feeling to fill his life. Whenever man tries to grasp, acquire or possess this sweetness - it betrays him and changes into something else. Seen years of friendship turn sour, tainted by greed, envy, jealousy? What happened to the two day old rice and potato can happen to age-old friendships. They turn sour. Too much sweetness turns sour. And the sense of satiation slips away, making way for envy, attachment and so on.

Our second experiment with salt demonstrated another aspect of 'tasteful mentality'. By pouring water into either lemon juice or sugar syrup, we make it palatable, which means the salt taste inherent in water creates appetite for more. The Siddhas have revealed the salt taste to be indulgent in nature; by spending and depleting it makes way for more. This is how one lands right back into the desire for sweetness in life.

I would like to add something more here. In the world today, there is a predominant attitude of 'Instant'. Most people thrive on sharp, instant lifestyles and experiences. They strongly adhere to and depend on all that is fast, instantaneous and fast-acting; in food and in medicine - a highly result-oriented attitude. Unfortunately, all this only agitates and aggravates an individual leaving him volatile and hot! The way of the pungent in you! Ironically, man craves for sweetness. He has been consumed by the mechanical pattern of running after the memory of Sweet, grasps at it and then watches it turn Sour. His fundamentally indulgent side pushes him to try once again, some other 'instant' way. When he meets with a rude shock, such as a crisis, it leaves him with strong Bitterness. Life confronted him! Man finds himself staring in the face of Truth, which he finds Bitter. Bitter only because it demands a change and this he does not like. Man cannot palate this easily and according to the nature of Bitter, it doesn't leave so easily. This is, in fact, a guiding light, but before he sees it, he first has to face his inability. If he proceeds to digest the bitter truth, it converges and brings him back to himself. If not, it erupts as volcanic anger, a Pungent reaction to Bitter truth. If he recoils from the undigested Truth, he falls into an extremely Astringent place, such as anti-social behaviour; an isolated and withdrawn attitude or mentality. Notice how by making 'satisfaction' our yardstick of craving, we deviate from our integrated-ness and repeatedly externalise ourselves.

The fiery tastes - sour, salty, pungent and their qualities make you relate with the external world; they draw you outward. On the other hand, constricting tastes work to bring you back: astringent and bitter. If the diet of an individual is primarily astringent and bitter, he would remain withdrawn and isolated, unable to relate comfortably with the external world. This is imbalance, which brings us to the importance of a Centreline; balance between the Externalising tastes and the Converging ones - a place and quality that relates with one's inner world just as well as with the world around - with a complete sense of contentment and grounding. This is why the Siddhas call the heat governed tastes as '*Boga*' - enjoyment or indulgence. They continually rope you in for more and more.

The body is made of food, which is made of six different tastes, each bearing distinctive expression. Some tastes are expansive i.e. move outwards and some are constrictive, i.e. move inwards. Mind identifies with the body (and therefore food) and through this, to the world around. In this way, the intake of external food connects him to the world around. Food and Lifestyle are basic imperatives that govern man's quality of existence. What man eats and pursues as lifestyle is what his mind imbibes and also is his expression of livingness. This brings us to a vital question. Where does disease come from? The Siddhas say, 'Diseases don't fall from the sky, we create them.' An Integrated Life can be defined as a perfect blend of the six tastes of Nature; a harmonious coming together of expansion and convergence, empowering one to abide with one's inner self as well as with the world. But, diets confined to *'Boga'* lock the individual into a circle of persistent indulgence in search of contentment. Eventually, he disconnects from his individuality and feelings of disintegration gradually build toward an Integrity Crisis. This confinement deprives man of vital qualities required for a balanced mind-body. This over-emphasis of expansive qualities results in heavy outward-spending, depletion, agitation and always wanting to acquire and possess. The individual is consumed by a 'Utilitarian Mentality'. On the other hand, excessive convergence results in feelings of separation and isolation from the external dimension of existence. Exaggeration of either group of tastes imbalances *Ahamkara*, but life does go on, even in imbalance. But eventually, the body suffers derangement and demands attention. By now, constant attention to the external is a crystallised habit which ignores the suffering of the body and does not recognise signals for help. The body is forced to live with a growing derangement.

An Integrity Crisis - spoken of in the *Tattwa* chapter. There are four *Antha Karanas* or inner instruments. They are *Manas* (mind), *Buddhi* (intellect), *Chitta* (memory retainer) and *Ahamkara* (individuation or identification factor), all of which are vital for *Gyanendriyas* (knowing senses) and *Karmendriyas* (working-senses). Even though there are four names, fundamentally it is only one inner instrument, called our mind or psyche. It is similar to a person having different names depending on his role, situation or relationship - such as father, son, boss, husband, etc. The psyche also takes on different names, like while being analytical or doubtful it is the mind, when it is determined, synthesised or deliberate it is called intellect, when it recalls information it is *Chitta* (memory), etc. Identifying with each activity, it gets individuation. For example: I am going out to a restaurant. After I leave the house, somewhere on the way I suddenly wonder, 'Did I lock the door?' This is mind. When I feel assured I did lock it, it is intellect. When I think of my lover waiting for me at the restaurant, it is memory. All these are thoughts and bits of external information. When 'I' identifies with each available information or process as...

...I doubt I locked the door, I have identified with mind aspect.
...I am sure I locked the door, it is identification with intellect.
...I have to meet my love at the restaurant, is the identification with memory. Most importantly, *Ahamkara* or individuation is a subjective process, an internal aspect, while the other three have an external source.

Post modernism is about being fast in multiple dimensions, because of which our *Manas*, *Buddhi* and Memory, process a lot of data and undergo frequent, fast changes. What's wrong with fast? *Ahamkara*, which makes each of these processes a subjective experience for our identity, rapidly fluctuates and changes. What happens when *Ahamkara* is unable to digest vast amounts of information or tries to possess it in this mass-level conditioning? It hangs! This impairs the body. Common present day diseases are auto immune disorders; the right word being 'pseudo immune disorders'.

Over time when the human body lives with growing imbalances of *Pitta*, *Vatha* or *Kapha*, confined, unattended and ignored due to our insensitive attitude, they begin to collect. A derangement, of either *Pittam*, *Vatham* or *Kapham*, over time turns into *Kapham* - it gains 'form' and 'shape'. The Siddhas call this '*Megham*', which literally mean 'Clouds that travel'. *Megham* erupts in any part of the body and/or just as clouds travel in open skies and burst, they can rain several chronic diseases. A chronic disease is too debilitating to be ignored. Who is responsible for this? The Siddhas say such diseases are 'hard to heal'. Man at first depleted, then deprived the body of wholesome qualities by adhering to *Boga* tastes and left his body with almost no immunity to protect it. Such diseases are common today - Diabetes, Cancer, AIDS, etc. Siddhas declare these as, 'Integrity Crisis' - the clouds that cause rain. Turning a deaf ear to the calls of our body, we adopted habits and made choices under the pretext of building a 'better life', but what did we actually do? We denied ourselves wholesome qualities Nature herself provides. We set out to conquer the fast-paced world but what did we actually destroy? We trampled on our platform of existence - our Integrated Individuality - not knowing that the platform of an integrated individuality stands on a harmonious integration of all the six tastes and not only on the half circle of *Boga*.

The six tastes play the vital role of upholding our Individuality and decide how we integrate with the world within and the world without - a bridge. 'Body is made of food and mind identifies with body and through it to the world'.

ಶಿ ಲ

TAPPING THE ANCIENT SOLUTION

Disease is a lapse in integrated function. In reference to the seven tissues that make up our human body, let us see how that stands.

WHOLISTIC FUNCTIONING

The instance below exemplifies integrated function using a compensating process. It describes how an imbalanced part of the human body tries to balance itself by taking from another - a compensating process.

Leucorrhoea first erupts in the generative fluid - the seventh tissue of a woman's body. The symptoms are burning/itching of the generative organ, accompanied by a white fluid discharge. Under Allopathy, the common diagnosis is of an infection for which a strong dose of antibiotics is prescribed. Recurring Leucorrhoea is a chronic condition and affects the body on multiple levels. Associated symptoms are low back pain, cracking sound from joints, giddiness and exhaustion. In the Siddha system, chronic Leucorrhoea first affects bone marrow tissue and then the bones. As the disease depletes the generative tissue through chronic discharge, it spreads to the bone marrow, establishes new roots and spreads, melting it to continue the vaginal discharge. From the bone marrow, it spreads to take from bones. In the sequential seven *Thathus*, bone marrow precedes the generative fluid tissue and bone tissue precedes bone marrow. An allopathic doctor treats each symptom separately. Ancient medicinal texts elucidating the interconnectedness say that unless Leucorrhoea is cured, rejuvenation of bone marrow will not take place and symptoms continue.

༚ ༙

SIDDHAS REMEDY FOR AIDS

The ancient Siddha system speaks of indications and symptoms of the onset of a host of diseases which closely relate to present day AIDS. The works of Siddha Ramadevar (also known as Yakop), Agasthiyar, Thirumoolar and many others describe in detail the subjective cause, the symptoms, the associated diseases and amazingly enough the remedies and cures. Today, the world fears these diseases for their tough resistance to treatment and cure, their multiplicity (syndrome), complexity, their infectious nature and their ability to spread through unsafe sex, etc eventually leading to death. AIDS is defined as an 'Acquired Immune Deficiency Syndrome'. The breakdown of the immune system paves the way for all kinds of opportunistic diseases and finally death. Modern practitioners are still at loss when faced with this incurable, deadly and greatly feared disease.

What is Immunity?

The Siddhas' understanding of immunity is holistic. Immunity is the binding inter-connected nature and balanced function of the seven basic constituents, (called *Sapta Thathus*). Their combined function establishes a nature of immunity within us. There is a popular maxim in the circle of Siddha healers that says, *'Thathu kettal palamum kedum'*. It means, 'if the basic seven tissues are impaired, immunity is impaired'. The physical aspect of immunity is called *'Deha Vanmai'* and the subtle aspect as *'Amritha Nilai'*.

Clouds That Gather To Cause Rain……

A group of disease triggered by the fragmentation of immunity are classified as *'Megha Noi'*; the 'Clouds that gather to cause rain' (*Megham*). 21 such deadly diseases have been named under this classification. Diabetes is one of them.

DIABETES

Diabetes sprouts from excessive, habitual indulgences and frequent stimulus of pleasure, stress or misery that demand recurring indulgence. A prolonged obsessive indulgence leads the body to multiple imbalances which affect the quality of the binding fluid in the fundamental seven constituents of the human body (*Sapt Thathus*).

This is what is hard to cure. The Siddha system calls this disease as *'Neer Ellivu'*, literal meaning - dissipation of the fluid system. Although, diabetes is mostly seen as a metabolic disorder, the Siddhas' way concentrates on healing the impaired function of the liver and associated *Pittam* dosham. My own experience found that saliva and its segregation also play a significant role in diabetics. The diet of a diabetic holds great potential. Restrictions of sweet, rice, dairy products and refined flour foods, etc. I found two reasons behind this. Soft foods don't require much chewing because of which they pass into the stomach quickly without being mixed well with saliva first. It means the sugar level in these foods requires a longer time to assimilate into the body, causing imbalance in hormone levels. This is known as *Thathu* imbalance - already known for its low curability. The second reason is that after a diabetic consumes something sweet, he experiences drying up of saliva. Whatever food he subsequently eats would not be met with enough saliva to mix with, before entering into the digestive system. The valuable role of saliva is highlighted here because when food is chewed well and mixed with saliva it gets partly digested, making it easier to become one with the body. Saliva is the first sensor. It informs the brain about the kind of food that has entered to enable it to segregate appropriate enzymes and hormones to help digestion. It is of vital importance for a diabetic to chew his food thoroughly to avoid the system from carrying and holding onto excess sugar levels. In the Siddha and Ayurveda medicinal systems, *'Nellikkai'* (Amla fruit) and *Vilvam* (Bilva) are leading medicines for diabetes as they enhance the production and secretion of saliva. Modern day lifestyle, rush hours and fast-paced daily routines include quick meals and fast foods, all gulped down in haste. These are open invitations for imbalance, and it is no surprise that the number of diabetics are increasing by the day. In the old days it was a matter of pride to have diabetes! It afflicted only the rich. A sugar assimilation problem impressed others, indicating one was either rich or at least didn't belong to the labour class. A matter of false pride. Although strange, there is some truth behind it. It pushes us to ponder the role of lifestyle. The rich could frequently indulge in pleasure activities like food, sex, alcohol, etc. A peasant would either drink rice water, eat left over rice and go work in the fields. His breakfast was rice water or old rice, which is now categorised as a sugar-increasing food. This is true for modern day human situations. But a labourer or poor man works hard and spends his energy constructively while the rich just indulge. Today, rich or poor, most prefer a hippy sort of way. It is said that the effect of a prolonged deprivation of nutritious food has registered deep into Indian genes. An early exposure to the opposite sex, engaging in multiple relationships and spending idle time (watching television, etc) are leading reasons for the higher percentage of diabetics in India.Taking advantage, India applied Western technology in a relatively short period and also latched onto western lifestyle, and invited trouble. The genetic coding or mental attitude of Indians was/is not ready to digest the invasion of multiple new outlooks and lifestyles and this reflects as disease in physical as well as social structures. In the olden days, the exogenous factors for disease were only natural calamities, but we have added to that by eating pesticides in food, junk food, polluted environment and occupational disease; the result being, life-style diseases.

ಬಿ ಧ

Another of the 21 deadly diseases revealed by our Ancients is AIDS. The sacred texts refer to a particular Acquired Immune Deficiency Syndrome by the name of *'Vettai Megham'*. It is described as the deadliest of all. The poetic composition found in the work *'Theran Venba'* of the Siddha Theraiyar gives a beautiful comparison to opportunistic infections.

CHAPTER FIVE: MEDICINE OF THE SAGES

The poem says:
> When one is affected by *'Vettai Megham'*
> Diseases attack the body devoid of immunity
> Like 'Clouds that gather to cause rain' (*Megham*),
> Likewise, various infections take ground in the infected individual to spread as numerous diseases.

Most minds question the subjective factor and its role. For instance, we all get bitten by mosquitoes but only some get malaria! The subjective aspect plays a pivotal role. One of the major ways of transmission of AIDS is through improper sexual acts, but why? During sexual relations, partners open up to each other, which psychologically reflects as vulnerability of our inner environment. In these states, it is most agitated and exposed. The word 'improper sexual acts' is to be emphasised, because it implies perversion and/or loss of inherent balance. Indulging in 'improperness' is open ground for perversion to mingle with the agitated vulnerability which triggers severe hormone imbalance, nervous agitation and most importantly, the generation of a lot of heat within the body. This heat consumes and dries up the existent *Ojas*. Once *Ojas* depletes, the body instantly tries to replenish it by opening up energetically. (*Ojas* is the resultant unifying factor from the function of the seven basic constituents that express themselves as *'Rasa'* within the human psyche). A depletion of *Ojas* during uncontrolled agitation and improper sexual act stimulates craving, urging one to invite and unify with the contaminated *prana* (deranged *Vatham*), toxic heat (deranged *Pittam*), bad fluids (deranged *Kapham*) segregated by the generative organ of the afflicted partner.

What is the cause of AIDS?

Contaminated and stagnant *prana* (deranged *Vatham*), toxic heat (deranged *Pittam*), bad fluids (deranged *Kapham*) within the body begin to fragment the balancing nature of immunity which eventually leads to a complete breakdown. This invites deadly diseases to flourish as there is nothing to fight back. The earlier verse speaks of the cluster of three saturated black clouds of Bad *Prana*, Bad *Kapham* and Bad *Pittam* coming together to bring a rain on the 'depleted immunity' (the word 'Bad' implies severe imbalance).

Siddha Ramadevar depicts *Vettai Megham* in his poetic verse as follows:

"Patta Maram Pollakuum Vettai Megham"
('*Patta Maram*' refers to a withered, rotting tree.)

This poetic reference states the body affected by the disease '*Vettai Megham*' will slowly lose its '*Amritha Nillai* State' (Immunity) and become like a withering, rotting tree. The co-relation between present day AIDS and *Vettai Megham* and its associated symptoms mentioned in Siddha Agasthiyar's 'Vaidhiya Kaviyam' (the great work of medicine) can be established after reading the verses.

"Matharall Vantha Vettai Van Megham
Chenni Vali Odhu Suram Vizhi Noi
Odungkaan Baethiodu Makkattam
Seethamaru Maa Mooli Yam Vellai
Chem Parathai Mega Vettai
Theera-Diramiyamodu Vampirathai
Vellai Vazhuvazhu
Thutta Vidam Paandu Veppu
Aripakki Kon Kudal Noi
Ketta Kandamaalai
Mega Vettai Weer Churukku
Veera Thridotam Punvenga
Surathagam Veppam Vitozhiyam…"

CHAPTER FIVE: MEDICINE OF THE SAGES

"...Daasi Veedu Chendratharut Halaikku
Chemmaiyai Tharugaue Cherupadi Than
Athawal Kaasamilagum, Kabum Athuvidum..."

Ancient Text Siddha Terminology	Modern Day Terms
Chenni Vali	Pain in Spinal area. This may be compared to Tubercular spine disease
Odhu Suram	Recurrent Fever
Vizhi Noi	Eye disease (maybe EBV viral infection which is common in AIDS)
Bedhi	Recurrent diarrhoea
Seetham	Dysentery
Thira abirumiyam	Leucorrhoea discharge
Vellai	Gonorrhoea
Paandu	Severe anaemia
Soolai Vetham	Neuritis
Kuttam	Dermatological Infections
Aripakki	Herpetic lesions
Konkudal Noi	Gastric intestinal disorders
Keta Kandamaalai	Nodular Growths in cervical lymph nodes
Kiranthi	Syphilitic adenitis
Megha Suram	Leucorrhoeal or Syphilitic fever
Neer Churukku	Urinary Micturition

The afflicted seven *Thathus* sprout disease from every *Thathu*:

- Fevers are caused due to the first *Rasa Thathu*.
- Skin rashes, anaemia, herpes and itching are born from *Raktha Thathu*.
- The third *Thathu*, *Mamsa* suffers weight loss, deterioration in muscles, etc.
- The fourth *Thathu*, *Medha* suffers heat, excessive sweating, dryness of mouth, and stomatitis.
- *Asthi*, the fifth, brings intense body ache, joint pain, hair loss, and brittle nails.
- The sixth *Thathu*, *Majjai*, suffers neurological complications, disorientation and improper co-ordination between the brain's signals and the body's response to it.
- The last *Thathu*, *Shukra*, causes insomnia and memory loss which finally leads to a state of semi-consciousness and then unconsciousness.
- The depletion and deterioration of all the seven *Thathus* leads to death.

According to ancient texts, victims of '*Vettai Megham*' through '*Daasis*' (commercial sex workers of old days), first suffer a continuous cough, combined with spitting of phlegm via short coughs called '*Kasam*' (Pulmonary tuberculosis). Today, the early symptoms of HIV are pulmonary tuberculosis typically seen in tropical weather, as claimed by modern practitioners.

ॐ

THE ANCIENT APPROACH

Apart from learning of these fatal diseases from Siddha's ancient texts, native Siddha healers, who studied under the traditional *Guru Kula* system, have implemented therapies and remedies with remarkable success. There is a distinct difference between today's modern approach and in the cures and remedies revealed by the ancient Siddhas - in its theory as well as treatment. All formulations of the Siddhas are designed in a specialised manner. They not only treat specific disorders sprouting under this condition but aim to rejuvenate the *Thathus* (Constituents) entirely. This approach is based on the Three Doshams Concept. (*Mukuttram*-in Tamil). Modern day theory treats infections caused by the AIDS virus with an anti-viral treatment - a symptomatic approach. But the Siddha's theory doesn't limit its attention to the disease. It dives to the root to eradicate the fundamental causative factors.

What does 'medicine' mean to a Siddha?

The interesting theory of 'REFUSING THE DISEASE' as revealed by Siddha Thirumoolar stands unique to the Siddha Medicinal System.

> "Maruppthu Udal Noi Marundhuenalakum
> Maruppthu Ula Noi Marundu Enalakum
> Maruppthu Ini Noi Varathiruppa
> Maruppthu Savai Marundu Enalakum"

> "Refusing The Disease Of The Body
> Refusing The Disease Of Mind (Psyche)
> Refusing Further As A Prevention
> Refusing Death Itself Ensures Real Medicine"

Sacred teachings state...

> ..."Medicine is that which ensures and regenerates balance in physical and psychological dimensions, leading to prevention as well as construction and last but not the least the conquest of death par excellence."

This divine tradition continues to offer remedy and cure for extreme diseases, upholding the eternity of its theory. A wise and competent native Siddha healer approaches AIDS according to its nature of affliction. Deterioration of health can be prevented and gradual eradication of the syndrome from the individual's constitution can happen if it's a recent affliction. In case of a 'full-blown' affliction of AIDS, the Siddha system aims at reducing the suffering of the individual and offering longevity.

Some native Siddha healers cure *'Megha Noi'* diseases using only herbal medicine, others use compounded formulations after considering their synergistic action. Some basic medicinal approaches prescribed for AIDS may be divided as follows:

Purely herbal preparations,
Herbo-mineral preparations,
Herbo-mercuric preparations,
Herbo-mercurial-mineral preparations and
Higher Kaya Kalpa rejuvenative treatment etc.

The formulation *'Kala Bairava Ennai'* (main ingredient being purified mercury), revealed by Siddha Sage Agasthiyar, works well for skin-related diseases.

The formulation *'Sengottai Rasayanam'* (main ingredient being purified Semiecarpus Anacardium), revealed by Siddha Bogar, works great as an antibiotic and can be incorporated for cancer treatments also.

The formulation *'Markandeya Melugu'* (both metallic and rare herbs formulations), received from my Siddha Master, cures all kinds of tuberculosis, including Insipidus tuberculosis.

There are several other successful formulations used by native Siddha Healers in Tamil Nadu. Academic Siddha Physician's clinical research successfully proves the cures Siddha medicine has been offering for several chronic diseases. The Tamil Nadu Government has recently established a Research Centre for the Siddha Medicinal System and supports it in a constructive way.

The success behind Siddha's remedial medicines is the ability to enhance bio-availability of the cells. The pharmacodynamics (the working nature of Siddha medicine after intake) of this system is unique. There is no single medicine for AIDS. It varies as per the person's constitution (*Prakruthi*), the nature of disease (the *Prakruthi* of the disease) and associated symptoms. But the healing potential does not depend upon medicine alone and includes the competency and dedication of the healer as well.

KAYA KALPA

Human existence paves its way through a maze of intermingling influences, all of which are variables of nature's ever-changing momentum. The five natural elements, as rising incarnations get bifurcated into the Exogenous and Endogenous. We discussed the endogenous ones - the three *doshams*, the seven *Thathus* and the *Malas*. The exogenous ones are the *doshams* around us, such as rhythmically changing seasons and daily rhythms. Man lives amidst macro and microcosmic patterning. The human body functions by the inter-connectedness and inter-dependence between exogenous and endogenous factors. From the moment a human body enters existence, it is governed by the three *doshams*, and is nourished by the seven *Thathus* continually. Tissues are replenished, formed and nourished by the intake of food. From the proper balanced function between *doshams* and *Thathus* emerges a Quintessence - the Siddhas call it *Amritha*. This water element is the collective quintessence and the immunity factor of the body. But all these factors are ever under the influence of larger cosmic factors. Assuming the variables of nature to be harmonious, the Siddhas point to yet another vital variable within the human organism - the Fire Element, represented by the conversion catalysts of the seven tissues - the *Sapta Thathu agnis*. They say: unless these *agnis* perform their best the circle is not complete. The fiery intensity of the seven *agnis* equally determine the strength of immunity - *Amritha*. The Water element, cooked by Fire, releases as Vapour which is called *Vaasi* - the life-giving *Prana* or force. Human existence is based on this process of core combustion. Something further is revealed at this stage. The three *doshams* are descendants of the three primordial essences' of Existence - Air, Fire and Water. This means the primordial essences exist within us prior to the birth of the three *doshams*, which supports the proclamation of the human body to be a microcosm. We now know that the quintessence of *doshams* and *Thathus* cannot sustain human life alone and that human existence essentially depends on the three primordial cosmic essences. The balanced function of *doshams* and *Thathus* actually replenish these primordial reservoirs of life. Lifestyle is activity and we drink from these reservoirs to accomplish it. Demanding lifestyles and post-modern food habits cause us to drink more of the reservoirs but replenish less; proved by fast-reducing lifespans. Sickness and chronic disease further deplete these life-giving reservoirs. Siddhas scripted a therapeutic dimension called Kaya Kalpa Therapy. Kaya Kalpa is rejuvenation of the Primal fire within the body and revitalisation of all the seven tissues, which encourages a greater lifespan and efficient living. The Siddhas recommend Kaya Kalpa for chronic or near-fatal illness, for the effective rejuvenation of the subtlest essentials responsible for human existence. Ill health is the imbalance of this core, as the three primordial essences - Air, Fire and Earth are vulnerable to external factors such as food, seasonal changes, daily changes, lifestyle demands, etc. These external factors acting as doorways between our inner and outer world, so are supportive as well as causal factors for disorders. As long as we depend on these doorways to exist, the possibility of disease remains. Higher Yogic practices point to a path that transcends these to accomplish Siddhahood - the way of Immortal Masters. Kaya Kalpa Yoga stands unique to Siddha Tradition.

The path of Kaya Kalpa Yoga involves rigorous practice and stretches over a long period of time as the foremost principle is de-conditioning. The primordial doorways are gradually eliminated one by one. By incorporating basic changes at first, one's entire diet and way of life is altered and eventually eliminated until the doorways are rendered invalid. The body is urged to function as its true nature - a microcosm — self-sufficient in itself. All energy-spending activities are gradually brought to a minimal until almost no energy is spent. The unspent energy is redirected within and used to nourish the inner world. The reservoirs are continually replenished in this manner with minimal depletion which multiplies core functionality. Ordinarily, human existence is sustained based on evolutionary principles, but in Kaya Kalpa Yoga, the journey involutes and a series of transformations are encouraged where the temporal meets its end in existence, which brings an Internal Rebirth.

ॐ ॐ

INTERNAL REBIRTH

This rebirth is on an inner platform. Air and Fire give birth to *Vasi*, the primordial life *Prana*, which when conserved results in an internal conception. The foetus is nourished into an embryo and so on until it nourishes itself to a complete rebirth. This new life functions on the core platform of core functionality. The conserved life force gradually transmutes the primal elements of Air, Fire and Water to their primordial essence; a state prior to evolution. Space, and its quality of non-resistance, involutes to its primordial essence of 'no change'. Air, and its quality of mobility, reverts back to the essence of 'expanded-ness'. Fire, and its quality of combustion, falls back into its essence as 'Light'. Water, known for fluidity, reverts to its essence of life-giver. Earth and its solidity, revert to 'unhindered' form. Each of the elements now exist as their primordial essences - exhibiting qualities of full potential, devoid of the trait of depletion. New life stands upon this platform; a life beyond conditions, change and limitations - life of the Immortal One.

KAYA KALPA - THE HEALING DIMENSION

Disease is an ever-present menace since ancient times. Diabetes, HIV, heart and vascular disease have always been a threat. Our Ancients fought the scourge of disease with what modern historians term 'a competent medical faculty'. Drugs, anaesthetics, complicated surgical procedures, even the vaunted antibiotics, were used to war against ill health. Rather than the static way of organ-wise application, they used it based on functionality, a holistic approach. The Siddha system of medicinal treatment is designed to return the propelling forces of disease to balance. Their approach focuses on human life rather than the symptoms as each individual has his own specific balance of these three forces, which is their *Prakruthi*. The Siddha system of medicine carries an extensive herbal and mineral industry including what is probably the greatest variety of herbal and pharmaceutical preparations in the world. These include herbal decoctions (kudineer), medicated powders (choornam), herbal pastes (lehyams), essences (satthu), pills (kuliga), medicated herbal oils (ennai), aromatic oils (thailams), jellies (kulambu), waxes (melugu), tablets (mathirai), incinerated bhasmas, chendhurams, balsam (kalimbu), powders for external application (patru), higher metallic preparations (kilangu, kalpam, karuppu), distilled medicated drops (dheenner), etc. Siddha treatment includes multiple therapeutic methodologies: medicated emesis, medicated purgation, medicated enema, nasal medication and collyrium for eyes, oil massage, mud therapy, moxibusion, etc. are the procedures of purification and removal of accumulated toxins from the body. Siddha Agasthiyar describes complicated Kalpa procedures in his work, 'Antharanga Theeksa Vidhi', dedicated to native Siddha Kaya Kalpa techniques which are divided in to two principle types.

ಙಃ ಆ

Reduction and Rejuvenation

Reduction
The method of reduction is further divided into Palliation and Purification.

Palliation:
Palliation is the gradual reduction of aggravated *doshams* at their respective sites as a means to cure disease or contain its symptoms. Disease-causing *doshams* when eliminated by the purification therapy do not recur but chances of recurrence still stand when treated under palliation therapy. But as palliative treatment relieves symptoms for the time being, it is the most widely used type of treatment.

Palliation consists of seven types of treatment:

> Withholding hunger or thirst or fasting;
> Various types of exercise;
> Exposure to sun or sun bathing;
> Exposure to fresh air or wind;
> Taking herbs which increase digestive power and taking herbs which destroy accumulated toxins.

These supportive therapies are used prior to or after purification. Applied prior to Kaya Kalpa procedures, they prepare both, the bodily tissues and the mind for the exhaustive elimination therapies to come. All palliative treatments can be used independently but purification cannot be done without prior palliative treatment.

Purification:
Radical Purification removes the aggravated *doshams* from the body. It is mentioned earlier in the chapter 'Hallmark of Siddha Medicine' how one medicine can be used for different diseases by only changing the carrier (the *Anupanam*). Another unique feature of Siddha medicine is Purgative medicine. Not merely meant for stomach cleansing, it acts as a curative medicine for each disease by its purgative and purification action. These are the three traditional Siddha preparations that are used by both, native Siddha healers as well as academic Siddha physicians in Tamil Nadu.

Vedanta Melugu:
Like its name, *Vedanta Melugu*, has the unique spiritual aspect of *'neti, neti'* (not this, not this). This cleansing medicine triggers de-identification of the disease identified with the body.

Major Ingredients:
Sublimated mercury, yellow orpiment, red arsenic, borax, rock salt, terminalia chebula, black cumin seeds, long pepper, asafoetida, purified croton seeds, etc. (all purified).

Used for...
- All kinds of poisons - betel leaf juice
- Nocturnal emission due to excess body heat (*pitta*) - infusion of Terminalia chebula

- Persistent cough powder of Terminalia chebula
- Bleeding piles, haemorrhoids - cow's ghee
- *Vatha* disorders - coconut milk (juice of coconut pulp)
- Gastritis - Oil
- Body pain and rheumatism - Vitex negundo juice
- Fever - ginger juice
- Urinary calculi, kidney problems - tender coconut water
- Anaemia – cow's milk

Agasthiyar Kulambu:

This preparation is named after Sage Agasthiyar as it may have been revealed by Him.

Major ingredients:
Rock salt, asafoetida, mustard seeds, borax, long pepper, aconite root, red arsenic, mercury, yellow orpiment, inner parts of jatropha curcas, croton seeds, etc. (all purified).

Used for...
- Septic ulcers and skin diseases - juice of caltrophis gijandica
- Urinary calculi, venereal ulcers and syphilitic abscess - clerodendran inerme juice
- Bleeding piles - cow's ghee
- Fever - Dry ginger

Kausikar Kulambu:

This single preparation, revealed by Sage Viswamitra, cures over 430 diseases just by combining and changing different carriers (56 in number), which has been accepted by the Indian Medicinal Council of Research.

Major ingredients:
Terminalia chebula, mustard seeds, rock salt, asafoetida, borax, mercury, red arsenic, cumin seeds, orpiment, picorrhiza kurroa, aconite root, croton seeds, daemia extensa juice, coconut milk, palmyra jaggery etc... (all purified).

Used for...
Fevers - with warm water
Easinophelia, cough - Terminalia chebula infusion, juice of calotropis gigentia
Shivering fever - decoction of dry ginger
Throat cancer - Solanum tribolatum juice
Vomiting and stomach ulcer - Cassia tora juice
Asthma - Aibizzia amara juice
Stomach pain - castor ghee
Gastritis - Centella asiatica juice
Ulcerative colitis - Oxalis corniculata juice
Intestine cancer - castor oil with breast milk
Phlegmatic diseases - Adatoda vasika, Alipinia chinensis butter
Abscess - butter milk
Madness due to excess *pitta* - juice of palam pasi with buttermilk
Orchitis - goat's milk
Leprosy - cow's milk, ghee and sugar
Haemorrhoid - breast milk with butter
Dysentery - cow's ghee
Jaundice and oedema - castor oil
Ascites and dropsy - urine of goat
Anaemia - Thriphala (terminalia chebula, phyllanthus emblica, terminalia bellerica)
Spasms and all kinds of *vatha* disorders including paralysis -Clerodendrum phlomides juice
Skin diseases and poisonous bites - Caltrophis gijandica juice

During *dosham* purification, the *Thathus*, being interconnected, get affected by the eliminating procedures. For instance, an intensive elimination of *Kapham* by herb-induced emesis affects the nutrient tissue fluid pool containing water and electrolytes, plasma, muscle and fat. A strong purging of *Pittam* indirectly affects the total colouring material in the body or blood. *Basti* or medicated enema is somewhat different as it is meant to nullify excess *Vatham*. *Basti* contains warm oleating substances. By extended contact with the membrane of the large intestine it separates, eliminates layers of faecal matter, enhancing absorption which is responsible for nourishment of all tissues. Nasal medication cleanses the sinus and opens cranial nerves, enhances bio-circulation and improves the function of sense organs. In normal course by day, night and during digestion, the *doshams* appear in the hollow organs of the trunk (*Asayams*), from the circulatory channels (*mandalas*). This occurs in different stages of digestion. *Kapham* appears in the chest and upper abdomen, *Pittam* in the mid and *Vatham* in the lower abdomen. A centripetal movement of the *doshams*, toward the gastrointestinal tract is natural course. The aim of the body is to eliminate unwanted substances through gastrointestinal secretions. The appearance of the biological humors in parts of the gastrointestinal tract is enhanced by Kaya Kalpa and excess bio-humors get eliminated. During pathological conditions, the normal rhythm of the bio-regulating forces is disturbed and the vitiated *doshams* move and settle in solid tissues in circulatory channels or head and neck regions commencing pathogenesis and forms of disease. Excessive exercise, extreme climate, excessively spicy food and erratic behaviour also aggravate accumulation. Physical rest, avoiding hyper-stimuli and calming the mind aid the *doshams* back toward the gastrointestinal tract. Massage and sudation therapies also help. By eliminating the vitiated *doshams*, recurrence of the disease is prevented. Siddhas Kaya Kalpa recommends dark room therapy and underground living in cases of fatal disease and yogic alchemical procedures to avoid external stimuli and continuous sensory inputs. After aggravated *doshams* are removed, purification of the body increases the capacity of the *agnis*. The sense organs work with vigour, and after a certain time strength increases, old age ailments are prevented and diseases cured.

ಸಿ ಲ

FOOD AS MEDICINE

> "Andam Surungil Atharkorazhivillai"
> Bindam Surungil Pranan Nilaiperum
> Undi Surungil Upayam Palaual
> Kandang Karuthu Kapaliymame"
>
> "If the universe were to reduce itself, it is immaterial
> But if the body, is reduced, (made lighter) life would become (is) permanent
> If food, is eaten sparingly, much goodness/auspiciousness would flow
> Then you verily become the Lord with the 'dark-hued throat"
>   Thirumoolar's Thirumanthiram, Verse 735

In the verse above, *Undi* means food; the essence of the verse is that the less one eats, the healthier one remains. A moderate diet carries strong benefits and prolongs life by reducing excessive toxin accumulation. A proverb of Tamil Nadu says: "Langanam parama ausatham". It means "Fasting is divine (or supreme) medicine." (*Langanam* - 'fasting'; *parama* – 'supreme' or 'divine'; ausatham – 'medicine').

CHAPTER FIVE: MEDICINE OF THE SAGES

In the work Thirukkural, a Tamil-classic written more than 3000 years ago, Siddha Sage Thiruvalluvar devotes ten stanzas to diet restrictions that promote physical stamina and mental equilibrium (vide MARUNDU Chapter 95, stanzas 941-950). A few have been translated below if the reader may choose to contemplate and imbibe these nourishing principles into their lives.

The learned physician says:

- Excessive or deficient food upsets the three humors in the body and causes disease.
- There shall be no need for medicine if one eats only when he feels hunger.
- When one feels very hungry, let there be moderate eating; it leads to a longer life.
- After what is eaten earlier has been fully digested, when one once again feels hunger, one should eat only wholesome food that does not upset the evenness of the three humors.
- No disease attacks the person who eats in moderation according to the laws of health; eat therefore, such kinds of food as suited to the three humors of one's body.
- Perpetual enjoyment of health exists in one who is moderate in eating; perpetual trouble of illness dwells in one who eats like a beast.
- There is no limit to sickness in a man, who immoderately eats incompatible food paying no attention to time and calorific value factors, etc.

For good health of mind and body, one can follow the core-principles of diet formulated by Siddha Thiruvalluvar in the world famous Thirukkural, chapter 'Marundu' (medicine). He says, 'Man does not survive on what he eats, but rather on what he digests.' The body is nourished by nutrient fluid and the quality of this nutrient fluid depends upon the quality of one's diet principles. Below is a list of food combinations that according to the Siddha System should not to be eaten together. They are classified into food, herbs and metals as *'Chathru'* (unfriendly), *'Mithru'* (friendly). If an unfriendly food combination is taken, it triggers abdominal pain, gastritis, skin disorders, constipation, diarrhoea, urinary retention, lethargy, sleep disorders, depression and anxiety, as different classes of food require different digestive enzymes.

Food Item	Chathru – Incompatible or Unfriendly
Honey	Ghee (Equal proportion should not be taken)
Mangoes	With yoghurt, cheese and cucumbers
Tomatoes	Milk, Melons
Lemons	With yoghurt, milk, tomatoes
Radish	Milk, Bananas
Milk	Fish, Curd, Meat and Sour fruits
Chillies	Yoghurt
Yoghurt	Milk, Melon, Meat & Fish, Hot drinks, Sour fruits, Mangoes.
Corn	Bananas, Dates
Potatoes	Yoghurt, Cucumbers
Egg plant	Yoghurt
Honey	With hot drinks

Also,

- One should not bathe or indulge in sex two hours after eating.
- Cold drinks should not be taken immediately after hot drinks.
- Tender coconut water should not be taken on an empty stomach at morning time.
- Drumstick leaves should not be taken at night.

CHAPTER FIVE: MEDICINE OF THE SAGES

Fasting may not be beneficial to all. Fasting to reduce weight can anger *Vatham* and *Pittam* without affecting *Kapham* and sleeping on a full stomach tends to increase *Kapham*. Eating attuned to one's *Prakruthi* is the key element here. In order for a meal to be *Prakruthi*-friendly, a few guidelines or components are:

> An individual of *Vatham prakruthi* should avoid dry and light foods and eat more lubricating substances like oil, sweet, sour and salty items.
>
> A person of *Pittam prakruthi* should prefer cold items which have sweet, bitter and astringent taste.
>
> A person of *Kapham prakruthi* should avoid sweet taste and prefer hot, spicy foods. *Prakruthi* should resonate with food tastes and daily and seasonal rhythms.
>
> The quantity of food as well as the individual quantity of dietary components is important. The latter is dependent on the *prakruthi* of a person.
>
> A *Pittam prakruthi* could eat more *Kapham*-increasing items such as rice and wheat. While a person of *Kapham prakruthi* needs more vegetables, oil quietens *Vatham* and ghee counters the anti-kinetic nature, cumin or mustard seeds contribute to the bitter taste to increase *Vatham*.
>
> The state of *Agnis* is also an important part of our diet. The proper time for breakfast, lunch and dinner are based on the maximal functioning of the *Agnis*.
>
> The seasons are to be considered too.

A typical Tamil meal is systemised in a particular order to quieten down and balance the three *doshams*. At the start of a meal when one is very hungry, *Vatham* is upset and causes hunger pangs. Eating rice and dal with ghee increases *Kapham* and soothes *Vatham*. The next course of ghee, rice, vegetables and curry increases *Pittam* and helps digestion. The final course is usually buttermilk, which reduces *Pittam*. It could also increase *Vatham*, to counter which, betel leaf and supari, which are astringent in taste, are taken after the meal to enhance digestion.

Siddha Theraiyar quotes some principles as life regimen in his work "Noy-Anuka Vithi".

The verses are as:

"Take food only twice
Sleep only at night
Have sexual intercourse only once in a month
Drink water only between meals
Don't eat bulbous root vegetables except Karunai kilangu.
Don't eat any unripe fruit except tender plantain.
Take a short walk after a delicious meal.
What then, has death to do with us?"

"Once in six months, take an emetic.
Once in four months, clean your stomach by a purgative.
Once in a month and a half, have nasal cleansing.
Twice in a fortnight, have the head shaved.
Once every fourth day, anoint our selves with oil bath
Once every third day, apply collyrium to the eyes
Never smell perfumes or flowers around midnight time.
What then, has death to do with us?"

ಶ ಡ

CHAPTER SIX

VARMA - VITAL SPOTS

> "When the stem of a flower gets slightly deviated,
> The florescence doesn't diminish.
> When the sugarcane stalk is deviated,
> The sweetness flows.
> When an iron rod is bent,
> It controls even an elephant,
> But, when a nerve gets bent, what can be done?"

This is an old Tamil saying, which the Siddha Healers challenged!

'The human body is an organised living manifestation that is constantly being broken down and built up, without its identity being denied in any way.'

Ancient Tamil Saints made no precise distinction between arteries, veins, lymph nodes, nerves, tendons, meridians or for that matter even between mind and matter. They concerned themselves with the 'system of forces' that enable the human body to move, breathe, digest and think.

Varmam is an ancient Siddha Science that identifies a vast number of locations on the human body, vital for holistic function. *Varmam's* (points or locations) can either heal or harm the human body and act as connects or junctions between the physical and pranic body (subtle body). They are psychophysical in nature and not gross like bodily organs. Ancient palm-scripts describe the importance of each *Varmam*, it's inter-connection with others and how these can be therapeutically used to cure, heal injuries or ailments afflicting the body. In this chapter, we will read about the *Varma* therapists and the system they practice. I will also introduce a valued dimension of *Varmam* Science - Martial Arts. The knowledge of *Varmam* is the foundation of all ancient combat. Skills used in *Kalari* system of martial art flourish in Tamil Nadu and Kerala to date. *Varmam* Science is taught strictly under the *Guru Sishya* (Master and disciple) mode. Teachers are called '*Varma Asan*' and a *Varma* combat soldier is called '*Varmanian*'. Therapeutic *Varmam* Masters impart their knowledge only after elaborate scrutiny and careful selection of a disciple, implying this art is meant for only a chosen few. Once selected, the student is taught the exact location, frequency, pressure and treatment protocol which could take as long as 12 years. These techniques are considered sacred and strict conditions are adopted to prevent misuse. To learn and master the *Varmam* system, one first needs to understand the three core principles of the Siddhas science of Bio-nature.

The first principle

The body or any matter in the universe is not static, but acting and reacting with external forces all the time, as a result of which, *prana* is in constant motion and adjustment within a body.

The second principle

Amritha ascends through *Varma* points situated on the left half of the body after the new moon and descends through the right half of the body after full moon.

CHAPTER SIX: VARMA - VITAL SPOTS

The third principle

A student needs to master the understanding of 96 *Tattvas* that organise the entire human living system, and is the basis of *Varma* physiology. Some of this has been explained in earlier chapters.

First principle:

Prana (life energy) is in motion within the body. Based on food and lifestyle, *Prana* is affected and responds quantitatively as well as qualitatively. The human body absorbs *prana* through the senses:

- Through food
- Through breath
- Through listening and hearing of information or music
- Through visuals of various incidents
- Through daily habits and lifestyle
- And even our mind absorbs *prana* by the mode of thought

Apt Pranic absorption allows a person to lead a balanced, constructive and authentic life. But in cases of poor Pranic consumption, such as a regular smoker would have weak pranic assimilation in the chest, which affects all kinds of pranic exchange throughout the body leading to anything from body pain to a weak immune system. Liver is the accumulator of energy and named the 'seat of the subtle body' as per the Siddha system. An alcoholic's liver would not serve as a good assimilator nor sustainer of energy as it would be severely impaired. This physical disorder would reflect in his personality as a trait of impulsiveness. (This kind of contaminated *prana* in the body can also be treated by Tantric Siddha system).

The pranic energy, as a breath of life, is always in motion in the body. The Siddhas call this breath of life as *Vaasi*. In locations where this pranic energy is vulnerable to influence are called *Varmam* points. The Siddhas give a short definition - 'Vaasi Thadai Padum Idam Ellam Varmam', which means 'the place where the flow of *Vaasi* gets obstructed becomes a *Varmam* or vital spot'.

Second Principle:

> "To reveal the size of life-breath, Jiva
> it is like: splitting cow hair, soft, into hundred tiny parts
> and then each into a thousand parts divide,
> The size of Jiva is, that, one part of the one hundred thousand."
>
> Thirumanthiram, Verse 2011

Not many theories offer explanation to where life is located within our body. The Siddha system accurately describes, 'life' within holds a particular location from where it operates throughout the entire body. It is called *Amritha Nillai*, the position of *Amritha*. This location isn't one permanent spot and instead travels from place to place according to the lunar cycle. In ancient Indian mythology, the moon is said to symbolise the 'bowl of nectar', due to its nourishing and cooling influence. One can find a crescent moon in the matted locks of Siva's hair indicating the flow of nectar from the head region. Just as waves of the ocean create different tides under the influence of the lunar cycle, likewise *Amritha Nillai* shifts and affects the flow of *prana*. For instance, during the new moon, *Amavasya*, the *Amritha Nillai*, would be found in the right big toe of a man and the left big toe of a woman. An injury to the toe at this time would take an unusually long time to heal. Surgery on the big toe on this day would lead to severe adverse effects as it is where 'life' is and any direct damage to it can damage the entire body.

Once, my Siddha Teacher said,
"Just like the external lunar cycle, there is one within our body which has a known path. Based on this inner function, one can ascend to an experience of Truth."

(Tantric Siddha system is based on this vital principle. It is called *'Parianga Yogam'*. The word *'Pari'* means bed and *'Anga'* means portion of the body and the word *'Yogam'* indicates union. He said Siddha Bogar and Siddha Gorakkar are masters of this yoga. The work 'Thirumanthiram' by the Siddha Thirumoolar carries an exclusive section on this.)

The first principle states, the internal pulse of life is vulnerable to influence in specific places. The second principle says, the pulse of life and its flow is also under the influence of the diurnal cycle of the moon by an inherent connection.

Third Principle:

Tattwas are interconnected with the vital spots. An in-epth understanding of *Tattwas* plays a vital role for a *Varma* therapist. In the chapter, 'Creation of Tattwas', we discussed 26 *Tattwas*, the remaining 70 have been briefly touched upon in the course of the book.

They are:

> The 6 yogic chakras,
> the 10 kinds of vital air (*Prana, Apana, Samana, Udana, Vyana*...),
> the 10 different important *Nadis* (*Idakala, Pingala, sushumna, singuvai, koorma*...)
> And the 3 *Doshams* or *Prakruthi*.
> (An elaborate discussion of these 70 *Tattwas* is beyond the scope of this book.)

A self-explanatory example of *Varmam*:

> A vital spot called '*Kallidai Varmam*' is situated in the *Mooladharam* (basal Chakra), the region of *Apana* (downward moving *Prana* responsible for excretory functions). Injury to this vital spot affects the associative movements of *Apana* and the excretory functions also feel the impact.

Names of some available ancient palm leaves (manuscripts) dealing mainly with *Varmams*, the effect of blows and injuries and ways to treat them are given below. Also described are the qualifications and ethical parameters required to study *Varmam* science. Averse in '*Varma Sutra*' it says:

> "As science of *Varma* deals directly with the lives of people, if it is taught to those of unworthy character, it would spread as evil in society. Hence, it is imperative that science of *Varma* be taught to those of pious nature and righteous character."

It also implies that one should learn this sacred art from an authentic and competent *Varmam* Master.

- Varma Sutra
- Varma peerangi
- Varma thiraugole
- Varma ponnosi
- Varma kundoosi
- Varma odivumurivu sari
- Varma Jeevakandam
- Varma Nalokolmathirai
- Varma villumvisayum Sara sutra
- Varma Guru nadi
- Varma Alavugoal
- Varma Oosi mugam
- Naal Mani Thiravukol
- Varma Sara Sutra
- Varma Kannadi
- Varma Suchhadhi Succham
- Pavai Thiravukol
- Agasthiyar Kambhu Sutram

VITAL SPOTS

There are several hundred vital points in the human body, of which 108 are considered as major. 12 of these are crucial as adverse effect due to impact, injury or accident could be fatal. Harm and injury to the remaining 96 have the possibility of being healed, provided it is attended to by a *Varmam* therapist within a stipulated time. The 108 vital points are seated throughout the five broad regions of the body as described below:

    25 are found around the head region
    45 are between the neck and umbilicus region, (naval area)
    9 are found between the umbilicus and anus region
    14 vital spots are spread through the upper limbs region
    and 15 vital spots are scattered throughout the lower limbs region.

Even though 108 *varmams* are mainly considered, their number varies from work to work. Some ancient works mention *Varmams* to be 200 in number. Ancient work 'Varma Vimanam' speaks of 827 vital spots related with disease and its cure.

Vital spots found in the six Yogic Chakras:

And a few others are described below:

CHAKRA	Name of Varma Spot in Tamil
Mooladharam	Andakalam Varmam
Swadhistanam	Kallidai Kalam
Manipoorakam	Urumi Kalam
Anahatam	Ner Varmam
Visuddhi	Thummi Kalam
Agnai	Thilartha Kala Varmam
Sahasraram	Kondai Kolli Varmam

Locations	Name Of Varma Spot in Tamil
Big toe of foot	Booli kalam Varmam
Sole	Vellai Varmam
Knee	Sanni Varmam
Thigh	Amaikala Varmam
Abdomen (lower Stomach)	Anna Kalam Varmam
Chest	Dhusiga Varmam (8 Spots)
Neck	Sangu Thiri Kalam Varmam
Fore Head	Moorthi Varmam
Eye Brow	Mel mantra Kalam Varmam
Medulla (Back Portion of head)	Pitari Kalam Varmam
Skull (Top of the head)	Kondai Kolli Varmam

A vital spot gets its name based on the nature of occupied energy. (This approach is not seen in the Ayurvedic Marmam system.) Stable energy at a spot is a *Varmam*. (*Javvu Varmam* - located four fingers below the inner armpit). Its name indicates that energy is stable and localised in nature. Vital spots with oscillating energy carry the suffix, *Kalam*. (*Thilartha Kalam* - located in the centre of the two eyebrows). The names given by the Siddhas describe the type of energy movement present based on which the attack or therapy is styled.

౸ ౾

Rings worn on the fingers have an effect on the body. Each finger results in a specific curative influence.

RING WORN ON	AREA THAT GETS VITALISED
Middle finger	Lungs
Ring Finger	Heart
Little Finger	Kidney
Thumb	Brain

The physical location corresponding to *Varmam* points are found spread over major neural plexus, major endocrine glands, muscle junctions, joint spaces, important blood vessels and soft parts. In these locations, the vital body force, *prana* is present. The subtle body is called *Suksma Sarira* according to northern tantric system and *Puri Attakam* according to the ancient Siddha system. An accurate blow or precise touch to any of these points, applied with calculated force (*Matrai*), frequency (*Illakam*), and pressure (*Alutham*) can affect and result in a minor to major injury, instant to insidious illness, paralysis or even death.

Some standard treatment protocols prescribed by Siddhas:

	Tamil Name for Treatment	Explanation
1	Ellakkumurai	Neutralizing the damage
2	Thadavum Murai	Massaging The Particular Spots
3	Kattu Murai	Bandages
4	Maruthuva Murai	Application of Medicine like Oil, Decoction
5	Santhi Murai	Divine Treatment

In *Varma* therapy, the first basic steps adopted are:

Relaxation of *Varma* points by massage (Varma Ellakkumurai)
Relaxation of adjacent muscles by massage
Application of medicated herbal oil through massage and internal medicines
Fomentation with herbal pouch, if necessary with hot water,
Or with navaraikizhi (a type of rice)

Anthropologists discovered *Varmam* science was martial art learnt by soldiers for self-defence and attack. The Indian state, Kerala is famous for its martial art, Northern Kalari (Vadakkan Murai). In Tamil Nadu, the Southern Kalari system (Thekkan Murai) prevails.Originally, in the hay days of Kalari-fighting systems, *Varma* science was used as combat skill as well as for healing purposes. Present day finds *Varmam* science mostly applied therapeutically.

Varma science is classified into five major areas:

1. Padu Varmam
2. Thodu Varmam
3. Tattu Varmam
4. Mei Theenda Kalam (*Mei* means body, *Theenda* means without contact)
5. Nokku Varmam (*Nokku* means by sight)

From the main five classifications, the first three are related to blows received from attack or injury solely by physical contact. The remaining two are afflictions without physical touch or body contact. Few minor ones are listed below:

1. Naal Varmam
   The *Varmam* spots that have a corresponding relationship with the movement of the lunar cycle.
2. Oodhu Varmam
   These are a few secret vital spots that can be afflicted or healed by a concentrated blow of *prana* through the mouth.
3. Vatham Varmam
   Vital spots connected to *Vatham Dosham*

4. Pittam Varmam
   Vital spots connected to *Pittam Dosham*
5. Kapham Varmam
   Vital spots connected to *Kapham Dosham*
6. Sundu Varmam
   Vital spots that can be afflicted or healed using the flick of one's index finger and thumb, etc.

Padu Varmam

A *Padu Varmam* is a major vital spot and *Thodu Varmams* are minor ones as each *Padu Varmam* is connected with eight *Thodu Varmams*. If a *Padu Varmam* is injured, there are chances of more than one of its corresponding *Thodu Varmams* also to be afflicted. There are twelve *Varmams* under the *Padu Varmam* category that can be influenced by force, blow or accident or trauma. Upon injury, the *Varmam* region gets chilled. (Only '*Thilartha kalam*' and '*Kallidai Varmam*' under this category do not show this response), and the person falls unconscious. If suitable treatment is not given in time, death may occur. The appropriate treatment is '*Varma adangal*' and '*Varma elakkam*'. After *Varma adangal* and *elakkam* are administered, the convalescing patient should be monitored carefully for the next few days.

Thodu Varmam

Varmam spots of this category get affected even by minor injury. The primary difference between the earlier category and this one is that the affected area responds by getting 'hot' upon injury, generally there is no loss of consciousness, but sometimes if the blow is of great force, giddiness, numbness of the muscles, contraction of muscles or paralysis may occur.

SECTION TWO: TREE OF LIFE

Front of Body

1. Moolai Varma
2. Koombu Varma
3. Thilartha Kalam
4. Kannadi Kalam
5. Mundelumbu Varma
6. Vilangu Varma
7. Thummi Kalam
8. Sulukku Varma
9. Ettu Muka Varma
10. Kumbu Varma
11. Ner Varma
12. Adappa Kalam
13. Kariral Varma
14. Muthu_---- Kalam
15. Kalladai Kalan
16. Vithu Varma
17. Mani Pantha Varma
18. Moli Varma
19. Kaal Muttu Varma
20. Nai Thalai Varma
21. Kuthirai Muga Varma
22. Komberi Varma
23. Pooli Kalam
24. Paatha Chakram
25. Kona Channi
26. Thida Varma

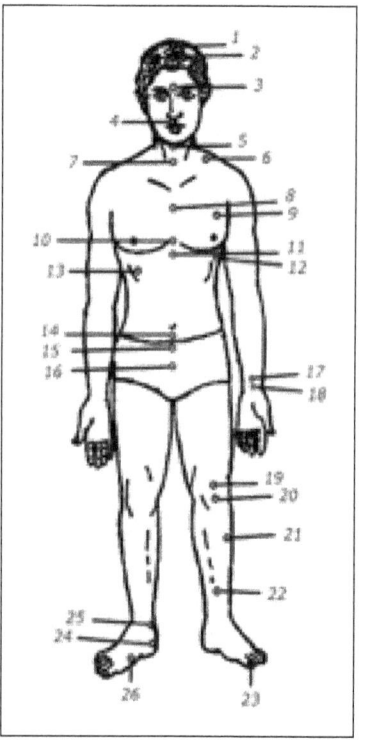

Rear of Body

1. Poondel Varma
2. Athi Varma
3. Pidari Varma
4. Mel Suliyadi Varma
5. Porsai kalam
6. Puya Varma
7. Kara Koottu Varma
8. Maiya Varma
9. Keel Suliyadi Varma
10. Keel Sangu Three Kalam
11. Nodi Varmam
12. Kulirchi Varma
13. Asagu Three Varma

Chest Area

1. Thallal Kuli Varma
2. Thivalai Kala Varma
3. Kai Puga Naangam Varma
4. Adappa Kala Varma
5. Ananda Vaasa Kalam
6. Kathir Varma
7. Kathir Kama Varma
8. Koombu Varma

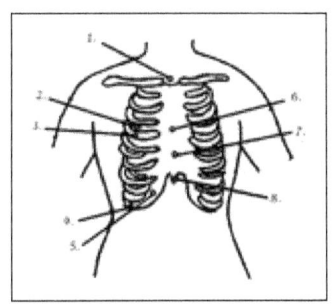

BASIC TREATMENT

Varmam adangal is administered when the vital force is blocked due to injury. The first basic step therapists perform is this *Adangal* which re-channelises the blocked *prana*. After *Adangal*, *Varma Elaaku Murai* is done. *Varma Elaaku Murai* revitalises the afflicted *Varmam*. It is administered by applying counter-pressure or relaxing massage after which the bio-energetic flow is expected to return to normalcy. Internally, a herbal decoction is given. An application of medicated herbal oil is administered externally, if needed.

Mentioned below is a self-explanatory case study:

NATCHATHIRA KALA VARMAM

> "Chathi Ennum Natchathira Kalanthanai
> Thalakkumamkal Viaparmudan Sarrak Kelu
> Jothi Ennum Kadai Kannin Irraikullethan
> Thulanku Kinra Kuzhivathile Kalamappa."
>
> Poem from a Varma Sutra

Position of Varmam:
  Natchathira Kala Varmam is found in the middle of the lateral margin of the orbit close to the lateral angle of the eyebrow.

Important Associated Parts:
  The frontal bone and the zygomatic bones meet at the zygomatic formal suture that is palpitating (throbbing) in a living individual. This region is covered by circular oculi muscles and is fed by the zygomatic orbital vessels.

Effects upon injury:
   A yellowish discolouration of the face and eyes is seen which soon disappears and is followed by sweating of the face. Hearing could be impaired. The back and the sides of the trunk remain cool. For treatments to be effective it must be carried out within 11 hours of injury.

Treatment:
   A rapid, careful tapping on the opposite Natchathira Kalam; a general massage on either side of the nose (Kampothi Varmam) is to be administered following which the healer should place his left hand 3 inches above the patient's head and with his right hand administer three taps to his left hand (which is placed over the apex of the patient). This is expected to restore the individual to normalcy. Dietwise, the individual should take Rice kanji (porridge) prepared in milk. Blowing dry ginger powder into the nose could also help. The healer, at the time of blowing, ties a cloth on his own face and covers even the patient's face with a light cloth so that the powder does not blow into the patient's nose as only its smell is to be administered.

In case of mistreatment or no treatment, following are the symptoms observed:
   Gradual loss of eyesight and/or refractory errors in young people may be noticed at later stages.

೧೧ ೧೩

Matthi Varmam
(Matthi means centre or middle)

Position of the Varma Point:
This *Varmam* is found in the centre of the spinal cord.

Important Associated Parts:
Damage to this *Varmam* affects heart-related nerves and liver. Subsequently, veins suffer damage from this impact and blood circulation is also affected.

Effects on this Varma Spot by injury:
Pain spreads throughout the chest region. The injured person is unable to breathe with ease and neither can he bend forward. Incase he tries to bend forward, the pain enters into the rib cage and spreads. If treatment is not administered within five hours of injury, the heart is rendered functionless.

Treatment:
First, the affected individual is asked to sit comfortably. The *Varma* therapist then clasps the hair in the centre of the patient's head with one hand and administers eight taps with the knee on the centre of the spinal cord. The patient is then made to lie down and the therapist gently massages the affected area in the spinal region. For hot fomentation, gingili oil is first boiled and fomentation is given by dipping a fistful of crystal salt tied in a piece of cloth. After the fomentation, the individual is asked to stand up. This treatment is administered for nine consecutive days. Internally, '*Karunkoli Ennai*' (medicated oil prepared from black hen and herbs) is administered.

Thuthikai Varmam

Position of *Varmam*:
From the palm of your hand, towards the wrist and above at a four finger width; on the centre region of this curve.

Important Associated Parts and Effects caused by injury:
Assault on this spot stiffens the entire body and eyesight begins to diminish. The individual feels weak and cannot lift the affected hand. If treatment is not administered within 6 hours, the hand could be rendered functionless.

Treatment:
The individual is made to sit in a comfortable position. The *Varma* Therapist applies Gingili oil or *Varma Kotari Tailam* on the affected area. Fomentation is administered by dipping a salt-packed cloth into Gingili oil twice a day for three days. *Kurunthottiver* decoction is administered internally for 15 days.

૭૦ ૦૨

A BEACON OF LIGHT FOR DISEASES

Even though this science is portrayed as martial art or injury therapy (sports medicine or accidents), it has the potential of healing disease. The function of the human system being holistic, allows it to balance excess or lack in energy patterns of the subtle body which can heal and prevent disease in the physical body. Unlike external medicine, *Varma* therapy targets healing the seed of disease located in the subtle body. Hard to heal disorders such as cerebral palsy, muscular dystrophy, paralysis, brain tumours, hydrocephalus can be treated and cured by a competent *Varmam* healer.

According to the Siddha *Varma Sashtra*, there is a *Varmam* called *'Bhoomi Kalam'* situated in the mound under the big toe. This spot has direct relationship with the pancreas. I recommended a toe-jumping exercise along with pressing of the *Oorami Kalam* vital spot to some diabetics with success. It resulted in stimulating the function of pancreas, liver and spleen. In ancient times, this exclusively-recommended activity was actually mingled in day-to-day living. They walked everywhere; the farmer ploughing the fields walked behind the bulls using his front foot to soften the earth before seeding. People would climb trees using the grip of their front foot. These lifestyles still prevail in the villages of India.

৪০ ০৪

COMBAT CULTURE

"It was a small town, with tea shops, restaurants, small gardens and a fair amount of houses. In the centre of the town, stood a popular restaurant where people gathered for evening meals. One day, a villager came asking for a job. He looked frail and innocent. The owner appointed him for serving people food. That evening, a big man came walking towards the restaurant. Seeing him, people ran away and the innocent newcomer didn't understand why. He stood waiting, ready to serve the big man. On seeing someone still standing in his way, the big man got irked. "How dare you," he hollered. "I cut whoever stands in my way!" Saying this, the big man drew his sword. In a trembling voice the newcomer spoke, "I am here to serve food." The tray dropped from his trembling hands to the ground spilling tea and food onto the big man. Outraged, the big man called the frail man out for a fight. In those days if you were challenged, you had to oblige or it was a shame. The shaken up villager, once again in a trembling voice asked, "Sir, I will come to fight, but please give me some time." The big man agreed. Promising to return in six months, he left.

An old woman washing dishes in the corner called out to the villager and asked, "Now what will you do? Shall I give you a solution? On the outskirts of this town lives a Master, adept in the art of fighting. He may teach you. I sent many to him but none believed him to be a true Master and left. You keep faith and stay there until he himself sends you back." The villager went to the outskirts of the town where he found a small hut. Around 500 metres from the hut stood a large tree, under which sat an old man, smoking. Approaching him, the villager noticed how the old man was inhaling smoke but not exhaling any. With childish innocence, the villager explained his reason for coming. The old man accepted him on the condition that he would bring him tea five times a day. The villager agreed. He brewed tea in a large pot and brought it to the old man under the tree. The old man said, "I cannot drink tea from the pot. Bring me one cup of tea at a time." For the next few days, five times a day, the villager did as told. The old man didn't teach him anything. All the villager was asked to do was serve tea. A month later the old man said, "I am bored with this cup. I want tea in a cup of thumb size. Offer me tea in that cup as a mark of respect to me." The next day, the villager brewed tea in the big pot and poured some out into a thumb-sized cup. By the time he walked to the old man under the tree, the tea had spilt and the cup was half empty. The old man remarked, "Is this the way you respect your Master?" Apologising, the villager returned to the hut, poured out more tea and walked back, but again it spilt. The villager spent the entire day like this. He grew more and more cautious while walking with the tea. He forgot the problem for which he had come. Gradually, he learnt the skill of carrying tea to the old man. In the coming months, he would offer tea without spilling even a drop.

One day, the old man said that his teaching was complete and the villager was free to return. Recalling his problem the villager asked, "Master, you have not taught me anything. I still have one month left, why are you asking me to leave?" The old man answered, "I have made you a Master. A perfect disciple is a perfect Master. A Master never fights as he is agreeable to everything and no situation arises for a fight. A Master proves himself by this." He said, "Have conviction in my words. The sword is like the big pot of tea that you brought in the beginning. There is also a sword within like the thumb-sized cup. Always greet everybody with this thumb-sized cup."

The villager left, returned to town and rejoined his job. The day came when the big man returned. "Are you ready?," he asked. "What is the hurry, let us have a cup of tea," the villager calmly replied, recalling the literal words of the Master to greet everybody with the thumb-sized cup! Taken by surprise, the big man accepted. He wondered how the frail man showed no fear. The villager brought tea in a thumb-sized cup. He carried the cup atop the first two fingers of his left hand and skilfully tossing it up in the air, he received it on his right and offered it to the big man. Seeing such skill the big man stood up, stunned. Placing his sword before him he said, "Both of us are equal, why fight?" He bowed and left.

CHAPTER SIX: VARMA - VITAL SPOTS

The villager thought that his Master's advice of greeting everybody with tea in a thumb-sized cup really works!!! People began calling him Master.

ॐ

The following paragraph has been mentioned in the songs of Dakshina Murthi Kaviyam - 1000, one of the Ancient Siddha Treatises.

"Ancient Sages observing forest birds and animals jumping, hiding, standing ground, confronting, and swiftly attacking formulated various stances and techniques and compiled palm scripts for the well-being and benefit of mankind."

Colonel Welsh, based in Tamil Nadu during British rule, wrote in his, Memories of Military life:

"Once, hunting with King Periya Marudhu, we were faced by a tiger. On seeing it, the King jumped off his horse, caught the tiger by his tail, swung it around and threw him at a distance of twenty feet. When the tiger came back with jaws open wide, the King kicked him with his leg and gripping the tiger's jaws tore him into two. On returning home, he proudly showed the fangs of the tiger, to his friends, that he had plucked and laughed. I learnt the skill of spear fight from his brother, Chinna Marudhu, a highly skilled warrior of a weapon named Valari, exclusive to Tamil Nadu. His throw was accurate to a target 300 feet away and could retrieve it after. Such a skilled warrior was Chinna Marudhu."

ॐ

The *Kalari* system, under the influence of ancient *Varmam* science formed two branches - techniques of offence and defence called *Verumkai prayogam*, the 'bare hand' fight. All combat techniques require thorough anatomical knowledge, specifically of vulnerable spots which the *Varmam* system provides. Though the use of martial art seems to have diminished at present, one can still learn *Kalari* in the present day Kerala and Tamil Nadu (southern states of India), where genuine *Asans* (Masters of Combat Science) are available. In the Kerala style of *Kalari*, all techniques used in combat are taught as one system, while in Tamil Nadu, over time the techniques diversified into branches such as *Silambam* (stick combat), *Kai varisai* (hand combat), *Kuthu Varisai* (boxing), *Malyudham* (wrestling), and Esoteric martial art.

ಞ ಇ

ESOTERIC MARTIAL ART

The 'Big Bang' theory could pose as an example for the standing practices revealed by the Siddhas, which states, energy and matter condense into an infinitesimal point of immense density and then explodes as an unimaginable explosion. The singularity point mentioned above is '*Bindu*', and the explosion is '*Natham*' according to Siddha texts.

The underlying principle of Esoteric martial art lists three types of energy phenomena:

Centripetal energy
Centrifugal energy
Combined rhythm
Centripetal energy

Centripetal energy being receiving in nature is shown by actions of yielding, deflecting, guiding, borrowing, trapping, wrapping and coiling around. It is a pulsation or an incoming force; from the periphery to the centre.

Centrifugal energy

Methods used for centrifugal nature of energy have multiple principles such as discharging the full force and power either in smooth wave-like motions or in short pulse-like actions, arising from various parts of the physical body or from the *chakras* of the subtle body. This energy has a delivering nature in the form of a pulsation or ongoing force; moving from the centre to the periphery.

Combined Rhythm

The combined use of both, receiving and delivering, creates a spiral wave of energy.

Siddha Masters designed standing meditative stances to experience the three phenomena. The stances teach us to be aware of our own tension and how to release it. It makes the entire body sensitive to the nuances of balance and motion, and by our own experience of this rhythm, we can feel the same existing in nature and other living beings. The first type teaches how to fill a balanced and emptied body with energy, permeating from the feet to the top of the head, combined with the intention of contracting or expanding. The second teaches how to take this energy and project it at will in a chosen direction at a general or specific target. The third is a state of perfect balance of energy where one's senses are finely attuned to combining both the receiving and directing energy. All three principles reflect in *Vasi Kalari* and *Vasi Varma* as the Esoteric Martial System of Siddha tradition. The pelvic region, in the human body, holds the centre of gravity. It is where the weight of the body rests, is balanced, co-ordinated and integrated. After a prolonged imbalance at this centre, the body begins to alter in shape or contours, to counter this imbalance, such as protruding hips, broad and heavy shoulders, bellies that hang out. Problems in bodily elimination, procreation or digestion could also develop. The *Kalari* system specifies the centre of gravity to be in the *Basal Chakra*, *Mooladharam* and teaches how to find one's own centre and strengthen it. After which, it teaches to use the gathered energy and transform it into an active burst of movement. The word '*Kalari*' is derived from the root word *Kalam*, meaning 'Field'. Using a balanced wholesome movement for a big impact with minimum effort, the centre of gravity and the nature of the field should be attuned as 'One', in complete harmony.

For a Combat Master, the Earth is his centre of gravity.

Training involves practice in different fields such as sloping, flat, slanting and steep, under ground, in a water hole, high altitudes and even in trees. This awakens deep awareness of the changes in the nature of gravity with a change in field. In this ancient art, attention is not narrowed towards the opponent, but to one's own grounding. The perfect grounding leads to a perfect up-lift. The stances are called '*Suvadu*'. *Suvadu* includes both standing and moving stances. Three standing meditative stances are of fundamental importance to Esoteric martial art which are ancient techniques evolved over time.

Three stances of specific attitude:

    Verumena Nitral Suvadu   (Fully open or empty stance)
    Karuvena Nitral Suvadu   (Womb stance)
    Malaiyena Nitral Suvadu (Mountain stance or universal pole)

These three stances generate an inner energy skill/strength. Under the guidance of a Master, a student develops and explores the mysterious power of energy. At the start, the student learns to feel and correct misalignments within his body through standing practices. Then he learns to develop a nature of control over physical tension, life's mobilising power, within his body. In practicing the first stance, the quiet posture of emptiness is used to create stillness and reduce external influence.

ಖ ಛ

Inherent Centre of Gravity

- Stand with feet together, body relaxed, hands loosely dropped by your sides, knees soft.
- Draw imaginary marks on the spots where the little toes rest on both sides.
- Keeping the heels together, move and place your big toes on the imaginary spots. (The place where the little toe was earlier).
- Now shift only the heels and bring them in line with the toes. Now the feet are straight and slightly apart.
- Notice - An imaginary line drawn upward from the place of the little toes all the way up passes the body, the toes are in line with the hips, the pelvic region.
- Feel the weight of the body. Try and sense where the weight rests.

This is the natural stance where the centre of gravity of the body drops to the perineum area, the region between the anus and generative organ. Now, the earth where you stand is bearing the weight of the body. No isolated part of the body is bearing any major weight. The centre of gravity can be collected, accumulated and shifted to a different location as desired.

Shifting the centre of Gravity to the hips

- Standing in the natural stance described above, once again draw an imaginary spot on the location of the little toes.
- In the manner described above, move the front part of each foot so that the big toes now occupy the place of the little toes.
- Bring the heels in line with the toes.
- The feet are now wider apart than before and wider than the width of the hips.
- Drawing an imaginary line upwards from the little toe, you will notice it is now further apart than the shoulder line.
- Once again sense the weight of the body by swaying or moving the body without lifting the feet. Observe where the weight of the entire body is collected and held. This is the new centre of gravity created by a shift in position. The weight of the body now rests in the feet instead of its original place, the pelvic region. No more in its natural position, the weight has accumulated in the leg area.

In the martial art system, it is imperative for the centre of gravity to always reside in the perineum area, its original resting place. From there, one must learn to be aware of its movement to different places according to different stances and movements of the body.

Moving the centre of gravity to a front foot:

- From this position, lift the right leg and take a comfortable step forward. The knee is soft. The knee of the back left leg must be straight and act as secondary support with not much pressure on the left leg.
- Body weight has now moved ahead to the front leg, thigh and come to rest in the big toe.
- The centre of gravity has now shifted from the pelvis to the big toe of the right foot.

Our centre of gravity is always moving and shifting by our movements. It travels. It journeys to different points, collects, accumulates and functions as the centre point or works as our 'ground'. This phenomenon is applied in the ancient system of martial arts and is a skill to be mastered. Due to a fragmented lifestyle, the mind lays scattered in an assortment of directions and so does our bodily energy, which settles and stagnates there, preventing life force to flow freely throughout the body. Sharp attentive awareness can free blockages and the weight energy of the body can stop withholding itself and flow. Communion augments strength and power. A lack of insightful sensitivity and deep communion between body-mind is the foremost hurdle for people today which prevents them from knowing themselves as enriched and wholesome life forms of energy.

೩೨ ೧೪

Imagine holding a ball in your arms, parallel to your belly, where the pranic energy ball gathers. Remain in this meditative standing posture and feel your internal energy build up as if air is being pumped into this ball. When an opponent touches you, imagine how your entire being would dispel energy by unleashing the *prana* in a thousandth of a second. With keen awareness of free-flowing energy within the body, it can be accumulated and directed to a location of choice, putting its power and strength to intended use. (Dispersed energy is of no use). The key implementing factor in martial arts is the natural filling of vital breath in the space between the navel and loins when the centre of gravity is established and crystallised in its origin. With the support of intention, this crystallised ball of energy is made to burst forth combined with whole body's synchronised co-ordination. The action occurs in a fraction of a moment but the impact is immense and multifold. If done correctly, the slightest action on your part, even of one inch, will push or bounce the opponent away. Your compressed energy expands, gently at first, and as you imagine it erupting like an air bag, it instantly bursts out, not in a linear fashion but in all directions. The internal force is so tremendous that it can project objects away without any apparent effort. Integrated muscles, (from feet to hands) work in synchronicity with *prana* for this to happen. This force can be carried into linear and circular movement stances, and with a command over this skill one can almost imperceptibly move the body to create a wave of energy over a short distance with a surprisingly powerful force. After advanced Standing stances, one learns to move slowly and smoothly in a unified manner, co-ordinated with a rhythmic breathing pattern. Next comes learning to contract and almost instantly expand the muscles of each joint: leg, hip, spine and arm, and thereafter instantly and simultaneously locking them all in place in the moment of contact with the opponent. In time, this can be done standing still, walking or circling. This skill is the essence of using the available internal power - the first stage.

෧ ଔ

Gathi Manifestation

In advanced practices, one crosses beyond the physical body and works using the subtle body in the web of *prana*, to influence. Siddhas have formulated Esoteric Yogic practices called *Gathi* (Gait). *Gathi* is the creation of a rhythmic pulsation of *prana* at a specific speed. There are 18 *Gathi* practices for working and channelising *prana*, such as *Siva Gathi, Hanuman Gathi, Mayil Gathi* (Peacock), *Simma Gathi* (Lion), *Nadana Gathi* (Dancing), *Pranava Gathi* (Om), etc...and lastly...*Vaasi Gathi* (Primordial pulsation). Today, these types of internal sensory practices are available only under Oral Siddha teachings.

CHAPTER SIX: VARMA - VITAL SPOTS

Symbols of Various Gathi

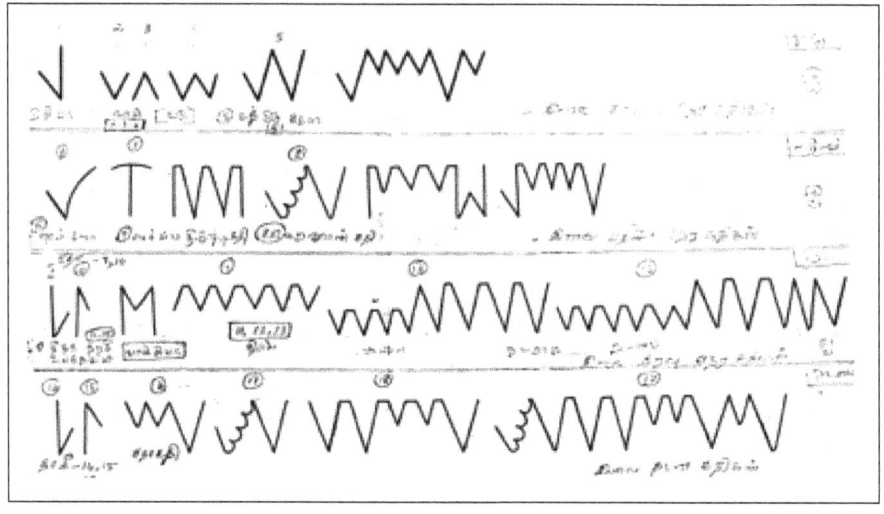

ෂ ඥ

OTTIYAM

Ottiyam is an ancient Tamil word, and this art is rarely seen in present times. *Ottiyam* is the art of absorbing, sucking or depleting an opponent's energy. An incident in Ramayana where Vali absorbs half the power of his opponent into himself is an example of this art. Lord Rama, considering this divine blessing bestowed upon Vali, didn't make a confrontational attack on him.

A short story of a friend named Raju. (A disciple of Yogi Devaraj Swami.)

> "Hailing from the lineage of Sage Patanjali, Devaraj Swami was a Brahmin householder. Only few locals living around knew of him. One day, when Yogi and Raju were returning home, on the side of the street sat a black magician, holding

a human skull and performing black magic. He did it as a means for livelihood. The black magician called out to the Yogi and Raju in a challenging voice. Devaraj Swami ignored him. He preferred to avoid confrontation but the unrelenting magician continued to aggravate. When the magician didn't give up his offensive behaviour, the Yogi walked up to him and swiftly moved his hand before him in a wave-like gesture and said, 'Now go ahead and do whatever you can.' The Yogi and Raju left the place. The black magician sat paralysed. He couldn't move a finger. It was around 10.00 am.

Reaching home, Devaraj Swami and Raju did their daily chores and ate lunch after which they stretched out for a short nap. Suddenly, Devaraj Swami said, 'Let's go, he is crying.' Walking back, Raju saw the magician seated in the same spot, paralysed, crying and pleading, 'Enough Swami, I won't do it again.' The Yogi once again waved his hand before him. The pleading magician was freed. The Yogi said to him, 'The art you learnt is for you to earn your livelihood; not for quarrelling. Nor is it something for you to be proud of.'

On the way home, Raju asked the Yogi what he had done to the magician. He said, 'Ottiyam.' Raju asked if he could learn this art from him. 'Why, what is the need?', was the reply. Some years later, the Yogi attained Maha Samadhi. He never taught Raju this art but he did mention how he had come to learnt it. Before this village near Madurai, the Yogi lived in the Andaman Islands where disharmony about caste and creed was dominant and occult practices were common. A simple method to kill someone was to drop a coconut from the tree using occult methods, on the head of the target. The Yogi had learnt this art for survival."

Early in the chapter, we read about nectar points or *Amritha Nillai* - the life force that shifts from point to point. In an ordinary person, energy is constantly mobilised like a stream, from point to point, according to the lunar cycle. An esoteric martial art Master has the ability to sense the exact location of life force within an individual at any given moment and time. With this knowledge, he can absorb the life force of the individual, who would drop dead to the ground. Invoking the centripetal mode of energy is the key point in the art of *Ottiyam*.

ഊ ଔ

SALLIYAM

A coconut can be made to fall without any physical contact. It's a nature of psychokinesis. *Salliyam* is the art of dispersing natural forces and individual energy in an explosive way.

A short incident in relation to my Tantric teacher, Swami Poi Sollan.

"In India, it is common to approach a Tantric Master for solutions to vital or life-threatening problems. A man and his three children approached my teacher, seeking refuge. Their lives were under threat and their property had been taken over by his opponents. When one of his opponents learnt that the man had taken refuge at the feet of Swami Poi Sollaan, he approached a young popular Tantric of that locality, who was always surrounded by no less than fifty students. The young Tantric had received his teachings and initiations directly from his Master's Samadhi. After he had gained direct contact with his Master's Samadhi, he was able to converse and get resolutions for different cases he was dealing with. Choosing an auspicious night, he decided to perform a mystical ritual to kill the man and his three children. Seated before the Samadhi Shrine of the Guru, the young Tantric began. That night, Swami Poi Sollaan sensed the intentions. He quickly woke up, and lighting a single incense placed it in the sandy ground. Internally, he generated *Gathi* and blew it in a specific direction.

Ten days passed. A person belonging to the young Tantric's group came to Swami Poi Sollaan and asked refuge. Sharing his experience, he expressed feelings of desperation and frustration about the (left-hand-path) tantric teacher's motives and applications. Speaking to the frustrated newcomer later, I discovered he was present the night they performed the ritual for killing the man and his children. He said that around midnight a cyclone had suddenly appeared. It dispersed and blew away the ritual preparations. The four people seated for the ritual had also been blown in four different directions!"

Modern scientists now concur that in the quantum field, everything is inter-related, but ancient Tantra has been applying this science in various walks of life since thousands of years.

CHAPTER SEVEN
STRESS

On a cryptic note...

> "There is a story about the Indian King Akbar. One day, King Akbar drew a straight line on a wall. He turned and asked his courtiers if they could shorten the line without touching or cutting it. The courtiers looked at each other puzzled. It was a problem. Birbal was a clever and intelligent Minister of Akbar's Court. He came forward, drew a longer line beside the line drawn by King Akbar."

HANDLING THE FIRE FOR COOKING

Newspapers are filled with violence, betrayal, chaos, accusations; a compilation of pessimistic expositions. Is there something wrong with the newspaper? One of the most common projections is, 'life is a struggle'. Human issues are on a similar note. 'Fighting for Rights'; 'Eradicating Cancer'; 'Fighting for women's liberation'; 'Conquering Peace'; 'Struggling for Excellence'; 'Demand of human rights', etc. Why don't we say, 'Healing cancer', 'Nurturing human rights', 'Sharing our rights', 'Living in peace', 'Unfolding our potential', 'Mothering women's rights', etc. We paint the world by the way we express, not only to others but to ourselves too. The colours of our mind are the colours we use. The way we relate to ourselves is how we relate to the world. As within so without! Believing ourselves to be co-creators of our life, we assert control.

RESPONSE OR REACTION

Situations beyond our capacity run chaotic and turn to stress! Confining mechanical routines and chains of compulsion lead to depression. Stress spits irritation at the psychic level and builds a non-receptive psyche; a depressed and closed individual breeds a suppressive mentality and a psyche devoid of vitality. How do we suddenly find ourselves incapable of coping? The root of incapability is in our obsessive involvement to assert control; in trying to push a situation as per our programmed wish. The first step - restoring harmony within. Discovering the cause of disharmony and disarming it naturally restores the mind to balance. An initial search may point to feelings of hurt and pain. We might even recognise that our failure to heal injured feelings led first to frustration and then anger. Only after this, do we see it was our unprocessed anger that burst out so violently on the outer world at being pushed away.

One who embodies contentment and happiness can be instrumental in restoring and maintaining the same in the external world.

A short incident about 'inner unrest' and its causes:

> During my Siddha healing practice, a software programmer came in for a consultation. He worked for a well-established company and put in nearly 12 hours of work a day. Somewhere along the way, he began drinking (alcohol) regularly after work. He said it helped him relax his overactive rational mind.

CHAPTER SEVEN: STRESS

His job demands were high. He found himself frequently arguing even with his family. This was when he came to me, asking for de-addiction from alcohol. I explained that the root of his addiction had erupted from the demanding nature of his occupation; one which constantly agitated and assaulted the rational side of mind. Persistent agitation had brought imbalance which reflected on his stagnant emotional side which plunged him into catharsis.

We may not be conscious of stress and anxiety assaulting the internal balance of our body, but the body is, and it finds a way to express its suffering. At some point or another, we all behave similar to that man. An incident could be assaulting us within, and not knowing what to do we hurt and assault others - project it. World violence has similar roots. Imbalance comes from high-level stress and severe physical exhaustion, both results of mechanical routine. A man loses his temper and turns abusive not because he is inherently bad, but because he has a hard time coping with fragments of his conflicted life. Violence increases in direct proportion to fragmentation; fragmentation of relationship with our self and others in our daily environment. Inner unrest is the inability to distinguish if our actions are responses or reactions. Stress is a conditioned fixation. Anger, hatred, jealously, greed, attachment, fear and desire are some root fixations and ego, the primordial root. Transformation begins somewhere for each of us. The most obvious starting point is the depleted body, reflecting the imprints of our fixations. Once, a parent brought his five-year-old son for a consultation. The parent confessed being puzzled by the child's abnormal adamant behaviour. The child's pulse said - chronic constipation. The parent admitted that his son passed bowels once in three days. Constipation is the body's tendency to withhold which, over time took root in the child's mind and showed up as adamancy. Duality of mind and body stands invalid in this child's case; it shows body-mind continuum. The mind fills each and every pore of the body! An individual is an 'organic unity'. A whole, in whom the objective as well as subjective work in unison.

There is a medical proverb in Tamil:

> "Mala chikal mana chikal uruvakkum. Mana chikal mala chikal uruvakkum."

This means,

> "Complexities in bowel movements lead to mental complexities. Complexities in mind lead to bowel complexities."

Toxicity of body generates toxicity of mind. A body lacking in energy, suppleness and strength cannot support endurance, clarity nor flexibility of mind.

৩০ ০৩

Accepting ourselves as the root of unrest and chaos is hard, and looking inward bears little or no significance in busy lives. It is felt unnecessary, difficult and unsettling for most. And so, we blame the world! But, the cause of our problems does not exist 'out' there, even if we wish to believe so. This is the essence of what psychologists call 'projection' and the ancient Sages call *'Maya'*. It doesn't end here. After presuming external factors to be responsible for our circumstances, we anxiously attempt removing or fixing them, and when we fail to justify our projections we are angered. Non-acceptance of inability has led to the anger we still carry around. Ironically, anger is momentary; a mild skin-deep reaction; a passing cloud. The moment we become aware of its temporality, it opens up a different possibility. Awareness or recognition allows the energy of anger to transform into heightened awareness. Recognition is the light breeze that quickly disperses this passing cloud. But unawareness bottles it up and rarely discharges it - due to social norm, self-image, etc. This anger settles as depression; a self-inflicted suppressive act. Each such act is a shock to the dynamic nature of the human organism. Both anger and depression incur deep damage on sensitivity of the human organism. A loss of sensitivity indicates a lurking incorrect perception because of which we no longer see clearly. We lose lucidity in evaluating the logical chain of cause and effect and are forced to behave in an indiscriminate and erratic manner. We invite chaos into our world. It is our own creation. Damaging approaches and attitudes are open invitations for a host of vicious cycles to take root. Layers of encrusted habitual mental patterns build upon our perception, like moss on the surface of a pond. This damp and insensitive accumulation restricts the flow of awareness. The thick moss blocks the rays of the sun, making our waters stale and dark. Persistent physical, mental and emotional stress leads to fear, dullness, poor discrimination and lack of faith and courage. The example of the constipated boy shows body-mind continuum. We are interwoven down to the subtlest tissue. Ingrown habitual fixations in the body turn psychological, and vice versa and mental suffering triggered by a psychological block can be far more draining than physical blockage in the body. As resonates the mind - so resonates our body. The swirling currents of hurt, pain, stress, frustration, anger, depression and violence don't diminish over time. The stimuli of stress patterns gather and regather, adding new impressions to existent layers that get translated into action. Whether we accept it or not, our actions reek of rancid impulsiveness and impure intention. For the subjective and objective aspects of life to integrate, there is the need to remove the dividing factor - egocentric desires. The damage began with an encounter with stress! In stress, the body prepares for a 'fight or flight' response and adrenaline sets off an alarm. Out of fear, our reflex is to turn inward in an effort to find stable ground but all we find is our inconsistent personality, which we clutch onto. We have just strongly identified with a wavering, unstable identity - but that is all we could find! Reactively grasping to some form of identification is known as *Ahamkara* or Ego. The Siddha's perspective of the Ego: A 'weaving power of identity' that functions on habitual, insensitive patterning. The Siddha path aims for mankind to be free of fixation and conditioning: mental, physical, cultural, racial and gender.

We are the sum total of all that has happened to us!

We are replicas of our past, which is how we call upon the 'same' in our life to happen again and again. Scars from strong stimulations at physical, emotional, mental levels change one into an uptight person. Every block felt by our body has an unresolved thought-pattern or emotional fixation preceding it. This is how we are responsible for our actions and its effect. Our mind and body are vulnerable to each other. The human body retains all past experiences, actions, events, emotions, traumas and memories within its system, affect its function and influence the kind of events we attract into our lives. To cut down the growing chains of stress and break free from the feedback-loop of reaction what we need is 'De-automation', which, translates as Mindfulness and Perceptive Sensitivity. (discussed in Being and Sharing).

The Siddha system of healing names three kinds of stress:

Emotion-Related Stress:

The root of emotion-related stress is primarily relationship. Loss of a loved one, betrayal, hurt, etc. are few reasons. Emotion-related stress triggers irritability, depression and emotional agitation. Physically, it could show as intermittent waking-sleep-waking patterns or disturbed sleep. Emotional stress afflicts *Pittam* for which *Pittam*-pacifying foods can be taken. Another effective way of reliving this nature of stress is a balanced routine and lifestyle.

Mind-Related Stress:

The cause of mind-related stress is the misuse or abuse of mind. Long hours of intense mental work is an overload to the left-brain which imbalances *Vatham*. A chronically-deranged *Vatham* expresses as inability of handling simple day-to-day situations and poor coordination between *Manam, Buddhi, Chittam* - thinking, understanding and recalling. The mind is hyperactive and the ability to make clear decisions and think positively diminishes. A person begins to lose sight of the purpose of an activity. In this state, first *Vatham* should be pacified and then *Pittam*.

Physical Stress:

Physical stress comes from misuse or overuse of the body. Hyper-exercise or over-exertion for prolonged periods proves taxing, especially combined with poor eating habits. Another cause is lack of physical activity resulting in poor digestion, laziness and lethargy. Physical fatigue and dullness of mind eventually convert into irritability only to later explode as violence. Primarily, *Kapham* is treated for this kind of stress along with other *doshams*. The ideal solution would be to balance *Kapham* and stimulate *Vatham* by inculcating a food and lifestyle regimen to that effect.

ೞ ಣ

SECTION TWO: TREE OF LIFE

TAMING THE WILD HORSE
The Right Attitude to Stress

Fire is an integral and indispensable part of daily life. Stress is a fiery wild horse that needs taming to be a good ride. The fire of stress can be tackled just like fire used for cooking or sacred worship. Stress instinctually sets off 'the big red fire alarm' within the body-mind in response to a sense of danger. Each time the body is charged with adrenaline to help stay alive BUT there are times when these are false alarms, when there is no real and immediate danger. False alarms are frequent in present times. Stress management is a simple skill. A lack of self-efficacy arises when we forget our innate capacity to accept facts and circumstances, overcome hardships, meet our life situations and accomplish our tasks. Instead of hiding behind habitual patterns of dominance or avoidance or succumbing to the pressure of past known actions as reactions, a useful approach would be to remain aware of the stress, without prejudice or past conditioning. A state of open-heartedness and trust makes us receptive to new possibilities in the moment. Attuning to the dynamics of the situation helps bring true solutions. Factors influencing the shape of a situation are ever-changing. Preconceived ideas and known solutions fail to resonate with ever-changing scenarios and turn into barriers. The habit to resort to known solutions narrows our perspective, making it static.

"You cannot jump into the same river twice".

Heraclites

CHAPTER SEVEN: STRESS

Dynamics

Taming the wild horse is to be in the openness of a situation; independent and free. Leaving the situation in its own place and making no attempt to be rid of it. Not being lost and submerged amongst struggles or manipulating situations to our expectations. The displeasure and discomfort of stress is always accompanied with tension. Tension by itself has no specific effect on our body and is an energy-response instinctively summoned when confronted. Mild tension is actually a form of excitement.

Tension is the dawn of life's mobilising power to overcome barriers.

A natural solution to each moment exists and unless one recognises this appropriate inner response, stress remains. Unfortunately, we get caught up in confusion unable to recognise the ideal approach which vitalises stress and pre-learnt tips prove temporary. Come to think of it, the attitudes we learn in kindergarten might be quite enough to live and survive in the world! The key is to attune to the natural, inherent drive of spontaneity, allow it to grow and actualise to full potential. Seeing things as they are can actually bring solace, comfort and freedom. By dropping known, habitual reactions, you mobilise Rising Life, a dynamic energy within that unfolds the appropriate response. It empowers us to walk our path unhindered, crossing stressful situations and leaving our authentic presence in it. An authentic response not only changes the situation but, transforms the one who suffers.

Lord Siva is the most beautiful icon worshipped in the Siddha Tradition. *Sivam* means, both deathlessness as well as consciousness. (What dies is called *Savam* - corpse.) Tantric Siddha practitioners worship Lord Siva dancing, symbolising the dance of immortality flowering in the realm of mortality. It is known as the fiery *Tandav Nritya* performed by Lord Siva amidst the *Savas* (corpses) in the cremation ground; the realm of mortality and inertia. This dance is the divine representation of light penetrating darkness or a lotus blooming on a muddy lake.

Losing ourselves in the corpse of stress is to be in bondage; to find ourselves in every experience - it is true freedom!

༄ ༃

REMEDY TO STRESS

Breath retention is a common reaction to feeling suffocated by the situation. Stress gets patterned onto our consciousness when we unconsciously hold our breath. Exhalation (described below) helps relive accumulated-stress patterns. Breathing practices described below should be done on an empty stomach, in the morning and evening, starting with 10 minutes and gradually increasing to 30 minutes.

o Relief from stress by deep exhalation and cleansing breath practice: Sit in a comfortable posture, with your head slightly tilted upward. Place your thumbs on the two ears, gently closing out sound from each ear. Place both middle fingers at the inner edges of your eyebrows, and let your index fingers rest naturally on the forehead. Place the ring fingers and little fingers of both hands gently on both sides of the nose, so that the little finger rests just above the flares of the nostrils, the ring fingers beside the bony bridge of the nose. Gently exhale that which has stagnated inside your body, through your nose, making a humming sound. (You should feel the humming vibrating in the nostrils). When the entire body is pulsating with the humming sound while exhaling, accumulated stress patterns of improper breathing are relieved and disperse, enabling *prana* to flow freely throughout the body. One can experience an immediate sense of relief from stress.

- Deep Belly Breathing:
  After relieving existing stress patterns by the above practice, one can energise the spirit by deep belly breathing. This helps one to meet oncoming situations in an integrated and collected manner and skilfully assimilate accumulating stress. Before starting deep belly breathing, observe your breath and gradually exclude all thoughts and sensations. Focus your attention on the navel, remain aware of the contraction and expansion of the abdomen with each exhalation and inhalation. Allow the breath to regulate itself into a low, deep and rhythmic pattern. Continue the perception of your navel region for about 5 to 10 minutes until you feel the comfort of breathing in a slow calm rhythm. This practice brings integration and inner grounding, which prevents one from being swept away by overwhelming situations. The ground that develops by this practice helps master a skilled tackling of any nature of crisis.

The practice described below, if done consistently, helps one imbibe the above into his life.

Continuing from deep belly breathing practice, observe the slow, deep and rhythmic breath. Gently shift your attention from the navel to the inside of the nostrils; at the junction where the two nostrils (sun and moon) meet. Let the perception of breathing fill your entire mind. Maintain the continuity of perception throughout the practice. Try not to be distracted. If distraction does occur, without dismissing it, observe patiently until it naturally goes away. If distractions get frequent, hold your breath for a brief moment which helps bring you back to your inner ground. As the perception of breath fills the mind, mind and breath come together in perfect co-ordination; one orderly movement. By this practice, one naturally enjoys a clear perception with the capacity to assimilate the entirety of a situation just as an eagle takes in the view of the world below from aerial heights.

SECTION TWO: TREE OF LIFE

RELIEF BY BALANCING THE DOSHAMS

	EMOTIONAL	MENTAL	PHYSICAL
1.	Eating sweet fruits.	Eating foods with sweet, sour and salty tastes.	First getting moderate rest.
2.	Eating foods with sweet, bitter and astringent tastes.	Taking warm milk at evening time	Moderate exercise
3.	Eating lots of juicy vegetables.	Warm oil massage twice weekly.	Having proper understanding about one's real physical ability
4.	Attending bhajans (Devotional songs) or singing devotional songs	White lotus petal jam (or Decoction)	Avoiding long term vices, bad habits (such as smoking, drinking, drugs) that induce negative side of Kapham nature
5.	Self-massage with cooling oil such as coconut oil	Moon visualization technique	Performing full-body warm oil massage four times a week
6.	Cucumber, rose petal jam, ghee, cardamom, in food have a balancing effect on emotional stress	Staying in open space at night time before sleeping like under the sky; walking on seashore or riverbed	Eating two figs (with warm milk or warm water) each night before sleep for one month

7.	Faith in guru or God	Meditation--silencing the mind - not concentration	Every six months, clean stomach using herbs
8.	Not expecting much from relationships	Planning, but not programming every activity	Following proper lifestyle routine for the changing seasons
9.	Early morning waking	Playing games which don't demand much thinking	Moderate sex
10.	Surya Namaskar (Sun salutation)	Listening to Satsang (attending spiritual discourse)	Maintaining proper digestion

CHAPTER EIGHT

ARDHANAREESWARA
Dancing Lore of Feminine and Masculine

Dinosaurs weighing not less than few hundred tons have two pea-sized brains! The brain in the head governs vision, hearing, etc. and the one in the tail controls locomotion and procreative instincts. For humans, Mother Nature kept it simple. She created one brain with two hemispheres - the greyish left half and the white right half. The highly-developed cortex located in the upper brain distinguishes man from animal. Science has only recently attributed man's dichotomy to these two halves, while our sages have detailed this thousands of years ago. Siddhas describe the left and right hemispheres are man's masculine and feminine aspects; dual forces permeating his physical form (the brain) and his subtler realm such as pranic and psychic levels. At the pranic level, the solar and lunar breath correspond to masculine and feminine natures respectively and aggressive and passive state of mind is evident in human psyche.

"The infinite gracious effulgence
Has established woman in man and man in woman."
                                    -Verse 703

"The infinite gracious effulgence,
Has reserved femininity in man and
Masculinity in woman in a concise manner."
                                    -Verse 709

CHAPTER EIGHT: ARDHANAREESWARA

"The infinite gracious effulgence,
Has instilled feminine mind and masculine intelligence,
In a concise manner."

-Verse 713

"The infinite gracious effulgence,
Has infused masculine and feminine natures,
In different levels, separately, as different body frames."

-Verse 715
Arut Perum Jothi Agaval, Siddha Saint Ramalingam

The two hemispheres are in an ever-progressive interplay; a dance between the masculine and feminine natures in man, instilled by the infinite gracious effulgence. The Siddhas emphasise an ideal and harmonious coming together of the seemingly divergent sides for it to serve as a platform for the Divine to unfold. The Siddhas draw attention to the distinction between the right and left-sided functions of our personality and its roles. A harmonious interplay of hemispheres facilitates lateral and linear growth, creating a doorway for the possibilities inherent in each human being to emerge and flourish.

The two hemispheres develop, flourish and interplay throughout life and depend on a set of internal and external dynamics for their development. The internal dynamics are meticulous patterns formed by ever-changing *doshams* (stages of life) and the external ones are our social order. These two sets of dynamics impress upon and modify the universal platform of basic modes of survival and this is what grooms 'individual' personalities. Commonly, the masculine and feminine aspects are seen as opposites, but are in fact complementary. Like two different travellers bound together on a journey called life, the right and left hemispheres require to strike an amicable balance for an individual to enjoy deep harmony. But before this melodic poise can be realised, the journey holds many interesting nuances. An overemphasis of either oppresses the possibility of a balanced combination of lateral and linear growth. The social canvas of today exhibits disparity and it is not hard to recognise an overemphasis of the masculine aspect at mass as well as individual levels. Our surroundings are undeniably leading to an exaggerated linear growth!

༄༅

FROM IMPULSE TO INTUITION
The Nature of each Hemisphere

Areas of specific functions within the human brain are woven together into interdependence. (Similar to the development of seven *Thathus*). Just as instinct rises to intuition at psychic level, the growth of the brain proceeds from the lowest to the highest; from the tangible to the abstract, or non-substantial. The lowermost rung of this ladder is Survival Impulse. Next is what science terms the limbic system or the mammalian brain - the area responsible for all primitive emotional response in man. These two rungs of this hemispherical ladder are common to man and beast. The third, more distinct and refined rung is absent in animals, and excessive to man; the Neo-cortex or cortex. The Neo-cortex is bifurcated into two halves - right and left. Sequential development from the limbic system grooms into the right hemisphere, the emotional or the new mammalian brain. The next and superior half of the neo-cortex is the left hemisphere, which deals with more abstract levels such as calculative and analytical functions. Beginning at conception, the brain grows through these stages but the progress of each stage depends on the qualitative development of the previous one. Based on this, an ideally nurtured child would grow up to have a nourished and balanced development.

CHAPTER EIGHT: ARDHANAREESWARA

Distinctive attributes of each section of the human brain:

R-system

At the lowermost rung of the hemispherical ladder, is the R-system or Survival Brain which consists of the Medulla Oblongata with reflex centres to control heartbeat, breathing and is responsible for sending out signals for sneezing and laughing. It is also called the reptilian or primitive brain as it is solely concerned with survival instincts, using two modes - attraction or repulsion - a simple defence mechanism. An infant sees and experiences the world through these reticular movements.

Limbic system

Passion and drives such as fear, grief, anger, lust, etc. arise from the primitive region of the brain known as the limbic system. The limbic system works with the neo-cortex (above) and the brain stem (below). This connection permits the interplay between reason and emotion and is called either the mammalian or emotional brain. The limbic system predominantly influences learning at one or one and a half years of age.

Hemispherical dominance and how the left and right hemispheres of the neo-cortex govern the functioning of our body in distinct ways:

In his book, The Psychology Of Consciousness (published by Jonathan Cape, London, 1975), Robert Ornstein sums up the position thus: "If the left side is predominantly analytical and sequential in its operation, then the right hemisphere is more holistic and relational, and more simultaneous in its mode of operation."

Neo-Cortex

Neo-cortex is found in the upper section of the brain and lies bifurcated into two hemispheres; left and right. This section distinguishes a human brain from that of an animal, and is known as the New-mammalian brain. We commonly know it as our conscious, or waking state. Occupying two-thirds of the brain, it is where human thought and creativity originate. The left hemisphere relates to the right half of our body and the right hemisphere relates to the left half of our body. This reference is merely in regard to gross movements and body sensations, and the entirety of complex information from within and outside the body is available to both halves of our brain. A thick broad band of fibres called the corpus callosum connects the two halves and is the pathway to mutual influence.

The Feminine

The right hemisphere is responsible for feminine traits and attributes and deals with refined feelings of compassion, love, spatial arrangements, and holistic understanding. It is simultaneous in its nature of thinking and has the faculty for instantaneous computation of available information without being bound by time. Its operations are based on the perception of total patterns rather than the principles of linear sequencing. The seemingly straightforward act of pointing to one's nose requires information to travel to the nose, finger and hand, the position of head and body, the blood supply requirement for muscles, etc. all of which are instantaneously and simultaneously processed. This is a right-brain function. Over and above simultaneous tasks, the right brain does dreaming and intuition, simultaneous and pattern-oriented direct perception. Executing simultaneous tasks that call for higher faculties happens through 'Lateralisation' - an optimally co-ordinated and harmonious blending of both hemispheres to function as a unified whole. The finest possible merger of the right hemisphere being incorporated by the left reflects the intensity of lateralisation. This happens through the quality of perception - the kind of perception that surpasses human intellect and its limitations. Through expanding lateralisation, simultaneous faculties like intuition, holistic clarity of situation, etc. unfold, leaving behind narrow, petty, isolated views. But if the reverse happens and the right hemisphere gets incorporated by the lower-brain instead of the superior left hemisphere, personality traits like impulsiveness, haste, reactions, recklessness, short temper, etc. are born. The inclination of the right hemisphere (whether it bends to the lower end or rises to the higher end) truly decides the nature and level of human perception.

After a spiralling journey through intensities of lateralisation, between the two natures, the peak of their resonance opens the door to non-cerebral living.

The Masculine

The left hemisphere governs attributes of analytical thinking, numbers and quantities as well as higher abstract level functions such as abstract symbols of language and numbers. It works on logic and its processing ability is sequential. It can be described as a verbal, logical, sequential operator, linear in its experience of time. The verbal function is an outstanding example of linear or sequential processing in time where one word succeeds another. This mode of function attracts material suited to its operational purpose and ignores information that does not. Even though the left hemisphere is seen as most evolved in the history of brain development due to its high evolutionary functions, its overemphasis results in imbalances that surpass individual levels and affect broader ones. Reminding ourself of the reason this evolutionary rung appeared, could help deter an over-emphasis. Its development arose in response to the need of the right hemisphere, and its lower associates. Overlooking this, humans invest in exclusive indulgence of the left hemisphere, assuming it is solely responsible for advancement in Man. This isolated and excluding approach disregards that this evolution was brought by Nature to serve the call of the feminine; not to replace or substitute it. The industrial revolution continues to blindly favour left-brain faculties and accelerate progress in technology, the consequence of which is the largely retarded progress of the right side of the brain: the emotional, the paranormal, ESP and other hidden powers inherent to man. An individual functions from the combined use of his right and left hemispheres and it is impossible to confine individuals as left-dominant, right-dominant or even mixed dominants. Mixed-dominants are those who equally use both sides of their brain, but vary in lateralisation. Mixed-dominants, who lack the skill of lateralisation, may experience an inner competitive tension between two sides, which could show as indecisiveness or stammering. Sequential growth and development in an individual runs through vital milestones, starting at birth. An infant experiences the world based on its available faculties - its survival impulse of attraction and repulsion. By age 1 or $1^{1/2}$, the second rung of the brain ladder, the limbic system or the emotional brain comes into play. After the age of three, the child learns through both, the limbic system and the right hemisphere. Between the age of twelve and fourteen, the analytical left hemisphere predominantly influences the teenager.

Hemispherical preferences are determined by our genes and psychological, social conditioning. The factor of one-half-dominant function influences our way of thinking, our skills, inclinations, interests and ability to gather specific kinds of knowledge. It also determines our attitude to life, our relationship with people, our material possessions, our attitude toward work and even the manner of work.

A left hemisphere-predominant individual:

Is objective
Is abstract
Focuses on the content and construction of a statement; not on the tone and feelings behind it
Analyses the structure of research and requires supporting logic before accepting new ideas

Is unwilling to take risks
Is not open to spontaneous decisions and not in the habit of trusting impulse and intuition
Is willing to follow rules
Gives importance to analysis, rather than integrating points to come to a decision
Experiences time as linear, successive
Programs before starting anything
Has a definite aim to fulfil tasks
Is ambitious
Prefers science subjects to art subjects.
Has right-eyed vision.

A right hemisphere-predominant individual:

Is imaginative
Is intuitive
Is concrete
Does not seek empirical evidence before accepting new ideas
Is uninterested in programming or planning and is impulsive
Enjoys taking risks
Is attentive to the overall message
Takes immediate decisions or comes to conclusions without excessive thinking, based on what he feels to do
Experiences time as simultaneous
Prefers art subjects to science subjects
Thrives on leisure, recreation
Likes change
Has an interest in anything that is extraordinary
Has predominant left-eyed vision

While a verbal, logical or mathematical task is solved by the left-brain, the electrical activity of the right half is depressed. Likewise, the electrical activity of the left-brain is depressed while an emotional or intuitive task receives attention. One can identify if an individual is tackling a math or an emotional problem based on the right or left deviation of his eyes. The traits of each zone of the brain are typical and move from instinct to higher abstract levels through the process of maturity from infancy to adolescence. Our social order plays a definitive role in making or breaking overall qualitative development of the hemispheres. One can't help but acquire a few narrow ideas side by side the talent and wholesome traits, passing through the stages of life. The intention of *Sadhana* (daily spiritual practice) serves the sole purpose of gradually bringing into balance our acquired derangements, which is why *Sadhana* should be according to the call of one's psyche for it to actually bear fruit.

The magnitude of experiencing an idyllic balance between the two opposing inherent natures, serves as an irrevocable call for Self-Actualisation. Harmonic vibrancy arising from the union of these two opposites resonates at levels beyond reason and understanding, and soars to the inexplicable realms of intuition wherein a monopoly of neither feminine nor masculine natures prevail - the realms of Absolute Unfolding.

Life unfolds from the physical to non-physical, concrete to abstract and substantial to Non-substantial.

ஐ ஃ

NATURE'S INTENT

Life is a maze of individual volitions and collective cultures in a meticulously prepared divine recipe intent on human Self-Actualisation. The process for growth in each hemisphere is paced to meet the demands of human existence, from birth to death, demonstrating the undeniable function of a higher intelligence – Nature's Intent. To support idyllic growth, nature has added the interplay of the three bio-regulating forces, or *doshams*, as inner dynamics. Nature's foremost intent of Self-Actualising each life stage is seen in the common platform. How does nature intend to accomplish her intent without ruling out the ever-changing external world? The Siddha system of life science classifies human lifespan into three phases. The first phase experiences *Vatham* dominance, the intermediary phase *Pittam* dominance and the last phase experiences *Kapham* dominance. The span of the first phase falls between birth to 24 or 30 years of age and so on.

An additional subdivision of each phase:

1st Phase	Vatham			
		Vatham	-	birth to 8 years
		Pittam	-	9 to 14 years
		Kapham	-	14 to 24 years
2nd Phase	Pitta	Vatha		
		Pitta		
		Kapha		
3rd Phase	Kapha	Vatha		
		Pitta		
		Kapha		

In the sub-classification, the initial 24 years of human life are further sub-divided into *Vatham-vatham*, *Vatham-pittam* and *Vatham-kapham*. In which case, the first 8 or 10 years of the initial 24 are completely *Vatham*-dominant. The next 8 to 10 years are influenced by the dominant *Vatham* along with a secondary *Pittam* influence, and the final 8 or 10 years of the first 24 years, *Kapham* is the secondary influence along with the central influence of *Vatham*.

Let us re-visit an infant's state of consciousness, this time through the underlying *doshams* and try to recognise nature's perfect design. An infant at birth subsists in the pre-reflective state, one with the world, having no division of object and subject, but without being conscious of it. As she grows, this state alters. She first begins to sense and explore her own body parts and her attention is predominantly captured by locomotive functions. *Vatham Dosham*, a part of the perfect design, is the primary functioning bio-regulating force. At the same time, all sensory functions related with the R-system in the brain are active in this period. Followed by this, change in a child's consciousness comes by learning by touch. By touching and feeling different objects, she undergoes concrete learning function. For instance, if you say 'leg' to a child under the age of 4 years, she responds with a combination of moving her own leg and uttering the word 'leg'. If you say the word 'plate', she responds by an action of showing a plate and uttering the word 'plate'. This is to say, word and object are not separate for the child. This is typical of right hemisphere incorporated by the lower brain instincts, such as reticular system. So far, only the *Vatham* has been the acting support for self-actualisation in the early learning process. Approximately after the age of 8, *Vatham* is joined by *pittam* and the child now begins deeper learning. She wants to know all about personal possibilities. Science describes this function typical of the right hemisphere majorly being incorporated by the limbic system. At the age of 14, the bio-regulating platform is *vatham-kapham* and left hemisphere is dominant. The *vatham-kapham* combination incorporates the mentality for choosing her own learning dimension - such as her main subject at school, etc., pointing toward a career or job. At this age, the higher cortex is dominant. In this way before closing into the age of 24, she would have more or less chosen a life course or browsed through career options, under the playful support of all three *doshams*. First, her

CHAPTER EIGHT: ARDHANAREESWARA

active search of options offered by the world is pressed on by the prevalent sub-dosham *Vatham*. Her learning, exploration and study of the one correct possibility are overseen by the sub-dosham *Pittam*, thereby forming a *vatham-pittam* combination. Then, to narrow down her search into a single choice and being grounded in her chosen purpose, is the sub-dosham *Kapha* in the boosting role, a *Vatha-kapha* combination. Between 24 to 30 years of age, she would have settled in her chosen life course, after which *Pittam* takes over as the dominant bio-regulating *dosham*. She would be active in actualising her chosen area, using the supportive sub-doshams *vatham*, *Pittam-Vatham* combo. And so the pattern continues. Self-Actualisation is available to all humanity - by way of this common platform but invariably, it gets left behind as 'a possibility of being an authentic person', because very few fulfil nature's intent and get tangled elsewhere.

ಸಿ ಆ

Abstract learning instils its way much later. Grasping the abstract is based on the quality of concrete learning in baby years. Language and understanding are similarly learnt. Just as a young child cannot comprehend a mathematical hypothesis, chemical equation or formulae, he cannot understand electricity, which is abstract compared to his concrete living experience. After the age 14 or 16, learning non-physical aspects - the abstract world can happen under the dominating left-hemispherical influence. Competency to assimilate the broad possibilities of our abstract world is relative. Deeper facets of the abstract successfully instil themselves into a young adolescent if his early stages were exposed to good parenting, stories, tales and a vivid imagination. These prepare the ground within her psyche that eventually transforms into understanding metaphors, visualisations, images and blossom into inspiration.

If this ground is fertile, she would be equipped to grasp the essence of abstractness of life. But a child deprived of a nurturing environment, metaphoric listening and wholesome concrete relationships will experience trouble as will his relationship with life. It could mean poor communication skills or a weak living expression. A person encountering the calculative and mechanical nature of the abstract (left hemisphere domain), supported by a poorly nourished right hemisphere, would be unable to derive any meaning from it. The person would react and compensate the empty experience by grasping at the encounter in a dry intellectual way. This is how 'acquiring' activities get cultivated within a growing individual. These tendencies channel pseudo-satisfaction which eventually betray and release as perverted claims of the right-hemisphere. History has written of many renowned philosophers or great intellectuals known to have a dark side. Some were notorious drunkards, alcoholics, etc. Many suffered failure with emotional ties and few even turned senile in old age or committed suicide. There is a vast difference between a philosopher sipping alcohol and a poet. For the philosopher, alcohol is a vent, a catharsis, but for the poet it is inspiration, such as Rumi and Tennyson. The Siddhas say, a great *Gnani* is a great *Bhaktha*. A good discriminator is a good devotee!

ಐ ಆ

THE SPLIT

A child recognises her mother as the source of learning and relationship. A mother provides her opportunities. Given a rattle, the baby shakes it, and the sound makes her surprised and happy. This triggers the 'Self-Similar' instinct to manifest and the baby shakes everything she grasps. A mother accepts certain attempts of

CHAPTER EIGHT: ARDHANAREESWARA

self-similar experiences and forbids others. When the baby picks up a knife, the mother instantly takes it away. At first, this new response from the mother brings shock and confusion. It introduces suffering coming from her mother who, until now was always the source of happiness and love. This unexpected mix coming from one primary source, her mother, triggers an individualistic sense in the baby and initiates the 'struggle to prove'. Hereon, she is self-conscious and incorporates defence, or retreat in all relationships. If the situation permits, she willingly opens herself to relate and learn, but, in an oppressive situation, she retreats in attempt to fulfil herself by way of a 'compensating approach'. At this significant juncture, in each of our lives, our 'whole energy' splits into two - energy related to learning and energy related to defence. From this point on, we no longer invest all of ourself, wholeheartedly, to anything without reserving defence energy. After the inception of this inevitable early split, whenever the child feels vulnerable to the world, her defence mechanism kicks in. And to replace the unpleasantness of this inner partition, she uses a compensating process. Henceforth, this is the point from which we all live. And the outcome of always living with a strong sense of vulnerability brings an 'in-built hollowness' arising from a lack of spontaneity. The difficulties that tumble down from this hollowness are discussed in the chapter 'Reluctant Masters'. Before long, a defined approach to face most circumstances in a reserved manner begins to crystallise in these early stages.

Drastic extremities and how they reflect

The above is a common description of the inception and rooting of the 'split' but each of our stories change in relation to our personal environment. Infants, children exposed to improper nurturing and trauma unfortunately bear a harsher 'split' with deep-rooted scars. Dissolving this nature of crystallised split demands more. If healing doesn't come around in the progressive stages of childhood then our social structure and ties (our mother in adulthood) need to provide relief. Native spiritual traditions, say surrender, mindfulness and unconditional involvement are imperative to be freed from shortcomings carried from the split.

༄༅

In individuals influenced by both the right and left-brain hemispheres, one might expect the two halves to work in harmony but facts speak otherwise. Typically, the two halves share an unhappy marriage where friction supersedes cooperation. Conflict is a ground-bearing disease which triggers major disasters in society. An unfortunate bias made by social and cultural sectors not only gives less importance to right brain activities but even to the left half of the body; the left hand presumed 'inauspicious'. This bias has even infiltrated spiritual lore by the Tantric energy practices to awaken and unleash deep-rooted archetypal energies being called the 'left hand' path.

༄༅

The hemisphere dance of existence also reflects at broader social levels. It's happening in our towns, cities and countries. At mass levels, we are primarily employing analytical, numerical and calculative faculties cultivating a left-brain dominated social order alongside a string of technological advances. Repercussions have seeped from individual levels into the social order. In an individual, left-brain exaggeration increases the distance between traits of both hemispheres because of a lapse in combined use. The reactive deficiency of the right hemisphere expresses aggressive or overly passive behaviour. The broken or deranged psyche instinctively attempts to replenish the dearth by a compensating process and grasps at addictions or abnormal behaviour patterns. Such glaring extremities compile our society - great progress on the technological front versus a steep decline in the quality of human nature. Additionally, our manmade mathematical model of society and its asymmetrical abstract mode of living are being introduced far too early into the lives of children. Early exposure to an array of left-hemisphere encounters especially during the initial stages with the R-system and the limbic system still needing attention is leaving young minds 'hanging'. A child needs to pass up the hemispherical ladder in an evolutionary way by relating first to one's body and its movement, if not, the limbic system grows asymmetrical devoid of the vital support coming from concrete experience of listening to inspirational stories, etc. These pillars that nurture the future ability of visualisation are prematurely skipped.

ఞ ఞ

CRYSTALLISED HEMISPHERES REFLECT, EXPRESS AND REACT
(Consequence of which is seen in global societies)

A left-brain dominated society converts every spiritual and artistic contribution (right brain) into a marketable commodity. On one hand, large quantities of milk was destroyed due to surplus and poor profit, while simultaneously, in a society close by the discovery of increasing milk production by injecting cows with drugs was practiced. We bombed whole populations, and on the other hand, organised relief foundations like Red Cross Society to aid the disabled and provide burial services to the dead. We fought legal and armed battles to decide who holds the rights to water a particular tree, while the tree is actually dying or dead. Our loveless, heartless, cold and calculating commerce rests upon a plethora of dead religious formulae of precept, precedent and is considered the crown of such left-brain dominant societies. These instances illustrate deranged hemispherical decisions that manoeuvre social order. It is no wonder that people opt for spirituality when they find themselves buried in the dire consequences of living an imbalanced life. The surge in Zen and Vedantic spiritual teachings spreading across America and Europe is not without relation to hemispherical influence. On a mass scale, hemispherical dominance rose from the nature of work, too rapid a scientific progress and an artificial mode of social life. People of western countries drawn to the 'no-mind' of Zen or to the 'Self beyond the mind' of Vedanta sought relief from the exerted left-brain. The Zen No-Mind and Advaitic teachings say that there is none other than Self, both of which suggest the limitation, the invalidity and the illusive nature of mind. Those who find nourishment through this are either intellectually-obsessed or approach life with comparative and relative conceptualisation. Interestingly, people from Africa or west Asia show little interest in Zen and Vedanta. Their lives are full of physical hard work and strong emotional and often fanatical attachment to religion, caste, tribes and race. People of underdeveloped and developing countries are excessively conditioned in the right-hemisphere which is why they fight for religion, creed, caste and communal differences.

ಸಿ ಧ

ARE THERE ANSWERS

To be free from both extremities and to be able to stand in idyllic natural balance, an integral education is needed. The coming generations should claim their right for a total integral education as individual transformation leads to a collective one. Educational systems should teach science and art subjects alternatively and timetables can be drawn up with attention to blend subjects in a balanced way. The intent should be to educate the whole of the brain. A fresh perspective to what a child actually absorbs would be useful. An over-feeding of large amounts of data just to achieve new standards is shameful. Wouldn't it be more important to verify how much of what is taught is actually assimilated and actualised in a child's daily living? Learning is authentic only if the child assimilates the information and is able to enjoy it as a living experience. Several schools and education centres are now incorporating methods such as juggling of balls, optical illusions and other games and tests that encourage a balanced hemispherical development. The Siddhas recommend letting go of ideational accumulation so that lives hanging from the hooks of 'ideational world' stagnation can naturally fall into their existential conditioning or the imperatives of life. Magic hides in daily life. Unfolding true potential in spiritual life lies hidden in what has been given.

> "Once Narada, the mischievous sage, came to Mount Kailash for the *Darshan* of Lord Siva. Goddess Parvathi welcomed him. It had been long since he had visited the Lord. Narada offered his salutations to both. 'Does your visit here have a purpose, Narada?' asked Goddess Parvathi. Narada nodded. Lord Siva said, 'Yes, wherever you go, Narada, you start a play by creating an unresolved situation. Today you have chosen my place!' Narada replied, 'Oh Mahadeva! You are the great player. *Leelas* are your profession not mine!'
>
> 'Ok Narada, you have come here with some idea so why the delay?' said Lord Siva. Narada held forth a mango fruit toward Goddess Parvathi and said, 'This is a rare mango and is called the wisdom fruit (gnana palam). Eating it can make you a *Gnani.*' Surprised, Goddess Parvathi said, 'O really? Then

both my sons, Ganesha and Subramaniam can share half and half.' Narada prompted, 'No *Ma*, the fruit should not be cut. It should be eaten whole or it will have no effect.' At this point Lord Siva spoke, 'Narada, you have done your job here!' At this crucial moment, Ganesha and Subramaniam, their two sons playfully skipped in. Seeing the mango they both asked for it. Mother Parvathi grew sad. Lord Siva said, 'The fruit of wisdom should be given to the deserving one.' Sage Narada nodded in agreement. Turning to Parvathi Lord Siva said, 'Put our sons through a test.' 'But how?' asked Mother Parvathi. 'The one who travels around the world and returns first will be the winner of this fruit,' he replied. Hearing this Subramaniam, the second son said, 'Oh, it is easy. I can do it in a second.' He alighted his peacock to around the world. Everybody turned to Ganesha to see what he would do. Ganesha was calm. He asked Narada, 'What is meant by 'world' and what is meant by 'mother and father'?' Narada replied, 'The world is mother and father and mother and father are the world.' Ganesha's eyes opened wide, 'Thank you Narada.' Ganesha walked around his parents, Lord Siva and Goddess Parvathi, saluted them and graciously received the fruit.

A tricky situation most often brings anxiety; a 'reactive linear approach' that prevents us from seeing the solution. A person mature in emotion as well as perception is naturally competent to recognise the complimentary side of anything but present day society operates on a linear mentality. It tends to separate the complimentary feminine and render it as 'opposite'. For instance, sleeping is labelled as an inactive state instead of being considered as 'refreshing our ground for the next day'. The utilitarian attitude fails to see all utility arising from the ground of non-utility. Society pushes us to be competitive right from early years. They call it 'survival of the fittest'. Psychologists say a good psyche comes by

CHAPTER EIGHT: ARDHANAREESWARA

strengthening the ego. Positive thinking workshops are based on inculcating the masculine aspect.

We miss to recognise the place of real strength; of being flexible and nurturing the spirit of a 'yielding' approach. Man's fear of the feminine aspect of his psyche comes from its suppression due to masculine overemphasis. By persistently suppressing the feminine spectrum, man ends up with a purely competitive social structure which is calculative, mechanical, overly technological, jealous, and violent

Lord Subramaniam is the God of "accomplishment' and Lord Ganesha the 'remover of obstacles and the commencer of new beginnings'. Lord Ganesha is the inspiration aspect of accomplishment! The accomplishing or acquiring spirit is masculine with attributes like calculative planning or the stages of 'doing'. But the spirit of inspiration is feminine that unleashes strength to accomplishment. Lastly, our relationship with the world is determined by the quality of relationship we share with our parents. Growing up in a good-natured environment with the mother develops a balanced feminine aspect and sharing a good-natured relationship with the father reflects as matured performance later in life. The world begins from one's mother and father and Lord Ganesha, the source of divine inspiration, to burn all obstacles circumambulated his parents!

ಸಂ ಆ

BALANCING THE HEMISPHERES

Four different practical aids have been described below:

- Marching exercise
- Swara Yoga
- Omkar Breathing
- Nadi Suddhi Practice

A predominant hemisphere can be brought to balance by consistently following techniques given below.

- Marching Exercise

Imagine yourself as a puppet with strings at the knees and fingertips. Standing, raise your right foot, bent at the knee until your right thigh is parallel to the floor (as if you are climbing a high step). As you lift the right foot, simultaneously raise the left arm and reach high, fingers pointing to the ceiling. Keep the arm close to the ear. Keep your other arm relaxed. Do the same on the other side: lift the left foot and right arm in the same manner; thus shifting the weight from side to side. Coordinate the movement of your arm and foot, so both reach the peak at the same time. For around two minutes, keep alternating these movements in a vigorous manner; marching. Rest for two minutes and repeat. Do this three times. Begin with one minute of movement, then rest; and build to two or three minutes of movement with rest periods in between.

- Swara Yoga - The Science of Breath under the Yogic dimension of the Siddhas and its relation to the harmonious function of hemispheres.

Avvai Kural, chapter 11

> "The breath pass in and out by left side
> At (the dawn of) Friday, Wednesday and Monday."
>
> Verse-2

> "The breath pass in and out on right nostril
> At (the dawn of) Tuesday, Saturday and Sunday."
>
> Verse-3

CHAPTER EIGHT: ARDHANAREESWARA

> "On Thursday during the waxing moon and waning moon day,
> Breath will pass in and out on-left
> During the other waxing moon days, on right nostril."
>
> Verse 4

The flow of breath holds many secrets! According to astrology, the first hour of each day is under the governance of a particular planet. Likewise the flow of breath at daybreak has a rhythmic path alternating through the nostrils, every one or two hours through the day. The breath begins the day (one hour before sunrise) and ends the day (beginning of sunset) through the same nostril. Through the day, it changes course every one or two hours alternating from right to left and left to right. A change in this rhythm indicates an illness on the horizon. Siddhas' Swara Yoga deals exclusively with indications of health and life incidents based on the principles of the cycle of breath. The nostril through which the breath flows indicates the mode of energy currently available to the body which is a practical key used to consciously attune one's behaviour. To find through which nostril you presently are breathing, close the right nostril with one finger, inhale deeply and exhale the breath through the left. Then close the left nostril, inhale deeply and exhale through your right. After two or three times, you will recognise which nostril breath is dominant, similar to which hemisphere is predominant.

The connect between the right and left breath and the hemispheres of the brain has been only recently scientifically understood. The dominating hemisphere is the one opposite to the dominant breath side. In Yogic Physiology, the flow of breath through the left nostril is called lunar breath (Chandra Swara) and is influenced by 'Ida nadi' and the breath flowing through the right nostril is solar breath (Surya Swara) and is influenced by the 'Pingala Nadi'. The breath establishes our relationship with the nature of the

Inner Moon (passive, intuitive, surrendering) and with the nature of the Inner Sun (active, rational, will-oriented). The left nostril lunar-breathing is feminine and is primarily influenced by the lunar cycles, lunar planets and by the days of feminine nature (Monday, Wednesday and Friday). The day-to-day health of our body-mind is reflected in the synchronicity of our alternating breath cycle with the external world. An overly-predominant breath in any one nostril signals stress in one of the hemispheres. Swara Yoga plays a vital role in Siddha Tantra and Yogic system. Swara Yoga is the base in Astrology, Kundalini Yoga, herbal and alchemical preparations, etc.

ಸಿ ಇ

Methods to shift the breath from one nostril to another in Swara Yoga of the Siddha System:

Standing Position:

> In a standing position, use the right toe to press down on the left toe. While breathing keep the stomach in a mid-position (not pushing out, not pulling in). Soon the breath will shift to the left nostril. If you do the opposite, it will shift the breath to the right.

Sitting Position:

> Keep the left hand slightly behind you, using the ground for support and/or even placing the left shoulder against the wall. In that sitting position lean to the left, bend both knees, placing feet on the ground before you. Bring the left heel close to the right buttock and let the knees fall to the left, so the left bent leg lies on the floor and the bent right leg is

over it. Using the thumb and middle finger of the right hand, press the right ankle, with your thumb resting on the back of the Achilles tendon and the middle finger in front, at the mid-ankle point, pressing on the tendon coming from the big toe to the ankle. Apply light pressure to this tendon repeatedly, by pressing and releasing the middle finger. The breath will shift to the right nostril, crossing Sushumna Cave behind the forehead. Repeat the procedure on the opposite side of the body to change the breath to the left nostril.

Reclining Position:

Lie on the left side, pulling in the left elbow towards the left side of the chest. Support your head with the left open palm beneath your left ear. Both legs are extended, the right leg resting atop the left leg. Let the straight right arm rest on the right side of the body. Soon the breath will shift to the right nostril. One can also sleep in this position at night.

- Omkar Breathing

Actions and behaviours are also ruled and motivated by keywords. The ancient martial arts system, *Kalari-Varma*, has a practice called '*Vaithari*', where words and movements are simultaneously coordinated. When speech and body movements coordinate, synchronise and get simultaneously expressed, a communication between the two hemispheres takes place. This is the fundamental principle an expert practitioner in *Varma* Martial Arts uses to create whole-body alertness and sensitivity to his surrounding. Esoteric martial art terms it 'when the whole body becomes the eye'. These practices are done under the supervision of a teacher. In this book,

I recommend the Omkar breathing technique - of sound and breath coordination.

The Tamil, 'AUM' is written as above. It is a spiral form i.e. converging in a particular spot. 'AUM' is the *Bija Mantra* (seed mantra) of the Mooladharam chakra, in the Siddha path. This mantra is the upholder of all deities residing in other chakras. Chanting the mantra 'AUM' is most invigorating as it creates a coordinated vibration that resonates within the entire system. The harmonious vibration ultimately leads to spiritual dimensions. It also benefits the physical body by creating new cells, by removing unwanted toxins, by calming mind-agitation and soothing the nerves.

Chanting AUM coordinated with breath:

AUM is the sound of Universal energy, from which all things manifest. All words are fragments of AUM, just as all images are fragments of the cosmic picture. AUM is the symbolic sound that brings you in touch with the 'resounding being'; the Universe. A-U-M symbolises birth, coming into being and the dissolution that cycles back. AUM is called the 'four-element-syllable', and what is the fourth syllable? The silence out of which AUM arises and falls back into. The underlying substratum of Silence.

Start in the back of the mouth, 'aah' and then 'ooh'. Fill the mouth, and 'mm' closes the mouth. When you chant, all vowel sounds are included. Breathe in first, filling the abdomen from the mid-thorax to the upper thorax; hold the breath for 5 seconds, and breathe out chanting 'AAAAAA', continuing 'OOOO' and finishing with 'MMMM'. While doing this, place your attention on the heart centre. The vibration of 'AUM' harmonises any dissipation of energy and slows down the heartbeat. A perfect rhythm is necessary for attaining mastery in this practice. If practiced properly and regularly, it stimulates the five vital forces of the subtle body, increases flow of energy to the five senses and clears obstructions in energy channels. It reduces fear, anxiety and stress. This practice can be undertaken ten times in the early morning and ten times in the evening.

- Nadi Suddhi Practice:
  (Chanting AUM a single time, 1 matrai is equal to 1 second)
  Sit in a comfortable and relaxed position, keeping the back and neck comfortably straight. Place your right thumb against your right nostril and the index and middle fingers between the eyebrows. The ring finger should be on the left nostril. Exhale through both nostrils, slowly and completely. Closing your right nostril with your thumb, inhale slowly and silently through your left nostril for 5-matrai potential. At the end of inhalation, close the left nostril, release your right nostril and exhale slowly through it for 5-matrai potential period. At the end of the exhalation and without pausing, begin to inhale through the right nostril, (the same nostril that was just used for exhalation). Inhale slowly for 5-matrai period. Now close the right nostril and release the left one, and exhale slowly for 5 matrai. Complete the exhalation. This completes the first round, as the original starting point is reached. Without interruption, this practice can be done for ten rounds. One can attempt to maintain a rhythm without actually counting. This practice must be done on an empty stomach and should not be undertaken for more than ten minutes until one attains mastery. Keep in mind that the use of fingers is temporary and that ultimately one uses will to alternate the right and left breath by thought.

SECTION THREE
BEING AND SHARING

Yogic and Tantric System
of the Siddhas

CHAPTER NINE

INTRODUCTION TO THE YOGIC SYSTEM

THE WAY OF THE SIDDHAS

> "Sleeping, envisioned Siva's world in themselves
> Sleeping, envisioned Siva's Yoga in themselves
> Sleeping, envisioned Siva's Bhoga in themselves
> How then speak of the state, those who slept, envisioned?"
> Thirumanthiram, Verse 129, By Siddha Thirumoolar

It was once hoped that modern science would rid us of all superstition, human problems and solve the mysteries of the world. But making sense of a cluster of multiple approaches is much harder - and today, knowledge can disable. The way of the Siddhas de-conditions the inessential and provides grounding in the Existential, which leads one beyond - to the Unconditioned. They speak of two types of conditioning, Acquired and Existential, present day examples and instances of which are described as seen commonly in all of human society today.

Does wisdom of Ancient Siddha Yoga hold true for today's fast paced life? Massive industrial revolution has made us more automated but modernism has also brought exclusivity, singularity and separation. Experts, consultants, specialised jobs, specialised professions, specialised doctors of medicine, etc. are trending and multiple opportunities are flooding the career market. Everything is readily available to all. Streams of opportunities allow high-end qualifications and proficiency in specific fields. 'Specialisation' is choosing one and leaving the rest, and is better defined as 'isolated study'. It has brought adversity in the form of fragmentation. Knowledge and experience can no longer be called holistic. True knowledge brims with awareness of the inter-connectedness and understanding of the whole. So, even though new age prospects appear unlimited, glamorous and inviting, they provide isolated knowledge instead of wholesome deep-rooted experience. Yoga is most commonly called 'a practice of Asanas for health purposes'. Yoga classes are fit into busy schedules to manage stress. The new age idea of yoga cannot be more further from the truth and is titbit knowledge that makes for nothing more than superficial change. New age yoga is not about transformation and the core of our being remains hidden and untouched. Transformation, in the post-modern world means 'adding to what you already have', and not, 'losing what you don't need'. We cram office yoga, meditative cooking, healing vastu, management program on vedic thought, and Bhagavat Gita classes into our life. But meditation is not a solid, concrete activity and cannot be added to current activities! Meditation is the quality reflecting off the activity you are involved in! It is true, anything can be meditative, but effort to make something meditative? Effort is the part creating conflict.

    Today's 'individual' is 'a reaction of many'. Trapped in a multitude of circumstances, he is constantly reacting to oncoming influence and yet believes his actions to be of his own accord. But most of his actions come from a bunch of entangled, confused ideas called mechanical reactions which are all he has. Man is under the illusion of having one steady self. Present day spiritual teachings insist upon finding the 'Self' by understanding the illusory nature of "I'; or one's limited 'self'. How can man recognise his limited self while under the sway of multiple ones? When man is living with multiple inconsistent and incompatible selfs, is it even possible to act with any one specific attitude? Can any activity enjoy a wholesome channelled flow? With so many centres fighting to be the main base, the Socratic Maxim should now read 'Know Themselves'. Having a single belief structure plays a vital role in life, but then maybe the very nature of belief has changed. Very few adhere to one solid belief. Most are won over by several often conflicting beliefs and the majority feel justified in moving through different, changing belief systems, sometimes even in the course of a single day! Man moves from (re)action to (re)action, without any attitudinal link. He puts on many masks, and has no degree of clarity to what he truly is, what his goal is and what are the guiding principles of his life. He is a fragmented entity, fashioned from the bulk of many impositions. Caught in a constant state of anxiety, he lives a fragmented, confused life, alienated from his nature. The only individuality he knows and asserts is his 'prejudices'. He is his prejudice.

> "Madu than analum oru pokkundu
> Manitharkku athuvum illaiappa"

> "Even a bullock walks his own pace
> But man doesn't have even that."
>
> Agasthiyar Gnanam 6, Verse-2

ಲ ೧೩

Flow of life is, constantly swinging multiple energy levels transpiring within us and the entire living community. We constantly derive and spend energy through breath, food, thought, environment, etc. We experience constant change in inner energy levels and operate from these ever-shifting resources. Individual and collective factors contribute to this ever-shifting energy-phenomenon and unless we are careful, we grow conditioned under its weight. Conditioning puts on layers that interfere and digress from the original impetus of life, which brings ill health, disease and suffering. The way to reclaim our unconditioned nature is following a yogic way of life, which is shedding inessentials and imbibing a holistic attitude to living. The present day dense and unforgiving conditions have taken the mind-body much farther from simplicity, making it much harder to cut through the multiple conditioning hiding our true nature. From the current complex energy maze, can the wisdom of true yoga teach humanity the yoga of relationship and art of living? Can we shed the conditioning?

ACQUIRED CONDITIONING
THE INDIVIDUAL DOMAIN

Pavlov, the famous Russian psychologist, once performed an experiment. Before feeding the dog, he rang a bell. After a period, he noticed the dog would salivate each time he rang the bell. The dog acquired a conditioning connected to food. The dog's survival instinct converted into a reflex conditioning under the influence of its surrounding. The human brain also functions on associative memory. We rarely adore a flower for its beauty and mostly associate, interpret and link it to prior experience. We end up seeing our own likes and dislikes - not the actual. The first approach is an existential experience; the second is interpretative, ideational one. Association is the only way mind keeps memory and mind needs memory to re-live experiences and perpetuate itself! The longing to perpetuate comes from the mind's anxiety of non-being. We derive a pseudo sense of being from an association with the 'other'. Not accepting the natural existence of what already is, we prefer to impose our idea and bring conceptual existence in, personalising a simple natural happening. The tendency to acquire by association is a reflex conditioning that eventually hampers man's health and individual domain. Heavy consumerism, cut-throat competitiveness, environmental destruction and a horrifying rise in addiction and terrorism form the part of the social conditioning we live by. Disease, disorders, habits, behaviour, choices, lifestyle and mental makeup are conditioned factors of the individual domain. Obesity is not a natural state of health. It is derived off simultaneous, conflicting reactions on the part of an individual as the persuasive nature of post-modernism overpowers man's natural faculty of discrimination. We ignore natural wisdom and push away simplicity in exchange for 'more' and 'better', rising from a deep sense of deprivation. We make an arbitrary settlement for pseudo satisfaction using a substituting approach - a masking game. Unnatural and insensitive eating habits trying to fill the lack of nourishment lead to obesity. Today, obesity is a common disease as the body-mind weigh heavy with acquired conditioning. A majority of people choose fasting as a method of weight reduction but for most, it ends up aggravating the condition. In my healing experience, I found a common factor tying most obesity-related cases. Irregular intake of food and virtually no routine. I recommended a basic lifestyle change. Eating at regular times and in case they missed the allotted time, they should try to skip that meal altogether and eat at the next allotted mealtime. With an irregular and inconsistent intake of food, the brain messages the body to hold on and store the nutrients coming from food as it is never sure when the next meal will come (a *kapham* tendency). A conditioned memory of starvation signals the brain to store as protective measure.

When habitual consumers of meat suddenly change to eating small vegetarian meals, they often suffer acid-related disorders such as acid eructation, bilious headaches and ulcers, etc. How does a positive diet change cause adverse reaction? Long-term habits turn to conditioning. A brain conditioned to secrete bile for meat could not incorporate the sudden change. Inappropriate bile secretion leads to acidity-based disorders. Abruptly breaking a conditioning triggers an angry revolt from the ego, called 'withdrawal symptoms'. According to the Siddha system, six tastes nourish the body which explains how food influences our body and mind. In turn, the ego is nurtured by identifying with the body as well as the influence of the six tastes. Food connects to ego and mind-set. So, there is no harm breaking old habits but it should be done using a suitable, gradual approach.

Diseases don't fall into our bodies from the skies... we create them. We create disease by insensitive lifestyle, food habits and erratic perceptions. A long time smoker's throat and lungs become desensitised which affects his breathing channels. In reaction to the demand, there is an increase in cell growth in the breathing channels. The affected area starts creating its own localised territory to demand identity. When we ignore or suppress a part of our body, it longs for identity and to fulfil that it generates an abnormal growth in cells to re-establish presence. It creates a localised ego. This is Cancer triggered by mind-set or lifestyle, the individual domain.

૪૦ ୡ

SOCIAL DOMAIN

Adulterated food, crops and vegetables cultivated by chemical fertilisers are major causes of cancer. Causes sprouting from society as a whole are more or less unavoidable acquired conditioning we are subject to. Chemically fertilised food, processed food and allopathic drugs cause disorders of the glandular system. Another socially-acquired conditioning is stress. Unable to change the root cause, people follow fitness programmes, yoga, meditation, tai chi, etc. to reduce stress. Even though these methods may help the nervous system, the glandular system remains untouched as it depends on food. Such substitute approaches could disconnect us from our sensitivity and an ignored body sooner or later rebels and gets sick. Illness and pain turn our attention inward and we come to face our conditioned mind making even the most stubborn people, flexible. It is nature's call for de-conditioning. Another collective conditioning we subjugate ourself to are pills. Techno-pharmacies manufacture painkillers, antibiotics, sedatives and sleeping pills - all of which make us mechanical and chemical. Unfortunately, rigid post-modern lifestyle pushes the body-mind to its limits until it is forced to send out a drastic alarm. Too many alarms and we pay the price. Due to deterioration of natural habitat and growing pollution, there is a rising scarcity of natural herbs. On the other hand, even the number of native healers are dwindling. Indians doubt and fear their own ancient healing system for its lack of scientific documentation and are leaning toward modern medicine, while the West is turning toward alternative healing systems. Along with technological advances, India has hastily adopted the likes of chemotherapy, diet supplements, etc., forgetting that less than hundred years ago, India depended entirely on ancient medicinal and healing values. Ironically, the common man is in the dark about the hidden agenda of specialised sectors of camouflaging the truth in pursuit of monetary interest. This discussion intends to draw attention to our choice of life-shaping factors. Every choice indirectly or directly is a life-governing principle and misinformed ones collectively contribute to a weak and unhealthy social structure.

Western medicine is another intimidating conditioning of our social domain where theory is learnt through autopsies, examination of tissue under microscopes, blood, urine and other isolated analysis of the body, etc. Even the anatomy of 'living beings' is learnt from a dead one! Experiments are carried out on animals. Health is managed through hospitals, not rehabilitating health farms. One might think the true purpose of health insurance to be prevention or health care, and not a paying proposition or financial compensation for treatment post illness. The hypothesis of advanced medical science is built on fear of death and suffering - conditioning society with a pessimistic outlook to life and humanity. Western medicine learns from death and disease, not life and healing.

Western medicine criticises Siddha, Ayurveda, and Unani medicinal systems for using metals and mercury. This is well known. An article in 'New Scientist Magazine' dated May 30th 2006, is about the use of mercury as vaccines. The article states how vaccines turned poisonous due to an adverse amount of mercury content and lead to juvenile diseases like autism, asthma, diabetes, etc. Some common flu vaccines are found to contain mercury, which proves hundreds of times more toxic than hazardous waste. The world has no clue of the number of vaccine-toxic bodies walking the earth today. Modern day health industry defines health in 'numbers' - calories and nutrients. They reduce a complex living phenomenon to caloric counts, age-height ratios and weight measures. Calorie charts and dietary tables state the amount of vitamins, minerals and protein a man or woman should receive in a day. One such table states, an average person should intake 3000 calories per day. Another one states, 11 calories per day, per pound of weight just to meet the basic metabolic needs and then to increase according to the demand of work, i.e. if engaged in heavy work. Neither of them specify the ratio between the calories of carbohydrate, fat or proteins. Take carbohydrates, for example. Should they be taken cooked or uncooked, refined or unrefined, processed or unprocessed? And what should the ratio between calories and nutrient density be? Should we dare to imagine how far we have gone from nature? Thousands of research papers each year declare the importance of vitamins, proteins and minerals but without holistic knowledge of the human metabolism, an excess of single supplement can easily damage the metabolic process. It is not easy to know precisely when the body utilises its own reserves and when it draws from food.

But with each day on a schedule, we are compelled to ignore instinct. Several diseases spurt from time-factor conditioning. Hypertension, panic attacks, headaches, acidity, psychiatric disorders and other stress-related disorders are common complaints. People pop pills to cope. Instant-relief medicines are promoted through commercials and are a part of every home. Accepted for instant effectivity, the common man has little knowledge of its dangers. Steroids are used for speedy relief from even common ailments. All these methods bypass the vital process of recuperation by overriding body-intelligence and assaulting hormone function. Either way we continue to push the body beyond natural boundaries by popping a pill. We are that far from our existential nature.

The glamorous sensational media is another psychologically contagious persuasion. Uncensored exposure at an alarmingly early age has contaminated pure young minds with improper perceptions, violent notions and straying ideology. Such early contamination only multiplies with age. Early sex is a part of this alarming change. As per primal archetypes, this aspect of life blooms within the psyche after the mind and body get groomed into readiness, by Existence. But social life has indiscriminately and liberally crossed the natural boundaries and brought in illicit relationships, pre-marital pregnancy, child pregnancy and divorce along with a hoard of physical and psychological disorders. Family values have been hastily discarded and chastity is outdated! The early exposure speeds up the mind and by middle age, one is bored and yet incomplete. The speeding mind pushes on and ends up crossing more boundaries in search of thrill and satisfaction. We take whatever society offers. We don't discriminate. We feed our children junk food. We live on painkillers and sleeping pills to cope the next day. We buy health insurance for when we get sick and live in fear of disease. We vaccinate ourselves. We obsess with calorie charts to bring health. We run by time-management and play the role of the post modern man - hungry for success. And we turn a blind eye to the deterioration in human nature. This is proof enough of growing insensitivity toward oneself and toward biological wisdom.

There is a link between Life and Health!

Health is a spontaneous, dynamic, nurturing pulsation. Rejuvenating trillions of cells, our healing intelligence resides somewhere in this amazing complexity. The human body's native intelligence runs the body so that you can live your life. Come to think of it, until you don't suffer a headache, you don't think of the head. Each cell, within and around, is governed by native intelligence. Health becomes Life! As long as life exists, health flourishes. If living is the capacity to heal then health is inherent and natural. Anything existential remains dynamic if potent spontaneity continues to flow. The living body, an organised pharmacy, produces healing resources in timely optimal levels/dosage with zero side-effects. It is skilled at extracting minerals, vitamins and salts from the food we eat. The body stores and utilises specific quantities of vitamins. Do we really need to invest, research, manufacture and externally consume what already exists within? Additional supplements and vitamins tend to overload our system fairly quickly. Sensing the overload, the nervous system initiates an additional task to either temporarily dump the excess somewhere in the system or eliminate it for which the body shifts to an agitated mode. Ironically, this stepping up of metabolic activity is what makes us 'feel' good and eventually this boost becomes habitual. When the intake is stopped, the body evidently suffers deprivation and sinks to an unexpected fast felt low which is NOT a disease. It is a reaction. Indiscriminate consumption of vitamins, mineral, supplements disturbs the native intelligence. And the reason we might feel the need for additional vitamins or supplements is only when our food contains poor levels of natural enzymes responsible for strengthening the endocrine gland and its hormones. But all in all, supplements are fundamentally pseudo-nutrition. The body recognises food, fruits, vegetables, nuts, sprouts, etc. as it chews, digests, extracts and absorbs nutrients, vitamins, etc. in its rhythmic process. Readymade vitamins, mineral supplements, in direct form, bypass these vital processes and change the inner rhythm. With this happening repeatedly or daily, the native intelligence renders that process obsolete and inessential, so when the vitamins/supplements arrive in direct form, the body sees it as overload and experiences internal stress. This stress sends panic signals to other areas of the body which leads to complexities.

ಖಿ ಆ

INTELLIGENT BODY

I observed a common factor tying most cases of prolonged bacterial infection - anaemia. Bacteria multiplies where iron is abundant! Which is why the body takes away some amount of iron-content from the circulatory system and transforms it into another tissue (*Thathu*). Intentionally throwing the body into an anaemic state is a protective measure. The native intelligence withdraws bacterial support thereby preventing the spread of infection. A blood report at this point would indicate anaemia but it must be understood that this is pseudo-anaemia and should not be medicated as a primary treatment. The healing approach of the Siddha system instead of attending to the infection, focuses on eliminating the bodily circumstance the infection is using for survival. The body already performs all functions the medicine aims to, which is why the Siddhas' way is to accelerate, not over-ride native intelligence of the body. For instance, in my opinion several phlegmatic diseases are due to heat and not cold in the body. In tropical countries, common symptoms are runny nose, eosinophilia, recurrent sneezing, allergic rhinitis, fever, etc. In the case of runny nose suffered by a *Vatham/Pittam*-dominant individual, the pulse showed accumulated stale heat in the lower abdomen, particularly urinary tract area. Now, cool energy by nature travels downward and heat upward. Eating foods of cooling properties or taking a cold shower first thing in the morning evaporates the stale heat of the lower abdomen, and phlegm begins to collect in the upper regions which the body eliminates by a runny nose, sneezing or fever combined with a cold. Reverse osmosis happens through the *nadis* connecting the urinary tract region to nasal cavities. As another instance, heat can accumulate even due to sexual intercourse which explains the common phrase, 'honeymoon sneezing'. Stagnant heat must be eliminated through frequent urination and the simple remedy of drinking warm water cools the body by flushing out unwanted heat. Frequent urination during the monsoons or winter is also an example as it is the only appropriate and possible process of heat elimination from the body in such weather conditions due to reduced sweating. Bilious discomfort, vomiting or sudden diarrhoea is commonly seen as illness but most often (for a *Pittam* constitution) it is the body eliminating excess *Pittam*. It would be a mistake to interrupt this natural cleansing by taking allopathic medication as it would open our body to skin disease, severe itching, red heat rashes, etc. Discrimination is vital before medicating the body. And it is better not to forget, our body is communicative and intelligent.

CHAPTER NINE: INTRODUCTION TO THE YOGIC SYSTEM

COMPENSATING PROCESS

In order to prevent chemical deficiency, the body secretes each chemical in two or more places. For instance, a major percentage of erythropoietin is produced in the kidneys. In case of low oxygen in the blood, this chemical reaches the bone morrow *Thathu* and the formation of blood starts from there. In cases with both kidneys showing poor function, the liver can produce this chemical too. Siddhas founded the *Varmam* system based on this very premise of all causative bio-factors created in this holistic way. When one gland is weak, another gland is activated to take over through *Varmam* treatment. This intelligence works through the *Prana* which is why *Varmam*, Yoga and Tantra of the Siddhas hold the working knowledge of this pulsation in high regard. The human body is a nexus of multi-participants in continuum with each other.

Spontaneous cancer regression continues to puzzle western medicine. But the body knows. The living system is a symbiotic integrated process; everything happening at once, in sync and support. Nourishment is nature forging a relationship to awaken the connect between the human bio-system and life, which analytical data cannot comprehend. This nourishing relationship is a living phenomenon - life form gives itself up to transform into another. Giving the body its rightful place is true transcendence of the body. Responsibility is the ability to respond and man has the individual and social responsibility to restore his personal and collective universe into a state of harmony. Life, by its very movement, calls us to engage in its flow to be alive. To be alive, is to respond to one's 'life-calling'; responsibly living in connect anywhere within the continuum - is Life. But post-modern educated citizens fail to illustrate harmony and expanse - the tribals do. Having lived with tribals up in the mountains, I have seen unbelievable sensitivity towards Existence. They sense oncoming events, rainfall and even an approaching wild animal. They chase away snakes or poisonous insects by emitting specific sounds. These commonly used faculties appear strange and miraculous to the urban man. They live in self-referral, depending on themselves for survival, not upon a mechanical social structure. They live free of conflict with their surrounding. Living by existential conditioning taps into our faculties and inherent potential - here emerges authentic living.

༄༅

MECHANICAL PATTERN OF MIND IN DAILY LIFE

Is 'Work' the opposite of 'Play'? Both are actions! Work makes man time and self-conscious; Play helps man forget his self-obsession. Work is a time-bound daily pattern, defined by rules and norms, consciously restricting free movement and activity. Action is movement in relationship. When movement is restricted by a quantitative approach to increase efficiency and productivity in pursuit of 'more', it splits natural action into Work and Play or Conformity and Release. Soon 'Work' turns repetitive, compulsive, mechanical and renders the mind uncreative. Many argue work as being productive. If it is not creative, it is nothing more than a psychological and social fixation dulling us by its monotony - an imposed mechanical life pattern. This imposition gives birth to a persistent need for release and we seek freedom through recreation, entertainment, excitement, thrill, addiction - a temporary escape.

Life is movement; a network of relationships based on action. Action gives experience. A joyous experience fuels the desire for more. Identifying with joy flowing from creative action crystallises into a goal and turns into an ego-centre. The desire to achieve 'more' is the drive for ego-expansion, responsible for the games we play to acquire false images. It triggers ruthless competition and weaves perverted multiple personalities in a person. Acquisitive restrictive action within a social structure self-perpetuates into mechanical patterns but action free of ego-consciousness does not degrade into self-perpetuated activity! By restricting natural action to a self-motivated activity called 'Work', we mutilate it.

ACTION AS IT IS...

Action coming from the core of life and the love of heart is Creative. Creative action implies no time barriers, no fragmented mind and no division. Creative action is whole, is its own means as well as end. Being creative, it looks for no reward being complete and incomparable. One cannot restrict creative action only to the likes of art, poetry, painting, etc. Creative action is the essence emerging from the immediate perception of the Whole; the unanimity of life. It is that which does not proceed from self-motive and so is free from the expectation of the outcome. Creative work is spontaneous and unconditioned! To know this, Mindfulness is the key.

WHOLENESS OF LIFE

To realise one's unconditional nature, one's conditioned state (acquired conditioning) needs de-conditioning. De-conditioning of the inessentials introduces one into existential conditioning or one's natural qualities and potential. A Siddha Master uses two approaches along the path of Siddha Yoga. De-conditioning of the inessential nature and grounding in existential conditioning. Ultimately, this leads beyond, to the Unconditional.

REALISING ENERGY PHENOMENA

Siddha Sage Valmiki says,
"Varuvathilum povathilum manathai vai."

Translation:
"Keep the attention of your mind in that which comes and goes."

Siddha practitioners, obsessive in breathing methods, interpret the above verse as "Put your attention on the incoming and outgoing breath" which is a limited perception. The state of mind is in a state of constant flux and to realise the nature of life force, one must perceive both externally and internally the cyclic phenomena of energy acquisition, conservation and depletion.

ENERGY SPENDING

A smoker after several smokes feels spent and to replenish himself eats. He experiences a rise of unassimilated energy and he smokes again, which is an insensitive catharsis that in due course fuels a meaningless attitude. An attitude inevitably spreads to all dimensions thus leading him to a meaningless life. Insensitivity to the phenomenon of energy conservation and its significance, the smoker's attitude stands applicable to all.

Losing peace of mind over trifles, we dissipate energy by giving vent to our anger. This is not constructive. Energy dissipates with each of the outward-bound million thoughts and agitations we suffer by the minute! Energy is constantly squandering away in a million different directions. Earlier, we read of energy stimulation and how receiving a large sum of money or getting a promotion can suddenly fill us with a burst of energy. The question to be asked is, do we conserve or dissipate this energy? Drinking, bragging, or stoking jealous opponents sound like common and insignificant catharsis. But consider the implications for a freshly-elected minister of a power position who names his impulsive reactions his decisions. This would end up affecting the entire social order. We are not self-aware of the energy-dissipating tendencies that arise on the accumulation of sudden energy which come because of a poor inner ground and the ignorance of energy conservation. Conserved energy held within firm ground is a platform for a meaningful living; a life where actions are channelled and energy is integrated, neither of which are nurtured in people today.

ಙಃ ಇಃ

PRIORITY LIST _ SWEPT OUT FROM UNDER!

"Once a teenage friend was expecting some money. He planned to join a computer course. When I visited him next, I found him listening to music on a new tape recorder! It cost Rs. 600/-. He said he had saved Rs.400/- and would replenish the Rs.600/- from the cash gifts of his upcoming birthday and join the computer class. But I knew he would just purchase something else. He hadn't been aware but the tape recorder had been his first priority all along." We all have priority lists hidden away from ordinary awareness. Priorities connect to associated energy levels and come alive the moment we experience that energy state which explains why my friend's decision to study computers didn't last very long. The moment he received the money, his energy shifted and out popped the associated priority - a tape recorder. Our relationship with material form is entirely energy-based. Latent desires cling to corresponding energy levels and a spike of energy could sweep out deep-rooted ones, demanding impulsive fulfilment.

ENERGY CONSERVATION

Siddhas mention two ways for energy conservation; familiarity or discrimination. To grow familiar with different life aspect energies by consciously attuning to them, practices such as the meditative stance mentioned in *Varmam* Chapter make one aware of their current energy levels. I also recommend deep belly breathing from personal experience. It creates 'grounding' by balancing the position of the solar plexus and is an efficient method for energy conservation. Practiced over a long period of time, it enhances digestion at the physical level and creates a psychic ability to assimilate and recover from impact of unexpected events. The second approach for energy conservation is the path of discrimination; being aware of one's latent tendencies and the transient nature of the world. Self-referral keeps our energy free of dependency. A practitioner of this method lives with crystal clear understanding and his activities flourish under an umbrella of cohesive strength that holds the flow and expression of life energy - assimilation and conservation. The River of Life flows between the banks of this attitude. Meaningful action enriches vitality. Inspiration derived from a trusting attitude to life must be conserved, enriched, strengthened, cultivated and nurtured by living the right values in life.

MINDFULNESS

We avoid our instinctive nature and foretelling sensitivity because it shows us what we rather not see and acknowledge about ourself. A mind built on the attitude of associative imagery, scatters its fluid energy into a multi-fold of split images and thought patterns. Emotions feel solid and real and not as a nexus of fluid energy. Before we can de-condition our inessentials, we need to recognise the multiple false 'I's by Mindfulness; by being present in what we do. A fluid mind knows mindfulness is being what we are doing; being the interlinking drift where watcher and watched vanish, where subject and personalised object disappear. Mindfulness is 'non-grasping awareness'. It pulls at nothing from the flow of life. By being involved and open in each moment of what we do, we become an active and present participant, not an onlooker. It is a wholehearted dive into oneself; within one's mind, body and emotion in a way that there is nothing or nobody left to see. There is no 'watcher', no fragmented self-conscious personality nor split of mind. We become present to ourself, to what we are doing and to the hidden significance of even the smallest of things — naturally, it brings meaning to action! Gradually, the imposing multiple pseudo-personalities thin down, leaving our perception clear. As the tendency to split diminishes, it reveals wholeness of life. Living deeply, we experience an inner openness that allows everything to come and go. Ultimately, sensitivity functions as perception. 'Letting go' is an offshoot of mindfulness. Letting go unnecessary identification becomes effortless.

A mindful look at 'acquisition', reveals its grasping nature. This open clarity allows our perceptive sensitivity to rise. When we humbly let-go of everything by keeping the perceptive sensitivity of the contents to be a passing show - a process and flow - we become present to the whole of our experience and a natural openness unfolds. To nurture a mind that clings to nothing is the path to wisdom. In the space of 'mindful letting-go' arises natural grounding. The words of Siddha Valmiki, putting one's attention in that which comes and goes, speak of this nature of mindfulness. Shedding ourself of a false image and dropping into the awareness of what is being felt, awakens us to the falsity of conditioning and reveals what we truly need. We learn to listen deeply and read how we respond to all that is coming our way as life. With the death of grasping and personalisation of these imagined acquired selfs', the false 'Is are no longer potent. Everything turns into an impersonal experience; a fleeting 'clinging' and ripple in the space of oneself.

ಸಂ ಡ

SECTION THREE: BEING AND SHARING

GROUNDING

Existential Conditioning, as the name suggests, is conditioning by birth. Prior to acquiring false ideational conditioning, the congenital centres of survival, emotion, power orientation, feeling, creativity, intelligence, etc. make up existential conditioning. Each centre has a mental disposition and can be described as the involuntary expression of *chakra* characteristics. Any one *chakra* predominantly governs each individual. Refining the qualities and features of the predominant *chakra*, harnessing the attitude and experiencing it as a whole in all dimensions of life is the standardisation, grounding and wholesome uniformity of Yogic living. Siddhas' Yogic system follows de-conditioning, shedding the acquired and imprinting of grounding. De-conditioning as a discipline includes everything from the intake of food to changes in lifestyle. Grounding is established by Yogic practice. Both features are implemented simultaneously.

I would like to break into a short story here. "I hold a keen interest in the game of cricket. Around 20 years ago, our Indian team experienced frequent highs and lows. My friends and I often wondered why every match was a struggle. While playing against the best, our team would often lose by a few runs after putting up a tough fight. No one was ever sure which side would win until the last ball was bowled. But our team struggled even playing weaker teams. Many cricket lovers may recall a time when one couldn't gauge our team's potential or standard. Even the players themselves were not sure! A strong team generally defeats weaker teams with ease but our team struggled either way. I would say this was because we played based on the strength of the opponent, not ours which brought fluctuation in performance. Our players depended on an external trigger - the opponent. Their spirit was entangled with the other side."

Standardisation requires recognition of one's strength and the implementation of its inherent potential, which was missing in our

CHAPTER NINE: INTRODUCTION TO THE YOGIC SYSTEM

team's perspective. Uniformity is accessed by playing on one's strength, regardless of the opponent's strength and position.

"During my brief course in American College, Madurai, I got acquainted with William, a student of Mathematics. Clearly not the mathematical type, he didn't belong and yet he sincerely attended class. One day, while we ate lunch on the college lawn, we watched a few students seated close by. One of them got disappointed seeing the contents of his lunch box. William immediately made a quick sketch of that situation and another one showing the boy's expression if the contents had been to his liking. I was amazed at how he spontaneously captured the moment with his witty sketches. They were visual messages. William's natural talent flowed as mere play. I suggested, "Somehow finish your mathematics course but continue your natural ability to sketch. Keep capturing what catches your eye." He promised. Two and a half months later, I left college. One and a half years later we met again. He was in his second year and seemed nervous and desperate. He had been discouraged by friends and acquaintances that sketching/art held no future and a doctorate in Mathematics was more promising. His friends had compelled him to joining a Computer course, explaining Computers also to be the future. I spoke to him strongly, "Don't give up your sketching and if you have to join a computer course, choose one related to drawing." Encouraging him, I added, "Choose any modern education just as long as it is related to your natural talent. William, keep doing what you love, other things will follow. By investing all your love into your natural ability, nature will surely respond." Four years later we met again. William was in Delhi working for a big firm dealing in consumer goods throughout India. He explained how he had landed this job. During the yearly campus interview for computer students, a few of them organised a small 'Welcome' for the Interviewers. William was asked to draw a picture on behalf of the Computer wing. He drew two pictures. One showed the delegates walking to the campus on

SECTION THREE: BEING AND SHARING

a path starting from their company factory. And the other picture showed the entire college building inside the factory grounds and the factory's name had been renamed the College name! Although his pictures were simple, straightforward sketches, what caught the eye of the chief interviewer was the unique picturisation of an existing scenario and the intelligent visualisation of the next desirable outcome. The campus interview was only for computer students, but William got selected in the advertising department of that company. Nature had responded!"

William didn't buckle under peer pressure and had refused the image being imposed on him. He remained devoted to his natural talent without compromise. This was his grounding. He firmly held the attitude I shared with him, to hold onto what you love; to remain with what comes natural to you. The mechanical is not in the present, and that which is alive can never be outdated.

The next story is a special one, told to me by my Master. A story that sunk deep into me!

"Once upon a time, in a small village lived a cobbler. Daily he would go to a nearby town, spread his tools before him on a street corner and sit there quietly. If someone brought their *chappals* (sandals) for repair, he would do the job without even glancing up. He would accept whatever money they gave and never bothered to count it. At sundown, he would return home. The cobbler lived his entire life like this. The day came when the old cobbler lay on his deathbed. It was the first time he prayed. He said, "God, throughout my life I accepted whatever you gave me. I never verified if it was more or less. I never verified if the money was genuine or fake. Now I am going to die; please don't calculate whether I am good or bad, whether I am spiritual or worldly. Just accept me as I am." Saying this, he died peacefully. The neighbours seated around him heard what he said and exclaimed "Alas, we missed a great spiritual Master who lived so close to us!"

CHAPTER NINE: INTRODUCTION TO THE YOGIC SYSTEM

Why did the neighbours call the cobbler, 'spiritual', and 'Master'? The cobbler never followed any philosophy or methods and yet was truly spiritual. Spirituality is the trusting attitude of living in humility with life. The cobbler gained firm ground by this one attitude throughout his life. Living devotedly, he brought it to life and in death he crossed over peacefully and naturally - in that very attitude. The cobbler's death came alive just as beautifully as his life. Spirituality is a preparation, an understanding of the phenomenon of death. The cobbler crossed over with simplicity and peace as he lived like that. Most people today, at the time of death lose their acquired spiritual knowledge all because it hasn't been truly lived out. In the very moment of death it turns invalid. But the cobbler lived his attitude and became it, which effortlessly reflected at the time of leaving his body. He is a Master."

ಏ ಆ

CENSOR

Censorship is removing or altering a part, or whole and retaining what you want. It is no longer the 'as is' original. Censorship happens all the time in the world as well as here within us. Man has an inner censor, a fixation that constantly distorts the experience of himself and the world, by applying programmed mechanical ideas or theories as a filter. This way man gets to perceive what he wants or expects and refuses the rest. The censor can otherwise be called Ego. It constantly resists the natural flow of life by making splits like, me and others, empty and goal, subject and object, inside and outside, past and future, mind and body, etc. Each moment gets recreated and conditioned based on ideas and inner programming that changes the experience from the actual into an interpretation. A filtered personal version! A collection of such personal versions builds a personal world in which man seeks refuge the moment he feels invaded. By not relating with what is, he sees a dead ideated world.

The censor is born from the hub of habitual energy patterns and is neither real nor solid. It takes the form of a pseudo well-wisher for the 'survival of the fittest' in man's projected personal world, a method employed to maintain a secure familiar world. The ego finds meeting the 'unfamiliar' extremely unsettling and instantly neglects or refuses it by switching on 'selective amnesia'. Through censorship, man avoids all contact with unfamiliarity, finding it disturbing. He forgets the potential held within unfamiliarity awakens him from habit, attachment and a numb dull sleep. Censorship thrives in the darkness of ignorance and man controls life through prejudice, presupposition, interpretation and projection, splitting the unity of natural fluid sensitivity of inter-connectedness. It is long forgotten how everything is a living whole and everything is in a living whole, in 'sensitive inter-connectedness'; a holographic phenomenon where all are participants and co-creators of life.

Humans have natural 'fluid sensitivity' that resonates with everything in this living whole. Reading fiction or watching a movie, we often become the character. We experience no conflict between us and the character. Sometimes, the sight of a beautiful mountain or vast ocean captivates us and we feel ourself to be a part of the whole environment. In moments such as these, our censor is swallowed by the immense presence of the mountain or by the love or affinity we feel with the fictional character. The 'censor' dissolves under the awakened sensitivity of inter-connectedness. As for 'letting-go' awareness, the dissolution of our censor gives rise to a new perception called 'perceptive sensitivity'; the awakened heart where your own sensitivity as 'Perception' relates, recognises and realises things just as they are. The ancient Siddhas call this awakened perceptive-sensitivity, *'Vasi'*, and the Tibetan Buddhists call it *'Bodhi Chitta'*. *Vasi* is the living-essence; a primal-pulsation that actively shapes one's life. Being 'Primal', it inhabits every individual, yet we are oblivious of its wondrous presence because of constant censorship and the assumption that we are controllers of life!

There are times when a child grows tired of his toys, thrusts them away and runs crying to his mother. His mother stops whatsoever she may be doing to hold her child close, and the child stops crying! He doesn't need his toys anymore. His sensitivity tells him that he is in a place worth more than all the toys in the world and will brush them away with a smooth wave of his little hand! When we say, 'I feel a sense of peace'; 'I feel all will go well', we are referring to a mind-process in terms of sensitivity. When we say: 'I feel the weather is too cold'; 'I find the floor too hard to sleep on'; 'the weight of the load on my head feels heavy'. Or sentences like: 'I feel fear'; 'I sense disaster'; or 'I feel it's going to rain'; we are referring to emotions as well as our body in terms of sensitivity. Whether we realise it or not, we inevitably refer to our body, our emotions, our mind, our feelings and our spirit in terms of sensitivity. For man, it is the only 'underlying link' to be realised and relived in inherent unity. Ultimately, acquired conditioning dissolves of its own accord under the 'letting-go' awareness as we awaken to the humble sensitivity that glitters within. Living in existential imperatives like remaining aware of your breathing, seeing, sleeping, hunger, loving, compassion, walking and running, turns into perceptive sensitivity... a non-cerebral life.

ಙ ಆ

INTER-BEING

"Keep your attention on what is coming and going,
the one that came and went would become Vasi."
- Valmiki Gnanam, by Siddha Valmiki
(Vasi means living-essence/experience)

Censored living is habitual. We take human consciousness to be a deterministic machine or calculator projected by the Cartesian model of 19th century science (based on Newton's influence). We believe in the limited and false view of our inner world. The sacred verses of the ancient Siddha texts liken consciousness to mercury. Back in school, we all experimented with it and learnt its properties. It has density as well as fluidity and appears metallic. It fragments into smaller globules and when brought together once again, it turns into one globule. It is sensitive! What is the nature of its sensitivity? Mercury is used in thermometers. Contained in a glass tube, it registers the surrounding temperature and rises while in contact. Once it is removed, it falls back to its previous level. Attributing these properties to human consciousness gives us a new understanding which doesn't seem limited or mechanical but more like an ever-flowing river of the sub-atomic world.

The ancient Siddhas picture consciousness as '*Rasam*', the inner mercury.

This sensitivity, characteristic to our consciousness, is always flowing as the ocean bed of all existence but our 'Censor' filters and alters the scene spread out on this vast ocean bed, picking and choosing according to prejudices. I hope it is obvious enough how high a degree of distortion the primal scene is subjected to. Lifetimes of habitual tendencies, acquired ideas and images, continuums of 'wants' or 'haves', mechanical lifestyle patterns, cathartic approaches... are the dust veiling the primal scene. The fragmented attitude of daily living is, in a single word, 'to have'. Life revolves around many 'to have' centres busy generating desire, wants, false images, acquisitions, all the while veiling simple livingness, 'to be'! Once the burden of our choices in the form of compulsive disorders, weigh too heavy to carry... we pick up a search. 'To be' in the direct 'as is' flow of the ever-flowing inner stream leads to the realm of Truth. It unfolds into the fluid-chain that links our inner spark of consciousness with all the facets of the larger one; the great world.

CHAPTER NINE: INTRODUCTION TO THE YOGIC SYSTEM

Unfortunately, we need to be guided to recall the stream of existence that flows within.

It is not hard to feel our fluid sensitivity... Relax your body and lose any tension. Make the body supple and buoyant and remain with it in a relaxed way. You will feel the inner warmth of your body and you can sense it as a mild warm fluid. Watch and allow the resonance of this warm fluid nature. You will suddenly awaken to the living presence of your body. This is your perceptive sensitivity filling every pore. The sensation of a constant stream of warm life energy is somewhat like having the whole body relaxed and yet remaining fully present in it. The nature of this sensitivity is distinct, pure, untouched, uncensored, un-fragmented, undistorted; free of imposition and ideation. It is true existential experience, untouched by mind.

ಸಿ ಆ

STEPPING IN...

'When I meditate, my mind doesn't settle down'. 'My mind wanders'. 'My mind is constantly crowded with thoughts'. There is no defect in the mind; activity is its natural function. We try to 'quieten the mind' and control its activity, aiming for a state of 'no thought'. Throughout our day, we involve in external activities and eventually, our inner feelings grow dependent on outer things for support which make the mind run about until it is satisfied. So how can sitting in a meditative posture and commanding the mind to be calm bear fruit? When we are not awake to our inner sensitivity, why would the mind turn quiet on a verbal order - a left-brain conditioning!

Our breath can be felt but not touched. Our mind is too fast to grasp. Our nearest most intimate and stable surrounding is the body which is why the Siddhas emphasise - start from where you stand. One needs to nurture the rediscovered sensitivity through the first stable footing - the body. Perceiving bodily feelings call for slowing down and remaining attentive to that which was so far ignored. It is a gradual and wondrous unfolding - not an overnight expedition. It is the journey home. Depending on the level of receptivity, the doorway of our body opens up a possibility; a possibility otherwise absent from the mundane and limited view of our self. Have you ever wondered if the physical boundary of the body is real? While watching the sun set, be attentive to the visual form of the object, the Sun. Allow your sensitivity to be taken from the form into the quality of the image; the feeling of its existence. Remain with it. By the resonance of becoming one, bodily sensations unfold and expand which dissolve the first believed boundary showing you how your perceptive sensitivity reaches out and beyond to the space around. Movements too can be perceived through this sensitivity. Perceptive sensitivity must slowly and surely reflect in each moment of day-to-day living and cannot be pursued as an exclusive practice in a closed meditation room. With this nature of livingness, things are not mere objects. You sense everything by recognising its qualitative energy. A dog is no more just a dog. You recognise its 'dogness' as a living quality, in the energy of your own body. You sense the unique quality of things and movements around you as 'energy feeling' in your body and begin to recognise the fluid intelligence of this sensitivity. Fluid intelligence is the heart of ever-flowing life through which the *'dharma'*, the inherent order of life, functions. This is the art of Yoga. Yoga is a part of our existence and not a separate practice. Yoga means relation or union by becoming aware of the inherent connectivity, the inter-link of how the ONE resonates as multi-facets.

> Among all the multi-facets of human nature, the body alone is steadfast. The *prana* or vital life force is dynamic; as for the mind, we can hardly get a hold of it. What if the stable quality of the body is instilled into the mind and the clarity and sharpness of the mind is made to resonate with the body?

CHAPTER NINE: INTRODUCTION TO THE YOGIC SYSTEM

The mind is now a stable reflecting body and its quality is light and clear, pervading as body-consciousness. The body-mind expresses the serene spirit naturally present in all. It brings about an obstacle-free inherent connection between all intrinsic human faculties - sensitivity is the real string.

The body becomes light, yet stable. Life force is freed from its customary restraints; the mind is fully present at what is being done in that moment, then and only then can the flow of awakened perception flow, even and continuous as perceptive sensitivity. As for fragmented consciousness, it reflects as a dull, inert body and a restless superficial mind. Don't miss the fluidity present at all times! Inertia too can take the form of its balanced counterpart - stability and steadfastness. Restlessness and superficiality can transform into its balanced counterpart - authenticity and sharpness, when one mindfully awakens to sensitivity.

Yoga is becoming sensitive to the relationship with oneself and with others, named *Yama* and *Niyama* respectively. Yoga reveals your conscious relation with your breath, your emotions, your mind and with your very core, the Spirit. Yoga is the art of relationship!

An initial ancient practice of the Yogic cult of the Siddhas recommends gazing at the sun in the morning and at the moon at midnight. The Sun appears static. We commonly use the terms sunrise, sunset, ascending moon, descending moon, all of which indicate the static and changing phases that resonate with time. In other words, the sun and the moon represent the primal patterns of movement and the static nature of the animate and inanimate - so declare the Siddhas. Ordinarily, objects are either static or moving, but the sun and moon have both natures. Recognising these primal patterns, one grows sensitive toward them and feels an inter-connectedness which naturally reflects in other things. Gradually, fluid intelligence of distinction unravels itself and one naturally learns to comprehend the qualitative changes in energy inherent to existence.

To understand, 'recognise the qualitative changes in the energy of the body in relation to objects' - one can gaze at the moon at night. Become aware of your bodily sense toward it. Feel the energy in your body-mind. Now shift your gaze to a lamp in your house and be sensitive to the change in the quality of energy in your body-mind. You may feel the subtle difference in your spirit. Sensitivity or the humble flow of feeling is the perception with which we physically experience our inter-being with others, our surroundings and the world.

ಙ ಡ

The next milestone we speak about is Time. No disposition remains constant through the course of a single day! A man's mood changes in relation to changing time - morning, afternoon, evening and night. Time, with its own quality participates in our day. If you notice, every space, however large or inconspicuous, demonstrates a disposition, mood, character and ambiance. Be sensitive to its intrinsic qualities like warm, cold, airy, chaotic, peaceful, wild, etc., it is another participant. Pay heed to the space between you and your lover when you talk and notice how that sense differs when you talk with a stranger or your boss, or mother or friend. The quality of space changes according to the quality of relationship.

We entered the doorway of our body via sensitivity and extended our self to objects, the surrounding, to our movements and actions, and to our relationship with Time and Space. The qualitative changes of varying energy feelings within our body resonate with all that we perceive as separate, rendering the separation invalid. Through the nature of ancient Siddha Yoga, we redefine our relationship with everything external. This ancient teaching guides you back to yourself.

CHAPTER NINE: INTRODUCTION TO THE YOGIC SYSTEM

The Siddhas encourage visiting power-spots such as *Samadhi* shrines, caves of the Siddhas in the mountains, holy springs, etc. as the prevalent presence heightens our sensitivity, with no effort on our part other than simply 'being' there. It is enough to just remain sensitive to oneself. Our inner journey reveals our sensitivity is always as our Heart. In other words, even if there are no forms or objects to relate with, we still are pulsating, sensitive heart; the *Atma Bhava*. One discovers he is beyond relative existence; *Atma Anubhava*, the experience of Self. This is inter-being. The inter-connectedness prevalent in all existence, within and without. Everything resonates with everything. Everything is alive as one.

৩ ৫

REMAINING HERE

Each milestone leads to the next, and transformation is inevitable. Milestones and landmarks lay open to flourish by, in none other than 'Authentic Living'. Abiding in and nurturing perceptive sensitivity builds firm ground in what is called the existential self; the most intimate of all surroundings and most tangible of given life situations. One cannot possibly hope to reach the intangible without walking through the doorways leading there - our existential ground escorts us to the otherwise hidden doorway of unconditional living; the ultimate ground of existence.

Even though the chapter of Inter-Being resonates with simplicity what is already within, one cannot deny the obstacles on this path. The mind is a cabinet stacked with lifetimes of information, conditioning and improper perceptions. Censorship, mechanical patterns, age-old urges, mediocre mind, fragmented and scattered attitudes toward one's self and so on, from time to time show their face reminding us that everything we have lived so far lies ingrained within each pore of our body. The awakening of perceptive sensitivity in our journey on the ever-flowing river of the quantum world also awakens the shunned, the ignored and the avoided. The only infallible means of nullifying these in-essentials is by holding steadfast to the flowing river of perceptive sensitivity and applying it to the rising conflicts within. It is the only way to expose them. Ordinarily, in anger we tend to blame others, but through perceptive sensitivity we find anger is just another type of energy. The distinctive intelligence of sensitivity brings to our notice the qualitative aspect of energy. And because we no longer mechanically and impulsively objectify it, the conflict between observer and external form nullifies. The slow yet sure journey of discarding the veil of a false and limited view of ourselves reveals that there is only a resonant sensitivity as Sentient. There is no 'other' to separate. This 'Sentient' is the only One whole that ever pulsates.

ಓ ಇ

FROM ACQUIRED TO EXISTENTIAL CONDITIONING

After acquired identification drops through mindful-letting-go and one is free of fragmentary up-surging images, the Yogic Path of Siddhas introduces one to the ground of existential conditioning by way of a conscious process. Perception, breath, dreams, sleep, hunger, etc. are all existential imperatives that even though appear natural, are a conditioning upon human consciousness; a limiting adjunct. Limiting adjuncts are a type of conditioning as they are not acquired. They don't demand interpretation, nor can they be influenced by new interpretation. These existential functions nourish living. Depending upon an individual's psychic mode, the Yogic Master prescribes an awareness-related practice that may be associated to any one existential conditioning.

CHAPTER NINE: INTRODUCTION TO THE YOGIC SYSTEM

BREATHING

Breathing and living, deeply entwined, co-relate and necessitate each other. After the practitioner drops what he thinks himself to be and abides as who he existentially is, his existential breathing demands total attention and involves his entire mind. In this precious moment, he observes his ever-occurring breathing with dedicated attention. He drifts as breathing itself and abides. This is *Dhyanam* or Meditation; perceiving the breath not by thinking or imagination, or by acquisition, but by humbly perceiving how he existentially is as breath itself. It is no longer called 'his breathing'. Breathing happens, whether or not he makes an interpretation or statement. Sensitive perception is as natural as breathing. Perceiving makes him aware of the existential fact of breathing! Both are natural and existential. And he cannot even call it 'his perception'. The mind is entirely involved in perceptive sensitivity of breathing, leaving no room for fragmentary urges or motives. This is Wholeness of Mind. Within him arises a state of silence in reflection of perceptive breathing. Under the guidance of his Siddha Master, the practitioner is taught how two existential conditionings are brought together in an immensely meaningful relationship, both being naturally entwined. We can no longer separate the identifier and the identified. The slight pause at the end of each inhalation and exhalation makes the practitioner realise that his drift in existential conditioning is not continuous!

Any natural process in the universe is not continuous.

The practitioner gains the parallel understanding that behind apparent continuity exists a repository discontinuity as its ground. The pause at the end of inhalation and exhalation lengthens and deepens. The sudden awakening of pranic energy rushes through a channel while simultaneously withdrawing from others, opening an enthusiastic new vista of the ever-existent inner realm. The perception of the practitioner shifts from the physical body to the subtle. He gains a parallel insight, more refined, of the discontinuous nature of the discontinuity he perceived. His insight shows repository discontinuity to open up into continuity of inner pranic circulation. A natural enquiry arises from the entire being of the practitioner - there must be a Source, a Primal ground from where the subtle *prana* emerges, circulates and manifests as breath! It's a mysterious journey, our inner quest. The breathing entity, he earlier thought to be 'me', is the significant Root Image on which the perception of the whole objective world converges. The Root perceiver, in search of the breathing entity, comes to confront the One who breathes. This confrontation is shocking; 'what he searches is who is searching'! In transition, the entire prana reverberates in the whirl of the Source, and is swallowed by IT. The perceiver vanishes!

ಬಿ ಔ

LEAVE IT

The realisation that movement of thought perpetuates the ego-centre and duality in fact quietens it, and from this quietude does the self-existent being shines forth. Unless identification is nullified through 'mindful letting-go', the mind continues to lapse into image identification in the want of 'becoming'; of desire, of hope and disappointment. As the Yogic path propels deeper transformation, the mind tires and desires to rest. 'Mindful letting-go' entails leaving everything where it belongs. Once you see things as they are, the masquerading world no longer hangs in you. A mind freed of craving further experience is capable of undivided attention. The alert and watchful eye of unbroken 'mindful letting-go' sees the awakening of intelligence; an intelligence that holds a vision of the eternal, no longer caught by false identification of circumstance happening between the content and the container,

CHAPTER NINE: INTRODUCTION TO THE YOGIC SYSTEM

the essence with the form, the eternal with the transitory. Instead, one must remain aware of this apparent duality by being truly established in oneself. But there is a trap. The tiniest intention of wanting relief from apparent duality, indirectly sanctions our chaotic identifying nature, justifies it and makes it real. As long as we sanction chaotic nature, the ever-peaceful state eludes. Of all the fragmentary roles we play, mindful letting-go is one such role we incorporate to remove other acquired ones. At this stage, our inherent intelligence prods – 'who plays these roles, who identifies with them and who empowers them? It is the primal role; the causative factor. Our presence as the Primal Role stands as an individual image; the Identifier. To drop the deluding Primal role of an 'identifying' person, the Identifier must be shed. All scattered experiences converge into one single experience - of an Identity, the Identifier, as the urge to identify. If the ever-ongoing urge for shelter is dropped, the refugee too drops. If our individuality as a refugee remains, it once again commences covering and motivating its respective dropping and letting-go. To realise this, we need Inner-Spaciousness.

Conscious de-conditioning uncovers and sheds the various acquired roles and brings to the foreground our existent individuality, grown solid by this process. This untouched 'identifier' individuality is the primal ideation from which all identification begins and it is what needs to be absorbed by the pre-reflective substratum. Nothing in the world truly belongs to us other than primal individuation that has been identifying in the game of owning and disowning. To renounce images and objects, they must first be ours. There is nothing to give up! One can posses the whole world, but the world never feels possessed; one can own this body, but the body never feels owned!

༄ ༅

SECTION THREE: BEING AND SHARING

THE PRE-REFLECTIVE

If a practitioner continues an acquiring approach, grasping 'more' in the pre-reflective substratum realm, it is because the 'identifier' wishes to survive as the possessor of ever-shining awareness. This individuality will encounter solid defeat, falling and succumbing to its own search. The individuality is wiped out in the process of transformation. The pre-reflective substratum is from where the reflective state of subject and object; identifier and the identified occur. The Ancient Siddha Sages describe the Absolute substratum with several names:

Vettaveli	(Grand infinite space)
Param	(One that is beyond)
Jothi	(Illumination)
Paraveli	(Space which includes all)
Sivam	(Supreme)
Monam	(Silent Spirit)

A Yogic journey to the Absolute comprises of specific designed practices that teach the balanced function of subtle energy-pathways, Yogic chakras and *Kundalini*. The rest of the Yogic chapters have been dealt with in a conventional manner with the intention of making original ancient values available to the reader.

ಐ ಙ

Nadis

- Brahmarandhra
- Agna
- Sushumna Nadi
- Pingala Nadi
- Ida Nadi
- Kundalini fire

CHAPTER TEN

THE INNER MAP

"Vaanukkul Isanai Thedum Marularkaal
Thenukkul Inbam Sivappo Karuppo
Thenukkul Inbam Sirunthu Iruntharppal
Unukkul Isan Olindhu Irunthane."

"You ignorant men searching for God in the heavens,
Can the sweetness of honey be explained as black or red?
Just as the sweetness of honey is in the honey itself
Thus God is hiding within the human body."
        Thirumanthiram, Verse 3069, by Siddha Thirumoolar

"Cease ye from man, whose breath is in his nostrils;
For wherein is he to be accounted of."
        Holy Bible - Isaiah, chapter 2;22

The conventional definition of Yoga is Union and the root word 'Yog' means 'to unite'. Yoga is the path to unite with our true nature. Yoga concerns 'relation' as Life in every moment expresses in relation; relation to nature, to our surrounding, our situation and to other fellow beings. Yoga teaches relating with our external world and with our self. As such to reach a destination, it always helps to have a path finder and in this case, it is an inner map that translates the abstract into concrete and lights up the way. Long ago, the Siddhas revealed the grace-lit path of Siddha Yoga that ensures the way home to our original nature. As our primal nature remains elusive to materialistic perception (mind nor spirit are grasped while oriented toward the physical dimension), we now explore the physical dimension through the next tangible doorway after the body, our breath.

Breath cannot be touched, but can be felt. Sacred verses describe breath and mind as two sides of the same coin. Breath mirrors the state of mind, bridging the physical and non-physical dimensions of our being. Leading us within, it introduces us to the non-physical state that enlivens our physical state... our *Prana*. *Prana* is the silent breath that gives impetus to physical breath. Consciously attuning to the physical breath makes it a door to the silent breath that, through subtle energy pathways called Nadis, opens to the subtle body; the realm of our chakras. As each chakra opens entirely and flowers, it triggers an unfolding of our 'establishment' in our individualistic consciousness by the involution of each of the five elements into their primordial nature. A true Siddha Master always ensures for his students concurrent breath, which is the first vital experience before all others along this path.

The complete journey of Siddha Yoga covers all vital milestones through the inner map of our consciousness. Various ancient Tamil treatises known as 'Siddhars Tattwa Katalai' enumerate 96 different constituent principles or *Tattwas* present in nature that intimately interrelate with one another even within a human body. Through the course of the book, we have dealt in detail with only the important ones. For our readers to recognise how closely interlinked they are to the doorway of breath, I have outlined below some of the other principles.

"The nadis 72000 are in human body,
Among them, 10 are chief ones."

Avvai Kural, Verse 1, chapter 4

"Among the 10, there is one chief Nadi,
That is full of power."
Avvai Kural, Verse 2, chapter 4

"The nadis spread and ramify, penetrating
Feet, hands and hip... like threads of a lotus stalk."
Avvai Kural, Verse 4, chapter 4

"Like the sun's rays, these nadis
Ramify and spread out."
Avvai Kural, Verse 5, chapter 4

"Verily these nadis spread throughout the body
Intertwining the bones and the nerves
Their ramification is the end."
Avvai Kural, Verse 6, chapter 4

Prana is the force of creation or life. We experience body-consciousness and its limitation when consciousness identifies with the body through the modality of touch. The attributes of the Air element are the sense of touch and sound. The *Gnanendriyas*, or organs of knowing, and *Prana* arise from these. A balanced Pranic flow ensures a harmonious alignment of body-mind-spirit.

According to the Siddha system, the human body (both physical and subtle) is made up of 72,000 *nadis* and seven vital centres (the Chakras) situated along the central channel called the *Sushumna Nadi*. The three important regions of Fire, Sun and Moon, the ten vital airs (*Dasa Vayu*) and other vital nerves (*nadis*) are all found here. Out of the ten vital *nadis*, the first three: *Idakalai* (moon), *Pingalai* (sun), and the *Sushumna Nadi* (central channel or lifeline) play important roles in human life. Several ancient Siddha songs mention that *Vaasi* (subtle air) begins manifesting at the centre of *Lalada*, the hollow behind the forehead, inside and above the *Agnai Chakra*. From here, it passes into and through *Chitra Nadi*, jumps down into the sacral plexus with the sound 'OV' and passes into the navel plexus with the sound 'AV'. From here, it enters into the *Idakalai* and the *Pingalai* with the sound 'SAV', and circles the cerebrum before finally entering into the nostrils. Siddha science describes the normal breath rate at 360 times per *Nazhigai* (one hour =2 ½ *Nazhigai*), which calculates as 21,000 breaths every 24 hours. (one day and night = 60 *Nazhigai*). With 15 breaths per minute, it works out to (24 x 60 x 15) 21,600 breaths in a single day and night. Ideally, every breath (both inhalation and exhalation) takes place from a length of 12 inches from the nostril, but we breathe out a length of 12" and inhale from only 8", losing 4 inches of breath each time. Therefore, of the available 21,600 total breaths, the human body takes, in a day, only 14,400 breaths and the balance 7,200 are wasted. If *prana* were properly utilised, the normal human lifespan would be 120 years. A large part of the energy that ought to enter our body is lost considerably reducing our life span which is expressed in this verse as:

"Nal Onrukku Irupathu Orayirathu
Arunooru Elunthirukkum Suvasanthane
Kolonri Nanooru
Kavi Moolatharathul Odungum Paru
Palonra Elayirathu Eranooru Moochu Palaga Painthum Enru Ariga Pinnai
Alonri Idathanaiya Utchathithal
Eppothum Balarai Irrukkalame"

"Twenty one thousand breaths are born in a day.
In that, fourteen thousand and four hundred breaths are absorbed in the Mooladharam,
The remaining seven thousand and two hundred breaths are absorbed in the surrounding space.
If you absorb these remaining ones, you will be ever youthful."
Yugimuni Tattwa gnanam-46

The *Ida Nadi* breath or left nostril breath inhales a length of 12" and exhales 16". The *Pingala Nadi* breath or right nostril breath inhales a length of 8" and exhales 12". Where does the extra 4" length of exhalation get its impetus? From within. Not from the external breath. This is how we are spending inner *Prana* during normal breathing and not really re-acquiring it. *Prana*, the pulsation of life, is responsible for the internal momentum needed for breathing. This is *Vaasi*. The Siddhas, through the path of *Vaasi* Yoga, show the way to consciously re-link with this pulsation of life. When the moon channel merges with the Sun channel, the remaining four inches of *Prana* begin to expand. This plays a vital role in the segregation of *Amritha* (Nectar). Saint Ramalingam says that very few are born with an activated *Pingala Nadi* while most are born with left nostril breath. Characteristically, the *Pingala Nadi* shows aspects of assertive human will; a hot nature, whereas the *Ida Nadi* is related to passion and emotions; a rather cooling nature.

෩ ෬

Our physical body is both, the temple of the soul and the microcosm of the entire universe. The bodily temple, as do traditional Hindu and Buddhist temples, contains gardens, rivers, sanctuaries and gates as well as the elements of the natural world: earth, water, fire, air, and ether. The nine gates to our bodily temple are: the anus, the male and female genitals, the mouth, the nose, the two eyes, the two ears and the 'passage of *Brahmam*' (The Absolute) or *Brahmarandhra*. The mysterious passage of *Brahmam* (the fontanel), is an actual opening that is visible at birth but closes as the baby grows. It is also known as the 'soft spot' found at the crown of an infant's skull. Tantric tradition describes the soul to enter and leave the body through this Gate of *Brahmam*.

Although the bodily temple may be entered or left via any gate, it is the Gate of *Brahmam* that leads to higher spiritual realisation. Tantra also describes the subtle body to contain the aura and chakras. The nature of chakras manifests through ductless glands. The two bodies are inseparable and both are worshipped as one temple. Taoists call the *Brahmarandhra*, the 'Mysterious Passage to Heaven', and the process as 'Returning to the Source'.

A current of centralised *Prana* is constantly moving upward and down from the *Sahasraram* to the *Mooladharam chakra*. When outward-bound operations of mind diminish and an indrawn pull arises, Yogic life begins. Under the Guru's guidance, an earnest seeker learns to perceive and attune with this current until his psyche rises from one chakra to the next and reaches its resting or uniting place, the *Paraveli*, (Brahmam). The centres of mind and *Prana* exist within our body and life-energy tends to go where mind is concentrated and mind is led to the place where *prana* is directed. The union of mind and *prana* reveals the secret knowledge of the particular *Tattwa* (basic element) of each chakra centre. The relation between the chakras, mind and *prana* is a wonderful mystery. By studying the work of different chakras and their presiding deities, we come to know how divine energy works through the different centres.

Siddha Sage Thirumoolar explains:

"Where there is mind absorption, there life's breath is:
Where there is no mind absorption, there life is none.
Those who sit in mind absorption are verily fixed in the yoga of whole absorption."

Thirumanthiram, Verse 620

Movement in the passage of vital air from *Ida* to *Pingala* is known as the *Uttarayana*, or northern course of the Sun. Movement in the passage of the vital air from *Pingala* to *Ida* is known as *Dakshinayana*, or southern course of the Sun, as is happening in the external world. Presiding over 'the path of the Gods' and 'the path of the ancestral spirits' respectively, are the solar and lunar energies. From the path of the sun in the posterior channel and from the path of the moon in the frontal channel, these energies move along the *Ida* and *Pingala* channels in the human body, day and night distributing pranic conversion all over the body.

> "Don't stand aside! Aside!
> Don't take *ganja* (Marijhuana) and be caught by its Tamasic sleep.
> There is nectar of moon with you, to dine,
> Drink it and happily clap your hands."
>
> Gnana kummi, (clapping the hands in way of wisdom).
> By Siddha Vaalai Swami Madurai.

Lunar energy, moving along the *Ida* channel sprinkles life-giving nectar over the 72,000 *nadis*. Solar energy, moving along the *Pingala* channel, dries the sprinkled nectar. The Moon passes through sixteen phases (*sodasa kalai*), changing phase each day of the descending moon. The new moon day is its first phase in the *Mooladharam Chakra*, when the sun and the moon meet (i.e. when the *prana* reaches the junction between *Ida* and *Pingala*). Yogis consider the new moon day ideal for awakening the *Kundalini Sakthi* or for giving or getting initiation. Siddhas in their mystical songs mention the new moon day as 'Ama Vasya'. *Ama* means mother and indicates the cooling nectar that nourishes the entire living process, like a mother nursing her infant with her own milk. *Vasya* means 'coming to stay'. All the lunar digits of the dark fortnight emerge from this source.

CHAPTER TEN: THE INNER MAP

This is referred in the poems of 'Avvai Kural' written by the woman Siddha, 'Avvaiyar', as

"Thondrum kathiravan mathi pukkidil
Sarrupan amavasithan"
"Mathikul kathiravan vanthu odungidil
Uthikkumam pooranai chol."

"If the moon meets with the sun
It is Amavasya (new moon)"
"If the sun is absorbed in the moon
It is Pournami (full moon),"

Avvai Kural By Woman Siddha Avvaiyar

With the help of five-fold *prana*, a yogi can keep the moon in the lunar sphere and the sun in the solar sphere. Arrested in their movement, the moon and the sun become incapable of oozing out the nectar or of drying it up. Once the moon conjoins with the sun, the fire in the sun can emerge from the *Mooladharam*, set ablaze in the body by *Vasi* yoga. The Siddha system calls this *'moola kanal'* (basal fire).

Chakras are inner phenomena experienced by Siddha Yogis during absorptive concentration and as such cannot be identified with nerve plexuses which are anatomical organs. The chakras are not material in nature but dynamic graphs of power operations. The power of each chakra can be manifested in a tangible way, by appropriate means.

ೞ ಆ

CHAPTER ELEVEN

CHAKRAS - THE WHEELS OF LIFE

"Ullanthinulle Ula Pala Theerthangal
Mella Gudainthu Ninradar Vina Geda
Pallamum Medum Parnthu Thirivare
Kalla Mana Mudai Kalvi Illare."

Within the body are many holy waters.
People do not take a gentle dip in them
And do not avoid karma completely,
Vainly they roam across hills and valleys-
Witless men of confused mind are they!"

                  Thirumoolar's Thirumanthiram, Verse 509

BEFORE THE BEGINNING...

Un-manifest and invisible divine energy or soul force is *Nirguna Nilai*; a state free of all attributes! *AdiSakthi* begins the course of creation, manifesting all beings - animate and inanimate. Energy directed toward creation and manifestation is *Saguna Nillai*; a state with all attributes. The microcosmic aspect of *AdiSakthi*, the *Kundalini Sakthi* enacts the same cosmic phenomenon at the microcosmic level by entering the foetus, bringing with it life-force that activates the pranic system of the body. The residual energy coils 3 ½ times into a small bulb of energy and goes dormant at the base of the spine. The onset of pranic activation engages the mind in the process of living, identifying with the body, the genetic heritage, mental, sensate and emotional processes, and it forgets the 'awareness of the Self' - the Source of all Existence. Thus, the *Kundalini* energy begins its life-long display of two movements: centrifugal - a movement from the centre outward and centripetal - a movement toward the centre. This dynamic flow continues until one of the two attains *Samadhi* experience or mortal death. The two opposing forces interweave, meeting at junctions in hierarchy. At each junction, it assumes a continued whirling-spiralling form called CHAKRA - THE WHEEL OF LIFE. Chakras are storehouses of past birth Karmic imprints. Due to the opposing current action, the mind (also a form of energy) gets whirled in attraction to the external world and its polarities according to Karmic imprints. All sorts of aversions, desires and egoistic propensities re-arise, move forward to materialise called *Pravritti*, the outward movement of mind. Once karmic imprints burn out, mind withdraws which is called *Nivritti*.

༄ ༅

WHIRLING PERCEPTIONS

"If you worship the wheels of life in a series,
If you happily emancipated the blessings of Sada Siva,
The wheels of life, the vision you saw,
Will surprisingly fade away and disappear."

Soumiya Sagaram-1200, Verse-72,
by Siddha Guru Agasthiyar

Mind, modifying due to continued outward movement, assumes gross form called mind-solidification, which carries a deep and solid identification with the body. In the waking state, the dark shadow of identified conditioning hides the 'unidentified' that stands by itself: the pre-reflective state. The associated forms of I - consciousness, such as my body, my house, my work and so on are solid and deep-rooted in the waking state, but don't hold true in the deep-sleep state. In the mind, thought after thought arises through the identified reflective state of human consciousness and rotates like a whirlpool, creating an incessant current of mental modifications. Hope after hope bewitches the mind by its magic charm. Just as the sun is not visible in a sky overcast by clouds, likewise the Self cannot shine as long as the mind identifies with the floating clouds of hope and desire. Humans, caught in the mesh of false identification and mesmerised by the three-fold misery of disease, grief and death, go on spinning in whirlpools of pleasure and pain.

An error cannot be corrected unless it is recognised. When man realises he is submerged in delusion, he decides to extricate himself and wake up to the consciousness of who he truly is. After experiencing the overwhelming agony of sorrow, he attempts to be freed of delusion. He knocks on all available doors, giving birth to the seeker in him. The dispersing current of identification gets set aside from his mind by spiritual aspiration and is replaced by the dint of a spiritual path. Gradually, conjured mind-identifications dwindle, interiorising the mind. Interiorisation deepens in proportion to the withdrawal of mental modifications. The chakras are formulated according to different levels of perception and correspond to the respective subtle attitude of mind. The seeker begins to realise how the quality and intensity of mental modification is impelled and navigated by the appropriate inner centres. He understands the seeds of tendency belong to specific chakras and that the six chakra centres of the subtle body are the whirling storehouses of the finer aspects of solidified mental modifications. As mind abandons the external play of identification, it interiorises and the seeker grows conscious of the gross, subtle and refined levels of perception. These altering, refining, energised perceptions are the Chakras. As long as the mind holds perception, the body carries it as energy-whirling chakras. In the natural state of who one truly is, all mental modification ceases. The chakras have no existence in the natural state.

A mind habituated to abnormal sense-gratification sinks into darkness. An overindulgent sexually-deprived mind remains caught in the region between the anus and the sex-organ, and its intellectual aspect gets sharply fragmented and loiters in the head area. The mind splits into duality - obsessive sexuality in the lower region and dry intellect in the head. The conflicted body gets engulfed by restlessness. 'My heart says one thing and my head another', is a common remark. Unable to conceive Truth, the individual clings to imaginary enjoyment. The will power is dragged and dissipated through tendencies - this is 'mechanical pattern'. Just as one cannot feel the existence of the world or one's body during deep sleep, similarly, in a mind steeped in the darkness of ignorance the *Kundalini Sakthi* remains asleep and realisation of matters beyond the sphere of the world do not unfold.

ॐ ॐ

OCEAN OF WAVES

The universe is in a state of constant flux; continually vibrating, generating innumerable waves. Recent geophysicists report the existence of a 'hum' emanating from below the earth's surface. By the Big Bang, dispersed fragmented segments went into a revolving motion, each generating a hum. It is the continuance of the Primal

Sound - AUM. According to the French scientist, Dr. Arnard, the vibration of the astral world is an octave lower than the vibration of the mental one. An octave comprises of seven notes and the eighth note is a repetition of the first - a recycle. Our universe is a maze of waves that are forming organic and inorganic systems (including humans), capable of receiving and emitting. Similarly, Tantric Siddha teachings for awakening the *Kundalini Sakthi* at the microcosmic level, describe seven octaves of vibration corresponding to the seven chakras, each having a specific *Bija mantra* (seed syllables) like AUM.

LIFE POWERED BY

The ten vital forces that emerge from *Maha Prana*, five main and five subtle potencies, empower the living process of the human organism and are responsible for all dynamic function.

The first vital force responsible for breathing is *Prana*. It originates and receives momentum from the *Mooladharam chakra*, rises upward to hit the top of the head and then works its way through the nose, accomplishing the process of breathing. Siddha Yugimuni, speaks in his work Nadi Tattwa, Verse 35,

> "Every time we breathe we exhale twelve units and inhale 8 units only and thus waste 4 units of vital air, this in fact leads to debility and diseases in due course."

Apana, the second vital force, originates from the *Swadhistanam Chakra* in the lower abdomen, (2" above the anus) and enables separation of excretory matter from the digested essence of food. It is also physiologically responsible for the contraction of the anus.

Samana, the third vital force, originates in the *Manipoorakam Chakra* in the naval region with the responsibility of assimilating nutrients from food.

Vyana, the fourth vital force originates from *Anahatam*, or the Heart Chakra in the chest region and balances and circulates throughout the entire body.

Udana, the fifth vital force, originates from the *Visuddhi Chakra* in the throat region and is responsible for distributing, stirring and mixing of the eaten food, etc. Failure of *Udana* leads to suffocation.

Amongst the five subtle vital forces, *Anga* enables us to open our eyes, mouth, etc. *Kirikaran* increases appetite. *Kurma* enables the contraction of limbs, cheeks, stomach, etc. *Devadatta* aids relaxation by opening the mouth wide for yawning. *Dhananjaya* sustains the body by ensuring the intake of nourishment and originates in the nasal region. It causes inflammation throughout the body and an abounding outflow of saliva from the mouth, after death. On death, after the nine vital forces leave the body, Dhananjaya breaks open the skull and escapes. Dhananjaya, for a Yogi proves as a vital tool in separating the life force from his body to bring voluntary death. It also explains the state of *Jiva Samadhi* and the Yogi's mastery of withholding it. The vital forces are the superior energies of the Lord that accompany the soul and reside in the spiritual heart, the central region - nothing escapes His guidance and observation!

WHEELS OF LIFE

According to the Siddha Tantra Yoga, there are twelve subtle energy centres within the human system. Siddha Thirumoolar names... six are *Adharam*, meaning base and the remaining six are *Niradharam*, meaning without or beyond base. The first six centres range from the base of the spine to the centre of the eyebrow in forms of Lotus plexuses or Chakras (Chakrams in Tamil) and are plexus centres of pranic dynamism, functioning both inwardly and outwardly. The remaining six signify the stages of interiorisation that ultimately lead to the merging of the Self. The *Niradharam* centres aren't accompanied by the experience of flowering or petalled formations like the six *Adharam*. In Yogic practice, the blossoming of these twelve centres generate latent forces and awaken powers that conquer the process of ageing, overcome disease, decay, bestow mastery over the elements, etc. The first six major chakras are the control centres for the areas related to five different sections of the spine:

(1) coccyx - Mooladharam
(2) sacrum - Swadhistanam
(3) lumbar - Manipoorakam
(4) dorsal - Anahatam
(5) cervical - Visuddhi

Above *Visuddhi*, is the sixth - *Agnai chakra* - the third eye, or point between the eyebrows. The seventh chakra, the *Sahasraram*, is not considered a chakra like the previous six and is located at the crown of the head. Each lower chakra is a portal to the energy of its higher one.

UNIFYING THE WHEELS OF LIFE

Awakening of the *Kundalini Sakthi* and the flowering of chakras is a mystery uniquely expounded by the Siddhas and is avidly sought out by yogic practitioners. The energy bulb of *Kundalini Sakthi* can be awakened in several ways such as intense devotion to God or the Guru, surrender to Existence, Dharma, the repetition of mantras or even by complete adherence to the words of the Guru. The most common awakening commences at the base or root of the spine and as the *Kundalini* awakens, She uncoils and ascends like a snake which is why it is often referred to as the Serpent Power. The Siddhas' literary poems sing the attributes of each chakra and the associated Gods, Goddesses, symbols, syllables, mantras, colours and characteristics, all relating to levels of spiritual revelations. It is more common for the male deity of a chakra to awaken and bless the practitioner with that aspect of consciousness after which consciousness rises in an involutionary way. Incidentally, the flowering of all the petals of a chakra is extremely rare and can happen only when both, the male and female presiding deities awaken. Using the *Mooladharam chakra* as an example, I have explained the implications of the flowering of all the petals.

The *Mooladharam Chakra*, situated in the basal area of the spine is an egg-like form surrounded by four petals. Within the egg is a downward pointing triangle. In one of the angles of this inverted triangle is an eight-petalled bud of a plantain tree, which has not been written of or revealed in other systems. The other corner holds the presiding male deity, Lord Ganesha and in the third angle stands his feminine aspect, Goddess Vallabai Sakthi. In the centre is a Siva Lingam, around which lies a coiled golden snake with its hood spread above the Lingam. The coiled maiden snake is Mother Kundalini Sakthi. Nandhi bull, the vehicle, is also seen.

> "Seeing, the root seems egg-like in form,
> Standing there as tri-konam, with reason,
> A ring surrounding three angles
> Four petals encircle,
> Approaching, four lotus Bija,
> Va, Cha, Sa, Sha,
> Nearing, then a vision of inner light
> Of the triad AUM-kaaram,
> Try to find within it...
> The first of AUM is 'A'-kaaram."
>
> Bogar Sapta Kandam, Verse 11

> "Upon the A-kaaram Ganesha presides
> In another angle the U-kaaram stands,
> Vallabai Sakthi presides on this U-kaaram,
> Then, is a plantain flower in the converging angle
> Below this, Kundalini Sakthi's calling face
> As like a coiled maiden serpent, ready to strike,
> Permeating, with ease within the edge of the whirl,
> Is the state Thuriyatheetham."
>
> Bogar Sapta Kandam, Verse 12

Siddha Bogar sings this description in his work: Bogar Sapta Kandam, of 7000 verses. He says the eight petals of the plantain bud remain closed and flower only by grace. Each petal holds a specific feminine deity, denoting the *Sakthi* of the corresponding Siddhi. The eight deities of the eight petals of the plantain bud signify the *Asta Siddhis*. During Yogic practice, when the male deity awakens, the latent eight *Sakthis* veil themselves by blessing the practitioner with an intoxicating experience which prevents him from perceiving the presence of the eight *Sakthis*. Siddha Bogar says, it is very rare for the opening of these eight petals which bestow the practitioner with the Goddess's *Asta Siddhis*. The *Asta Siddhis* can perform great miracles and is a rare occurrence. Ironically, nowadays casual practitioners claim that their third eye or eyebrow centre (a thousand petalled lotus) has awakened! Such is the ignorance. As per the sacred verses of Siddha Bogar, the egg shape he describes in the *Mooladharam chakra* is the seed of the universe and is potent with the dormant mysterious inner world which needs to sprout and flower. The name *Mooladharam* symbolises its divine essence of being the base for both internal flowering and external manifestation.

CHAPTER ELEVEN: CHAKRAS – THE WHEELS OF LIFE

THE VIEW FROM AN ANCIENT WINDOW

The impersonal revelations of the Siddhas' aim at non-egoistic living. They describe humans to be a combination of cosmic forces coming through planets and stars. The ego, which is our sense of personal identity, they say is mere fiction, an illusion, and does not exist. We all have the same basic nature, superficially and in-depth, and go through the same basic life experience, good and bad, solely for the evolution of consciousness. No soul receives special treatment. The differences we see actually arise from being at various stages of the process and not because we are truly different or separate, better or worse than one another. The essence of health actively flows within everyone as Divine Light. Snaking its way up through the subtle nerve-like threads of the body, called *Nadis*, it expels darkness of the past, un-knots traumas stuck in cellular memory and so on. Bathing in the Holy Springs within, a yogic practitioner gradually ceases to feel limited by past lives, present life trauma or old thought patterns. With an awakening, life gets freed from the ghouls and fears of the subconscious and all past life agony and grief appear faint and brief, as if performing their last turn on the stage of opposites before transmuting forever into the Light. It is the ultimate opportunity to be twice born. From the Siddha's perspective, illness or pain are not suffering but purposeful events within a universally ongoing evolution; a process of divine cleansing. Most chronic diseases such as - hypertension, arthritis, allergies, auto-immune disorders, diabetes, asthma, back pain - upon which the healthcare industry thrives, are, in fact, manifestations of energy encountering blocks or resistances to its flow which need liberation to continue on an unhindered path. All humans inherit the same potential as well as the same basic problems to work out as destiny. We also inherit a common spiritual goal to help us go beyond outer influence, primarily the need to feel important in the external world and to repeatedly prove ourselves. In this regard, every birth chart paints the picture of ignorance, our patterns of desire and our web of karmic imprints; the bondage by which we are caught. The mind lives in our body through the energy system, the subtle body, and affects our gross body. The consciousness of our mind reflects in our energetic subtle body. Wherever mind travels, energy follows. Energy blocks are areas one has turned insensitive to or is unaware of due to the absence of free-flowing perception. In order to understand where in our body our mind lives or does not live and how it has come to be this way, we can start observing our energy phenomena. But that it is hard to do in a world that bombards us with so many influences. Recent neurological studies indicate that the human brain with its electromagnetic fluids is constantly processing and generating waves that affect our sensitivities. Our reactions show we are sensitive to sound and light waves. Noise can be jarring to the ear and music can stimulate us in different ways. Fast-paced music can generate pulsation enough to push us into over-drive, while melodious music can be a soothing experience. Ancient Indian myths metaphorically picture the process of creation and destruction by the Cosmic Dancer Siva dancing to the Cosmic Tune. The Siddhas prescribe *Bija Mantras* (seed syllables) in the practice of *Kundalini Yoga* because just as external waves affect us, the resonance of *Bija Mantras* lead us to experience the vibration of the relevant whirling chakra of our subtle body. Light waves also impact the brain causing different reactions to shapes and colours. We feel different around shades of red, brown or shades of blue, green. We are affected differently by the noise and visual pollution of urban and semi-urban cities and the open countryside.

The exhibitionist approach of humans created a visual and descriptive world-view, which also made him insensitive toward himself. Subtle energy practice requires high-level sensitivity, awareness and clarity in perception. Even though subtle energy functions are always at work, to be aware of it requires more than a mediocre level of sensitivity which is why it is not easy to experience the dynamism of chakras and its various dimensions such as colour, vibration, inherent nature, characteristic traits and each of the presiding deities. Modern day practitioners follow the practice of visualising the chakras and its attributes. This cannot be considered true experience. The revelation of each chakra is an undeniably spontaneous experience.

ಶ್ರೀ ಕೃ

MISSED CONCERN

The Siddhas say - human life is meant solely for growth, transformation and expansion of consciousness. Every individual may be at different milestones but our journey is one, like rivers converging into the ocean. Whenever we move farther and farther away from ourself, the iron hands of life bounce us back through a spiritual crisis, where we experience utter inability of our will and are made to confront the masks disguising our existential nature. A long-standing conflict between free will and fate, born of poor understanding triggers a spiritual crisis. Unresolved conflicts turn severe and reflect in one's personality as confusion, un-clarity or more intense states like schizophrenia, multi-personality disorders, paranoia, psychosis, etc. A spiritual crisis almost always precedes a medical condition. It is the 'overload', the 'too much', and the 'too fast'. When our logical mind and parts of our personality fail to process experiences, we fall into an abyss of chaos and confusion. We begin to feel the genuine need for an awakened guide; one who has travelled the road and emerged victorious.

Energy-practice and awakening the *Kundalini sakthi* are not paths to be travelled unaided, but ironically, those who can guide are busy mystifying themselves rather than spreading the light of awareness, and those who do make it forward in the social world end up making it a business! We are left with the sole option of making this ascent by feeling our burning quest for Truth with our genuine longing and our sincerity calls forth the shower of grace required for true transformation. When enthusiasm for transcendence is intense, inviting experiences are bound to follow and the teachings of ancient Siddhas are never more relevant than now.

ॐ ॐ

SECTION THREE: BEING AND SHARING

LADDER OF HEAVEN

The experience of chakras are revelations that cannot be studied, memorised or worked out. Some modern day books approach the subject in a technical fashion and provide a lot of data but this book describes the chakras with only as much detail as required for the moment.

Mooladharam
Root or Base for both the Physical and Inner World

This chakra is situated at the base of the spinal column in the perineum area between the genital area and anal orifice. It is a deep red-coloured lotus of four petals, surrounding an egg-like circle. Within this circle is a green inverted triangle and its downward point symbolises a *yoni* (a downward triangle). In one angle of this triad, there is an eight-petaled plantain-tree bud. Another angle shows the presiding male deity, Lord Ganesha and in the third angle stands Goddess Vallabai Sakthi. In the centre of the triangle sits a Siva Lingam. Coiled around it is a golden snake with its hood spread above the lingam. Nandhi bull, the vehicle, is also seen here. The coiled maiden snake is Mother Kundalini Sakthi. Its *Atcharam*, or seed syllable, or *mantra* (Bija in Sanskrit) is 'AUM'. And the characteristics of this chakra are related to aspects of physical survival, anxiety, groundedness, etc. The word *Mooladharam* means foundation, base or receptacle. It carries our past *Samskaras* (karmic imprints). Experiences and residual sensations of previous lives are stored here as dormant potential. Other yogic schools consider this as the chakra of the Earth element, but the Tamil Siddhas attribute no element to the *Mooladharam* and is perceived to have a centrally-independent and vitally-significant function, which is discussed in the section 'Rivering the Fire'.

Swadhisthanam
Own Place

Moving up, the next chakra is situated in the *Sushumna* channel between the genital and navel region. This yellow chakra is square in shape and is encircled within a yellow lotus of six petals. At its centre is inscribed the letter 'NA' signifying the Earth element. From within this square-shaped chakra shines a yellow green colour. The Tamil Siddhas attribute *Prithivi*, the Earth element, to this region. The presiding male deity is Lord Brahma and the female deity is Goddess Saraswathi or Goddess Vani. The meaning of the word *Swadhistanam* is 'home' or 'own place' of the individual self. Its inherent nature is procreation, passion, over attachment, impulse and emotion.

Manipoorakam
Gem of Rays

Manipoorakam is situated in the *Sushumna Nadi* in the area corresponding to the navel. The lotus here has ten petals. Within the circle is a white crystal-coloured crescent moon, submerged entirely in water. The space above the water level has a rising light shining forth. The light as well as the submerged crescent moon carry deep significance. The submerged crescent moon denotes subconscious mind tendencies and the light refers to the conscious mind. 'MA', is the seed syllable. The presiding deities are Lord Vishnu and Goddess Laxmi. The symbolic posture of Lord Vishnu asleep on a milky white ocean influences all living beings by making them identify and attach to apparent things in a delusive way. This is the nature of Yoga Maya. Lord Vishnu is the presiding deity of Yoga Maya. The element or *Tattwa* attributed to this centre is water. The meaning of the word '*Manipoora*' is 'city of crystal or rays'. The Siddhas have another definition for *Manipoorakam*: '*Poorakam*' meaning inhalation and internal assimilation: the gem of assimilation. Its characteristic traits are related with pride, confidence, achievement, competition and personal power. This area marks the climax of all material possession, power, name, fame and authority. As dispassion unfolds toward power and other traits mentioned above, the practitioner gains a fuller understanding of the futility and transient nature of worldly things which allows the love for truth to flower, naturally enabling the practitioner to rise to the next chakra.

Anahatam
Uncaused Mystical Throb

The chakra in the region of the heart is the seat of Lord Rudra (Lord Siva's aspect as the destroyer of the manifest worlds) and Goddess Rudri (or Bhadrakali). Its seed syllable is 'SI'. The element attributed is fire. It is red in colour and its form is a triangle with its apex pointed upward. There are twelve blue-coloured petals. The function of this chakra is in the realm of personal love, feelings and compassion. *Anahatam* means the uncaused or un-agitated. When the *Kundalini* rises and this chakra flowers, an entirely new realm blossoms for the practitioner. Its awakening transcends the lower chakras and the material identification that goes along with them. The individual is reborn into the spiritual realm. Its traits are love, benevolence and devotion, flowing ceaselessly from within, without being triggered by external factors. The experience and expression is of Universal Love; love of God, love of human beings, love of one's self, all three in ONE, everywhere, for everyone and everything.

Visuddhi
Beyond Obstruction

Visuddhi is located in the throat or neck region, at the junction of Medulla Oblongata and the spinal column. It is the seat of Lord Maheswara and Goddess Maheswari. This plexus is related to the Air element. The chakra is a smoky grey formation of a six-pointed hexagonal star with 16 petals, inscribed with the mystic letter 'VA'. The characteristics of this chakra are expression of feelings, clarity, sharing, communication and creativity. A spiritually-integrated and devoted practitioner, expresses creatively with unobstructed flow on the awakening of his *Visuddhi*. Divine creativity such as devotional poems, music and singing and divine art forms flourish through him. Conventional Yogic practitioners of other schools withdraw the pranic current from dissipating through the nine orifices of the body using *Bandha* and *Mudra* techniques which is called *Prana Pratiyakara*; withdrawal of *Prana* from the senses. The Siddhas name the *Visuddhi* centre as the origin of the Air element and its awakening naturally leads to the withdrawal of the pranic current from the nine orifices of the body and *nadis*. Therefore, concentrated withdrawal of each aspect of the pranic current from its respective orifices is unnecessary as the Air can be restrained in its own house itself. The word *Visuddhi* also means 'extremely pure' which is why the personality of the Yogi manifests as pure beauty, pure goodness and pure truth.

Agnayam
Non-duality (Agna in Sanskrit)

The Agnai chakra is situated at the end of the Sushumna Nadi, in the centre of the skull - at the junction of two imaginary lines drawn to the centre from between the two ears and joining at the midpoint of the eyebrows. The seed syllable 'YA'. The two-petaled lotus is indigo in colour and is the abode of Lord Sadasivam and Goddess Manonmani. The related element is Ether. Here the two nadis Ida and Pingala finally merge.

> "Left hand, Right hand,
> Change both hands!
> If you eat with the hand of worship
> Not depleted, you forsake sleep
> And become realised.
> You need not die, but live eternally!"
>
> Thirumanthiram by Thirumoolar

The function of this chakra relates to qualities of intuition, divine contentment and perceptive sensitivity. Awakening of this chakra facilitates dropping of objective consciousness and the individual remains intoxicated as subjective consciousness. The Siddhas call this state as *Thar Bodham* which too must be transcended. Here, absolute knowledge unfolds within the yogi. Knowledge is contentment, freedom and bliss but there is still a limitation to be surpassed. Subtly, subjective consciousness remains, implying truth to be as the 'object' of perception and oneself being the 'subject' in it.

Sahasraram
Field of Flowering

The *Sahasraram* is above the *Agnai chakra*, near the point corresponding to the 'soft-spot' of a baby's head. The word *Sahasraram* means 'thousand-petal lotus' - the symbol of the transcendental state of absolute existence, knowledge and bliss.

CHAPTER ELEVEN: CHAKRAS – THE WHEELS OF LIFE

Here, subjective consciousness flowers with un-ebbing flow. The state is *Nirvikalpa Samadhi*, a state devoid of any thought or movement of mind. One is beyond time, space and causation. In fullness, the innate divine nature manifests in pristine glory and infinite bliss. With the full culmination of the thousand and eight petaled lotus, the blissful consciousness finds its settling place either by descending through the *Amritha Nadi* to the Spiritual heart or by travelling twelve inches upward, above the *Sahasraram* and merging into the *Dwadhasantham*; here 'Dwa' means two, 'Dhasa' means ten, and 'antham' means the ultimate or end.

ॐ ☙

Each chakra has its own specific deities:

CHAKRA	GOD	GODDESS
Mooladharam	Ganapathi	Vallabai
Swadhistanam	Brahma	Saraswathi
Manipoorakam	Vishnu	Laxmi
Anahatam	Rudra	Rudri
Visuddhi	Maheswara	Maheswari
Agnai	Sadasiva	Manonmani

The presence of a presiding God and Goddess within each chakra demonstrate the inner significance, spiritual nature and aspects. If the Goddess is the power of identification of the particular modes in each chakra, then, God is the consciousness presiding over that specific (Goddess) force. *Ahamkara*, the power of identification, is the basis of all addictions, i.e. identifications. The Goddess nature is *Ahamkara* (*Aham* means inner and *Kara* means propelling, rising, or projecting). This power of identification is also *Kundalini Sakthi*. *Ahamkara* deceives herself into believing she is mated to the limited physical body. And in order to de-identify from her limited identification as body-mind, she undertakes the journey through the chakras. On reaching the top, *Sahasraram*, She discovers her true identity by the withdrawing of karmic *prana* from the solar and lunar channels into the central channel, *Sushumna nadi*. The slumbering *Kundalini Sakthi* completely 'uncoils'. Goddess (Sakthi) realises that She belongs to Siva. Realising the vast conscious space of Siva, *Sakthi* sacrifices her limited individuality, surrenders to Him and what happens is instant enlightenment. For an uninitiated or inexperienced person, if his power of identification (*Kundalini*) awakens to its true nature in a sudden or rash manner, it causes a sudden, forcible and overwhelming de-identification with the limited body-mind, making it an un-assimilable experience. An individual, ungrounded in crystallised consciousness cannot assimilate the huge influx of *Kundalini Sakthi* upon suddenly transcending the identified limitation, and both time and body-mind adversely lose their ability to identify. This leads to several complications like brain haemorrhage, seizures, nervous debility, mental disorders, cancer, coma and in extreme cases can cause physical death due to an overwhelming damage to the nervous and immune system. One is therefore advised to be supervised as an incredible amount of energy is released on the path of energy practice. The proper way to go through the energy practice that transmutes Goddess Sakthi's binding limitation by merging her with her conscious nature, Siva, is under the guidance and blessing of a *Sat Guru* (A Master of Truth), who is none other than the manifestation of the presiding consciousness, Siva, in human form. By His Grace, the limited personality is transformed by expansion into the '*Vettaveli*' (the Space, Infinite) of the Siddha (*Sat Guru*), abiding as 'Grand awareness'. Siva signifies the nature of endurance, assimilation and transcendence as the eternally presiding power over *Sakthi*.

> "Tapas, performed in the mountain valley within my head,
> Lo! I beheld the Lord with consort Sakthi,
> I crossed the river of birth in this fleshy body,
> And met the Thief, hiding in Kailash."
>
> Thirumanthiram, Verse 2597

ೞ ೲ

CHAPTER TWELVE

KUNDALINI - RIVERING THE FIRE

"Once upon a time, a Master and four disciples had been walking day and night for two days to reach a particular village. Along the way, they passed through many small villages. At dusk, the four disciples were exhausted and couldn't walk further. One disciple said to the Master, 'Enough! We cannot walk even one more step. We have already walked much further than we ever have. Now let us rest here.' The Master said, 'O.K. You may stay here but I will keep walking. You can join me tomorrow morning. But, my dear disciples, I have heard there are tigers attacking people at this place, so take care.' Saying this he started to walk. Suddenly, crossing in front of the Master were all four disciples. The Master caught hold of one and asked, 'Wait! You just said you didn't have any energy. From where has all this energy come?'"

Our relationship with energy is conditioned according to our way of life and social needs. The level of available energy depends upon personal traits and social conditioning but in situations of shock or sudden fear of survival, the conditioned pattern loosens giving way to a miraculous change! We realise a boundless reserve of energy becomes available in a state 'free of conditioning'. This unlimited, unconditioned energy, is *Kundalini Sakthi*.

Flow of Pulsation

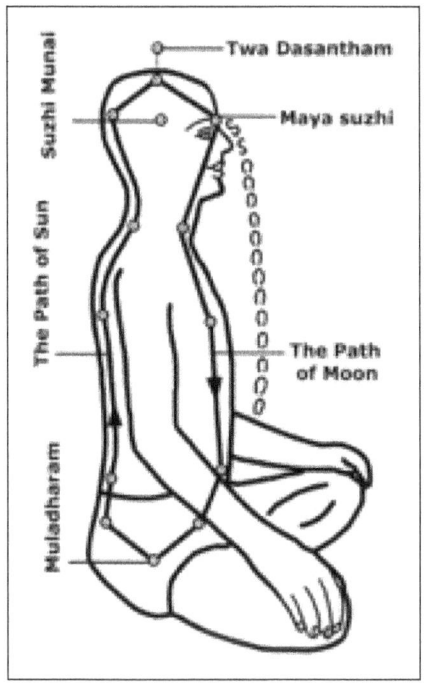

RISING OF THE KUNDALINI

> "Igniting a fire, pouring ghee, daily doing Pooja,
> Keenly you bathe in water and listen to the Vedas.
> The fire and water is within, if you reminisce,
> Then you will merge with the never diminishing Light."
>
> Siva Vakkiyar Padalgal Verse 31

The *Sushumna Nadi* begins at *Mooladharam*, the basal chakra, where Mother *Kundalini Sakthi* lies dormant. The *Sushumna Nadi* blocks spiritual evolution in an individual until the arousal of *Kundalini Sakthi* along the divine path, known as the Sun path. The block opens by the fire of *Kundalini* rising through the chakras, commencing the burning of tendencies and karmic imprints stored in relevant chakras.

> "Below the Earth, the path of Sun,
> Being a rare one, none see,
> Then rises between Fire and Water,
> Reachable to none, the Sun is He."
> Thirumanthiram Verse 1982

ಙಃ ಛ

Before reading about the Rising of *Kundalini*, we must first get familiar with the three basic lower chakras that play a vital role in the identification with the external world.

Mooladharam

The Siddha tradition assigns no element to the *Mooladharam chakra* in the evolution of the *Tattwas*. The formation of the five elements begins with ether at the *Agnai chakra.* and ends with the earth element at the Swadhistanam Chakra. What then is the nature of element in the *Mooladharam*? It is the residual part of evolution which we identify with the physical world. This chakra is also the point from which we mingle with *Moola Prakruthi*, the Primal Substance. The *Mooladharam* stands as the entrance to both worlds: the outside world and the subtle inner world. All five elements merge here, enabling functionality with the external world. Of all the many forms of Lord Ganesha, Ucchistha Ganapathi is the ruler or presiding deity of the *Mooladharam chakra*. *Ucchistham* means auspicious, blessed or sacred remains of either the food eaten by the Guru, or food offered to a deity: a special form of *prasad*. This implies that

Ucchistha Ganapathi is the *prasad* of Creation. When consciousness is interiorised in the *Mooladharam chakra,* the practitioner experiences a strong sense of grounding within.

Swadhisthanam

The second chakra carries a vital influence in identification with the external world, and represents the Earth element, according to the Siddhas. The presiding deities are Lord Brahma and Goddess Saraswathi, the presiding rulers of the Earth element. The Primal nature of *Swadhisthanam* is related to the faculty of procreation. It is from here we feel the sense of 'How can I create more to strengthen and enhance my sense of "I"; my existence. How can this "I" endure even after bodily death? By having offsprings, I physically create a replica or reflection of myself that survives and continues from generation to generation.' When our attention is externalised at the *Swadhistanam*, concerns related to generation and sexuality arise and when consciousness is directed inward, a creative nature flourishes.

Manipoorakam:
(*'Mani'* means gem; *'poorakam'* means internal assimilation)

This chakra is distinctive in nature. In the practice of *Pranayama*, '*Poorakam*' means inhalation and the literal meaning of *'Mani'* is 'gem', or crystal, implying crystallisation or centring. A crystallised part can be called a gem. Personalities dominated by extrovert energy of this chakra show predominant traits of possessing fame and power but if consciousness is indrawn, the energy crystallises and prevents dissipation which gives perfect momentum to the rising *Kundalini Sakthi*. The practitioner recognises that all power resides within and prior extrovert cravings dissolve. Today's way of life is built on an imbalanced function of the three lower chakras. Survival anxiety imposed by the likes of terrorism or vulnerable situations affect and awaken the negative aspects of *Mooladharam*. Poor ethics and values lead to a lifestyle of over indulgence and addiction which impairs the *Swadhisthanam*. The hustle bustle of society and frequent inventions tempt man to possess more and more to fulfil his fantasies. But man alone cannot be blamed. The speeding world runs in the name of survival of the fittest and in order to survive this mass hypnosis, each one is driven to use the same approach of competitiveness, jealousy, power, position, and fame. These neurotic tendencies, mistaken as Life, severely damage the inherent function of *Manipoorakam*.

༄༅

RISING FIRE

Factors that participate in the arousal of the *Kundalini* and their existential significance.

> "There is no lineage without the Seed, either above or below,
> In what way can the Palace take shape without an architect?
> You ignorant one! You sell your mother and turn her into a slave!
> Where there is no emancipation, there is no Life!
> Never, Never, Never!!!"
>
> Siva Vakkiyar Padalgal Verse -15

We have no right to call *Kundalini* 'Mother', when we sell her to a multitude of fragmentary images! To worship Her is to give Her, Her rightful place of properly awakening the Mother consciousness in oneself.

CHAPTER TWELVE: KUNDALINI - RIVERING THE FIRE

MAYA SUZHI - THE WHIRL OF MAYA

The extrovert function of senses is due to energy being projected outward through the eyes (seeing), mouth (speech and eating), nose, (smelling and breathing the air outside), etc. To begin with, these are survival-based existential externalisations, by birth. But, living in an overemphasised head-dominant thinking world we become head-dominant, localised and fragmented. We exclude the rest of 'us' and identify predominantly to the physical world. When a head-dominant individual turns his attention within, the mixed energy of external and indrawn consciousness first accumulates and whirls in the frontal centre of the forehead between the eyebrows. The Siddha tradition names this place *Maya Suzhi* or the whirl of *Maya*. It is our first encounter of ourself. The whirling energy then descends through the frontal channel, *Chandran*, located in the frontal line of the body. This is the path of the moon, anterior channel, the descending line or procreative channel. Another channel beginning from the Basal chakra to the eyebrow chakra is called the posterior channel or the path of the Sun. This is explained further as we go on. As the practitioner becomes aware of the whirl of energy, he may misunderstand it to be the eyebrow centre, *Agnai chakra* to be active, but this is not so. This is not *Agnai* activity. *Agnai*, the eyebrow or third eye centre, is located behind this place, within the skull. Moreover, at the *Agnai chakra* the energy whirls in a clockwise or centripetal direction, whereas here, at *Maya Suzhi*, found between the eyebrows, the whirl is anti-clockwise. This should clear any misconceptions of each of these energy-whirl experiences.

ಐ ಐ

SECTION THREE: BEING AND SHARING

ABDOMINAL BRAIN

In the foetal state, consciousness is located in the posterior channel and operates only up to the naval area of the frontal channel. Consciousness is centred here, providing the foetus food and energy through the belly button or naval (colloquially called *Nabhi* in Tamil). The navel is called *Arutha Adaita Vassal* in Siddha terminology. *Arutha* means 'cutting' (the umbilical cord is cut); *Adaita* means, it is 'blocked' (the belly connection with the mother); *Vassal* means 'entrance or gate'. By cutting the umbilical cord our psyche's connection to 'home', the place where consciousness is centred and which sustained our foetal body, is cut. In the moment it is cut our 'belly-located' consciousness gets thwarted upward from the *Manipoorakam* through the frontal channel to the head region (Pseudo-Agnai or Maya Suzhi point) and the concept of subject and object gradually begins to manifest. Now the newborn has to identify with the external world for survival, will take food through the mouth and recognise his mother by sight.

ಲ ಆ

FALL OF THE 'OBJECTIVE'

During a meditative mood or while lost in the divine melody of *bhajans,* the world outside fades and outward-looking eyes now carry a vacant look. By not identifying with the eyes, the eyes don't focus on anything particular and they appear to have a vacant look. (A meditative state need not be confined to a seated posture and closed eyes.) The breathing spontaneously slows down and outbound energy begins to gather between the eyebrows at the *Maya Suzhi* - the mid-eyebrow point in the frontal channel. There it mixes, converges, aligns and begins to whirl in a counter-clockwise direction. The spin of *Maya Suzhi* pulls it downward and the whirling energy descends through the frontal *nadi*, the path of the moon. Usually, the whirl does not descend speedily except for ripened individuals, in which case it descends and settles in the belly area. This can also happen by the grace of the Guru. But more commonly, first there is a throbbing pulsation moving back and forth between the Pseudo *Agnai* point and throat. As meditation deepens and the withdrawal graduates, these swift pulsations descend further down from the throat to the chest area. A person carrying emotional suppression over a long period of time could undergo emotional upheavals and strong reactions when this whirl of energy hits the chest. With continued meditation, the whirl of energy descends lower through the frontal channel to the belly area. This entire process of descending pulsating energy is a thrilling experience and can be described as an 'energetic inner conjugal relation with oneself'. This exhilarating experience enhances the spirit to awaken the fire in the Basal chakra. It is like the blacksmith blowing air on the fire to set it ablaze and make it fierier. In the Siddha tradition, terminology differs according to context. For example, the left-nostril breath and the left eye are governed by the moon (lunar principle). While referring to the breath, the left-nostril breath is called lunar breath and while referring to pranic or energy pathways, the frontal *nadi* or channel (through which energy flows from *Maya suzhi* downward) is also called the path of the moon, *Chandra kalai* (*kalai* means fragmentary path). Likewise: the *Suzhi* - the counter-clockwise whirling is called *Ida* and the clockwise whirling is called *Valam* (*pradakshina*). (It is always better to be careful and understand from a genuine Siddha Master the authentic terminology of the Siddha tradition to avoid being misled.) As meditation deepens, the *Maya Suzhi* descends further until it settles in the *Mooladharam*, the basal/root chakra. From here *prana* takes the path of the posterior channel, the path of the sun; *Surya Kalai*.

Just as the cosmic Moon reflects light received from the Sun, similarly, our reflective awareness localised in the frontal channel gets its impetus from our centralised awareness of the posterior channel, the Sun. The solar and lunar symbolism is the central principle in the mysterious cult of the Siddhas. Even according to ancient Hebrew tradition, the Sun is masculine and paternal and the Moon is feminine and maternal; Taoist Chinese tradition considers the Sun - Yang - Hot, and the Moon - Yin - Cool.

"The Solar breath leads to transcendence;
The Lunar breath is a form - giving substance."

Prana Upanishads

With deepening meditation, when the *Suzhi* (whirl) descends and joins the *Mooladharam*, it awakens the *Kundalini* and the four-petaled *Mooladharam* flowers completely. The practitioner temporarily loses his sense of smell or may experience a trembling in the whole body or torso. Some may even experience suspended breathing along with profuse sweating. When *Kundalini* moves again, it is along the posterior channel, the path of the Sun. Now, with its upward rising journey it begins the involution of *Tattwas*.

For a moment, let us speak of the state of a newborn. Immediately on birth, if the newborn doesn't cry it is hung upside down and slapped on the back until it does. This is done in order to start the breathing process which happens with consciousness thwarting upward through the frontal channel. The crystallised *Prana* is channelised to the head. Interestingly, the seed of the first sound comes from the posterior channel, through the *Mooladharam*, into the frontal channel and up the belly, from where it starts to eject as an audible sound. Focused seeing or attentiveness to the external world is not immediate for a newborn. For some duration, a newborn carries a vacant gaze as its attention is still directed inward.

CHAPTER TWELVE: KUNDALINI – RIVERING THE FIRE

As we play with the newborn, its sight or attention begins to get drawn outward through its eyes in response to this play of the other. Our sound, breath and consciousness are interlinked, which is why the Siddhas use various breathing practices and the chanting of *mantras*, etc. to once again realise the true nature of consciousness.

> "The oracle of breath unfolds its secrets to those who know the keys. The elements in breath are known as Fire, Water, Earth and Ether."
> Swara Chintamani (Sanskrit work)

> "When the breath is unsteady, all is unsteady:
> When the breath is still, all is still:
> Remain aware of the phenomena of breath, carefully.
> Inhalation gives strength and a controlled body,
> Retention gives steadiness of mind and longevity,
> Exhalation purifies the body and emotional spirit."
> Goraksa Sathakam (written by Gorakkar in Sanskrit)

As meditation deepens, the indrawn *prana* carrying localised consciousness to the Basal chakra, now begins to move vertically from the *Mooladharam*, centre by centre, through the posterior or Sun channel. When the *Kundalini* rises from the *Mooladharam chakra* to the *Swadhisthanam*, all the petals of this chakra bloom completely and the practitioner temporarily loses his sense of taste. *Swadhisthanam*, the procreative chakra, is innately related with one's taste buds, explained by the phrase "palate and passion". An involuntary contraction of the lower abdomen towards the backbone also happens. When *Kundalini* reaches the *Manipoorakam chakra*, the external breathing process changes and inhalation and exhalation happen as *Inner Pranayama* or internal breathing with the absence of nostril breath and the presence of some amount of heat waves from the nostrils. This shift represents the turning in of the identifying nature toward its original identity and until it finds it, merges and settles, the internal breathing process continues. With the *Kundalini* reaching the heart chakra, *Anahatam*, the practitioner has the first glimpse of his subjective nature or identified consciousness having a singular mode of perception instead of a fragmented or multi-faceted one. For example, when the consciousness of a Yogi, who is an earnest seeker of Lord Krishna, localises at *Anahatam*, he will find himself always with his beloved Lord Krishna. When his consciousness rises to the back of the throat area, to the *Visuddhi chakra*, he will see his beloved Lord Krishna everywhere. To him the whole world is Krishna as his singular perception shifts to universal singular perception. The creative nature of *Visuddhi chakra* must not be mistaken as the procreative nature of *Swadhisthanam*. In the *Visuddhi chakra*, even though the sense of self expands to encompass the entire universe, it remains gripped to a specific mode or attribute such as the perception of Lord Krishna in this particular example. The being begins to have its 'inter-being' in the throat chakra. In the *Visuddhi chakra* state the experience is of clean, infinite, vast spaciousness, yet with a specific attribute. Even though the power of identification with form is greatly reduced, there still exists a sure but subtle veil of objectivity; 'I' and the 'other-ness'. When consciousness merges into *Agnai chakra* within the skull at eyebrow level, objective consciousness manifests into a pure attribute-free consciousness holding only the subjective nature. From here, when the practitioner's subjective consciousness rises to *Brahmarandhra* (in Sanskrit) or *Suzhi Munai* in the Tamil Siddha tradition, it flourishes as an un-ebbing flow. The *Brahmarandhra* 'opens' only once the *prana* merges, before which it remains closed as embodied consciousness is gripped externally due to being projected outward through the nine orifices of the body. The nine orifices are: the two openings of the eyes, ears, nose, one of the mouth, one of the genitals, and one of the anus. When *Suzhi Munai,* or the 'tenth hole' opens, the other nine orifices render themselves functionless.

The arousal of the *Kundalini* in the chakras begins at the point of *Maya Suzhi* with the dissolution of objective consciousness and ends in *Suzhi Munai* - the vortex of the dissolution of all embodied objective nature. '*Suzhi*' means vortex or whirl; '*munai*' means edge. This "vortex edge" is the end of the solar path. Its location is the midpoint of an imaginary line drawn from between the eyes and another line from between the ears, to meet. When consciousness merges at *Suzhi Munai,* everything objective disappears and the world ceases to exist in or to our awareness. In the fire of the third eye or in the eye of Siva, the subtle body merges with the causal body and the *Samskaras* of all past births begin to burn. After this comes the flowering of the thousand-petaled lotus. The journey continues to the *Ucchi Vassal* or *Ucchi Kan* - this means 'eye in the top' (*Ucchi* means top). When the ethereal eye in the crown region of the skull blossoms, it grows supremely sensitive and starts to see the inner cosmic space. This stage is prior to abiding in the Ultimate Truth. Next, the flourishing subjective consciousness in the *Sahasraram*, has to fall to its settling place for one to vanish in the Absolute; the pre-reflective consciousness where there is no reflection of subject and object. Consciousness can settle in the following possible ways. Subjective consciousness descends through the *Amritha Nadi* and settles in the spiritual heart after cutting the *Hridaya Granthi*. The Siddhas call this as '*Pinda Anubava*'; realisation that manifests by relinquishing the identification with the body. (*Pinda* means limited or form). In *Pinda Anubava*, there is no experience of body consciousness. Consciousness can be said to have settled in the right side of the chest, the spiritual heart, although, in truth there is no physical point of the spiritual heart as it is beyond localisation. Alternatively, consciousness could take an upward course and merge 12" above the head (*Dwadhasantham*), with the inner cosmic space, the Source. This is called *'Anda Anubava'*, liberation in the Un-manifest.

> "In twelve finger measure within the head,
> The moving life-breath rising high,
> Seeking the place of beyond sound where the Lord Dance
> That verily is the sacred temple."
>
> Thirumanthiram Verse 2764

Siddha Kaga Busundar and Siddha Saint Ramalingam Swami, both speak of these experiences giving them two different names: the first, *Pinda Anubava*, is called *'Poorvam'* (meaning 'Here' or 'Primal') and the second, *Anda Anubava*, is called *'Utharam'* (meaning beyond).

> "The eight-fold yoga, the six chakras of the body, the five states: all have gone, erased in the infinite space of nothingness, leaving me amazed. Drinking the white milk from the fountain of the red-rounded moon, being delighted, the unobtainable bliss has engulfed me!"
>
> Siddhar Pattinathar (Pothu Padal Verse- 25)

I would like to clarify that although throughout this chapter we have implied consciousness to rise, move, etc. we have done so to make it easier for the reader to grasp the essence. The word 'consciousness' has been used in reference to the journey of the re-falling of reflective consciousness to its pre-reflective state.

ಖಂ ಲ

CHAPTER THIRTEEN

ALCHEMY - Internal and External

A story better elucidates the knowledge and true spirit of the hidden science of mystery and cryptic terms.

RISYA - THE REMINDER OF OUR LOST SPIRIT

From a tiny patch in the otherwise large and looming forest was heard noise! The forest air hummed with shrill, squeaks, snorts, sniffs and the sounds of scampering feet. It was a small Rat village. A marked terrain hidden beneath thick bushes and tall wild grass was home to many rat families. It was a crowded rat community that revered a head, elders, young ones and all.

It was common protocol and long established norm to not venture beyond the boundaries of the thicket. The rest of the forest was forbidden and lay unexplored, for among other dangers the eagles circled above. Every rat grew up learning to fear the soaring eagles ready to prey on them. Generations inherited this conditioned terror and not one ventured beyond the thicket to walk under open sky.

Risya was one of them. An active, playful and energetic rat, he was always eager for some fun. He had a gentle, kind and caring heart and like any other rat in the village, he too was always busy scurrying about in search of food, running hither thither all day long, sniffing out places and digging little burrows. Risya's mind nurtured an added curiosity for the enigmatic touch of life. His perspective, unlike others, was a bit more far reaching. Now and then, he would be overcome with curiosity to what lay beyond The Boundary. One day, while scurrying around, Risya's sharp ears heard a sound. He stopped dead in his tracks, pricked up his ears and listened. He listened hard. It grew louder – it was a roar...'ROAR'... Risya's heart beat loudly and eyes grew wide. He listened in sheer astonishment for it was like nothing he had ever heard before. Lifting his able nose, he sniffed the air carefully. It twitched and turned trying hard to pick up a telling smell. Then the sound slowly faded away and stopped. He had no idea of where it had come from or what it was. A little alarmed by the strange incident he looked around to see if any of his brothers and sisters had heard it. Nothing had changed around him. No one had stopped like he had. They scampered around as usual - doing what they always did. Unable to stop himself, Risya asked his friend if he had heard anything strange. He hadn't. Then he asked another... he hadn't either. Risya soon realised he was the only rat in the whole rat village who had heard 'the sound' - the 'Roar'. He thought that was strange! Well, the sound had faded away and Risya couldn't do much about that now, so he went on with his mediocre life, and mediocre ways, doing his mundane activities day after day. Life was passing by again.

 A few days later, it happened again. Once again, the bewildered rat stood transfixed in his place. It was the same 'Roar'. Risya listened hard. The sound was enthralling and this time he didn't feel so afraid as before. Then again, it faded away and left, bringing back the old and familiar sounds of the forest to fill Risya's sharp ears again. But it didn't leave Risya's mind. Risya couldn't stop thinking about it. Thoughts and memory of the sound wouldn't leave. He wondered and pondered about what it was, where it came from and why hadn't anybody else heard it? Why was he the only rat that had heard it?

CHAPTER THIRTEEN: ALCHEMY - INTERNAL AND EXTERNAL

Was there something wrong with him? All these questions haunted Risya's little head until finally he did the unthinkable. He took a bold step - the kind never taken before by any other rat in the whole of Rat Village. Risya decided to cross The Boundary in search of the 'Roar'. He was to do the unheard of! The other rats looked at him in sheer disbelief, their whiskered mouths wide open. They glanced at each other with enquiring looks, shrill voices rang out from the community, 'Nobody has ever gone beyond The Boundary.' 'It is unheard of.' 'You are walking to your death, Risya.' 'Risya! Don't be foolish, how can you face the unknown?' 'Brother, don't be stupid, don't throw your life away.' 'Young man, listen to the elders, they know best.'

Risya stood silent. Some noses turned away in disgust at his outright disobedience. Some eyes grew wide with fear at the thought of the danger that lay ahead. All in all they thought him foolish and crazy and it didn't take long before most of the village made Risya into a laughing stock. Everybody mocked poor Risya. Not one voice concurred with his but Risya stood firm. He knew he had to find the 'Roar'. He set off early next day. The community stood whispering amongst themselves, smirking and laughing, as Risya walked by. They watched as he scurried into the forest and crossed The Boundary. The Search had begun.

Novel sights met Risya's eyes. He looked around, amazed at the novel forest. Away from familiar sounds of the Rat village, the forest stood in an immense silence. The grandeur of it all left Risya wonderstruck. He had never been out here and what he saw filled his heart with marvel and awe. Risya felt happy. He felt free. Risya kept walking. Suddenly, scampering around a bush, Risya stumbled upon a strange animal he had never seen before. Taken aback Risya stared at the queer yet beautiful creature before him. It was so different. Bigger! Risya didn't fear so easily and felt the creature meant no harm, so he bravely spoke, 'Hello, my name is Risya, the rat. Who are you?' The graceful animal came forward and called himself Deer. He said,

SECTION THREE: BEING AND SHARING

'They call me 'Runner from the Masses'.' Both stood in the morning green and exchanged friendly words. Deer enquired, 'What are you doing so far from Rat Village? There are many dangers.' Hesitatingly, Risya narrated his story explaining how he had set off in search of the 'Roar'. He was afraid the Deer would laugh and mock at him as his community had. But to his surprise, the Deer smiled and said, 'I can take you there.' Overjoyed at the Deer's words, Risya happily agreed and together they walked into the unknown.

For Risya, this was a wonderful journey. His heart felt lifted, light and wide, wide open. Excited by every little thing he saw and smelt, the brave little rat, so far from his village took in every new feeling, sight, smell and sound with great eagerness. Soon, Risya and his new found mate, the Deer, could hear the faint sound of the Roar. As they walked on, the sound of the Roar grew loud and strong. It didn't fade away anymore. As the sound grew closer and closer, Risya fell silent! He felt the 'Roar' was calling. Passing a bend, suddenly without warning, in a fraction of a moment they were met by a deafening sound and a sight that completely took Risya by surprise. His heart skipped a beat. They had reached the place of the Roar. Risya found himself standing right before a Roaring River. Deafened by the sound and over-whelmed by the sight, Risya merely stood there, unable to move or utter a single word. He had reached!

Risya felt the 'Roar' strongly saying something... he turned and asked the Deer, 'What is it the 'Roar' is saying?' The Deer laughed a sweet laugh and urged Risya to follow him. He led him to meet a new friend. She sat on a leaf - a fresh green leaf! The Deer walked up to her and introduced Risya. Then bidding goodbye to both, the Deer left the two new friends to get to know each other. Risya had never seen a frog before. Her very sight struck him. His gaze didn't leave her as she leapt high in the air and then to Risya's complete surprise, she jumped right into the river and out, right before his puzzled eyes. He thought she was terrific! She could go everywhere.

CHAPTER THIRTEEN: ALCHEMY - INTERNAL AND EXTERNAL

He looked shyly at her and asked, 'Who are you? Both land and water is home for you?' She smiled back and replied, 'Yes, both are home for me. I am a frog. The Elders call me 'Oceanic Moon'.' Risya politely introduced himself and explained he was a rat from the Rat Village far, far away. Coyly, he confessed he had never quite met anyone like her before, someone who could live on both land and water. The frog smiled at his honesty and innocence. Gathering some courage, Risya asked, 'I felt the Roar saying something, something I couldn't grasp, can you help me?'

She didn't reply at first. Instead she leapt about and Risya watched on in silent wonder. She then quietly turned and looked to where he stood and asked, 'Do you want a food that sprouts from the earth and reaches the skies?' She paused. 'Will you listen to what I say?' Keen Risya eagerly asked, 'What is that food?' Oceanic Moon said, 'It is the food elders took and became The Elders'. But, Risya still didn't understand. He was just about to sprout a new question when the frog spoke, 'Crouch down low, as low as you can go, then jump up high, as high as you can try!'

So Risya crouched down low, as low to the earth as he could go and then jumped up high, as high as all his strength could. To his disbelief and astonishment, Risya found himself up in the air... so high as he had never ever been before. He was almost flying... something ordinarily not known to him. From here, Risya saw the river down below, he saw how the land looked from up above ... and suddenly his eyes turned and he saw 'the Holy Mountain' with its oracle of golden rays. The sight of the holy mountain stunned him. It put him in awe greater than what he had felt on first seeing the Roaring River. In that moment, Risya became ever so happy that he entirely forgot everything else. He forgot the frog seated below, he forgot the Roar, but most of all he forgot he was up, up in the air! Suddenly Risya found himself falling; falling downward with great, great speed. He looked down just in time to see his widely spread arms and legs closing in and touching the rushing waters of the Roaring River flowing below, and within moments he got swirled away under the fast speeding waters.

Below the waters, Risya struggled. He was drowning and gulping water fast. Frantically waving his arms and legs, Risya somehow managed to push himself to the surface of the water and out popped his head, desperately gasping for air. Swimming with all his might, in one way or another he managed to touch the riverbank and cling on for his dear life. Risya climbed out.

Drenched to the bone, tired and completely shaken, Risya fell to the earth exhausted but relieved. He saw the frog. A sudden rage of anger welled up in him filling him with new energy and he jumped up shouting, 'Are you crazy, what did you ask me to do? I could have died.' She smiled and waited until Risya had finished shouting all he could. Then she gently asked, 'Risya, do you remember what you saw?' He grew silent. He whispered, 'Yes...' He had seen the Holy Mountain. A sight that had captured his tiny little rat heart! Risya knew he had been blessed. All his anger dissolved and a warm feeling of love filled his entire being. The frog said, 'What the roaring river murmured was an invitation to its home, the Holy Mountain, the Eldest Ancestor.' In a strong and forceful voice, Oceanic Moon declared, 'Risya, now you are the Jumping Rat!' Exhilarated by this adventure and the unbelievable vision, Risya thanked the frog profusely and hurriedly scampered back all the way to his tiny Rat Village to share this with his entire rat community. But Risya was to meet with a rude, rude shock.

He reached the village dripping, drenched, panting but all smiles. The rats stopped and turned to look at approaching Risya. They stared at his ragged condition and all of them stopped doing what they were doing. Their noses lifted up to smell. He smelt different! Once again, they exchanged looks. Something had changed! Risya, in a panting voice, eagerly shared everything he had seen and everything that had

CHAPTER THIRTEEN: ALCHEMY - INTERNAL AND EXTERNAL

happened with him to the nearest detail. His voice sounded strong, calm, and penetrated into the hearts of all, but, to his perplexity no one was ready to believe and accept what penetrated their hearts in that moment. They hurriedly refused the rippling changes that stirred the stagnant waters of conditioning, not allowing their torpidity to be made volatile. Instantly, their denial reflected as adverse reaction to what Risya had brought. Some completely ignored him, some walked away. Some grew angry and shouted rude remarks at him, 'He is an outcast. He abandoned the village. He no longer belongs.' Deep, deep inside, each rat secretly wondered how he had not been eaten by Them! But nobody dared speak it aloud.

Sad and broken-hearted, Risya listened to all the words thrown at him and his brave act. Finally, unable to bear the rejection and the anguish of standing alone, Risya made a huge compromise. He chose to walk back into his own rattrap - the mechanical mediocre living with the masses. With head hung low, Risya re-entered his same Old World and began to live as he always had. He followed the same vegetative routine, did the same habitual activities and life was no different than before he had left, but for one thing. This time Risya found himself unable to live this vicious routine. He was not happy. He didn't feel at home. The confused little rat struggled to pull through each passing day. Grappling with emotions of sadness, he encountered his aloneness, and life felt incomplete. Even though he tried hard to push his head down, it refused... Risya was caught between two worlds. Lonely in his sorrow and grief, Risya found no one to turn to. None of the rats came to care for him in his suffering; none recognised the pain in his heart. Risya watched them sniff around all day in search of food, keeping their heads down low, very busy gossiping with each other, telling tales. Risya tried and tried until he could try no more. Emptiness overtook him and he found himself failing miserably at his pretence. He could pretend no more. He stopped sniffing with the others and retreated to a corner of the village, sitting idle, alone. On one such day, as he sat in idleness, darkness gently fell around him and a sudden roar filled his ears. It shook his boundaries of idleness and filled his heart and entire being. Exhilarating memories poured and flowed. Risya shed tears of joy. In this tearful and joyful moment, each tear turned into climbing inspiration. He was taken in by a sudden revelation, 'If ten fools criticise one, then that one must surely be on the right track.' Risya jumped up strong and anew! Gone was his idleness. Gone was his sorrow. He had decided something for himself. The Mountain was calling. Risya didn't waste any time. Early next day, while the others were busy doing their sniffing activities, Risya slowly and steadily walked through them all, breaking ties with their grasping eyes. He walked on and watched his family, friends, loved ones turn into mediocre memory of the past as he passed.

Spread before Risya was the vast and deep forest and another unknown journey. It was silent, but a terrifying one. He felt watched even by the trees as he walked through the dense greens. A sudden thought disturbed the hanging silence. 'The eagles'. He felt an overwhelming fear engulf him and for a moment he halted in his tracks, almost sure the eagles were already above. Vulnerability clung to him like a shadow, going everywhere with him. Although he had left his entire village behind, fear had stuck with him. But Risya didn't stop for more than a moment. He still had bushes around him into which he could run and hide. Soon, the tall trees were thinning out showing more and more open sky. He knew the time for real danger had come. He had reached the outskirts of density and now what lay ahead were vast barren plains. There was nowhere to hide and the eagles were above. How would he make it? Would he make it? Risya continued holding to one choice - he had to cross the plains.

A strange thought dropped, 'If I have to see the Mountain, I need to fly high in the sky. In the sky, where there are eagles... How can that ever happen, it is a paradox. 'Danger' and 'the Calling-Home'

CHAPTER THIRTEEN: ALCHEMY – INTERNAL AND EXTERNAL

lay as the same place, so close to each other.' Holding his beating heart firmly, Risya stepped out of the sheltering trees and tall grass and felt the sun beating down hard on his head and back. He knew he was not safe anymore. Seeing an isolated bush a short distance away, Risya scampered there and dived under. Safe! Peeking out from it, he noticed another. Scurrying to it, he hid himself. A few such bushes helped him on. All of a sudden, as he rushed into one such bush, Risya noticed two equally surprised eyes peering back at him from the darkness. He knew those eyes. They were of a rat! How unexpected to find a rat in these parts. Risya spoke first. 'Hello, my name is Risya, who are you?' A rat voice replied, 'I am the Old Rat. What are you doing so far from the rat village? Are you lost?' Risya, once again, shared his story with the Old Rat. The Old Rat smiled in an understanding way and spoke, 'Risya, when something new begins to emerge it has to pass through three stages before it fulfils its purpose and attains its fullest form. It first confronts the teasing masses. When the masses see a new rising, their foremost instinct is to ridicule it. This way they ignore and push away what comes at them with an unknown strength. Soon after, when they discover it still survives and grows, their indifference and mockery climbs to vehement opposition. Their refusal is forceful and their anger towards it is no longer hidden. Something has managed to make a difference within them and they don't like it. It has begun to matter! We can say the unknown strength with which the new rising emerged has reached far enough for them to feel their being carried by it too. This is what they don't want and fear. But a final and inevitable turning point stands as the last stage. Acceptance! Whatsoever was put through their dislike and tease, whatsoever was mauled by their words in protest, they receive. So never-mind what has happened with you so far. It has its own course. You are more than welcome to come live here with me. There is plenty of room in the bush. Here we are safe from the hunting eyes of the eagles above.'

SECTION THREE: BEING AND SHARING

It was a dear old scene as Old Rat shared himself with Young Risya. They had already spoken late into the night when Risya asked the Old Rat how he had come to live in the plains. Out poured a story of long, long ago. 'A long time ago, I belonged to the Rat village way down south from where you come from. One day as I was sniffing for food I heard a 'Roar'. I was stunned, even afraid. It grew loud and then even louder. I couldn't move until it had completely faded away. But even after it faded, I didn't forget it. And for good reason too, for it came back. It kept frequenting only me. So, ultimately I approached our village head. He confided, 'Yes, I have heard stories of it from our ancestors. They said it is a river and the sound is, the Call of the River. It is known to be eternally calling. Calling all of us, all the time, but only a few open-hearted ones can hear its call, and even fewer are the ones who answer. The ones, who do embark on The Journey, are not known to be seen or heard of again.' After I had heard about the River and its Call, I felt the strongest urge to answer. I left, ignoring the angry protests of my fellow rats. On the way, I was often chased and threatened by the eagles and had to run into hiding. I lost my way. Whenever I lost my way, I admit contemplating returning back to the village while I was still alive. But until I hadn't seen the enchanting Roaring River, I didn't want to return. So I kept going, taking each step forward slowly and cautiously. Well, there is not more to tell. This took me many long years. But at last, I reached the Roaring River. It was something indescribable. I felt I had regained all the lost years. And now I hear the elders call me, 'Hair on Fire', but I am not, I couldn't be it...'

His face suddenly fell heavy with sadness and he stopped speaking. He sat there lost in thought for a long, long while. Risya had listened keenly and had been waiting to hear about the Mountain. He now wondered why the Old Rat's story had stopped short of the Mountain. Why hadn't he spoken of it? He couldn't contain himself anymore. He asked, 'Did you ever see the Holy Mountain, the Eldest

CHAPTER THIRTEEN: ALCHEMY - INTERNAL AND EXTERNAL

Ancestor?' All of a sudden the Old Rat's face wore a twisted look and he abruptly finished, saying, 'Never mind all that now, it's all myth and legend. Take some rest. It is late.' That was that. It was the end of subject, but Risya couldn't sleep. He lay awake all night, pondering the Old Rat's story and what it meant for him. Thoughts of the Mountain didn't leave him all night. He couldn't let it go. However, he did wonder how the Old Rat had relaxed and pushed aside the Journey. He knew he couldn't. He had to go on. So, Risya stayed the night in the comfort of shelter but was ready and waiting for the wee hours of the sun so that he could be on his way.

After offering gratitude for the hospitality shown by the Old Rat, Risya set off. He had gently explained that although the Old Rat's offer was kind and generous, Risya couldn't accept, as he knew he must find the place he feels at home. Initially, the Old Rat had been reluctant to let him go, fearing the immense danger ahead. Further, down the plains the bushes got scantier and scantier, the vulnerability heightened to its most. It was not easy for the Old Rat to see Young Risya go. Risya was ready for it all. He had kept only one choice for himself. There was no other way but ahead. Risya could see the eagles circling far, far above in the sky. Keeping his eyes on the ground ahead and his sharp ears wide open, he scampered along open plains, finding a bush or two for a moment's shelter and then to move on again. Suddenly, loomed ahead of him a white mound. Almost like a little hill of a sort. Intrigued, Risya wove around to investigate. As he scurried along, his eyes met with another pair of eyes; large brown eyes. It is an animal! There was so much pain in those eyes, Risya thought. Instantly his heart reached out to the strange creature lying there.

Edging closer Risya politely introduced himself, 'Hello, I am Risya the rat. Who are you? And what has happened?' There came a feeble response. 'I am a camel, a white camel. I am soon to die.' Risya's heart wept tears for the grand animal. 'It's a pity the big white camel was to die,' he thought. He sat there beside the waning animal, speaking soothing words. Unable to bear the anguishing state of the Camel any longer, Risya felt a rising hope to help, if he could. He asked, 'Is there something I can do for you? Is there any way I can help you feel better?' In a pained voice the Camel said, 'Yes, actually there is. The only way I can heal is if I get the eye of a rat.' Stepping aside Risya fell deep in thought. The suffering of the Camel had troubled his heart and he truly wished to see him healed. Now he knew how that could happen, even though it meant being blind in one eye. Risya was ready to give an eye to his ailing friend. He thought to himself, he would still have his other eye and that can't be so bad. Returning to the Camel's side, Risya said that he would be glad to give him his eye if it meant he would be well again. As soon as he said these words, out jumped his right eye! Miraculously, in that very instant the Camel rose from the earth, where he had lain in pain just a few moments ago. The Camel was healed.

Standing there tall and strong again, the Camel expressed immense gratitude to Risya. Risya was taken aback at the size of the Camel. 'Risya, you are my brother,' so spoke the Camel. He enquired why Risya was wandering in the dangerous plains, away from the shelter of the forest, and so far from his family. Risya once again shared his tale. The Camel told Risya, he would need to cross the vast barren plains to reach the Holy Mountain, and would have to confront the great danger of the eagles. Risya nodded in agreement. A surprise awaited. The Camel offered to help in return for the kindness shown by Risya. Risya could walk under him, between his legs all the way to the edge of the plains. Hidden in his shadow, the preying eyes of the eagles wouldn't spot him. Knowing it would have been extremely difficult to travel the entire distance with only one good eye to keep watch on both the road ahead and the danger that circled above, Risya was so relieved. Comforted by the protection, Risya gladly accepted and they set off. As the tall Camel

CHAPTER THIRTEEN: ALCHEMY - INTERNAL AND EXTERNAL

walked under the strong overhead sun, Risya scurried around below, between his legs, all the time carefully remaining in the shadows. Eagles circled above. After a very long walk, they reached the edge of the plains where once again grew tall trees and thick bushes. Risya stood at the beginning of another dense forest. At last, he was safe from the eagles. The Camel said, 'I cannot go further than this. If I do I will fall, for I am an animal of the open plains. You are on your own now. Goodbye my brother and thank you.' Thanking him for walking him this far with shelter and safety, Risya confessed how he had been afraid of being stepped upon by one of the long legs of the Camel. With a friendly laugh the Camel said, 'That couldn't be, for they called me the 'Sun Descendent',' he said. 'I know where each of my feet step.' Smiling happily, and sharing a farewell filled with warmth and gratitude, the two brothers parted, leaving little Risya to scamper off to continue his mysterious voyage to the Holy Hill.

Risya scurried along engulfed by the beauty of this forest. A freshness captivated his attention which he playfully explored. This brave little rat, so far from home was merrily journeying on when all of a sudden he spotted a Lion. Risya's one good eye opened wide as he looked at the beautiful and noble Lion seated in the cool shade of the forest. He looked regal and grand. But something was odd. The Lion looked confused and lost. Risya leisurely approached him, smiled and said, 'Hello, I am Risya the rat. Are you lost?' His reply was met by an even more questioning look from the majestic animal. He had no answer. So Risya spoke some more and soon gathered that the Lion couldn't remember who he was. Risya gladly reminded him, 'You are the magnificent Lion.' The Lion seemed to gain some memory by this, for he explained to the intrigued Risya how he often slipped into states of oblivion. As they spoke, Risya noticed the Lion drifting again. In time, Risya witnessed his frequent drifting. It was clear how often the Lion lapsed into a state of no recollection of who he was and it saddened and distressed Risya to see the plight of this beautiful creature. Sitting beside him in his moment of distress, Risya spoke with tender consideration. Risya wondered how this novel creature could be helped out of his misery. A fresh thought penetrated his mind. 'By giving one eye to the Camel, he had been healed, maybe an eye could heal the lost Lion too.' Risya knew if he gave his other eye away, he would be completely blind and helpless. But the Lion would be cured. Voicing his thoughts to the Lion, Risya shared his willingness to give away his other eye to the Lion. The eye leapt out from his body and in that instant, inexplicably the Lion healed! Risya sat in the dense forest, sightless, blind. But he knew in his heart, the Lion had healed. Risya experienced a flowing happiness. The Lion sat beside him, shedding tears of joy. Grateful beyond words, the Lion knew he had been given a new life. Risya had saved his life. He now knew who he was and he shared this with the little blind rat. Thoughts flooded Risya's head. 'The Journey is meaningless and impossible now. How can a blind rat see the Holy Mountain? But there is solace in the fact that two creatures have been helped.' 'Risya, what purpose brings you to this dense forest?' the voice of the Lion interrupted his thoughts. Risya explained he was on his way to the Holy Mountain. To this, 'I will be ever so glad to escort you Risya, for I am none other than the Guardian of the Sacred Mountain,' the lion exclaimed. Elated by the unexpected turn of events, Risya knew his Journey hadn't ended after all. The Guardian would take him further. The 'Guardian of the Sacred Mountain' asked Risya to walk close and follow him through the forest path. Travelling through the weaving forest paths, Risya and the Lion reached a lake. The Guardian shared precious knowledge seated beside the lake.

It was no ordinary lake it was, the 'Sacred Lake'. 'The waters of the Sacred Lake are no ordinary waters,' he said. 'They are holy and healing. All creatures of Creation as well as the Sky and the Earth are

CHAPTER THIRTEEN: ALCHEMY - INTERNAL AND EXTERNAL

reflected in it. Those who drink from it gain Ancient Wisdom.' Saying thus, the Guardian of the Sacred Mountain led Risya to the edge of the Holy waters and Risya bent forward and drank from the Sacred Lake. After a moment's pause the Lion said, 'I must take your leave now dear friend. I have to return to my purpose of helping others toward the Holy Mountain.' The Lion bid farewell and they parted with a loving sadness. It saddened Risya that he had to go, and he also feared for he would be alone now and could not see. He sat by himself, beside the Lake. There was nowhere to go now and nothing he could do.

Far above he heard the flapping of eagle wings. He heard their cries spreading through the skies. There was nowhere to run. He sat. He felt a rush of air touch his head as though an eagle passed through his entire being. He accepted his helplessness and stayed vulnerable with no urge to run. Risya was ready to die.

The sound of flapping wings grew close. Risya closed his eyes tight, ready for whatever was next. A sharp gush of wind hit his body. They were close. Too close! In an instant, he felt a hard brush against his body and Risya fell to the earth in a daze, losing his senses. The last thought in his head was, 'I am going to die!' The sound of flapping wings continued. As they grew close, Risya felt himself growing transparent to the flying eagles. The eagles were passing through him. Suddenly, an overwhelming silence descended through him and everything grew perfectly still! Some time passed. Risya lay there on the bank of the Sacred Lake. Not dead. Something extraordinary was happening. He blinked in wonder. He could see! Faint and blurry, but he could see! Leaping to his feet, overcome by excitement, he began to jump for joy. He skipped and leapt around, screaming with all his might, shouting for joy, 'I can see. I can see. Yes, I can see.' But it was not to end here. Amidst his own uproar and ecstasy, Risya felt someone come very, very close. Someone whispered, 'Risya, do you want the food of the Elders', the giver of Life to all creatures?' Risya spontaneously replied by moving his whole body like a wave, 'Yes,

SECTION THREE: BEING AND SHARING

yes...' The voice continued, 'Risya, crouch down low, as low as you can go. Then jump up high, as high as you can try!' And so Risya did. He crouched down low, as low to the earth as he could go and then jumped up high, as high as all his strength could try. And once again, he was up in the air, high up in the air... Very slowly, bit-by-bit the blurriness left and Risya could see more and more clearly.

Up in the air, Risya felt a strong and rising wind come and carry him even higher in the air and then even higher. Risya was soaring... higher than he had ever imagined. He felt the air grosser than him and he was adrift, piercing through the wind. There was nothing he could do but trust its might and power to keep him safe. This time he wasn't falling to the earth. As Risya looked down, far down below he could see the forest, he could see the Lake and the vast stretch of land. Risya began to see much more than that. He could see all and he could see through all. Flying through open skies, crossing above the Lake and rounding a thick of trees, Risya suddenly saw a bright radiation, a brilliance that blinded him. The golden radiation of the Mountain...

His feathers were in gold. The very gold that stretched as the golden beams of the Mountain... He didn't stop but flew up above the Lake again. He saw the Sacred Lake reflecting his golden feathers. He saw the Frog. She was seated as before on a green leaf by the waters. She shouted to him, 'Risya! You are no more a Jumping Rat. You are the Eagle! The Golden eagle!' Risya's voice thundered in response, 'There is no way to overcome fear other than becoming that itself of which we are afraid, Oceanic Moon!!!'

৫ ৫

Alchemy is the art of recognising the 'conflict. Alchemically purifying the inessential dissolves the conflict and the participant factors fall back to their original complimentary nature. By the purification process, they are reborn to manifest in their inherent level of possibility, harmony and potential. The art of alchemy is about unleashing the transformational potential inherent in nature to manifest the hidden spirit of matter - animate and inanimate. The result born of alchemy is Elixir.

This art is classified in five, often overlapping forms.

External Alchemy	Internal Alchemy
Vaidhiya Muppu	Mantra Muppu
Vatha Muppu	Yoga Muppu

Gnana Muppu

External alchemy works from outside to in, while internal alchemy works from inside out. *Vaidhiya Muppu* is the art of alchemically potentiating the healing properties of herbs, metals and minerals. *Vatha Muppu* is the art of transforming base metal into gold. Existentially, all metals are already slowly evolving toward the perfect state of Gold. This natural transformation can be accelerated and made instant by the alchemical art of *Vatha Muppu*.

The Siddhas classify the agents participating in alchemical phenomena of transformation and purification, into four groups:

Outermost,
Outer,
Inner
and Innermost

Outermost and Outer are macrocosmic alchemical agents and Inner and Innermost are microcosmic alchemical agents.

Alchemical derivatives

CHAPTER THIRTEEN: ALCHEMY – INTERNAL AND EXTERNAL

EXTERNAL ALCHEMY

According to ancient Siddha works, the elixir that prepares one to attain heavenly treasure (*Vaan Porul*) by attaining perfection in Yoga is called *'Andakkal'*, the Philosopher's Stone. It is described as spherical shape that binds together all five elements. Westerners as well as Easterners illustrate as under:

> It is a small stone
> Having all colours that may appear in the sky.
> It is unaffected by chemical reactions;
> Capable of being played with, even by children.
> So ordinary to look at,
> That, ignorant servants may sweep it aside as refuse;
> But equal to the deadly poison (Hala Kala Visham),
> That emerged from the heavenly ocean of milk when churned, by the Devas and Asuras.
> Properly treated, it is soft to the touch,
> Endowed with a cool fragrance and sweet taste,
> It is fluid like water that does not wet and
> Comparable to the fire and the sun!

The philosopher's stone or *Andakkal* is also known by other names such as 'the vase of Ambrosia', *Amritha Kalasam*; 'the un-depletable bowl', *Akshaya paathiram*; 'the vase of philosophers', etc.

Unless the 'vase of philosophers' is identified and understood, the philosopher stone is impossible to attain. Just as planets orbit within the confines of space, the powers of these planets are confined within this stone, as if within a box. Just as the nine planets revolve around the sun as their centre, the powers of all planets revolve within the philosopher's stone. The Siddhas use the word *'Andam'* to describe the philosopher's stone. One meaning of the word *'Andam'* is Universe, implying All of Existence. While creation took place and primordial matter transformed and manifested into diverse multi-forms under the dominating influence of five elements, it also descended upon Earth in an 'as-is' state and lays hidden, buried, dormant and unseen, embracing all five elements within itself. Usually, the fire element is incompatible with the water element, and ratios change to accommodate each other in manifestation, but in primordial matter, all five elements are locked in a divinely compatible bondage.

Siddha Sage Agasthiyar has mentioned this in his cryptic and twilight verses saying,

> Siva, immersed in Samadhi lays buried under the Earth.

My alchemical teacher has said,

> 'The three treasures within the Philosopher's stone must first be separated to be purified, and then must be reunited to be ingested.' This is the Trinity!

The second meaning of the word *Andam* is Egg. A word signifies and indicates a phenomena or function. If one misses the true connotation of the used word, it can be highly perplexing, but if one does perceive the implied truth, it can unfold a chain of associated teachings, by Grace. In the words of my Teacher,

> 'If you understand the language of the Siddhas, then, to understand the human mind is not a big matter.'

An *Andam*, or egg has three parts. The white part called Albumin, the yellow Yolk and the *Prana* or living essence. All three parts are compatibly packed within, yet separate. This indicates three treasures; the three elements are compatibly packed within yet have

CHAPTER THIRTEEN: ALCHEMY - INTERNAL AND EXTERNAL

the possibility of separation for the above-mentioned process. If 'Andam' can be found and ingested after proper preparation, one will be freed of planetary influence that lays between us and the 'heavenly treasure'. Unaware of this great secret, many people recite *mantras* like Navagraha Panchatchara, 'the five letter mantra for nine planets', without truly obtaining any benefit and pass on from this world without attaining realisation. This is to say that the 'heavenly treasure' cannot be attained only through mantra or tantra.

The '*Amritha Kalasam*' (the Bowl of Nectar) or '*Pranava Peettam*' (altar of the primal nine) is actually a container. Naturally, the content is different from the container, which has been expressed by Siddha Saint Ramalingam Swami as follows:

> The treasure box has an immovable substance in it,
> You blessed me by offering the precious key that opens it,
> But, I am the ignorant who doesn't know what is Eight and two.
> Now, I am attempting to open and release the substance from the box,
> Don't object to it, I can't wait even half of a moment,
> Then I will get thousands of abundance from You,
> As an interest for the delay,
> I promise on you, oh! God dancing in the Hall of gems,
> Please come quickly and bless me."
>
> Thiru Arutperu, Verse 2, By Siddha Saint Ramalingam

He says,

> "I am trying to take out from the container these two grand and precious objects, by the name of 'A-kaaram' and U-kaaram'."
> "Don't think of objecting to it."

Afraid of losing it after getting so close, he prays to the Absolute to shower blessings.

Before knowing the single herb of 'Andakkal' (universal stone or philosopher stone) that contains both, demonic poison as well as Ambrosia that bestows eternal life, we must first realise the nature of the sacred container *'Amritha Kalasam'* (Bowl of nectar) that contains it. The inner surface of the container has three sides. One side is quadrangular, the second side is crescent-shaped and third is triangular. The external appearance is that of a *phallus* (lingam). Sage Agasthiyar explains how unattractive and repulsive its appearance is to the common eye and only the Sages know its true worth.

A-kaaram: The symbolic representation of 'A'

My alchemical teacher once explained that amongst all languages ever born, most have both verbal and scripted form. All of these languages have 'A' or 'A-kaaram' as the first letter of the alphabet. This uniformity is not accidental and the creators and linguists of these languages have given it the first place having realised its significance. Among vowels that can be used alone, 'A' is first. According to the ancient Tamil number system, 'A' denotes 'eight' (8); among genders, it denotes the Sun; among functions, it denotes the profession of Lord Siva, i.e. destruction – *samhara*; among the five elements, it denotes fire; among the arms, it denotes the right arm; and among the *Nadis* – (channels of Yoga), it denotes the palate.

U-KAARAM – the symbolic representation of 'U'

The letter 'U' or 'U-kaaram' in the Tamil language is the substance mentioned as the second part of *'Pranava'* (AUM). U-kaaram denotes 'two' among numerals; among genders, it denotes the 'female'; among functions, it denotes 'creation' (urpatthi); among the five elements it denotes water; among the arms, it denotes the left arm; and among the *Nadis*, it denotes the *'uvula'*.

A-kaara (a) and U-kaara (u) are Siva and Sakthi; the 'Bindu' and Female. If one realises and nurtures these two components of the philosopher's stone, all medicines become effective. The dried foam

CHAPTER THIRTEEN: ALCHEMY - INTERNAL AND EXTERNAL

of ocean waves form a sponge. Similarly, the union of 'a' and 'u' forms the philosopher's stone, or *Andam*. The Siddhas call it by many cryptic names such as *Andam, Pindam, Brahmam* and *Parai Uppu*, meaning Rock Salt.

A-kaaram denotes the Sun and U-kaaram denotes the ocean or the Moon. Keeping this fact in mind, someone sung the line 'the Mount Meru blown about by the waves'. Although the 'A-kaaram' and 'U-kaaram' are mentioned as two, they actually indicate one. A person of perfect eyesight cannot see in the dark. To see, external light is necessary. 'The light of the eye' and 'the light of the sky' are two different things and one is useless without the other, likewise, the two components 'A-kaaram' and 'U-kaaram' exist.

By distilling the mixture of 'A-kaaram', the fire, and 'U-kaaram', the water, we get the 'Ambrosia', purified of its toxic element. The 'ambrosia' is the 'M-kaaram', (the letter 'm') and the third aspect of "AUM". The Siddhas call this process of distillation, the 'Alchemical Pooja of Goddess Vaalai'. 'M-kaaram' is the *Kalpa* or Elixir, capable of permeating into '*Chunnam*' (the calcined). The beneficial qualities of this liquid have been greatly extolled by Siddhas like Agasthiyar, revealing how 'A-kaaram', 'U-kaaram' and 'M-kaaram' are intimately bound together. The state of union of these three is also called '*Monad*' (*Eka-Vasthu*). Attaining alchemical *monad*, what the Siddhas call *Vaatha Siddhi*, is usually through *Rasa-Vatham* - the process of transforming mercury into gold. Mercury is heated on porcelain and as the temperature gradually rises, Hg evaporates with a slight boiling motion on its surface. At that moment, A-U-M i.e. the three elements, fire, water and air are added. According to the rules laid down by Alchemy Siddhas, even a drop of these three elements, already bound into a single catalysis substance, cools and transmutes the heated Hg into high quality gold, on touch. In whatsoever manner one may attain alchemical success, all four elements - air, fire, water and earth are imperative. The absence of even one guarantees failure.

Most people after succeeding, begin to indulge in the world of pleasure and give up further effort to attain ultimate happiness. They forget that success in external alchemy is the first step on the path of Ultimate happiness. And then, there are those who try to attain success in alchemy as if it were an end. According to the Siddha cult, it is for the sake of those who practice '*Kaaya Siddhi*', immortalising the physical realm, and '*Yoga Siddhi*', that success in alchemy is offered as incentive.

The term 'Trinity' (mupporul) denotes the three elements - air, fire and water that are strongly bonded within the esoteric rock salt crystal which is called '*Muppu*' (universal medicine, elixir) in Siddha literature. These three elements exist all over earth in individual and bonded combinations. Similarly, A-kaaram, U-kaaram and M-kaaram are contained within the container called '*Pranavam*' or '*Andakkal*'. Earth and water are visible to the eye while fire is invisible but we know the earth holds hot molten lava at its core that has not yet hardened. So, although fire is invisible, we know of its existence. The three things within the philosopher's stone exist in a similar manner. This rock salt, mostly remains hidden inside hills or beneath the ocean and seems to have the quality/potency of mercury and sulphur.

A-kaaram, the fire element is bonded with both air and water. U-kaaram the water element, bonds with air and gives rise to the watery salt. In context of the union of A-kaaram and U-kaaram, the elements of fire, air and water are esoterically taken as mercury, sulphur and salt. The art of regenerating these substances from '*Anda Kalasam*' (the vase of ambrosia) and adding them after due process is known as '*Diksha*', initiation. To ingest the substance so obtained in the proper manner for one year is considered as 'one *Diksha*' or one initiation.

Siddha Sage Thiruvalluvar says,

"If it is taken for one year, longevity will be attained."

CHAPTER THIRTEEN: ALCHEMY – INTERNAL AND EXTERNAL

Siddhas say physical immortality (*Kaya Siddhi*) can be attained on the completion of ten such initiations called *Dasa Diksha* and is known as "the *Sadhana* of *Kaya Siddhi*". "*Kaya Kalpa*" is when it is undertaken twice a day, (morning and evening), along with diet restrictions like milk-rice, etc. along with inner alchemical practice, for immortality. Even though western alchemists succeeded in external alchemy, they died without incorporating inner alchemical techniques. Hidden within the earth, this magic wand operates at "God's intent" to stir up worldly animation. This treasure can bestow miraculous power and if mixed with medicine can create various new elixirs. This is used by Siddhas for sorcery.

The philosopher's stone is seeded by nature, on its own. It is the residue of cosmic creative energy. Siddhas name it *Brahmam*, the Primal Creator. Since it is the causative factor of all other substances, Siddha Thirumoolar calls it the "oldest substance". Siddhas say that even spiritually heightened souls cannot see this substance without the grace of ancient Siddhas. Just as an egg contains albumen, yolk and prana within its shell, the stone has three equal segments. The first segment signifies the pace of growth, the second is for breeding and the third part is its deterioration.

> "Opening the mysterious Box, three objects will emerge
> Opening the mysterious Box, three glitters will emerge
> Opening the mysterious Box, three divine fields will be revealed
> Opening the mysterious Box, three barren grounds will be disclosed."
>
> Nadhantha Saaram–100, Verse-13, Siddha Thiruvalluvar

Western alchemists say,

> "The copulation of the two is like the union of husband and wife, whose embrace results into golden water."
>
> Ascanius

Another says,

> "All things created by nature consist of three primal elements, namely, mercury, sulphur and salt, in combination. Three emerge from one and the one contains three, three in one."
>
> Paracelsus

Mercury, sulphur and salt are cryptic names for the three aspects of the philosopher's stone. The psychology of the human body, according to Siddha science, is based on five great elements that constitute the external world, and internally are at the root of man. They are found in all bodies by the process of transmutation and union. In their natural state, they are found more or less mixed-up and are apt to change from one to another. They are the fundamental principles of creation, preservation and destruction in the universe. They are so closely connected with one another that they lend and borrow their qualities amongst themselves. Each has two specific properties of which one is retained as original, belonging to itself. Fire changes into air, air to water, water to earth and again earth to water, water to air and air to fire. This cycle of transformation is the foundation of all bodies and its function. Of the five elements, three physical elements of the external world, air (wind), heat (fire) and water are selected in medical science as they form the three fundamental principles on which the human constitution is based. A detailed account of these elements, known as humoral pathology is dealt with in earlier chapters. Humoral pathology explains that disease is caused by a mixture of the three cardinal humours, viz. *Vatha*, *Pitta* and *Kapha* and the relative proportion of these humours are responsible for a person's physical, mental qualities and disposition. The three fundamental principles and essential factors in the composition and constitution of the human body are wind, bile and phlegm, representing air, fire and water respectively. External air corresponds to internal

CHAPTER THIRTEEN: ALCHEMY - INTERNAL AND EXTERNAL

Vatha (air dominant principle), external heat corresponds to internal *Pitta* (heat dominant principle) and external water corresponds to internal *Kapha* (water dominant principle). This links man to the external world and changes in elementary conditions of the external world result in corresponding inner change. The *Tridosham* theory or the doctrine of Humoural Pathology and Alchemical insights are based on this exchange of influence.

Each of the five elements is represented by a seed syllable in ancient Tamil letters:

'NA' represents the Earth principle (Tattwa). Its ratio is 1 ½. (earth)
'MA' represents the Water principle - Its ratio is 1 ¼. (water)
'SI' represents the Fire principle, Teyu - Its ratio is 1. (fire)
'Va' represents the Air principle, Vayu - Its ratio is ¾. (air)
And 'YA' represents Ether principle - Its ratio is 1/2. (ether)

The total of the ratios is 5. These five proportions create the physical body.

Ancient Siddhas converted this ratio of gross proportion into subtle proportions as:

'SI' represents the Fire *Tattwa* - Its ratio is converted - as 1 1/2
'VA' represents the Air *Tattwa* - Its ratio is converted - as 1 1/4
'YA', the ratio of this Ether *Tattwa* is converted as 1.
'NA', the ratio of this Earth *Tattwa* is converted as ¾.
and 'MA' the ratio of this water *Tattwa* is converted as 3/4.

Alchemical principles formulated by the Siddhas reflect on the medicinal system. For instance, a single medicine can be used as remedy for multiple disease by changing only the carrier or adjuvant.

The Siddha medicinal system uses raw ingredients such as herbs, minerals, metals and animal products for medicinal preparation based on alchemical principles.

SHELF LIFE

The following is a tabulation showing the shelf life of certain Siddha preparations

NAME OF THE PREPARATION	SHELF LIFE
Chenduram (calcined red powder)	75 years
Churanam (fine powder/pulvis)	3 to 6 months
Chunnam	500 years
Lehyam (confections)	6 months
Irasayanam (semi liquid)	1 year
Kalpam (Elixir preparations)	many years
Karuppo (calcined black powder)	1 year
Kudineer (decoctions)	3 hours
Manappaagu (medicated syrup)	6 months
Mathirai (tablet/pills)	5 years
Melugu/Kulambu (soft wax/semi-liquid ghee)	1 year
Nei (medicated ghee)	6 months
Parpam (calcined residue)	100 years
Patankam (sublimates)	10 years
Thailam (medicated oil)	1 year
Thiravagam (distillates of salts/minerals)	1 year
Thinir (distillates)	1 year
Vatakam (lozenges)	3 months
Vennai (medicated butter)	3 months
Velimarunthugal (external applications)	1 to 5 years

CHAPTER THIRTEEN: ALCHEMY - INTERNAL AND EXTERNAL

WESTERN ALCHEMY

Ancient Egyptian alchemists concentrated on making gold from metals. They used the term *'Chemia'* and researchers were called Alchemists. The Alchemical world spread and came to ancient Greece. The German word *'Chemie'*, and French word *'Chimie'* and the English word Chemistry are all derivates of that root word. When the Arabs invaded Egypt, they too discovered Alchemy. Jabirb Hayyan (720-813 A.D.) is known as the founder of Arab Alchemy and wrote Arabic and Latin books on it, and his words relate the information process. Al-Razi, (826-925 A.D.) was another well-known alchemist who authored the famous work, 'The Secret of Secrets'. Paracelsus, a 16th century alchemist is well known in Europe. Basil Valentine is another. The period of alchemy came to an end in the 17th century after the rise of Robert Boyle, who laid down the foundation of modern chemistry, after which the transmutation of alchemical processes was considered superstitious. But a few practiced secretly. On February 24, 1896, Henry Becquerel researched radioactive substances. In 1898, Madam Curie and her husband discovered radioactivity. This phenomenon destroyed many theories and once again proved that transmutation propounded by alchemists can be possible, as transmutation always occurs in some elements in a spontaneous manner. Based on this principle, an artificial process of converting elements into other elements was pursued and proved. The Philosopher's Stone is the residue of the primordial creative energy process. It has the seeds of transmutation. In the West, alchemy stands divided into two camps. One is the laboratory alchemists and the other 'spiritual' alchemists. I will discuss the second group first. The true art of alchemy is far from an external pursuit of deriving combinations. Unfortunately, new age thinking wears the causal attitude of 'anything goes', entirely unaware of the deeper psychology of this ancient art. This is very true as far as spiritual alchemy is concerned. I think Carl Jung began the whole idea. But their basic premise was that ancient alchemical instructions, not designed for laboratory work, were descriptions of inner processes and practices leading to enlightenment, for which the study of these texts from this specific standpoint was all that was needed. A few of these people are following Chinese techniques of yoga and meditation based on alchemy - in fact, there is a lot of similarity between these practices and certain forms of Tantric yoga, where a lot is concentrated on learning to utilise the semen energy, etc. Some people follow traditions that supposedly come from ancient Greece (which would mean they originated in Egypt) or the Hebrew Kabala, which is the occult path of Jewish religion. Today, laboratory (lab) alchemy finds the smartest of Western occultists, of whom about half a dozen I can think of are very serious and I highly respect their work. Generally, they work with what they call the Spagyric process, which separates the salt, sulphur and mercury of a given substance. In the case of a plant, salt is what you get after several incinerations of the plant's ashes. Sulphur is the essential oil, and mercury is the alcohol that can be drawn from the plant by fermentation. After these are properly separated, they are then recombined to make an exalted substance called a Spagyric Elixir. This is more or less the essence of the work, in the western way. Spagyrics are very powerful medicines, but rare, because there are very few who actually make them. There is a more complicated method of working with plants to create a substance called the 'first being' of a given plant which is an even more powerful medicine. Substances to support the separation and re-combination process are also created - this art is called creating a 'circulata'. There are specific techniques to make oils from gemstone and metal, but the metal work of this nature is considered highly difficult. Most of this work is centred around

CHAPTER THIRTEEN: ALCHEMY - INTERNAL AND EXTERNAL

making medicine for cure or to accelerate spiritual development. The ultimate goal is to make the Universal Medicine, which is said to come in two forms - the white form being the elixir that cures all illness and the red form being the medicine that turns base metals into gold. Many 'Greats' of the past, enjoyed considerable success with medicine, but due to political and scientific (I hate to use that word when I am discussing work done by corporate laboratories) climate, little is known to the outside world. Much of the western written material on alchemy is found in the symbolism of Greek and Hebrew traditions, but mostly it is general stuff. Majority of the best works are available in French, where the practice has deeper roots and in Eastern Europe (specifically Czechoslovakia).

Most lab alchemists are usually spiritual aspirants and take great issue with people practicing mixed paths that borrow from Indian occultism. To me, it seems that people into lab work are much smarter and have a greater understanding of nature, at the same time have a narrower view of spiritual development and the spiritual forces at work in the world. It also seems there is something of an alchemical revival going on at this time. Some universities are teaching courses; not teaching Alchemical and Spagyric preparations, but speaking of the history and symbolism of the ancient art. Several alchemists of the past were responsible for important developments in Western science. People interested in spiritual development are getting tired of the same old stuff they've been getting over the years from money-hungry gurus and supposed spiritual masters who are better known for their wealth and sex lives than for Siddhis. Also, word is getting around that Alchemy is the quick path where development can be accelerated by alchemical practice and medicine.

ಜು ೂ

SECTION THREE: BEING AND SHARING

INTERNAL ALCHEMY

This sub-section speaks on spiritual alchemy including the Elixir of Yoga and Elixir of Wisdom.

ELIXIR OF YOGA
(Yoga Muppu)

Yoga Muppu is the art of alchemical transformation and purification to bring the natural, inherent and harmonious order to shine, through the Yogic path. Alchemy demands to first know the nature of disharmony and prevalent chaos before bringing in harmony. Nature works the art of existential alchemy using the ground of inherent connectivity and by constantly reflecting, what we name disharmony, She sharply indicates what we fail to see - the harmony within. This is the alchemy of nature.

Inherent Connectivity

The universe is fundamentally an energy field and energy is universally ever present in both the animate and inanimate. Energy operates in a variety of patterns but the inherent pattern determines its character. Man is the only energy field that identifies with a particular pattern and grips onto its limited reflective consciousness. From all of universe's manifestation, man is the only one living a paradoxical nature. Taken in by the paradox, it seems man has poured his essence into a container and complains of being cramped, and in order to get comfortable in the container he decides to discard the discomforting excess. He is in this illusion.

The power to be free of conditioning or constraining influence is 'aspiration to fall into one self - the unconditional life'. The

CHAPTER THIRTEEN: ALCHEMY - INTERNAL AND EXTERNAL

object world is not separate from the observer and all natural phenomena are understood in terms of human experience, while human experience is viewed as natural phenomena. Every natural happening is personified with a specific will of its own and yet there is an inherent connectivity between man and nature. The renowned Saint Ramakrishna Paramahamsa once saw cranes flying across a horizon filled with dark clouds and instantly fell into blissful *Samadhi*. Dark clouds and white cranes appear contradictory but in truth are complimentary - a coming together of two participants of a whole. This evoked the blissful *Samadhi* in him. Every natural phenomenon has a fundamental and universal meaning that reveals the values of human existence.

In ancient mystic cults, gods, goddesses, demons and spirits are symbols and archetypes of 'unaware' potential which got personified and projected onto the natural world as trees, rivers, animals, mountains, etc. And vice versa, nature seems to provide a setting in which man can experience these archetypes within his psyche. Often a certain setting evokes a corresponding powerful authentic experience. Nature's functions are no different from the functions of the exclusive 'God'. For some, a heartfelt experience with a forest or mountain is an answer to a crisis or fulfils a deep longing at crucial moments in life. Saint Ramakrishna's illusive boundaries got instantly nullified and devoured by the simple vision of 'two' held within nature's wholeness. Nature everywhere is infused with feelings and values, a sense of enchantment lies in each particle and every wave is filled with meaning. Any moment can bring us face to face with ourself. It is the zero point of now here; there is no resistance between, nature and us. This is the alchemy of nature.

ಙ ಐ

SECTION THREE: BEING AND SHARING

The Subtle Body Is Really Our Inner Body

> "The deer-like identified consciousness is in body, physical,
> The magnanimous supreme consciousness - not limited, but
> As a body, subtle, mingles with the physical,
> By entering as a seed into the womb, physical.
> Even with both present, their working intelligence is different.
> If you can integrate both, then clench
> Your virgin primal life force.
> You can quit your body and enter another,
> You become an angel.
> Can travel thousand distances in a moment,
> Thus life span lengthened and crystal.
> You, free from the verdict of Lord Brahma, the Creator,
> With no interference with your life force,
> It will subside in itself, thus.
>   Bogar Janana Sagaram-557, Verse 505-507, Siddha Bogar

Losing Life

When chaos takes root in us, we lose life because we don't know of its harmony. When you place your hand on the surface of water, it responds with counter pressure. Likewise, a human body experiences pressure from manmade objects as well as nature. Man is exposed to air in the atmosphere, light from the sun, the *Prana* arising from the rotation of the earth, natural forces, etc. These intangible pressure factors trigger a response from within us and our intangible subtle body projects itself out as a counter response to nature. Kirlian photography proves this by capturing on film the projected protruding form of the subtle body. Manmade objects like artificial light, artificial sound, head-dominant thinking, social demands, etc. strongly distort and fragment the protruded subtle form. The universe is an energy field within which creation and manifestation happen. Being

CHAPTER THIRTEEN: ALCHEMY - INTERNAL AND EXTERNAL

a microcosmic entity, man has a sense of stretched-ness toward spatial orientation and an agitated multi-sense direction, in this energy field. If the energy field has magnitude and no protuberance, man has both, as a vector and the misalignment with the overall field creates a pressure. For instance, the electromagnetic field created by the earth's rotation interferes with the human magnetic force generated by the circulation of inner *prana*. Orientating and keeping equilibrium to adapt to the convergent energy without losing one's true identity has been a challenge, especially when boundaries are to be kept. It is as if we were standing on opposite sides of a room and the ground of that room is folding in the middle, we would be intercepting and collapsing into one another. We are as vulnerable as we are inclusive of the unnecessary and insignificant others in our life, which recklessly diffuses the vital spirit.

Siddha Sattaimuni sings,

> "The mosquito loses its life by the attraction of touch mode,
> The bees loses its life by the attraction of visual mode,
> The deer loses its life by the attraction of auditory mode,
> The fish loses its life by the taste mode,
> The ant loses its life by the attraction of olfactory mode,
> Observe simply how all these five creatures recklessly lose their lives,
> Just like, O Man you lose, your dear life entrapped in conceptual sense frames."
>
> Sattaimuni Mungnanam - 100, Verse 14

Man loses life by attraction to all five modes, sings Siddha Sattaimuni, and the governing factor of all five is majorly the mode of touch. We may think we are in the body but we are always stretched out and messed up in the foreground. Fragmented and caught in the web of five dissipative senses. When for an instance we lose grip over the foreground, we become receptive and return to our body. When we drop the foreground as our living reference, we fall back into the body and come together as our true earthiness.

ೞ ಇ

Utter Receptivity

In the path of Yogic Alchemy, the dissipative modes are brought in by utter receptivity which awakens the fire of life and leads to one's rebirth or coming together of the subtle body. The sole purpose of alchemy, the Yogic way, is to be engulfed by the Source. The first practice is separating the pulsating *prana* from the Air breath by utter receptivity flooding the entire being. *Hatha* Yogis use *Pranayama* and Taoists use their own breathing techniques for this. Body-based techniques may initially help but can lead to complications in later stages, the reason being the exclusive use of body movement for separating the *prana* as well as holding it after separation. This brings an excessive condensation of *prana* that tends to inflate delicate organs resulting in damage such as haemorrhage. Tense facial muscles attempting to concentrate on or pull the *prana* alter the authentic mode and instead of receiving *prana* and allowing its descent, it localises and stagnates. Siddhas emphasise the receptive attitude to be vital and the role of body-technique secondary. In a relaxed and receptive state, the *prana* naturally separates from the breath and gravitates, and all the five senses have an ingathering impetus when they drop the egress nature. A receptive mode triggers a spontaneous inherent impetus and unfolds the inner path. Falling into this new opening, the unfolding vital spirit awakens and nurtures us.

"Yogis never deviate their attention in this void external world."

ೞ ಇ

CHAPTER THIRTEEN: ALCHEMY – INTERNAL AND EXTERNAL

By the Body of Earth

The Siddhas' teachings shed enough light on the fact that spiritual life doesn't begin when embarking on a spiritual path or practice, but is always happening; our body is designed for it. Divine Elixir is commonly explained as the distillation of five elements: water, fire, air, ether and earth that associate with the five sense organs; eyes, ears, nose, tongue and body. How does one bring together these five within the human body and distil the divine elixir? The ancients have divulged the law of the five 'non-out' followings: when the eyes do not see, ears do not hear, the tongue does not taste, the nose does not smell and the skin does not sense any touch. Un-fragmented livingness, when, by way of a path, a quest or an ordinary life the senses are no longer vents dispersing and scattering attention in multitudes, becomes the way for spiritual evolution. Refraining from an improper use of senses, gathers, retains and nurtures un-dispersed energy in the *Manipoorakam chakra*. It subsequently descends to the energy storehouse, the *Mooladharam*, where this primal energy is constantly distilled into elixir. This phenomenon is always at work and the formation and maturity of elixir depends upon the effectiveness with which the energy is nurtured. Whatever may be our daily activity, if the law of 'non-out' is predominant, the rest takes its natural course. The law of non-out is based on how attuned the body-mind are and a Siddha is free of disease, enjoys lustrous health and is ageless. The vital breath (un-dispersed energy) must go on gathering in the space two inches below the navel which is the source of strength, and not be allowed to disperse as the entire being is nurtured and nourished from this source. When the vital breath fully accumulates below, it leaves no room for misfortune to operate, nor for evil to invade, from the outside. The circulatory organs work efficiently and the heart and mind brim with health. It is essential to keep the upper part of the body cool and the lower parts warm which implies that the upper parts of the body should be free of hot, agitated dispersing energy, and instead this energy must be directed within and down.

ॐ ॐ

Prime Movers

The Siddhas have named five types of impetuses that function as prime movers as Vital Forces.

The invigorating vital force	- Prana
The outpouring vital force	- Apana
The nourishing and assimilating vital force	- Samana
The all-pervading vital force	- Vyana
The uplifting vital force	- Udana

Initiation is imperative in the path of Siddhas Yogic Alchemy, but I have briefly described below an outline of the initial stage of practice to show the factors involved.

Inhaling slowly and steadily through the nose, one feels a subtle force separating from the air breathed in. After breathing in, until the lungs fill, the gross air travels on through the throat into the lungs. No attention be paid to that. A slight focus is kept on the spirit descending in the pulsating *prana*. A sense of proprioception will help feel it. The vital force likes to stick to the oxygen molecule O_2. This is the outer alchemical agent. Some tantric practitioners may need a prayer or incantation to invoke the separation during initiation. But in the Siddha path, the Master's breath with His spirit of life is blown on the practitioner's face which initiates the process.

CHAPTER THIRTEEN: ALCHEMY – INTERNAL AND EXTERNAL

In the early stages, the essence thus separated is very subtle and heavy concentration or grasping attention causes it to dodge away impishly. The descending pulsation conjoins with the inner alchemical agent that is Elixir saliva.

> "The great sanctum dwells in the heart,
> The fleshy body is the holy temple,
> God, the provider of all virtues, the mouth
> Turned to be the tower gate.
> For the realised, the life force itself is the idol of Siva.
> While the untamed five senses turn into fusion
> They glitter as the guiding light.
>   Thirumanthiram-3000, Verse 1823, Siddha Thirumoolar

Siddha Saint Ramalingam mentions five nectar spots within us.

> "The first nectar is under the tongue which has the taste of sweet spring water.
> The second one is in the uvula spot. And the taste is like melted sweet Jaggery syrup.
> The third one is on the bridge of the nose and tastes like boiled Jaggery syrup.
> The fourth one is at the centre of the forehead and tastes like ripened thickened Jaggery syrup.
> The fifth one tastes like sugar candy and exudes a deep coolness.
> The person who dined the fifth nectar attains the immortal body."

The Enchymoma saliva is the first nectar and signifies the inner alchemical agent. Both the inner and outer alchemical agents conjoin as a throbbing pulsation and descend. Once a person is floating in the descending pulsation through the frontal channel, a harmonic co-ordination of the subtle and physical body evolves and balance is attained. After being well-grounded in this practice, if a practitioner temporarily ceases the practice of collecting and descending the pulsating *prana* mixed with the sap of saliva, he will crave for it as if he hasn't eaten for a while. The next stage tackles another dissipative factor within our body - the sexual energy which is another factor governing the mode of touch and conditions the body to be dissipative in nature. The outpouring vital force *Apana* is responsible for this. Hence the next stage is separating virility from sexual fluid which is then sublimated from the water element of sexual fluid. Western countries show a higher indulgence in sexual activities so western practitioners, at this stage, may find a lot of heat generated within the body which could burn *Ojas* at the cellular level. Contrarily, in the east due to prolonged sexual suppression, the energy turns cold and frigid which demands a higher spirit from the practitioner. In either case, at this stage of sublimation the elimination of deranged heat or the channelisation of suppressed energy is to be considered first. The Siddhas' *Kalpa* system of internal and external alchemy insists on preliminary purification as a must. The descending pulsating *Prana* mixed with saliva and the arising *Apana*, all mix in the solar plexus area. Both these pulsating movements neutralise each other and assimilate under the governance of the nourishing and assimilating vital force of *Samana*. This assimilation spirals and descends to the basal chakra and ignites the fire of life, the *Kundalini Sakthi*. The pulsation in the frontal channel is characteristic of the Air principle and is signified in Siddha terminology as 'Va'. The fire ignited by it is signified by the letter 'Si' according to the five letters of Lord Siva, 'Na Ma Si Va Ya'. Sublimating the procreative nature of virility from the moon path gets transformed into creative energy for a new life in the Sun path, the posterior channel. This gives birth to the inner body, one creates oneself. The newborn subtle body is not actually newly born but is the earlier protruded and extended one - having come together now, de-fragmented and whole, as a seed. It sprouts like a baby, needing nourishment from the mixture of sublimated virility and the invigorating descending *Prana* conjoined with the rejuvenating saliva. A practitioner with serene awareness can enter into the subtle body by adopting a vacant look - a look not fixed on anything. Focusing on the subtle body, expands it to reach your physical size. After being well-grounded, one does feel the subtle body outside of one's physical body from above one's head. It is an exact replica of the physical one and is now positioned above the head. The Siddhas are adept in transmigration and multi-location by deploying the subtle body which happens in the *Mooladharam*, the basal chakra and the subtle body radiates and moves swiftly. This is not the same as an out-of-body experience commonly referred to as 'oobe'. Oobe happens through the naval area. This is not past life regression either, nor is it dematerialisation. Dematerialisation is when cellular memory entirely vanishes. As per the Siddhas' wisdom, this is considered a type of mishap; just like auto-combustion. The true purpose of Siddhas' alchemy is merging it into the source; an actual engulfing.

> "What can stabilise the body?
> It is the gracious primal Kalpam! Kalpam!
> If you consume that primal kalpam,
> It is the fruit from the fire of meditation.
> Now where has death gone?
> It has merged into the absolute intelligence.
> Where has gone the I, the ego?
> It turned to ashes in the fire of Nandhi, the Bull of Siva."
>
> Siva Yogam - 200, Verse 57, Siddha Ramadevar

> "When it is burnt in the fire of Siva's Bull,
> Those poisons that make one grey and wrinkled also crumble,
> In the inner cosmos where breath subsides,
> In the now emerging flame at the verge, Suzhi Munai,
> If you boil your body in this flame,
> The habitual impurities of body burn.
> If those impurities are burned,
> You are carried to the Hall of Gnosis."
>
> Siva Yogam - 200, Verse 58, Siddha Ramadevar

Siddhas typically mention two cryptic words in Yogic alchemical songs. *'Kama pal'*, which means the Milk of passion and *'Kanar pal'*, which is the Milk of Mirage. Glandular secretion plays a vital role in the function of the physical body and the two esoteric 'Milks' play a vital role in the function of the subtle body. The fusion of the separated *Prana*, the nectar-like saliva and the virile energy transforms the dissipative nature of the physical body. Milking the sublimated passion of dissipative mode enhances the fire in the basal chakra. This fire spreads upward through the posterior channel causing the three other types of nectar, mentioned by Siddha Ramalingam, to ooze and flow. The different nectars are called the 'milks of passion' and the fire spreading through the posterior channel is called the 'milk of mirage'. A mirage appears to be water but actually is heat waves floating above the ground. In inner esoteric *pranayama*, the Siddhas mention the release of this fire from the basal chakra and the spreading of it to be called *'Rechaka'*. The absorption of this fire in the *Suzhi Munai* at the third eye spot is called *'Puraka'* where the fire transforms into light, which steams the fifth kind of nectar to flow and permeate the whole being. In the words of Siddha Ramalingam, this nectar bestows immortality.

CHAPTER THIRTEEN: ALCHEMY - INTERNAL AND EXTERNAL

> "God abided supreme from my centre of eyebrow,
> in his luminosity like that of camphor flame,
> I see no smoke, no flickering, but steady vision,
> He unleashed the closed doorway of my mid eye.
> And liberated me from darkness to light everlasting.
> It was all His play, sanctified in the sacred expanse."
>
> Mahadeva Malai, by Siddha Ramalingam

The combined intermingling and repetitive internal copulation of the descending pulsation along with the ignited fire is called *Vasi*. The ignited fire then ascends to an ecstatic experience and spreads through the posterior channel to merge in *Suzhi Munai*. The spontaneous spread of this fire is called Rivering the Fire, and how it happens is a reflection of how highly potentiated the fusion of the three vital forces has been in the frontal channel. The ascent of fire is not so easily attained and Siddha Saint Ramalingam has mentioned in his prose work 'Pointers of Upadesha', as

> "Like we remove the moss from the surface of the water, we have to remove the blackish green veil that curtains our soul. This veil can be removed only by the extreme heat of devotion and meditation and not by any other kind. This heat is well understood through Yogic practice and cannot be created by ordinary human effort. Yogis enter into mountains, forest, caves, etc. to practice various disciplines of Yoga for hundreds and thousands of years to gain this heat. Instead if we heartfully think of God and pray sincerely even for a single hour, we can have this heat, increased many a million fold."

The human body has its own inertia which is cryptically described as a blackish green veil; a veil that can be burned only by the heat as mentioned by the Siddhas. How did this inertia come to be? Inertia is cellular level memory of a mechanical habit that binds, makes the body rigid and does not allow suppleness and light. When the heat mentioned by the Siddhas, rivers and merges in *Suzhi Munai*, it offers a gracious light experience. The effulgence melts the heart-full cooling energy, the nectar, and distils it to descend and engulf the entire body, making it immortal - Engulfing the whole body as one heart.

> "When the divine consort connived in sport to shut the eye of Siva,
> Dense darkness shrouded the Universe,
> With grace abundance, He opened His flawless mid eye
> And illumined in benevolence."
>
> Siva Gnana Siddhiyar, 1.2.24

ஸ ௐ

Metamorphosis

> "When the shadow of me will vanish?
> When my embodied body be without its dissipative composition?
> When a sword will pass unhindered through my body?
> When my body will be afloat above the earth?
> When my core self will engulf my body?
> In that moment, as a self generated pill, My whole being."
>
> Mathi venba - 100, Verse 8, by Siddha Yugimuni

Five consequential transformations happen in the physical form on attaining deathlessness.

- o Shadowless body
    A shadow is the reflection of a body influenced by light and lengthens, shortens or distorts as per the influence. It is like our double and never leaves us, yet is a separate entity that has thrown

us aside. There is a strange practice under the Swara Yoga school of thought that unfolds the mystery of the shadow by visualisations for predictions. Based on the colour of the shadow, one can find which element signifies this prediction. By this practice, the life span of an individual can be calculated based on his shadow. The practice is *'Saya Darshan'*, Mysterious Sight of the shadow. My Tantric master said, "A person practicing this will have a short life span because he gives his life to his shadow." But in the Siddha path, it is considered differently. With inner alchemical change, the biological components flowing inside to out, such as sweat, urine, faeces, etc. get transformed. There is no more ejection or dissipation of the subtle body as it is completely absorbed, assimilated and interiorised. Therefore, when light falls upon this form, there is no stimulus for reflection; light simply passes through unhindered. There is no shadow for Him.

- Floating physique

The nectar that engulfs the entire being when once again steamed by the heat of the radiant light, it crystallises into a throbbing pill which the Siddhas call *'Vasi Guliga'*, the primordial life pill. Siddha Agasthiyar explains its creation in higher Yogic alchemical processes, in his work, Agasthiyar Vatha Kaviyam. When this pill is whisked up to the crown area and left to glitter in this space, the cells within the body orient up toward it, relieving the Yogi of the gravitational vortex, allowing him to 'float' as an anti-gravitational force.

- Unhindered Form

Once all habitual patterns or cellular memories dissolve and are replaced by the enlivening light spirit, several bodily changes come to be and the seven-layered bodily skin starts to peel or loosen.

"Uttering for success in Pranayama
Consume first the Elixir of Lord Siva.
If you practice Pranayama ignoring the Elixir Kalpa,

Be it even till the world ceases to be,
Oh! Your life will escape from you,
You will fail."

Antha Ranga Diksha Vidhi-412, Verse 351,
by Siddha Agasthiyar

According to the Siddhas, it is imperative to start the alchemical process by consuming first external alchemical preparations, after which he can move onto orienting himself toward inner alchemical processes. This way the unfulfilled latent Karma starts to upsurge in the form of disease and loosens the dead cells of the body, such as nails, hair. etc. It is a heavy price paid for this metamorphosis and takes a few good years to accomplish at the end of which one naturally loses all craving toward bodily identification. It is a paradox. The Siddhas have detailed and described the changes that take place each year in their alchemical songs, but Siddha Saint Ramalingam speaks differently:

'When a person longs solely for divine grace and relinquishes himself to it and surrenders even his very life force to it, this immortality is gifted, without any pain-filled processes."

This is 'to be engulfed by Grace'.

"You will not fall in death,
No shadow of you,
Nor shadow against lamps light,
Nor shadow mirrored on still waters,
If these quantum qualities emerge in ones form,
The body's externalised coverings peel off one by one -
You radiate like the golden sun himself."
    Siva Yoga Gnana - 32, Verse 31, by Siddha Sundaranandar

CHAPTER THIRTEEN: ALCHEMY – INTERNAL AND EXTERNAL

Siddhas Koans

Like the Zen Koans, the Siddhas questioned paradoxically... For a body burning in the cremation ground, bodily fluids melt, the head burns and all organs decompose to ash, to which they ask, if there be an un-vaporising head and an un-flowable fluid within, then is there death? There are inherently deathless elements within. The five basic elements alchemically turn into the corresponding primal five deathless elements. The corresponding five elements are mentioned by the Siddhas as:

Idiyatha Puvi	-	Unhindered earth
Poga Punal	-	Non-flowing fluid
Oliyadha Kanal	-	Silent Fire
Saga Kaal	-	Undying Air
Vega Thalai	-	Un-vapourising Sky

"Shown me, Oh my Lord,
The head that never dies and
The leg that never burns to ashes,
For it is You who has shown me,
The water that never keeps flowing and
Thus seated, Oh You, in my heart,
Like a brilliant effulgence of wisdom,
To the unknowning person, it is unknowable;
To me, it is ever blissful."

Satguru Mani Malai, Verse 1382,
by Siddha Ramalingam

SECTION THREE: BEING AND SHARING

GNANA MUPPU - ELIXIR OF WISDOM

> "Trailing memory, the robust monkey,
> Jumping upon the branches of senses,
> And agitating them in ghostly madness,
> Fragmenting the mind to its very destruction -
> Not allowing the mind into the doorway of its liberating origin.
> It stands as darkness to glittering wisdom,
> Even a person blind and ignorant does consume
> The impetus of tracing memory,
> The path of wisdom then shall open and take him."
>
> Mun Gnanam-100, Verse-51, Siddha Sattaimuni

Although the Sun is much further above the earth, its rays spread uniformly over earth illumining, nourishing, extracting and vitalising all living beings with its fluid rays. Like the external Sun, there is an inner sun - consciousness that spreads its rays all over the body, permeating and illumining our personal world. Each morning on waking up, the egress fluid of consciousness externalises and reflects as objective consciousness and we begin to relate with the world which the Siddhas called *'Ninaippu'* or remembrance. Each night when we fall into deep sleep, we become oblivious to the world which they term *'Maraipu'*, forgetfulness or veiling; an inert state. Man enters a psycho-spatial and psycho-temporal mode once the egress spurt shifts into objectifying consciousness which is the reflective mode of experiencing the world after waking up. As he steps out of the inert state of deep sleep and begins to reflect upon his experience with the perceived world, he becomes the subjective entity thinking about an object or experience as if his consciousness is thrown before him. Once the reflected consciousness he sees thrown before him falls into oblivion. it is called sleep.

CHAPTER THIRTEEN: ALCHEMY - INTERNAL AND EXTERNAL

> "That we term death is just like sleep
> That we term birth is just like awakening".
> -Thiru kural – 339 by Thiruvalluvar

The Siddhas say, birth and death is nothing but the inherent impetus of egress fluid spurting into remembrance and falling back into inertness, respectively. This primal knot rules over our daily experience of identification with our personal world and of becoming inert when we fall asleep. This oscillation is two sides of the same coin; a fluctuation of active and passive states. Interestingly, this fluctuation also occurs every moment. There is a difference between 'thinking' and 'thought'. Thinking is an active process where the subjective influence rules over something whereas thoughts are streams of memories overruling a person; a passive state. We can be aware of this. On waking up, we actively think about what we must do today as the mind likes to program. As for sleep, if we try to sleep we cannot. The very effort to sleep is a hindrance. It is a passive state. When in bed trying to sleep, a stream of random thoughts invade, overrule and overtake us until we lose conscious control on the masquerading thoughts and fall into a dream, which is nothing but visualised thoughts. Everybody knows that we never see ourselves or our bodies in our dreams, but only sense ourself as a subjective person participating in the incidents of the dream. Where the dream ends, deep sleep begins and there is nothing subjective and objective, nor dreaming or waking. As we don't have awareness in this deep sleep state, it is an inert state.

> "Dine the A-kaaram that emerge at morning
> Dine the V-Kaaram that occurs Evening"

Invariably, all Siddhas give the above message in their alchemical songs. These cryptic words take on different meanings depending on external alchemy, yogic alchemy or spiritual wisdom alchemy. In the song, with reference to *'Gnana Muppu'*, (the process of wisdom-elixir), they mention the secrets of both phenomena, the reflective egress spurt and the falling of objectifying consciousness into an inert state. They say, "Let yourself feel all of your self. Be aware of this stream of reflective consciousness that objectifies everything. Each morning as you become fully conscious of this shifting reflective state, it will step back as a flow, a fluid consciousness. This is termed as 'A'-Kaaram." The Siddhas use several other cryptic words like water, divine water, water of Siva, Amuri, etc.

> "If you ask me to tell what is night and day
>
> > Oh son, I will disclose, listen now!
>
> The night is nothing but the shutting of eyes
>
> > The day is nothing but sight!
>
> Combining both these two fragmentary,
>
> > Whisk it into the supreme ground, which is as Inner Guru.
>
> And if you stand firm there, in meditative Yoga
>
> > To move ahead to its origin, the native beyond,
>
> That is known as 'true Siva Yoga'."
>
> > Siva Yogam - 200, Verse 160, Siddha Ramadevar

The primal sound 'AUM' has three syllables. A, U and M and another part called the *Artha Mathra*, the Silent Spirit. This is Its origin. 'M'-kaaram is the primal ground; the 'A-Kaaram' is the egress spurt, a reflective state, and the 'U-Kaaram' is the state of oblivion. Each evening when the sun sets, our urge to objectify recedes and matures even further into the night as we sleep. So, Siddhas sing in their twilight language,

> "Ignite your fire every evening."

CHAPTER THIRTEEN: ALCHEMY - INTERNAL AND EXTERNAL

Which means light the fire of awareness during the time of receding forces so that forgetfulness does not befall you. Before the light of day completely fades, it touches a point where it meets the darkness - the twilight time that holds both, the light and the darkness of consciousness. If we can find the moment where waking and sleep meet, then with a little more attention on this moment, it can be prolonged. At the time of sleep, the tendency of the mind naturally bends toward a cessation of restless activity which can be cultivated to emerge slowly, feeling its way. It is better one does not extinguish the lamp all at once but sinks into sleep just as daylight vanishes into the bosom of the evening; just as a child falls asleep but the mother stays awake. The child trusts his mother is awake. 'Ari Thuyil' mentioned in Yogic system of Siddhas pronounces awareness as, 'Sleep in the spiritual heart of the Mother.' In the depth of the night, the earth sleeps while the sky looks on through an unblinking gaze of myriads of stars. The sky is the heart of the Mother. To be asleep thus means to be awake to the vast awareness and peace of the sky, the grand infinite. Sleep does not mean extinction, but a silent wakefulness we need to sensitively invoke, and allow the wakeful silence to resonate and expand our consciousness to it, spreading into the core heart of the Mother. Sleep will reveal its infinite ocean of light.

Navigated by *Vasanas* (latent tendencies), the endless fluctuation is an inbuilt instinctive mechanism and burning each tendency would be an equally endless task.

> "More and more you pull water from the well
> More and more springs out
> The more and more you shun the tendencies of past imprints
> The more and more they emerge."
>
> —Mun Gnanam – 100, Verse-55,
> Siddha Sattaimuni

Burning each tendency leaves a distilled silence which in terms of spiritual alchemy is called 'mother tincture', but is an incessant process. Instead of burning each rising tendency and 'distilling' the mother tincture of serene silence on the fuming vapours of burned tendencies, focusing on the 'primal urge' or the origin of its momentum is a more direct approach. The fusion of water and fire creates a new life force, an infant. This is termed as 'Ma'-kaaram, the throbbing streamline of the primal urge of identification. This is the pseudo-self by relying upon its identified roles, objects. A derived sense of being! 'Ma'-Kaaram, the primal urge to reflect itself into subject and object now gets re-oriented to stand alone as a reverberation, a throb. Not to reflect but to fall back to its origin, the pre-reflective state. That state is signified by the fourth or silent part of AUM - A great Repose! The effort to grasp wisdom or undertake a practice based off borrowed knowledge is intellectual stimulation while the waves of silence held in the mere look of a True Master can make it real.

> "As lightening arises, spreads, recedes,
> So the Lord of my heart arises and spreads
> Who lay hidden within.
> Like the eye that does not know its own seeing,
> The lord who lay within I knew not
> As if He were not there".
>
> Siva Vakiyar Padalgal Verse-126, Siddha Siva Vakiyar

Here unfolds an understanding:

> 'Even though everything else depends on him to prove their existence, he depends on 'nothing' while abiding in eternal existence. This is disembodied awareness.'

CHAPTER THIRTEEN: ALCHEMY - INTERNAL AND EXTERNAL

'Be like a child.' - Christ

In a circle, the point of zero degree and the point of 360 degree appear the same but are qualitatively different by the embodied journey of the full-circle. We, born in a state of undifferentiated spatiality enter the world entirely 'pre-personal'. We live in the ground prior to the reflective state of subject and object but are unaware of it. We once again abide in this pre-reflective state once we realise this nature has always been everywhere as sentient, without fragment, non-reflective and as un-differentiated spatiality. And there is no trace, nor urge left to step out of the flow of pre-reflective living experience to project or think about what we are experiencing.

ಏ ಡ

VINAYAKAR AGAVAL

By Woman Ancient Siddha Saint Avvaiyar

"The anklets, in your sandalwood cool,
Red lotus feet, sing many a music!
The golden chain around your waist,
The soft flower like cloth draped
Around your torso shines aglow.

Your treasure chest like stomach
And tusk so vast, and limitless
Your elephant face and vermilion adorned forehead
So easily perceived.

SECTION THREE: BEING AND SHARING

Five hands, the Goad, Noose and
Body so blue is heart rendering!
Your wide hanging trunk, four strong protruding shoulders
Three sacred eyes, three implanted trails,
Two big ears, the golden summit of bun hair
The entwined holy threads, three, upon
Your glowing chest!

You, The true wisdom of Turiya,
Beyond all words
You yield all wonders
As a wish fulfilling tree!
Oh! You who rides the Mouse,
Dines three fruits, I pray to You
'Engulf me, as Yours!'

You manifested as Mother, showered
Your grace and severed the delusive
Nature of my Birth - this Illusion!
By the uniting of the pristine five Primal letters
You came and entered my heart!
Walking with Your Holy feet, this earth, in Guru's Guise,
Showing the essence of Truth by 'This'!
Gladly, You reveal the path of unfading life,
Your tusk as weapon, you remove and
End the vile fruits of Karma.

Poured in my ear un-cloying precepts,
You revealed to me the clarity of
Ever-fresh awareness!
Your sweet grace made me
Master the senses - five!

CHAPTER THIRTEEN: ALCHEMY - INTERNAL AND EXTERNAL

You proclaimed the way to still the organs of action,
Snapped my two - fold, dual karma and
Dispelled darkness, bestowing me,
A place throughout all four stages of Mukthi!

By grace, dissolving the delusion of
Triple impurities, showing me
A single Mantra, to shut
The five sense gates of nine door openings.
And the harmonious functioning of the chakras, Six;
You stood me firm and severed
All inner chattering!

You taught me the writ of Ida and Pingala
And showed me the end of Suzhi Munai, in the skull;
In the tongue of the rising serpent,
Came forth the force
Sustaining the triple bright realms
of Sun, Moon, and fire;
The unspoken Mantra - Ajapa
Entwined with Kundalini;

You explicitly uttered it, to impart
The skill of rising by life pulsation,
The raging flame of Mooladharam!

Revealed the secret of Immortality and
Taught me the nature of drinking Amritha,
The inner movements of Sun and the charming,
Moon - the friend of water lily.
Disclosing the wheel of moon and its 16 Kala stages,
And its relation with the inner sheaths of Body wheel,

SECTION THREE: BEING AND SHARING

Sweetly graced me to contemplate
The six faces of gross (chakras) and
Four faces of subtle (Antha Karanas)
Blessed the vision of subtle entwined body
And its eight facets, modes of being;
Showing the orifice of Brahmam and opened it!

Bestowing the miraculous powers and
Mukthi also by your sweet, grace.
Revealing Myself to me and Your grace
Swept away the accumulated Karma with its root;
Stilling my mind in Silence beyond speech and thought
Shining my mind by dipping me in ecstasy
And revealed, "Light and darkness share a common source"!

Boundless delight you have showered on me
Finished my, all afflictions, by the way of grace
Shown Sadasiva, at the core of Sound,
And Siva Lingam within the Heart.

Atom within Atom, vast beyond all vastness!
That stands like ripe sugarcane,
You made me realise the role of ash smearing
On the brows of your servitors, living in Truth,
And added me, one among them.

You made me experience, in my heart's core,
The inmost meaning of the Five letters.
Restoring my real nature and suffused me in Existence!

Oh! Master of Wisdom, Vinayakar,
Your feet alone are all my sole refuge!"

ಶ಼ಐ

CHAPTER FOURTEEN
TANTRA

Humans are drawn to take birth according to the pull of their karmic effects.

If perception changes according to karma and acquired conditioning, it means it is an illusion, and nothing but a collage of projected conditioning, thought form, emotional patterns and manifested un-mindful actions. Siddhas call '*Megham*' (AIDS chapter) a group of disease-causing clouds that rain down and deplete fundamental body-tissue. This view reflects here as well, 'What you call your nature is nothing but a cloud of stale vibrations of the sum total of all that has happened with/to you'. Our actions tend to arise from the stale programmed vibrations of karmic influence, the same influence that causes dreams/acts of life-drama to keep recurring. Our actions have deteriorated to being conditioned responses coming from our conditioned energy levels and cannot be called real conscious creative action or an expression of our inner spontaneity. Repetitive life patterns and suffering sprout from conditioned energy levels and we are often heard blaming 'karma', forgetting that it is Life commenting upon our inner conditioning!

The Siddhas, through divine vision found a specific heightened energy, residing in the depths of each human being, to dissolve the mediocre patterns of human conditioning. This gave birth to the formulated path of Siddha Tantra of unfolding and actualising the resident divinity and having it preside over the entire being.

Through Tantra, one transcends stagnant programming after a spectrum of designed possibilities dissolve the stale energy, after which an organising factor called *Samskara* then reveals one's innate supportive nature (*Swabhava*) that fulfils one's life theme (*Swadharma*). And action done toward one's *Swadharma* is called '*Swa-Tantra*'. The realm of heightened energy that defies linear logic resides as an opportunity to recognise the innate potent pace that accelerates one toward his divine nature. This inner 'potent pace', this gift, is *Swabhava*. Siddha's Tantric *Upasanas* work on one's pseudo nature and push one to fall into his innate potent pace to get synchronised in the river flow of existence of ever-moving life.

Some wrathful *Upasanas* and wild rituals pose impeccable aids in bringing to awareness the innermost stagnant conditioning and help its de-conditioning. This phase is often called the Left Hand Path. The process after, of actualising one's *Swabhava* is termed the Right Hand Path. In actuality, all aspects of this colourful journey are entwined and melt into one another according to each one's way of unfolding. I was initiated into an ancient Tantric *Upasana* called *Aswatha*, where God is worshipped in the form of a fire-breathing Horse that symbolising the destruction of the *Tamasic* (inertia) aspect of life. My Teacher explained how each conditioning has a limited vibration and speaks a language of its own. In the *Aswatha Upasana*, life force is symbolised by a formation of letters that indicate its programmed working nature, the vital factor being the splitting of the array of these programmed series of letters. Breaking the array of letters (*bijas*) implies breaking programmed chain-reactions of life force. Ultimately, it comes to changing the array into a different one to generate an entirely new and different energy level in oneself to produce desired life-situations in the pace of ones life. The *Aswatha Upasana* has several levels to peel different layers of external life situations corresponding to inner energy levels and is required to be practiced over a long duration.

ଖୋ ଔ

There is a vast difference between ancient Tantra yoga and today's new age practices. And the authenticity and true understanding of the path seems to have fallen to confusion on the part of the teachers as well as practitioners. Yet it has not failed to attract followers. Currently, the Tantric path holds quite a global following even though several Tantric teachings are being improperly imparted by present day teachers. Missing the true understanding of the path itself is what renders the teachings misleading and harmful, which is probably why this versatile path was a secret cult. A small example describes how the Tantric path differs from others.

Two ways a cow can be drawn into the shed.

One is by beating it and pushing it forward into the shed.

The other way is by offering it grass and allowing it to willingly and naturally enter.

The first approach exemplifies the Yogic approach and involves working on the human will by consciously adopting virtues like dispassion, austerity, etc. or imbibing a life of holy discipline. The second approach exemplifies the Tantric approach of how one's passion, feelings and emotions are used and channelised to become your path to realising Truth. If Yoga works on one's Fire aspect by burning of tendencies, then Tantra is the path of *Amritha*, the cool and nurturing way to Truth. The Tantric system claims two paths within itself: the 'Left Hand' approach, called *Vama Marga* and the 'Right Hand' approach, called *Dakshina Marga*. Ancient Tantric Masters would rarely disclose themselves except to a few carefully chosen disciples who would meet at secret remote locations such as in the depths of a field, mountainous regions or graveyards. The cause for such secrecy lays hidden beneath the authentic definition of the Tantric Path. It is the path on which, 'wherever one has fallen, one must rise up and stand'. This definition indicates that Tantra works on the wilder forces by influencing the deeper human psyche. The wild knots of passion, agitation, emotional constipation or diarrhoea are skilfully untied by the integrating approach of this sacred path. To an orthodox and religious mind, this path would seem bizarre but to a suppressed mind, it might pose as a glittering excuse for indulgence, which is the prime reason why the path has been kept hidden from most and revealed only to those of appropriate mindset and needed disposition. My Tantric teacher once said to me, "to follow Tantra you must have neither fear, disgust nor guilt." Think about how easily this could be misused for personal gain! As for new age followers, Tantra has become as a form of catharsis, after the changes over time have led to malpractice, perversion and a growing insensitivity toward oneself. A most common misconception is the Left Hand approach being a path of sexual activity.

A simple story about a small town wrestler who went on to become a Vaishnava Saint elucidates the true and authentic working nature of the Tantric Path.

"In an olden day township lived a wrestler renowned for his skill, courage and strength. People greeted him with great respect everywhere he went. One day a young and enchantingly beautiful *daasi* (commercial sex worker of those days) passed him on the street and swept him away by her beauty. The moment he laid eyes on her, the wrestler stood transfixed. As she passed him by, he turned and without a thought followed her. Unaware of the wrestler, the *daasi* continued to walk and reaching her house went inside and closed the door. Outside, the wrestler remained seated by the gate. The next day the wrestler was waiting outside her house when she emerged. Day after day he remained enthralled by her beauty, relentlessly following her everywhere she went. It was a small town and the popular wrestler's strange behaviour didn't go unnoticed. Word soon spread far and wide that along with other things, the wrestler had relinquished his wrestling activities too. Townsfolk, who held him in great respect, not understanding his strange behaviour, resorted to ridicule. But, the wrestler least affected by people's adverse reactions remained immersed in his feelings. He had courageously dropped everything for the one thing that had so overwhelmingly captured his heart.

One day, the sun shone strong and hard and when the *daasi* emerged from her house as usual the wrestler followed, this time carrying a palmyra umbrella above her as protection from the scorching sun. The town people now openly scoffed at him but the wrestler still didn't take notice of the mockery or scornful laughter. He continued following the *daasi* around. On this particular day, the *daasi* went into an old temple. It was completely dark inside. The wrestler followed. In the pitch darkness the *daasi* lit a lamp and as the light spread, it lit up the beautiful statue of Lord Krishna right before the wrestler's eyes. Something miraculous took place in this moment. The divine beauty of Lord Krishna captured the attention of the wrestler and once again he stood transfixed, this time his unmoving eyes immersed in the holiness and rapturous beauty that shone from the Idol. The wrestler had transcended his fixation of the *daasi's* and had been captivated by Universal Divine beauty of Lord Krishna. The wrestler went on to become a great Vaishnava Saint."

This story communicates the worthiness of a genuine attitude and imparts a true understanding of the Tantric path while exemplifying how the teachings are meant to bring transformation. The story also reveals how devotion to one's passion leads to a spontaneous letting-go; a natural renunciation of attachment. The dynamics of the Tantric path can refine gross passions into the sap of divinity.

ꕥ

A Tantric adores his passion, his emotions and every beauty he sees. He feels nourished just by admiring a flower, without plucking it, possessing it or crushing it in the name of intense adoration. He cherishes and adores its beauty as is. A tantric practitioner is taught to approach each moment with exclusivity. For instance, a Tantric would refrain from immediately quenching his thirst and thereby avoid a habitual approach. At the same time, his purpose is not to be insensitive or suppress his thirst, but to live in it and by doing so gain a deeper understanding of the fabric and nature of thirst itself. In fact, the literal meaning of the word Tantra is 'web of fabrication'. To sum it up, the Left Hand Tantric path is about adoring one's passion without suppression or catharsis and invoke an energy-awareness to the pulse of deeper inner forces. The Tantric path of energy-awareness is the link between the physical universe and its organising principles. All Tantric practices are premeditated to bring about a shift followed by refined transformation from overt physical pleasure to internal joy. It involves remaining focused and dedicated to the intrinsic flow of energy similar to the internal shift of focus that happens on experiencing sudden physical pain. One of the first avenues the path begins with are the human senses. A tantric practitioner builds upon the ability of his senses and grows in awareness of the movements and shifts within the energy spectrum in each present moment. His keen sensitivity allows each energy movement to become an experience in itself. In Tantric lovemaking, there is no goal for a sexual release or orgasm and instead involves total submission from each partner toward every movement of energy flow that demands attention. The level of attentiveness required along this path might bring forth a fundamental question - How to focus? But, the question itself is conflicting to the path by bringing in a mental approach, which is alien to energy flow. You play and learn. Sensitivity is spontaneous while watching a tree, bird, river; while witnessing the intrinsic intelligence embedded in each organism, in every moment. If you float on the dance of every emotion, every thought with sensitivity to the world within, then the thought withers away and brings a flowering to the emotion. This flowering is kind of spiritual mutation and grows to profound transformation. Abiding in this perceptive sensitivity or non-cerebral perception makes the mind exceedingly sensitive, pliable and creative, divulging a quantum energy potential that leads to quantum leap transformation. The path of Tantra not only benefits personal relationship but also establishes a visionary understanding reflecting in all aspects of life.

Tantra says...

> "To unfold is to discover, but to accumulate what one discovers is to cease to discover."

ಬಿ ಚಿ

RIGHT HAND PATH

The belief 'God exists' is said to be as old as human existence. Over the years, 'Chosen Ones' have perceived IT, realised IT, gone beyond the cycles of birth and death, attained *Moksha*, and remained immersed in eternal bliss, tasting the Nectar of Immortality. As long as man is bound by limitation, he cannot but worship God in symbolic human form, seeing Him as the ideal father, mother, husband, son or friend. Eventually, all names lead to the Nameless; multiple forms lead to the Formless; all words to Silence and all emotion to a serene flowering of peaceful Existence – Knowledge – Bliss. The Absolute. All Gods merge into ONE Godhood. But Man uses symbols, images, performs rituals and rites to invoke the supreme spirit. He renders the clay or stone images into embodiments of the Spirit identifying with life and consciousness. A *Gnani* abiding in Transcendental Reality sees the absurdity of material articles, rituals and rites but it is through these that an ardent devotee aspires to realise God as all-pervading consciousness. The second path of Siddha Tantra, the Right Hand approach, involves *Upasana* or worship of a prescribed personal deity through *mantras*, *yantras*, etc. In ancient times the Guru would prescribe an Upasana to his disciple based on his inherent character (swabhava) which would aid the *sadhaka* to forge a personal bond with that deity who would bless him and be his guiding light to Truth.

> "The Divine Mother's Magic
> is ancient all life itself.
> She existed before Gods and mortals
> and she will still exist even after the great dissolution.
> Mother is pure energy in subtle form,
> but in times of need
> or just out of desire to play, she manifests."

Nowadays, I find that followers of the Right Hand path worship not one but many deities and teachers prescribe *Upasanas* in a collective manner. This method could create adverse effects because it entirely overlooks the essential component of choosing the deity that resonates with the aspirant's inherent character. And only a *Sat*

CHAPTER FOURTEEN: TANTRA

Guru can see into one's character and qualities in totality, as shown in the short story below.

"In an ancient Indian Guru Kula, several boys were receiving guidance to fulfil their life-purpose. Knowledge learnt at a Guru Kula is different from schooling we know today. While the young disciples carried out seemingly ordinary activities, the wise Guru perceived their inherent nature, natural inclination and innate potential. One day while one of the disciples had taken the cows out to graze, a few boys from a nearby village beat him up. Injured, he slowly walked back to the Guru Kula in tears. One of his companions who saw him hurt and bleeding felt a rage of anger and he instantly demanded to know who was responsible for his dismal condition. Unable to tolerate this injustice, he set off to fight it out. Another companion approached him with great concern and began to clean and treat his wounds with herbs. A third boy enquired what had happened, listened silently to the entire incident without interruption and then calmly assured his friend not to worry, as God would take care of him. The Guru silently watched the three different responses. The boy who showed bravery and courage by fighting the injustice inflicted on his companion would be a suitable disciple for martial art. The disciple who felt compassion and wanted to ease his friend's pain would be a suitable student of medicine and healing. And the third boy, who showed the inherent character of surrendering to God would be suitable for leading a spiritual life right from a young age."

What is *Swabhava* and what role does it play? *Swabhava*, one's inherent character, is determined by a combination of past birth merits, and one's fulfillments as well as shortcomings. This combination takes birth with the individual, and urges one to lead life in a particular way, which is called *Swa-dharma*. *Swa-dharma* is one's life-mission. But, just living according to one's *Swabhava* is not enough. Life turns meaningful and authentic only if overseen by a constructive approach. All of humanity has one purpose - of realising Truth - and yet each of us walk a different walk, according to our *Swa-dharma* and *Swabhava*. The Right Hand path scripted by the ancient Tantric Masters divulges appropriate *Upasana* practices for different deities, which correspond to different inherent characteristics present in humans.

ೱ ೲ

UPASANA

The literal meaning of the word *Upasana* is *Upa asana* - close to one's grounding. Grounding can happen in two ways. Either by directly plunging into an inward journey, as a yogi would do; or by gaining external grounding, the by-product of which results in inner grounding. *Upasana* is the path of coming close to one's grounding by way of what one naturally loves. Each of us has a personal deity we feel intrinsically inclined toward - a bond arising from untouched ground, not acquired conditioning. And we get drawn because the deity is the refined embodiment of our own energy patterns. Our personal deity is an embodiment of the primal energetic patterns (*Samskara*) that predominantly influence our psyche. *Samskara* comes from past births and carries the influence of 'our collective' day-to-day life, which makes it individualistic as well as collective. *Samskara* can be paralleled to the word archetype. ('*Sams*' means - well, '*kaara*' means – making or creating, meaning – 'Making something refined or well'). One's predominant *Samskara* is to be consciously re-lived, while being aware of all its aspects. Through *Upasana*, the Tantric practitioner first recognises, then unwinds his *swabhava* into a greater pattern of creative awareness. In this way, a Tantric's life mission (*Swadharma*) shines to its fullest. The mystical ritual, *mantra*, *yantra*, esoteric processes, etc. of each *Upasana* lead to a loving union that evokes the primordial pattern, which is then consciously lived out. The journey introduces the practitioner to an alternate sense of time and space which he inhabits through his relationship with his personal deity. Scattered fragments of his inner psyche and conflicted life experiences come together and flower into one living whole. A Tantric practitioner's personal deity comes to life in every aspect of his living and he finds a living orientation to relate with existence. His personal deity is his primordial companion; a connection to his unified whole, that guides and consciously co-creates the course of his life.

An archetype, a pattern of energy, shaping an individual's psyche can be experienced only through one's personal deity. Gods, deities, demons, etc., are primordial archetypal energies. Mystical tales and myths are stories of the primordial, collective, unconscious realms and reveal how these forces materialise into the physical domain as *Samskaras*. As they are intangible, they cannot localise in their inherent state, but do localise externally in the form of deities or can even be seen in collective characteristic behavioural patterns. Unlike a western psychiatrist, the Indian mythologist approaches this constructively and positively, ascribing it a name - *Swabhava* and *Swadharma*. Consciously reliving the primal forces of our psyche with courage, tolerance and fortitude and by coming to know them deeply, we can grow to a new level of harmony and empowerment. *Upasana* is that journey. It is the adventure of seeing oneself in a mirrored room reflecting one's hidden aspects. An individual with insufficient inner ground would either get stuck or turn crazy as the encounter with primal patterns are actually lived out and actualised in a realm with a different sense of time. Deities embodying archetypal energies manifest at transitional realms - between the conscious and unconscious, sleep and wake or at kinds of physical spaces called power spots. The twilight time of dawn, dusk and the shifting transitional time zones during midday and midnight are considered vital moments in *Upasana*. Even in Hindu temples, *pooja* and worship are done during these hours. As the *Upasana* deepens, one sees the world in both its aspects simultaneously; the mundane physical aspect and the realm of *Samskaras*, the prime mover of archetypal patterns.

ॐ ☙

Goddess Chinnamasta

Goddess Varahi

Goddess Mathangi

Goddess Thripura Sundari

UPAASAK AND HIS DEVATA

The deity and *Upasana* is chosen based on the inherent character of the aspirant. A few *Upasanas* are described below highlighting the compatibility and resonance with a personal deity and how these attributes express as characteristics of the person. There are two kinds of practitioners (*Upaasaks*). Those whose inherent character or *swabhava,* naturally carry a majority of the predominant traits of a certain deity in which case the resonance and inclination is evident, effortless and natural. The other category are those individuals who are not necessarily of the particular nature of a deity, nor do they carry any relevant traits and characteristics, in which case they would need to imbibe by discipline the characteristics of the deity by worship.

Goddess Saraswathi

The *Swabhava* of an ideal *Upaasak* of Goddess Saraswathi would naturally have clear discriminative intelligence and an inclination toward reading scriptures. For him, insights and revelations would flow with ease. When the attributes and qualities of Goddess Saraswathi naturally resonate within an individual, performing Her *Upasana* would naturally lead to Truth by Her blessings and guidance.

Lord Anjaneya

For undertaking an *Upasana* of Lord Anjaneya, the person should be celibate and of valorous character. In case a person doesn't display such virtues, they are to be adopted as a discipline in the internship of the *Upasana.*

CHAPTER FOURTEEN: TANTRA

Goddess Kali

For the *Upasana* of Mother Goddess Kali, an individual should have an innate attitude of dispassion and renunciation matching the significance of the form of Goddess Kali as the destroyer of evil, attachment, sluggishness and other Tamasic characteristics. This *Upasana* would not fructify blessings for worldly and materialistic enjoyments.

Kali – The Goddess of Power

She has been conceived, worshipped and realised by the human mind in various forms. Kali, the terrific Goddess of Tantra; Kali, the pivot; the sovereign mistress; Kali as Prakruthi, the procreative nature; the destroyer, the creator - is greater and deeper to those who have eyes to see. She is the Universal Mother, the visible God who leads the elected to Invisible Reality. If She pleases, She can take away every last trace of ego from the created being and merge him into the consciousness of the Absolute or the undifferentiated God by Her boundless grace… The trembling and finite ego loses in the illimitable freedom – the Absolute! Tantra places Goddess Kali as first of the ten aspects of *Sakthi*; as the Goddess of Time who destroys everything. When the celestials were overpowered by Sumbha and Nisumbha (demons), they ran to the Himalayas and sought refuge at the feet of Goddess Parvathi, the eternal consort of Lord Siva. In response to their prayers, the beautiful luminous Goddess Parvathi chose to overpower the Asuric forces by becoming Goddess Durga, the remover of suffering. And to destroy Chanda and Munda, the acting Generals for Sumbha and Nisumbha, Kali, the fierce black goddess emerged from the forehead of the world bewitching beauty of Goddess Durga, and beheaded them, thereby earning Herself the name 'Chamunda Devi'. Rakta Bija, the fierce demonic general of Sumbha and Nisumbha had the mysterious power to multiply himself on the battlefield through the drops of his split blood. Goddess Kali asked Goddess Durga to spread her extensive tongue and drink away all the blood gushing out of Rakta Bija to prevent any more demons from emerging, and exterminate him.

With many forces at play within us at all times, if we have poor grounding we turn vulnerable by our inability to discriminate between that which has invaded and ourself, and become victims of invasions. *Asuras* or demons are symbolic representations of the various aspects of egoism within an individual. The demon Chanda symbolises the negative aspect of the subconscious tendencies of violence and the urge to cause harm. The demon Munda symbolises the negative aspect of the subconscious tendency of a provoking nature which instigates trouble and eats away harmony. The demon Rakta Bija symbolises the negative aspect of the subconscious tendency toward killing, terrorism, mass murder, etc. We can see the play of such Asuric forces in society today by the swell in terrorism and widespread acts of destruction happening in the name religion, race, capitalism and power. The demon Sumbha symbolises persistent inertia and laziness that everybody succumbs to more often than not. Each of us are familiar with this aspect at minimal levels but if this takes control and sweeps away all livingness and spirit for life, it hampers the flow of creativity, within as well as at the level of mass consciousness. It curbs evolution at an individual level and suppresses the development of society at a collective level. The demon Nisumbha symbolises ignorance, the illusory nature of egoism that veils one's true nature from oneself. The word Kali comes from the word '*Kala*', or Time; She is the power of time. Time, we are well aware, is all destroying. Since She is the supreme energy responsible for the dissolution of the created universe, Her form as depicted, instills awe and fear. But She is the created and the Mother too. She is ever engaged in protecting Her children. When pleased, She can remedy any disease but if displeased, She can destroy all that we love and like to possess. She is always reassuring Her fear-stricken children through the *Abhaya Mudra*, 'Don't be afraid! I am your own dear Mother!' She also exhibits Her wish to grant boons through the *Varada Mudra*. The Absolute is beyond name, form, attribute and activity, which is why Siva is shown lying prostrate like a *Sava* or corpse, under Her feet. Kali represents His *Sakthi* or energy. The energy, however, can never exist apart from its source, and can manifest and act only while firmly based in the source which is what Kali standing over the chest of Siva indicates. One need not hastily conclude Kali to be representing only the destructive aspect of God's power. What exists when time is transcended is the eternal night of limitless peace and joy. This is also Kali (Maharatre). She prods Mahadeva into the next cycle of creation. She is the power of God in all His aspects. She is the cosmic power, the totality of the universe, a glorious harmony of the pairs of opposites. She creates, preserves and She destroys the limited ego, offering it to Her consort Siva. As Her children we be blessed! Peace and Happiness! A prayer to Her, "Mother, make us men. Mother! Destroy all negative tendencies hidden within us."

Goddess Matangi

For Goddess Matangi, a creative and expressive character, inclined toward music as a form of expression is ideal. By undertaking this *Upasana*, the *Upaasak* could attain the *Siddhi* of oratory skill and music. The famous Meenakshi Temple of Madurai is also considered the Temple of Goddess Matangi. She guides one toward the inner ever-ongoing melody by the path of devotional music, as music is the only language of the Self. Goddess Matangi is the inspirer and carries in Her arms many of the wandering saints, spreading wisdom through their simple songs. An *Upaasak* of Goddess Matangi would feel music in every element of the earth and inspired by each, he would become an expression of the music of nature.

Lord Bhairava

A fearless individual, not easily horrified by hurdles thrown into his life could naturally undertake the *Upasana* of Lord Bhairava. He needs to have the inclination to overcome horrifying obstacles as this *Upasana* adopts the strange method of shifting one's consciousness by way of shock, as a way to lead him toward realising Truth.

Goddess Varahi

Goddess Varahi is also called Pantri Thalaichi (Boar faced goddess) in many ancient Tamil works. Three different aspects of worshipping Goddess Varahi have prevailed. The first aspect of Goddess Varahi is highly praised especially in the Atharvana Veda and the entire of Mantra Sastra is based on Her worship. The second aspect places Goddess Varahi as one among the seven virgin goddesses, where She is worshipped as the village deity by simple villagers and Left-hand practitioners undertake Her *Upasana*. The third aspect finds Goddess Varahi as the consort of Lord Varaha Murthi, one of ten avatars of Lord Vishnu where She is worshipped as one of the presiding goddesses in the Sri Chakra Yantra and Right-hand practitioners pursue Her *Upasana*.

The boar-faced goddess is known to have four subordinates named Swapnesi, Thirasgru, Giripadha Devi and Unmaddha Bairavi. Swapnesi makes others suffer from bad dreams, insomnia and panic. Giripadha devi chases enemies making them flee from one place to another. Unmaddha Bairavi turns the enemy mad and Thirasgru renders the enemy functionless or paralysed. As an example of the kind of practices involved in this worship, the left-hand theme worships Goddess Varahi during the hours of the night, on the fifth day after the new moon. Items like the milk and excreta of a buffalo, a red carpet, chik peas, etc. are commonly used during this ceremony. During the *Upasana*, evil elements like ghosts gain the intense desire to join in the invocation, which is why Tantrics perform the '*Thik Bandhana*' as one of the procedures to bind the eight directions. It is common that Goddess Varahi's worship attracts ghosts as they won't allow their destroyer to appear. Fulfilment of this *Upasana* depends upon the practitioner's courage and persistence. His fear and conditioning of death are destroyed by the divine *Darshan* of Goddess Varahi during Her *Upasana*. This boar-faced goddess presents Herself as an extremely powerful and wrathful Goddess and Her *Upasana* could grant many *Siddhis*. The blessings bestowed by this *Upasana* seem appealing and dreamlike but the Goddess has not made Her *Upasana* easy. Adversities are inevitable as the boar signifies digging deep into the earth which calls for tremendous stability and grounding on the part of the aspirant. An extremely specific attitude is required for performing the *Upasana* to this Goddess.

During the medieval period, there was a General by the name of Sunderesha Sarma in the Chola Kingdom of Tamil Nadu who fought many battles. He was successful and victorious in his generalship and found great beauty in his service and in the adventures of the battlefield. Post retirement he took up the *Upasana* of Goddess Varahi, had Her *darshan* and attained Her blessings. His *Samadhi* shrine is located in a village called Veerasolan around 60 kilometres from Madurai. He wrote beautiful verses adoring Her features and magnanimity in his work called Varahi Malai, (garland of the Goddess Varahi). This work also carries verses of the *mantra* and *yantra* for Her *Upasana* but their application (which is the

Tantra) remains hidden. The works of Varahi Tantra is unavailable anywhere in India. There are 32 types of Occult applications in Varahi worship under the base of *Asta Karma*. A character of strength, courage, stability and love for this form of adventure and battle is demanded from a practitioner. On fulfilling Her *Upasana*, Goddess Varahi graces the practitioner with mastery over the five elements along with the *Siddhi* of *Gnana*.

Sri Chakra Upasana

> "Behold the Sakthi as Chakra calmly,
> On the days meditating thus, Felicity be,
> Then your name and fame is equal to Brahma,
> From here you conjoin Siva."
>
> Thirumanthiram Verse 1367

Sri Chakra Upasana is the most popular and is common to all spiritual schools. In the Siddha tradition, the Sri Chakra Yantra is composed of 43 triangles and this divine *Mandala* comprises of intersections of downward and upward pointing triangles, symbolising each phenomena within existence. The Sri Chakra is considered the Master of *Yantras*, as all the Goddesses preside within, and Goddess Lalitha Thripura Sundari at the top centre. The Sri Chakra Yantra signifies cosmic creation, sustenance and destruction. According to ancient mythology, the sky symbolises the masculine nature while the earth the feminine. Similarly, the five downward pointing triangles of the Sri Chakra Yantra are the *Sakthi Yantras* and the three upward pointing ones including the *Bindu* are the *Siva Yantras*. As a whole, the Sri Chakra Yantra is described as the 'divine matrix of the union of Siva-Sakthi.' The nine outer circles are called *Nava-Avarnas* and represent the veiling or conditioning aspect of human consciousness that must be unveiled before the inner realms of this divine matrix are touched upon. Two different themes of Sri Chakra Upasana are followed in Siddha Tantra. The Mother Goddess Lalitha seated in MahaMeru as the presiding sovereignty of the universe is one. Here, She is as the ruling Ultimate, the one performing the *'Panch Kritiya'* - creation, sustenance, destruction, veiling and blessing. In the second theme, the *Bindu*, the Centre, is known as the doorway of 'Chidambaram' - the space of consciousness, where Lord Siva is ever-dancing.

> "The state of forty-three triangles, indescribable;
> The triangles pointing towards the Head in the centre,
> If you orient there, it is the best of all service that you can heartfully do.
> O Snake! Dance, saying this."
>
> Pampatti Siddhar Verses

On the divine union of Siva Sakthi, manifests Lord Natarajar - dancing in the space of consciousness. For this *Upasana*, a tantric practitioner requires to know the *Anga Niyasa* and *Kara Niyasa* procedures to invoke the Satvic divine nature within himself, and to awaken the deities within his *Nadis*. After purification, the practitioner worships the various other deities circling and guarding Goddess Lalitha. The great Chandra Sekara Swami, mentions, "The Sri Chakra is not different from Goddess Sri Vidya. One must not treat it as a mere *Yantra*, but as the very body of the Goddess Herself." This could be the missing link for *sadhakas* who perform *Upasana* with a practice-oriented attitude because one cannot find 'attuning' through technical knowledge. A worshipper and *Sadhaka*, require an optimistic character, adoration for prosperity, auspiciousness, purity and fertility. One who receives blessings through this *Upasana* will not face any form of deficiency, poverty, lack, pessimism or such in his life or would these aspects inflict themselves in his surrounding. A life of auspiciousness and wisdom would flourish as this *Upasana* grants both material prosperity and *Gnana*. Being the highest *Upasana*, it can be undertaken solely by the grace of the Guru. In the works and verses of the Siddha System the Sri Chakra is mentioned as 'Narpattu Mukkonam', which means 'The worship of 43 triangles'. Many verses depict how prized the Siddhas consider this form of *Upasana*.

Siddha Sattai Muni Sings in His Gnanam-4

> Listen the method of Pooja
> > Some do pooja for manuscripts with mudra
> Some do pooja of lamp
> > Some do pooja keeping woman
> Some do pooja regularly on chakras
> > The pooja, I do, is Meru
> Recite the forty-three triangles
> > Keeping this, did poojas, the Siddhas
> > > - Verse 1

> They, who do pooja of Meru, the self-illumines
> > If they curse, the universe be burnt
> The honey like Meru needs Deeksa (initiation)
> > Don't approach it as a kid
> They who did Meru-pooja
> > If they do teaching (upadesha) opening their mouth
> The Siddhis of alchemy, aerial fly
> > Can be attained (looted) by his disciple
> > > - Verse 2

CHAPTER FOURTEEN: TANTRA

Listen the three letters (syllables) of Valai
    After doing pooja of it skilfully
Then listen the eight letters of Tripurai
    After passing it by doing pooja
Listen the letters of on coming (succeeding) pooja of Buvanai
    Skilfully perform Buvani-pooja
Get oriented to the six letters of Yamala by listening it
    Do Pooja by praising Her feet
Listen the five letters of Yamala after it,
    After finishing the fivefold initiations

                                    - Verse 3

As a prelude for the fire like Vaasi yoga,
    Oh Son- do the inner pranayama within,
If you know and have insights all of these,
    Then no obstacles for Kaya- Siddhi."

ಶ್ರೀ

Unique to Siddha Tantra is the hidden Tantric worship of five Goddess - starting with Goddess Valai, moving onto Goddess Bhuvaneshwari (Bhuvanai), then Goddess Thiripura Sundari (Thiripura) and then Goddess Shyamala (Shyamalai) and finally Goddess Manonmani. A disciple undertakes this *Upasana* under the guidance of the Guru. In the beginning, Goddess Valai appears to him as a young girl of five or six years of age and engages with the *sadhaka* in play and teaches Her disciple, whom She has come to bless. As the journey continues She matures in appearance, in name and in Her teachings. The worship of Goddess Valai is a vital stage in Siddha Tantra, for without Her blessings one cannot attain Siddhahood. All ancient Siddhas have spoken of this on a highly secretive note. Another nature of worship of Goddess Valai has nine forms of Goddess Valai, with appropriate names and carries blessings for different attributes.

Goddess Kumari (2 years of age) -
> Her blessings destroy and burn away Karmic poverty.

Goddess Thirumurti (3 years of age) -
> Her blessings grant Wealth and prosperity.

Goddess Kalyani (4 years of age) -
> Her blessings destroy enmity and remove hostility.

Goddess Rohini (5 years of age) -
> Her blessings grant furthering in academics and learning.

Goddess Kalika (6 years of age) -
> Her blessings free one of agony, pain and trauma.

Goddess Chandika (7 years of age) -
> Her blessings break black magic spells and give protection.

Goddess Sambhavi (8 years of age) -
> Her blessings bring auspiciousness in the course of ones life, give pleasantness, and joy in the events in life.

Goddess Durgai (9 years of age) -
> Her blessings remove fear, phobia and paranoia.

Goddess Subhadra (10 years of age) -
> Her blessings grant all kinds of auspiciousness, abundance, affluences and contentment.

CHAPTER FOURTEEN: TANTRA

Those shrines in Tamil Nadu that depict the Goddess aspect as a *Tapasvini* are frequented by Tantric *Upasaks* to seek blessings during the internship.

	GODDESS	PLACES IN TAMILNADU
1	Kumari	Kanya Kumari
2	Tapas Kamatchi	Maangadu
3	Agilandeswari	Tiru Anaikaval (Trichy)
4	Gomathi	Sangaran Kovil
5	Kamalambikai	Tiruvarur, Kamala peeth
6	Parasakthi	Kuttralam, Yoga Peeth
7	Nitya Kalyani	Tiru Tala Turai (Lal Kudi)
8	Arum Tapa Nayaki	Balluvoor
9	Yogambika	Tiru Perum Turai
10	Karapagambika	Maylapur

௰ ௱

OCCULT

"We must not regard wonders and signs
As contrary to Nature but contrary to
What, is known of Nature."
              St.Augustine -deciv.dei.bk xxi, Ch.VIII

Life is a play of unseen hidden forces. We live and move among them but are almost unaware of their impact or potential and strength. The strength of these forces may be harnessed externally or from within our own being. For instance, the strength to fight illness can come either from external medicine, diet or can be derived from within the body's innate healing intelligence and ability. But in present times, lack of attention has dwindled and deteriorated our inner strength, and disease is mostly treated by external means. The use of powerful drugs and advanced technology has brought new disease in relation to the deterioration of the body's own immune system. In the present phase of human evolution, the difficulty in comprehending the subtle forces is due to the restricting nature of our ordinary limited consciousness. Only when it develops and becomes subtler will it come in more direct contact with inner reality and gain awareness of the working nature of unseen forces. This sort of inward and direct knowledge of things is the very basis of Siddha Tantric Science.

"Thannai ariya thanakkoru kedu illai
Thannai ariyamal thane kedukinran."

"Know thyself and this makes you free from all evil,
But man, un-knowing of himself, is a victim."

This is the basic dictum propounded by Siddha Thirumoolar in the science of Life.

ಸ ಞ

ASTA KARMAM - THE EIGHT KINDS OF OCCULT APPLICATIONS

The literal meaning of *Asta* is eight and *Karma* means performance. Ancient Siddhas describe the occult truth to be found within the very functions of nature and between the constructs of life. From an entire ocean only some water separates itself, rises as vapour and evaporates into the call of the Sun to form clouds in the sky.

CHAPTER FOURTEEN: TANTRA

Clouds come together in formations from which the 'whole' ones fall, separating from the sky, drawn by the attraction of the earth, as rain. For the cloud that burst into rain and fell to the earth, it was its death in the sky, but birth on earth!

OR

A predator exudes an enchanting presence to transfix his prey and render it immobile.

Simple, day-to-day processes of nature are built of different stages which amount to eight with a straightforward explanation to the series-phenomena created by their repetition or combination. The names and working nature of the classified eight occult aspects or performances within *Prakruthi* (Nature) are given below. The Siddhas' sacred verses describe these forces as intangible, elusive and subtle and therefore represented by a deity and its attributes. The form and worship of the relevant deity enables one to relate to the otherwise intangible world of occult and helps enter into a relationship which articulates the nature of the said forces. A force can be harnessed for an intended purpose by worshipping the particular deity. Through communion and interaction (worship) the subtle world is brought to light, expressed and actualised. The example of the Ocean and Predator given above elucidates the underlying natural occultism prevalent in day-to-day existence.

> Sthambana - restrain, transfix or immobilise
>> *Sthambana* is about different natures of restrain that render the enemy powerless; stopping, keeping in check or restraining the power of fire, the flow of water, the ferocity of wild beasts or making an evil person or spirit immovable and confined to one place.

Mohana - Gives the power of overwhelming seduction or enchantment.

Ucchatana - Confers the powers to exorcize
> It involves the power of expulsion. Setting demons against a person to ruin him by magical incantations. Dislodging them by proper procedure. Dislodging demons from persons or places.

Marana - Deprivation of life
> This force renders destruction and death of an enemy by killing either evil spirits or evil human beings.

Vasiya - Confers the power of bringing a person under one's influence.
> Confers fascination and attraction towards one.

Akarshana - Confers the power of placing men and things under one's will and desire or is used to summon or invoke a spirit or absent person visibly into one's presence.
> Vidvedanam - Triggers hatred toward something.

Bhedanam - Causes dissension, discord, etc.

Each of the eight classified karmas have eight sub-karmas or functions according to their application such as earth, friend, enemy, animal and world, therefore making a total of sixty-four *Asta karmas*, fifty-six of which fall under the first eight.

CHAPTER FOURTEEN: TANTRA

BOX OF DIRECTION

KINDS OF ASTA KARMA	DIRECTION
Akarsanam and Vasiyam	East
ThamBanam and Mohanam	North
Vidveshnam and Utchadanam	West

Mysterious herbs of occult nature used in Tantric practices:

Akarsanam	-	Acalypha
	-	Gynandropsis pentaphylla
	-	Calotropis gigantea
Utchadanam	-	Heliotropium indicum
	-	Crotalaria laburnifolia
	-	Lawsonia inermis
Tambanam	-	Spermacoce hispida
	-	Indigofera tinctoria
	-	Hygrophila auriculata
Vidvedanam	-	Aristolochia bracteata
	-	Phyllanthus amarus
	-	Euphorbia tirucalli
Vasiyam	-	Achyranthes aspera
	-	Desmodiuam gyrans/eodariocalyx-motorius
	-	Rhinacanthus naustus
Mohanam	-	Cyperus Rotundus
	-	Curculigo orchioides
	-	Hemidesmus indicus
Maranam	-	Plumbago Zeylancia
	-	Gloriosa superba
	-	Euphorbia hirta
Bedanam	-	Tinospora cordifolia
	-	Abutilon indicum
	-	Crateva Magna

SECTION THREE: BEING AND SHARING

The ancient Siddhas' working knowledge of unseen forces gave birth to the science of Occultism. They devised methods, practices, rituals, etc. to serve not only worldly success but spiritual intentions as well. The application of Occult practice involves *Chakras*, *Yantras* (mystical diagrams), *Mantras*, *Thithi* (a specific astrological time), specific herbs, particular beads, different kinds of seats for performing the worship, specific directions, particular elements and esoteric breathing applications. The following instance shows how six of the eight occult aspects are combined and applied for spiritual purpose.

For instance, in Esoteric-breathing practices...

> *Vasiya* is calling forth the *Prana* from Air.
> *Mohana* is involved in the process of settling the separated *Prana* into a specific *Chakra*.
> *Tambana* is retaining the *Prana* in that specific *Chakra* or *Nadi*.
> *Bedana* is separating the unwanted *Apana* from the Pranic current.
> *Vidveshana* is chasing the contaminated *Prana* or unwanted *Apana*.
> *Marana* is eliminating the chased unwanted *Apana* through the bodily outlets such as by exhalation, expiration, etc.

The Siddhas' poems caution us against learning and applying this warrior sorcery art for selfish purposes and encourage its use toward constructive means or the well-being of others. One must be aware of the unwanted karma of selfish acts as it returns, pointing the sorcerer against the bull's eye. Coming back to the application of this precarious and potent science, the first *pooja* performed before any ritual is the '*Ganapathi pooja*'. *Ganapathi pooja* or the worship of Lord Vinayaka is done to evoke the eight occult *Siddhis*. According to Siddha Tantra, *Asta Ganapathi pooja* is to be performed first with a *Yantra*, the appropriate *Mantra* and other Tantric procedures. After which one can enter into *Asta karma* practices one by one. Ritualistic or performed occultism has been described above, but on a final note I would like to add that a Siddha *Gnani* or *Gnana Chittar* never wilfully performs any *Siddhis*. It is by His very presence that the *Siddhis* emerge as an uninterrupted flow of Divine automation and perform the needed phenomena through Primal Intelligence and not a trace of acquisition or human intention stains its pure divinity.

ಙ ಲ

CHAKRAMS
(Yantras)

The word *Yantra* is derived from the root word *'Yam'*, which means to sustain, hold or govern. *Yantras* are called *Chakrams* in Tamil and is a field of concentrated consciousness that pulls together and controls different energies. Generally, *Chakrams* comprise of sacred Tamil seed syllables, numbers, a point, triangle, circle or square, lotus, etc. of symbolic significance.

- *Bindu* is represented by the dot in the centre, the point at which kinetic energy radiates to the outer circumference before subsiding into the nucleus again. It is the unitary state of Siva and Sakthi.
- A Triangle is symbolic of creative energy.

  - *Moola - Trikona* - the three lines of a triangle constitute the root matrix of Nature.
  - An Upward Triangle, a triangle with its apex pointing upward, represents the Siva aspect.

- A Downward Triangle, a triangle with its apex pointing downward, represents the Sakthi aspect.
- A Circle represents the cyclic and rhythmic contraction and expansion of Cosmic Energy.
- A Square - The Four corners of a square denote the four directions and thereby the totality of space. A square often appears as the base of *Chakrams*.
- Broken walls (of a Fort) - The shape drawn as the outermost layer signifies the Guardian Deities of eight directions.
- *Bija Mantras* represent the visual and auditory forms of a particular *Tattwa*, deity or any other quantum vibration of divine energy contained in the *Chakram*.

A special ritual performed to invigorate and enliven the *Chakrams* includes purification and energisation with specific *Mantras* for which an auspicious day, hour, *dithi*, *lagnam* and *nakshatra* are chosen to harness the required forces. This entire process is also called *Tantra* in esoteric practice. *Chakrams* help deal with human problems, external or planetary influence as well as meditative purposes. The human mind interprets every experience and associates it with a sound-symbol, a name and a visual form which is why Tantra uses visual form and sound-symbols to synchronise the mind with its Source. Naturally, forms are symbolic representations of a subtler nature. For instance, the ocean is a symbol of life. If one stands at the shore, the ocean appears endless and mysterious, full of depth housing many creatures within it. When people describe their view of an ocean, it symbolises their perspective to life. Likewise, a wall is symbolic of death. Certain visual forms invoke a feeling of an invisible phenomenon that can be felt but not grasped by the mind.

ಙ ಜ

CHAPTER FOURTEEN: TANTRA

A NATIVE TANTRIC TALISMAN

Siddha occultism uses herbal Talismans to resolve problems related to health, illness, spirit possession, planetary influence, stagnant situations, etc. A native Tantric follows a specific method to prepare a Talisman. Certain herbs have been cursed by the Siddhas as a measure of protection, to prevent misuse and before the Tantric can use it, the curse is removed by the chanting of a remedial *mantra*, 16 times, at a specific auspicious time. A part of the commonly-chanted *mantra* has been given below:

"Aum Mooligai Sabam NasiNasi
Sarva Mooligai Sabam NasiNasi ...
....
Oon Ooir Oon Oodalil Nirka Swaha."

(*Mooligai* means herbal, *Sabam* means curse, and *NasiNasi* means die, *Sarva* means entire, *Ooir* means life, *Oodalil* means body, *Nirka* means indwelling)

The Tantric must go to the required plant on a particular day and time and stand before the plant, naked. After chanting the remedial *mantra*, with his attention centred in the eyebrow *chakra* he must cut a part of the root running toward the North. Chopping it into small fragments he must then bind it with threads of five different colours. After this initial process, he can recite the *mantras* suiting the purpose of the talisman. Thus sanctified, the pieces of root, bound in multi-coloured threads, known as *Kulisam* (Talisman) or *Moolikai Ratchai* (herbal protector) is then tied around the wrist or worn around the neck of the concerned person to ward off/resolve the problem.

Another Tantric remedial procedure for warding off or resolving problems involves the preparation of a thin copper plate, of a minimum length and breadth of 5 centimetres onto which *Mantra* letters and a *chakram* or diagram is engraved. It is then rolled and bound by five coloured threads (symbolising the five *Bhoothas*) and offered to the deities along with *Prasadham* of rice and black dhal pongal. Lamps are lit in an *Agal* (small pit) made of rice paste with ghee, into which the threads are inserted and lit. The native Tantric performs *pooja* and chants specific *Mantras*. Camphor, lit in a plain plate, or a pot of offering is shown to the face of the affected person in circular movements while he sits facing east. Once this sanctifying process is performed, the *Kulisam* (Talisman) is tied at the hip or with a yellow thread around the neck.

The third remedial avenue involves the use of solidified mercury. An adept native Tantric uses solidified mercury as a more powerful remedy than the ones described earlier, the only drawback being that it employs a rather complicated process which is available only through the oral lineage. Solidified mercury, in the form of a bead, is commonly called *Rasa Mani*. Nowadays, the easily available mercury beads around temple areas or market places are actually 'dead' beads and not 'alive' as needed. The authenticity of a mercury bead can be verified by throwing it to the ground. If it rebounds, it is genuine. This test is a physical level test and does not verify the true potential of the mercury. Ancient Siddhas prepared 64 types of mercury-based remedy beads for difficulties ranging from health, affluence, meditation, aerial visit, etc.

৳ ব্র

SECTION THREE: BEING AND SHARING

AT THE HALL OF IMMACULATE GOLD

By Siddha Saint Ramalingam,
in His work Tiru Arutpa, Section Aani Ponnambalathe

Refrain
"In the Immaculate Golden Hall cosmic visions,
What wondrous visions - O Amma!
What wondrous Visions."

Stanzas:
"A mountainous light shone,
There was a street, - O Amma
There was a street."

"Walking this street, in the middle
There was a stage - O Amma.
There was a stage."

"Mounting this stage
There was a gathering point - O Amma
There was a gathering point."

"Approaching this gathering point,
Found a seven storied mansion - O Amma
There was a seven storied mansion."

"The wonders filled in those seven storeys
How can I speak of it? - O Amma
How can I speak of it?"

"In one level there was a glittering pearl,
It turned Blue Sapphire - O Amma
It turned Blue Sapphire."

"In another level of the multi-levelled world,
In making the Black blue, the gem turned red coral - O Amma,
It turned red coral."

CHAPTER FOURTEEN: TANTRA

On yet another level, the green emerald
Transforms itself, now a red ruby - O Amma,
Became a red Ruby."

"In the level after, a giant pearl,
Became a great diamond Gem - O Amma,
Became a great diamond Gem."

"In another different level, an augmented cluster of Coral,
Turned, White Gem- O Amma,
Became a white Gem."

"Next storey that I entered, organised multifarious Gems
Turning into Golden jewels - O Amma,
They turned into Gold."

"In the level after, where I settled, all the Gems that I spoke of,
Transformed to Crystal - O Amma,
Transformed to Crystal."

"Above all the seven levels - Was a Pillar!
A harmonious Golden pillar - O Amma,
A harmonious Golden Pillar."

"The moment I saw this golden pillar, climbing, I saw
A novelty! How can I describe it - O Amma?
That Novelty! How can I describe?"

While climbing, That confronts me,
Is of boundless measure - O Amma,
Is of boundless measure!"

"Sakthis are there, in thousands and thousands
They came - O Amma,
They came."

"When they came and intoxicated - I, undeceived by delusion,
Gaining the sovereignty of Grace - O Amma,
Sovereignty of Grace."

SECTION THREE: BEING AND SHARING

"By way of Sovereign power, climbing the Great Pillar,
I saw its jewelled peak - O Amma,
Saw its jewelled peak."

"Above the Jewelled peak, stood the crest of this peak,
As another, I saw - O Amma,
As another, I saw."

"Above the crest of that peak, a 1008 carat Gold
Temple was there - O Amma,
Temple was there."

"Seeing the Temple, with towering Gate
Went inside, un-hesitating - O Amma,
Went inside, un-hesitating."

"Inside the towering Gate, were Sakthis and Sakthas,
Crores and mutlicrores - O Amma,
In tens of thousands, many tens of thousands."

"There, their colours, white and red
Became colours five - O Amma,
Became colours five."

"There, they all asked, 'Who is here?'
I went beyond - O Amma,
I went beyond."

"Having gone beyond, and into a sacred entrance
Where there were Sakthis, Five - O Amma,
Where there were Sakthis, Five."

"Others standing there, showed the path ahead
I arrived at a jewelled entrance, O Amma!
Arrived at a jewelled entrance."

"On meditating in that entrance, a woman and man
Were there as two - O Amma,
Were there as two,"

CHAPTER FOURTEEN: TANTRA

'There they showed, a miniscule sacred opening
I looked in, with love - O Amma,
With love! I looked out."

"Through this holy entrance, found the Mother of Bliss,
As my mother - O Amma,
As my mother."

"Seeing the Mother, received Grace
And dined nectar - O Amma,
Dined Nectar - O Amma."

"With Her gracious support, the sanctum of
The Dancing King, I found - O Amma,
The Dancing King, I found."

"Entering the sanctum, the benevolence I attained,
Only God knows - O Amma!
Only God Knows!"

Refrain
"In the Immaculate Golden Hall cosmic visions,
What wondrous visions - O Amma!
What wondrous Visions."

ஐ ௧

SECTION FOUR
RELUCTANT MASTERS

CHAPTER FIFTEEN

RELUCTANT MASTERS
Spirit of the Siddhas

AWAKEN FROM ONE'S LIFE FICTION

"What we are looking for is who is looking."

-St.Francis

Did we decide our birth? Did we choose our parents? Did we pick the place of our birth? Once born, to live is a must. There is no choice to that. Is life imposed? From the beginning, right from birth, inability seems to have taken birth with us. Once born, can we remain idle? Here too inability stares us in the face. As humans, we are extended and related! Our first relationship is with our mother, which then, through her extends into a multitude of relationships. Doing or activity has meaning only if it is done with an orientation or relation. As infants, we move our hands and feet out of an instinct to 'do'. For instance, a baby cries to be fed or smiles seeing the mother, its first known face. 'Doing', begins at birth, expressing the inherent survival instinct born to fulfil life. For any life on earth, the 'doing' that begins at birth doesn't stop until death! Although the nature of activity does undergo change, physical and psychological, in relation to the stages of life.

SECTION FOUR: RELUCTANT MASTERS

Life is nothing but movement!

Infant activity is for survival. Craving for parental love and care gradually extends into 'play' and then into possessing toys. This continues as we grow and get introduced to the prevalent social, economical, political and religious conditioning around. Our first effort is toward 'fitting into' the setup and feeling accepted by the masses, or the collective consciousness - our immediate surroundings. Feeling accepted is the underlying motive behind most of our activities at this stage. After the primary stage of becoming a member of society, society rises before us as a performance field. The urge to excel now leads our every activity and life turns into a race for excellence. The end of each race spits out a winner and discards the losers. The struggle for excellence is the disguise to acquire power! 'To excel' implies others to be weak. This power struggle flourishes everywhere... in academics, specialisations, professions, politics, religion, socially, financially and even in spirituality. Our simple infantile, survival-oriented activities gradually are ruled over by our new found psychological cravings, in search of fulfilment. The psychological cravings come from a mix of our individual traits, type of upbringing and social structure transforming our simple needs into hoards of desire.

A child receives his first learning from his mother. A toddler explores his world in all openness, with no sense of discrimination or differentiation. But naturally, at some point his mother will deny him something and because both acceptance and denial came from one source (his mother) - that moment becomes an extremely significant turning point in the toddler's life. Being denied leaves the child in shock. He experiences an inner hollowness. Before the toddler-stage, in the waking state he had never felt a sense of separation from the mother - his secure centre around which his external world revolved, through which he moves and

CHAPTER FIFTEEN: RELUCTANT MASTERS

interacts with the extended world. But when the mother denies him something in relation to the external world, its impact hits his core - he experiences it as - refusal of his own existence. The anxiety born of this drives him to search a substitute and this marks the beginning of a compensating process; a method of substitution and the acceptance of the substitute, if he gets it. The event of denial could either provoke a stronger urge or desire or it could alter into a substituting process - used to overcome the feeling of hollowness. Failing both, the toddler could show the reaction of retreating.

This is the beginning of 'Fragmenting'!

The 'innocence, all openness, trust' fragments and hereon the toddler interacts with the world from these splits. The fragments gradually build and crystallise by each encounter with the external world, because it is the external social structure that plays the role of mother for our growing needs - either by providing or restraining. And this original childhood experience with our mother goes on to reflect into adulthood.

౩౦ ౦౩

Man, from birth is under the constant influence of his individualistic traits in the form of urges, emotions and feelings, which serve as streams of life expression. The mother, in childhood, plays the confining role of watching over our actions and desires, similarly our surrounding social structure doesn't always allow for the wholesome expression of our traits. The environment cannot always be conducive to each one's inherent traits as its own structure itself is built on boundaries. The consequence is that all traits beyond manmade norms remain neglected and unfulfilled. The restraining nature of our social setup acts as a canal for our

SECTION FOUR: RELUCTANT MASTERS

life expressions and man is at its mercy to fulfil his survival needs as well as psychological desires. Accommodating ourself within these boundaries, life turns into a search and we lose to the conflict between feeling our inherent spontaneity and following the structured social boundaries. Soon we grow a social face or pseudo identity as our individualistic traits submit to modification to suit social norms - only so that we are considered 'normal'. The majority of people make this compromise and sacrifice their inherent individuality but this highly discomforting process is against natural order and paves the way for hollowness in one's heart and mind. The process doesn't end here as man continues to shun himself until the point when external pressure climbs high and he finally questions his free will and stifled identity. It is only now that he realises the extent to which he is at the mercy of the social setup and how most of his activities are manipulated by this larger influence. Frustrated, he feels how far he has come from himself. The inner hollowness eats away, nagging him to notice his prolonged suppression until he is no longer able to ignore the discomfort. He makes efforts to fill the gnawing hollowness by playing a series of control games with the social setup - desperate attempts to re-establish his individuality. Most people spend their entire lifetime as a continued motion of doing and doing... a series of unconscious attempts to re-assert lost individuality by using acts of establishing and dismantling. Man's need to reassert his lost individuality arises from a feeling of imperfection. His acts to 'establish' are to prove himself perfect, similar to how a coward enjoys watching action movies. The force of the need to reassert is directly related to the weight of the external influence or projection. E.g. an individual with a strong inferiority complex obviously suffers severe feelings of imperfection because of which he attempts to assert a perfect individuality and compensate his imperfections with a superiority attitude. He ends up projecting a dominating personality.

CHAPTER FIFTEEN: RELUCTANT MASTERS

In all actuality, the struggle lies in the relative existence of things!

Our belief that the sole purpose of life is 'to Excel' hides our effort to substitute our sense of imperfection and deprivation that begins in infancy. As our attempts change according to the stages of life, gradually life becomes a pattern of oscillations between dropping old acquisitions and pursuing new ones. Fundamentally, the effort 'to pursue' is no different from the effort 'to drop'. Society calls this blind mechanical cycle 'growth', 'success' or 'progress', because somehow we find it is the only way we feel life is in our control. Our assumption of being in control is false and very few people are aware of how we continually use habitual patterns to escape the nagging hollowness within.

෩ ෬

CONTROL ISSUES

Within a social structure 'not to be in control' or 'to be out of control' is a taboo. Moreover, the society pretends to mother our individual as well as collective needs by manipulating our desires. Hypocrisy is common to most social norms. Alcohol is permissible as long as it is not too much. Dressing scantily is fashionable but to walk naked is shameful. Society says - those of fitting conduct are accepted members. The downside of this rigid, expectation-oriented structure of being in control, enforces the pressure to conform. It could also be a bargain, for us to be an accepted member of the society. Unfortunately, pressure seeks an outlet. And eventually we find ourselves overwhelmed, suppressed, imposed upon and suffering the deep pain of losing our innate individuality. Swallowed by the loss and overcome by hollowness, we yearn freedom - we turn to the path of spirituality! Do we really want freedom or just new answers?

෩ ෬

SECTION FOUR: RELUCTANT MASTERS

SPIDER - GOT BY ITS WEB

"A spider was wandering hither thither.
Freely!
Not understanding this freedom,
Considering itself vulnerable,
He wanted a home.
So, he spun a web.
Next day, he found a meal trapped in the web.
He was elated and happy
That by no effort food had come.
So he spun a bigger web.
Next day, the spider saw that dust was also trapped in his web.
But he didn't give up spinning webs.
Soon there was more dust in its web.
And then even more!
So much, that he couldn't move...
He died!
Even until the last moment, the spider
Failed to remember that
This 'world' he had made!"

While most don't mind the pressure factor, some of us conclude that society does not hold plausible answers and nor does it welcome what we have to offer. Any effort to contest the social structure lands us into deeper compromise with our individuality which lead to harsher confrontations with the hollowness. This is our turning point. Only after we accept we don't 'fit in', we approach a new world with new hope. Weary from the weight of our fantasies and exhausted from the obstacles, we don't realise that our intention to play out our unfulfilled fantasies this time on spiritual ground, still survives. Did we not flee from the intricate web of persistent day-to-day

CHAPTER FIFTEEN: RELUCTANT MASTERS

complications that we ourselves spun? But have we approached the spiritual realm with the attitude to escape our concrete reality? Unknown to us, all the aspects we claim to flee from have come along and we trudge into the realm of spirituality with a lurking motive to re-gain control over life and continue clinging to our fantasy-projected life. Ironically, we had initially hoped for change! Our new platform offers us simple teachings such as 'look within' to find true happiness, which we unconsciously interpret as - 'power lies here', and instantly our projections unite with it and turn into our interpretation; an idea that serves as the next starting point. We feel a sense of control coming over our life. And we once again channelise it favourably - at our pace - and begin to fulfil our desires along the way. A few of us realise from valued experience how the attempt to control life itself is futile and that life has a way of turning the tables on us. For the rest, 'looking within' becomes yet another adventure or process to employ - picturing a spiritual goal and setting out to attain it, in an exclusive way! We remain dangerously unaware of how our efforts are still fuelled by our 'same old' approach of 'acquiring' happiness. This habitual utilitarian approach to attain a new-found goal called upliftment is spiritual materialism. Our habit is a deep-rooted conditioning; a pattern of deciding what we want, structuring our view of life or restructuring our outer situations. What's our motive? The comforting presence of a specific and active working focus that provides the illusion of being 'in control'. But does this ideational approach free us from the nagging hollowness within? Temporarily! It does appear to bring it under control but little do we know that the driving force to reach a goal is actually a substituting factor and is veiling the depths of our unhappiness because we believe we are unfulfilled by this existing moment!

It is our restlessness and sense of abandonment that generates such a real feeling of un-fulfilment which is why rather than accepting things as they are, dreaming of a spiritual goal is in some way more appealing and comforting. We prefer to continue an external search to acquire or pursue some practice. It makes us feel fulfilled and secure. But our skin deep attitude doesn't allow us to 'be' and we affiliate ourselves to some establishment like an ashram or spiritual group. And we restlessly switch ashrams, groups or jump from teacher to teacher, as if shopping for Awareness, Kundalini, No-mind, Advaita, Tantra, Yoga or New Age Spirituality, in a spiritual supermarket.

But, this is not to say that anything external cannot bring temporal happiness. It also gives birth to a kind of enslavement, dependency or expectancy that carves a pattern of acquiring tendencies. It creates more than a basic sense of inner anxiety and we live harbouring a subconscious fear. A fear of change or that something won't last. We even dread losing what is currently fulfilling us. Fear and anxiety at once push us to assert the same kind of control as before to hold onto what we currently have. These need not be insidious forms of control and can be as plain as fulfilling expectations in order to remain a member of a spiritual group, or maintaining a relationship with a teacher, or even fanatically adhering to a teaching. Our neurotic grasping tendency enhances as our ego gets fuelled by the fear of deprivation along with our inner hollowness. The flaw in acquiring 'externally' is simple. When what we have added to attain happiness or fulfilment is taken away, we encounter the same nagging unhappiness. It shows its ugly face again and each time even more crystallised.

ಐ ಚ

Back to where we started, we confront the original problem. To keep what we want requires control and we reassert control to have what we want - this is still how we live. We are not free! For those who believe 'to control' is freedom, are they not diving further into bondage? Is there a silver lining around this dark cloud of a neurotically-driven habitual life? The hidden value in our external search is that it eventually exhausts itself, leaving us no other option but to be with ourself; with our Primal Knot.

My teacher once asked me, "A sword can cut other things, but can it cut itself?"

༄༅

WHERE WE MISS...

"Enlightenment is not something you can achieve; it's a state of being."
"I am not the body, I am the SELF."
"Don't analyse thinking, but forget the thinker."
"You are consciousness."
"Nothing ever happened."

These are powerful words uttered by the Knowers of Truth! In ancient times, such words instantaneously transformed beings, blessing them with the direct experience of Truth. In recent times, Nisargathatha Maharaj received only one teaching from his Guru, who said, "You are not this body." This statement was all that was needed for Nisargathatha to realise himself. He lived this single teaching and brought it alive. Today we read books, commentaries, articles, recorded questions and answers between Gurus and their devotees and so on and yet nothing happens! Can we honestly accept that from all the available questions none has proved to be 'our' burning one? By engaging in mere reading we are only in-sensitising ourself and are obviously not able to realise the true significance and potency of a direct teaching!

SECTION FOUR: RELUCTANT MASTERS

I recall a story:

> "One day a person heard of a sage in a nearby village, so out of sheer curiosity he went to meet him. Offering his salutations, he asked to know the nature of God or Truth. The sage looked at him and said, "If possible, please stay here until nightfall." Through the evening many people came for the sage's blessings. One asked, "This world is frustrating, what is the way to attain eternal peace?" The sage remained silent. Another asked, "What is *Samadhi*?" The sage remained silent. Many people asked questions but the sage remained silent through it all. Suddenly, a person entered the sage's place with a distinct sense of urgency, looked around at everyone seated there. Reluctantly, he showed the sage a piece of paper. Glancing at the paper, the sage arose from his seat and dragged the newcomer outside with him and returned a few minutes later. After *darshan* was over, people saluted and left. Watching all of this, the person asked the sage, "You didn't respond to most questions asked by people, but you instantly responded to the person with the paper. May I know what was in that? The sage smiled and said, "He asked about an address." The sage continued, "The people asked momentary and superficial questions which they wouldn't even think about after leaving from here. The questions weren't from their core but the newcomer's question was genuine. The only one worth answering. So I did."

We ponder on the words of the sage, play with it in the mind, turn them over and around and maybe, just maybe, have some success. It may seem for a while that we found 'the answer' which we fix in our mind as 'the path'. But sooner or later, it feels like tedious work. To keep on with the make-believe we fight, reassert it by some more

CHAPTER FIFTEEN: RELUCTANT MASTERS

thinking, do more practice or simply just cling harder to the belief. Eventually, we tire from the struggle, drop it or replace it with a new teaching and go through the same process - lifetime after lifetime. Spiritual fulfilment, sought externally through groups, practices or internally through ideas and teachings, usually tapers, repeatedly leaving us desperate and lost. We experience bursts of enthusiasm which wane and taper over time. Even though we spin the wheel again and again, we get nowhere. Is it time for another change of group or practice? Is it time to learn a new teaching or is it time to try harder? After all this effort and repeated waning of enthusiasm, the severity of slipping back into unhappiness and facing our inner hollowness is very hard to bear.

The knot left to be untied! Until you come home!

The acquisition and projection of interpretation is what we have been doing in the name of spirituality. We ideated our transformation to be waiting for us somewhere some place and devised a conceptual framework to reach it and adhered to some means to attain it. After that, we followed in the ways taught by groups, workshops, etc. to capture it. All the while, we ignored the demands of day-to-day life. At some point, we were compelled to co-relate our conceptual framework with our concrete day-to-day life when we tried to solve our day-to-day problems using our projected idea of spiritual transformation. How does an idea, a projection, break a barrier or resolve problems? It cannot. We felt let down, defeated by life and concluded that the teaching doesn't work. What happened? Entering the spiritual realm, our first action was to assign spirituality a label, an exclusive goal and attempted all possible dramas to perform that role. During a crisis, we naturally tried using what we knew but found ourselves empty-handed. Unfortunately, the belief structures we built from the practices we learnt left us with nothing to face our crisis. Nothing from the teaching was concrete enough to sweep away the sudden downpour of problems.

Was something wrong with the teaching?

> "A rich landlord had a rather spendthrift son who had no value for money. After the landlord's death, the son spent away all of his father's fortune. Then realising his relatives would not support him, the son decided to leave the city. What remained of his father's legacy was one very expensive shawl, which the son used to cover himself with. After suffering unbearable hunger pangs, for the first time he realised he needed to earn his livelihood. He took up work as a labourer. He didn't even own a pair of sandals so when he received his meagre pay he bought a cheap pair. He put on his sandals and stepped out of the shop. The wet and muddy street instantly covered his new sandals with muck which he began to wipe away using his father's shawl. A man asked, 'Are you foolish to clean these cheap sandals with that expensive shawl?' The son looked up calmly and said, 'The shawl my father earned. These sandals I earned!'"

We feel defeated when after exhaustive effort nothing transforms and the feeling of being deceived adds to our hollowness. What went wrong? How do we end up with unhappiness the moment something goes wrong in our life? Where do all our organised steps suddenly disappear in the time of need? Why do the teachings not work and how did we fall to the bottom? Have we honestly verified if there has been any movement?

Actually, life answers!

We pinned spirituality as our exclusive goal and excluded our own existential life. Whenever we assign ourself to a single goal, we turn

CHAPTER FIFTEEN: RELUCTANT MASTERS

away from the rest of our life. Existential life and spirituality are inseparable - two sides of the same coin! Any effort to separate them ultimately results in a strong disharmonious rebound of circumstances pointing precisely to the neglected. Our approach of highlighting one and sweeping the rest under the carpet has been ruling for a long time.

> In the good old days of school... it was the hour for English literature. We studied Wordsworth's poems on nature while seated in a closed four-walled room! Did no one want to take us outdoors to see the green of trees, grass or flowers to evoke the Wordsworth hidden within each of us?

An excluding approach destroys the heart of spontaneity!

In ancient India, living was a unitary movement. Life was an un-fragmented whole, rising from the unified participation of all. In the sweeping change from then to now, we lost familiarity with nature. The very first teaching in the Siddha system of healing says, 'If you are suffering from a disease, look around and there would be a plant growing nearby, waiting to heal you. Nature knows and provides for you!' I have seen plants miraculously appear in areas they have not been known to grow when the person living in the house close by is suffering a disease that the plant is known to cure. I have witnessed how well nature knows us and never betrays. It is we who live in concrete jungles and are proud of the concrete progress we make! The excluding approach has disfigured indigenous healing methods at individual as well as collective levels. Human functionality was the diagnostic instrument. The human pulse movement was likened to animal movements such as the slithering movement of a snake, the jump of a frog, the walk of a peacock, etc. Today, the medical system depends entirely on instruments for any problem in the body. Specifically designed devices identify specific problems - a narrow mode that is not equipped to pinpoint the root cause. Like so the cure also narrows down to that isolated area which most often proves a pseudo cure. Any localised diagnosis limits the possibility of complete healing.

Natural intelligence shines only where lives co-exist with Her with love and respect. Neem trees and palm trees flourish in summer, both of which have heat-reducing properties. Likewise, winter plants heal disease arising from the dire influence of the cold such as Ocimum Tenuiflorum (Indian holy basil), Leucas Aspera (wild). Today, plants are in nurseries and animals in zoos. The ancient time life principle was - 'Live by making others live'. Now, the life principle seems to be 'live by the destruction of others'. Man wants only for him to live, even at the expense of others. Turning a blind eye to all co-participants of life, man destroys natural resources in the name of enhancing his personal standard of living. Like a horse with blinders, man travels singularly, trampling natural factors in pursuit of desires. But spontaneity of life cannot be fragmented and it naturally comes forth as a whole which is when man comes to face dire consequences beyond his control like natural calamities.

How does one come in touch with one's nature of wholeness - the fountain of life?

෮෬

Actually, nothing can get excluded!

Exclusions happen only in our mind. Even though everything is inherently related and expressed through the spirit of life, the rebound impression of a long-held approach inculcates a subconscious utilitarian mentality of gauging what we can get out of something. Deformed by this ingrown approach, we lose creativity and turn into opportunists. Our calculation and analyses

CHAPTER FIFTEEN: RELUCTANT MASTERS

for gain navigates us to choose the most suitable and exclude the rest. We even calculate gain from relationship. A prolonged affinity to this makes us pretentious toward our children, friends, lover, even toward our mother. All our relationships remain skin deep. He, who targeted an exclusive mission, followed specific means, excluded everything else that he also is - now finds himself abandoned by his own nature. Man lives alienated from himself.

Rasa Siddhas, the Alchemists, have beautifully uttered...

> "The quintessence of immortality glitters in rotten things."

The quality of spirituality hides in concrete realities!

Assuming our projections to be true, we build our framework of reality. But it gives way under the spontaneity of life. As our pseudo spiritual journey comes crashing down, we blame, criticise and shun age-old living insights. Those of us who were betrayed by marketed spirituality write it off as a myth. In a way, it is true - a myth can never be grasped by the conceptual mind. It can only be lived. And there is nothing wrong with native spiritual teachings. The fault lies in interpretation and projection. Truth is not away from day-to-day life. Truth is not invisible in concrete reality. Life is whole.

> "Once a man teasingly asked me, 'Hundreds of commentaries have been written on Bhagwad Gita and Padanjali's Yoga Sutras. Initially, I found them interesting but now I don't find much significance in them.'
> I said, 'Yes, it is true! There is no significance in reading commentaries. Have you attended the workshops too?'
> He said, 'Yes, some. Of the Bhagwad Gita teachings related to attaining excellence in one's job performance.'

SECTION FOUR: RELUCTANT MASTERS

I asked him, 'At any time in your life have you felt compelled to fight your relatives and Guru and kill them?'

He simply stared. I continued, 'I believe you aren't familiar with such a crisis? Can you imagine how tremendous a crisis that would be? Arjuna was in it. Bhagwad Gita is for him!

You may think you are asking meaningful questions in the workshop, but those questions are not arising from your own existential crisis. It is your intellectual itch! If Lord Krishna appeared before you, would you ask him questions about the Bhagwad Gita or about your own existing problem? Wouldn't you show your love and adoration for Him? We have turned God into a consultant or counsellor!'

He walked out."

Ancient times have also witnessed spirituality as an exclusively-projected goal. People sought the other world - Heaven or imagined God seated somewhere in some world waiting to be found, etc. Nowadays, our projections take the form of 'transformation', 'sustained transcendence', 'altered consciousness'...

I recall a story here.

A popular historian published several books on the history of people and events. He sincerely gathered chronological data by visiting the actual places. Once he decided to write six comprehensive history volumes. His readers eagerly awaited the series. The author felt it would take him three years to write six volumes. In one and a half years he finished three volumes. Missing some hierarchal details in the fourth volume he decided to visit the place which happened to be in the neighbouring country. He began to plan his trip. Meanwhile, once on his daily morning walk he saw a man dead on the side of the road. Two or three people stood around the body.

CHAPTER FIFTEEN: RELUCTANT MASTERS

The author looked at the dead man and felt he may have died not even half hour ago. One of the men standing there said, 'I know this man. He drinks a lot of alcohol. He may have consumed in excess and died.' Another said, 'Somebody may have beaten him to death.' The author listened quietly to the various remarks. As the crowd increased, the author left and quietly continued his walk. On his way back he saw many more people had gathered around the dead body. 'This man was very ill. He suffered a heart attack,' said one from the crowd. Another voice said, 'He had business problems. His partner may have poisoned him.' The author thought, 'A man died less than two hours ago. Even with so many opinions and so much information floating around there is no finality about his death. People have projected their interpretations on a simple incident and turned it into an event! It is foolish to write about history!' He went home, burned the three volumes and vowed not to continue the absurdity of writing about the projections of others. His wife asked, 'Have you gone crazy?' The author didn't reply. As she left the room upset, the author wondered, 'Will my wife project my simple act of burning papers into an event!'

Once the projection formulae fail, one wonders if there is a way to exit the circle of acquisition, conceptual play and personal interpretations. Does a conceptual framework carry substantial reality? Yet we cannot escape it because the interpretational world is entirely conceptual. It is non-existent. How does one escape from that which does not exist? If someone does present you with a means to escape it, it is a guaranteed addition to your list of acquisitions! We needn't neglect anything from spirituality as well. If dropping anything is necessary, it can happen by life's humble movement. It is our projection or fixation that gets us stuck. With no success-guaranteed formulae at hand to rebuild our shattered conceptual world, we once again face our anxiety, our hollowness. We see the true face of our hollowness. It is our fear of non-existence which is also the root navigating factor behind building of the substituting framework. It is the seed that triggers our pseudo spiritual journey but once we understand the non-existence nature of our conceptual world, it drops. Out emerges our inherent potential to live in our hollowness, but this time our hollowness opens a doorway to the existence of flowing life; a self-unfolding flow of life. It is the door to the dimensionless existentially flowing life. Life cannot be stripped by projection. 'She' strips projections. She unravels Herself! Life has Her own pregnant vitality that unleashes by Her own ongoing movement.

This vitality is 'still'; living is dynamic!

Both co-exist, in truth, with no difference between them. It is non-dual. Life is always moving forth and we are its embodiment. Change happens by life's ongoing movement. A river flows its course without fear of change. If it fears, it stagnates and loses life! Life expresses truth in each moment, and if we are in life's flow, we express the way we are needed to. If life chooses to express its finer aspects by us seated poised with closed eyes, then we do and just 'be' which an onlooker interprets as meditation.

ஸ்ரீ

Love and compassion have becomes so alien that people 'do' these natural qualities as their 'practice'. Nowadays in Buddhist lore, people practice compassion as a *Metta*. Siddha Saint Ramalingam, who attained the immortal light body, a unique transformation in the Siddha path, recommended and showed the way to Truth as

'Jiva Karunyame Moksha Thiruku Thiravukol',
'The key to liberation is compassion to all living beings'.

CHAPTER FIFTEEN: RELUCTANT MASTERS

Saint Ramalingam says the nature of hunger overrides all other wants and intellectual itches. He recommends giving food to the hungry and says it opens and enhances the natural response of compassion inherent in every human being. Instead of advising complex practices or urging one to lead an intensely austere life, he says the basic human nature is more than enough to live in truth. But, many of his followers have turned it into a 'practice'. By 'practice', I mean a 'mechanical nature.' When one visits the Sangha or community of the followers of Siddha Saint Ramalingam, they compel you to have a meal without considering if you are truly hungry or not. They do it as a practice. They serve food with the intention of attaining liberation! This obsessive intention deviates one from the original native teaching of compassion that it is a spontaneous response. It is not a virtue to be adhered to. Nor is it an ethical garb to be worn. Nor is it a pedestal to be attained and neither can it be a curtain to veil anger. When, as a spontaneous response, we are ready to lose ourself for another, without an ounce of expectation, then and only then is it a wholesome loss of ourself, which is true compassion.

ಞ ಠ

Every word has a purpose of expression. Feelings and experiences use words to communicate. With spiritual terminology thrown about casually and irrelevantly, we have run out of words to invalidate and corrupt which is how new words have crept into new age spiritual books. Bored with the earlier words, we brought in new ones. Boredom indicates the repeated mechanical use of an intellectual or mental approach devoid of any link to the core. The journey of an excluding approach is long and draining. Whether applied to worldly circumstance or used for spiritual materialism, this mentality has harshly discarded the wholistic nature of life. Our societies stand on such excluding approaches and each of us suffer the consequence of this attitude on a day-to-day basis. It has led us to believe that it will deliver happiness to us someday and in that hope we keep playing out projection after projection. Why do we continue to fool ourself? We miss to see what is already given. And what we think we know is different from what actually is. What is happening through us? Life manifests in each moment with responses of love and compassion. But when we fail to be sensitive and attentive to such obvious responses, how can we expect to recognise deeper and hidden aspects of life, such as deep sleep, waking state, dreaming, etc.

ॐ ॐ

SO-CALLED REBELS

Nowadays, a lot of importance is laid on 'here and now'; another humorous ongoing sale. Every moment life moves ahead in open humbleness and what happens is only and always in the Grand Eternal Now. This eternal Now is a stated fact, but by insisting upon it, it turns static. By projecting a planned approach to live in the Now, makes it the past. A few ancient systems over time have turned into Neo Vedanta, Neo Tantra and Neo Buddhism, etc. and teach through workshops, boardroom teachings, seminars and strangely enough even offer correspondence courses. Some courses actually offer a certificate of enlightenment! Some establishments conduct teacher-level courses to teach enlightenment around the world. A few western tourist guides leading groups to spiritual spots in India sooner or later portray themselves as gurus, satsang teachers or even enlightened persons.

ॐ ॐ

CHAPTER FIFTEEN: RELUCTANT MASTERS

We want change - we want new and colourful interpretations and spiritual explanations. Books written in the 70's and 80's hold tremendous insights about the 'unconscious, subconscious mind' and back then people found it exhilarating. It was welcomed in the hope it may show the path to one's true nature. The writers dealing with these words, explanations and the people of workshops/seminars were taken to be imparting Truth! Today, books are filed with words like consciousness, holistic mind and enlightenment. The books back then and books now are dealing with the same human mind but the new books rendered the older ones outdated. The mind is still the same and the subconscious nature still prevails. Many new spiritual theories, vocabularies, practices or traditions have arrived. Suffocated by the multitude, the new bestsellers are redefining existing insights using a lighter approach. Many writers even condemn past spiritual approaches labelling them no longer relevant. In our boredom, we strangle existing solutions and seek new ones or redefine existing ones with fresh vocabulary. Our casual overuse of native spiritual words shows our ignorance of the innate power held in them.

The fault lies in our approach and not in the original system itself.

Buddha, the first well-known revolutionary in spiritual history, dropped all prevailing spiritual teachings because he felt them invalid. After enlightenment, he followed the *Sanyasa* system, initiating many into monk-hood. He used the word *Damma* (meaning *Dharma* in Poli), denoting *Dharma* of the Hindu spiritual system prevalent during his time. Buddha also taught *Vipasana* (breathing practice), also a part of prevalent teachings. His approach differed and he may have been a revolutionary against prevalent teachers, but not the Truth. After him there has been no revolutionary of his kind. In recent days, some teachers rebel or condemn native spiritual insights, masters and their native spiritual roots. The insights of Truth they themselves proclaim are no different from the contempt they throw. This is all they have to share as teachings!

SECTION FOUR: RELUCTANT MASTERS

The journey of pseudo spiritual teachers begins on the grounds of borrowed questions, posing as a quest for Truth. Their impulsive and rash words may even please and ease the ears of some. Considering their quest isn't a natural burst from their 'own' existential situation, their efforts get channelled toward fulfilling projected ideas. They grow weary somewhere down the line when they cannot find meaning in any of the teachings. And without meaning to one's core existence leads to an overload - turning it meaningless. Even after studying under many teachers and practicing many methods when nothing gave meaning to their living, leaves them with the root feeling of contempt. Their imitative minds and lurking expectations of fixed experience prevented the flowering of a true living experience because their very first steps began against the flow of life, un-truthful to their existential situation. The quest of realised persons bursts forth from their existential crisis. Their core questions weren't about spirituality. They were innocent to this dimension. The life sketches of our revered saints stand proof to that. Seekers need to find the right person to guide them and must embark with the right approach. None of the spiritual traditions, cults or teachings are ever invalid.

An interpretation can change and the interpreter can also change, but the interpreted is always one.

Teachers really care for us?

"Gooseberry heard that an Indian Swamiji had come to town; a Swami by the name of Strawberry. Wishing to meet Swami Strawberry, Gooseberry enrolled for the workshop. It was a small workshop for a group of four. Gooseberry decided he would be extremely polite and honest with Swami. The workshop began and Swamiji began speaking about life. 'Life is constantly growing. Life has many stages which depend on objectives. Objectives vary according to a person's age,' he said. Swamiji drew a table with three columns and titled them - Time, Stage and Object. He asked the students to write a particular year in the Time column; in the Stage column they should write their corresponding life position at that time; and in the Object column they should write their objective. After the students filled the chart describing the past ten years of their life, the Swamiji would assess their growth. Gooseberry was an idle but innocent young man. It was his turn to fill the table. Since he had decided to be truthful to his teacher, he went to the board and wrote on the left side of each title written by Swamiji, 'No, No, No'.

The board read, 'No time, No stage, No object!' Slightly irritated, Swamiji asked, 'How is it possible?' Fearing an adverse reaction form his teacher because he had achieved nothing in life, Gooseberry decided to show that he had achieved at least a little. Something is better than nothing, he thought and he did want to please Swamiji. So, he struck out the 'No's and on the right side of the titles Gooseberry wrote, 'Less, Less, Less'. The board now read, 'Time less, Stage less, object less.'

Gooseberry turned towards Swamiji. Swamiji had fallen off his chair!"

Pseudo teachers turn good teachings into a joke. They are insensitive to the vulnerable hearts of seekers when they aggressively impose what they claim to know. They don't verify if what is being said is relevant or significant to the seekers' day-to-day life. This is common in workshops and courses conducted by Indian and Tibetan teachers where the majority of what they speak is filled with native spiritual terminology, which is alien to people from other walks of life. For them, it is spiritual jargon of no actual relevance to the core of their life. These sorts of teachers tend to hide behind terminology because they lack something existentially worthwhile to impart.

Another common imposition comes as a part of the teaching - the practice of worshipping local Indian or Tibetan deities. This kind of sacred worship is suitable for those of the required archetype and commonly distributing this practice shows how the teachers are unaware of its Truth and significance.

Bhagwan Ramana Maharishi lived his entire life on the holy hill Arunachala. His words were simple and existential, making it impossible to differentiate spirituality and life. Saint Ramakrishna Paramahamsa narrated simple parables to explain complex spiritual dimensions. Below is a small incident that highlights how some teachers foolishly prescribe practices to their seekers.

> "Amrish, a dedicated seeker was involved in many spiritual practices for the past ten years. He came to me for a health consultation for an allergy he had been suffering since the past three years - runny nose, recurrent sneezing, itchy red skin rashes, etc. Both allopathic and herbal treatments hadn't brought relief. On enquiring about his daily routine, I discovered he was intensely practicing many traditional breathing techniques. I knew he wouldn't co-operate if I asked him to stop them, so I recommended strong medicines to be taken at frequent intervals for a week. He came back after a week. 'Nothing worked,' he said. He was suffering from severe itching at that time. I said, 'There is one way for some relief. Stop all medicine and stop all practice for one week.' He came back the next week. 'Surprisingly, the running nose and sneezing have moderately reduced. How did it happen?' he asked. I asked him a question instead, 'All ancient works say *Pranayam* practitioners never fall ill, so how is it that you are ill?' He didn't reply. I continued, 'Practices like *Kapala Pathi* (skull shining breath) purify the body by strongly eliminating toxins. By such intense practice your body has become pure, but you are not living in ancient society! You live in a highly

polluted world which is why your body repels everything as an allergy. Either you should live in a forest or if you choose to live in society you need to moderate the practice appropriately.'
Amrish's teacher had instructed him to practice for several hours a day and follow a natural diet. It was hard for me to break this conditioning as he had learnt it from his teacher. 'Because of a restricted way of life, your immunity has been fixated. You need to broaden and lengthen the range of your immune flexibility and for that you will need to gradually come into the world of dust and ordinary food. Come out of your puritan perspective.'"

A simple practice can turn dangerous if it is incompatible to the environment or strenuous to one's constitution. Many western people behave abnormally after practicing methods not relevant to them. Practices that remain as mere practice don't penetrate your flesh and blood, undoubtedly turn into stress-stimulating factors and instil a sense of alienation.

The practice valid to your day-to-day life will not and cannot remain a mere practice but will turn into a 'life-shaping source'.

Seekers today are encouraged to radically change their lifestyle by forcible renunciation, or initiation into monk-hood, etc. For some seekers, these are extreme measures that prove adverse and by no means are beneficial in their *Sadhana*. A mendicant or sadhu's life is alien to western cultural roots and forcibly following this path leads to suppression. Such cases are seen in ashrams too. Certain women seekers appear pale and anaemic reflecting their forced dispassion. Being a Master carries a responsibility greater than that of a parent. A Master's role calls for a tender caring approach as the master-seeker relationship strengthens on sensitivity, authenticity and is very rare in today's world.

SECTION FOUR: RELUCTANT MASTERS

THE BLIND AND THE BLIND...

> "They howl, like dogs in gallows,
> Peck like vultures, those of false wisdom,
> But, those of true Siva wisdom; dead to the world
> Though living in body and senses."
>
> Thirumanthiram Verse 1671

Several teachers in India as well as abroad impart their teachings after self-proclaiming themselves as Gurus. This is nothing but the projection of ego.

> "Having known the One, That knows him,
> Then, who is there to know oneself."
>
> Avvai Kural Verse 5, chapter two

The simple practices or techniques they introduce may even help some people. The problem arises when they claim to be in the natural state of *Gnana* or *Sahaja Samadhi* and conduct a lifestyle like that of a *Gnani*. Naive seekers believe these teachers to be sharing their Ultimate experience of the natural state of Truth by their sheer presence.

> "The ignorant say bliss bliss!
> None know the dance of bliss,
> Having realised the dance of bliss
> Where the me ends, there bliss."
>
> Thirumanthiram Verse 2796

> "Having known the One, That knows him,
> Then, who is there to know oneself."
>
> Avvai Kural Verse 5, chapter two

CHAPTER FIFTEEN: RELUCTANT MASTERS

How does one avoid being misled? How does one discriminate and recognise the authenticity of a teacher today? Below the different states of Truth are described.

When Bhagwan Ramana Maharishi was asked by Veera Subbaiya Swami, the head of the *math* (monastery), about how one gets established in the natural state of *Sahaja Samadhi*, he said,

> 'The *Satvidha Samadhi* (six types of *Samadhi*) includes both the *SaviKalpa Samadhi* and the *Nirvikalpa Samadhi*. And when both these states of *Samadhi* are established, it will lead to *Sahaja Samadhi*.'

SaviKalpa Samadhi is attained by a conscious and continuous effort on the part of the person, whereas *Nirvikalpa Samadhi* flourishes effortlessly. Therefore, *SaviKalpa Samadhi* is called the 'seed *samadhi*' and *Nirvikalpa Samadhi* is the 'seedless *samadhi*'.

> "Bereft of imagination, ascending the way of fire,
> Seeking the vast light, the sculptor of created all
> Reaching the mystic moon in union, becoming one with the unborn self,
> That, in soothe, is Samadhi's tranquillity."
>   Thirumanthiram Verse-628

When *Keval Nirvikalpa Samadhi* (*Keval* means spontaneous) occurs, the person drops effortlessly into the Self and there is no apparent external movement toward the world. As *Keval Nirvikalpa Samadhi* establishes, it leads to *Sahaja Nirvikalpa Samadhi* and the *Gnani* in the *Sahaja* state can enact and make himself available to the onlookers as a normal being.

> "At the young age of sixteen, Bhagwan Ramana Maharishi had his first death experience and realised Himself. After this, he

moved to the Holy Hill, Arunachala. He spoke infrequently and didn't preach or reveal many teachings. Thereafter, he had another death experience at Tortoise Rock in the year 1914. Only in his later years did he go on to reveal teachings. Vasudeva Sastri and Palani Swami were around him at the time of this particular death experience and witnessed Bhagwan's body experiencing death, including the colour of his skin turning blue. It was not a psychological death but death even at the physical level. Bhagwan's own description of this experience says that a pulsating energy suddenly emerged from the right side of his chest and moved to the left side, after which he opened his eyes. Bhagwan Ramana began to speak with people, share his teachings and accepted all who came to him for guidance after this extremely significant happening."

Both, Bhagwan Ramana Maharishi and Ramakrishna Paramahamsa say that a *Sat Guru* is preordained by Divine Will. So usually *Gnanis* who attain *Nirvikalpa Samadhi* either remain in this state until their *Prarabdha Karma* exhausts itself. If they have no reason to remain in the world, they leave their body while in *Nirvikalpa Samadhi*. The state of *Sahaja Samadhi*, (state of living in the natural state of the Self), in the phenomenal world has emancipated very few and rare *Gnanis*; those who have been blessed by divine ordinance to play the role of the *Sat Guru* never proclaimed themselves as *Gurus* or *Gnanis*. The ones who flourish in the *Sahaja* state of *Nirvikalpa Samadhi* are chosen entirely by Grace according to the presence of true and genuine seekers in the world, earnestly praying for guidance to be brought to Truth. In the state of *Sahaja Samadhi*, the mind may still survive as a very subtle enjoyer of bliss in order to keep the body alive. And this single subtle tendency gets burned when the *Gnani* leaves his body, usually known as *Videha Mukthi*. A *Gnani* to still be in the body while in the state of *Videha Mukthi* is very rare as it is beyond the state of *Sahaja Samadhi*. Bhagwan Ramana lived in this state and called it '*Ajadam*', which in truth cannot even be described as a state. It is better described as the 'indescribable'. Muruganar, a *Gnani*, mentions this. Muruganar, a very near and dear devotee of Bhagwan Ramana Maharishi was called his shadow. In one of his songs in his work Guru Vasaka Kovai he says...

> "To meet the needs of various seekers,
> Guru Ramana did expound,
> Various doctrines. But, I have,
> Heard Him say that His true teaching,
> Firmly based on His own experience, is Ajada."
>
> Verse 100

> (Ajada - no birth; unborn; the ever Immutable Self; birth, death and the world process never occurred)
> In the 40 Verses, Bhagwan himself speaks of the ever-existing nature of Ajada.

Devotees who lived with Bhagwan Ramana Maharishi would find him sitting motionless for long durations with his eyes open. During those days devotees could refer to him only as 'it', as they were unable to attribute any human or gender description.

> "When Maya veileth Jiva, the Truth by Vedas remaineth hidden;
> When Maya leaveth, that Truth of Himself revealeth;
> Those who can make Maya vanish, merge in God,
> No more is body, no more is mind."
>
> Thirumanthiram Verse 2548

Gnanis like Narayan Guru, Kanjankadu Ramdas Swami, who met Bhagwan Ramana praised his indescribable state, calling him the giant serpent in the spiritual lineage who comes only once in many centuries.

SECTION FOUR: RELUCTANT MASTERS

Once, Bhagwan ironically, said to someone,

> "People are coming here saying that they are longing for Enlightenment, (Mukthi), if I show even a glimpse of IT, even a crow and sparrow will run from here. Then only we will have to sit here."
> -Reference: Guru Vasaka Kovai, Sadhu Om commentary.

"In his early days when Bhagwan Ramana Maharishi spent all his time on the Holy Hill of Arunachala, a few people would come and sit near him. Bhagwan would be with a vacant look. One such day, Bhagwan Ramana Maharishi was seated near a rock on the other of which rice was being cooked. The cook placed the pot of steaming hot rice atop the rock. Suddenly Palani Swami, a devotee, noticed the pot had tilted and steaming hot rice water was pouring down Bhagwan's back. Bhagwan's back was burnt and scarred. A shocked Palani swami looked at Bhagwan and saw him still staring vacantly, unaffected!"

Bhagwan always said, 'We are not the body', 'There is only Self.' The teachings of Bhagwan are seen shining through many of his own life incidents. We can say, his experience of Truth was not separate from his life.

ಸಿ ಲ

Just as each flower exudes a distinctive fragrance, exclusive qualities shine through every enlightened being. This has been written and described as *'Muktha Lakshana'* in most ancient spiritual scriptures. An enlightened person is beyond the state of waking, dreaming and sleeping. By realising himself in all these states, he transcends them. As for us, we don't know what time we would sleep tonight nor what

CHAPTER FIFTEEN: RELUCTANT MASTERS

we would dream. These states are the true yardsticks that betray any fakes, no matter how they may pose themselves to be. Below are a few points for present day teachers for self-verification. Some teachers, mostly from Advaitic lore, are good at heart with a keen interest in helping people and highlighted here is a common pitfall - one that can be genuinely questioned. Teachers often say, 'I finished', 'I experienced self-realisation', or something like, 'What is there to finish? I am already the Self.' Without taking away their experience, I would like to clarify that what they actually experienced was the whole of their waking-state consciousness. Let me explain through an example. We hear a large deafening sound of an airplane, passing overhead. After it passes, we suddenly become aware of a large silence enveloping the room. This silence is not new nor has it just come from somewhere. It has always been pervading the room. It is we who just became aware of it through a relative experience. We scatter ourselves by strongly identifying with the chaotic world and are unable to experience the subjective nature of our own waking-state consciousness. A seeker, on his inner quest, plunges into himself by de-identifying or disengaging from all objective orientation which gives him an overwhelming experience of his waking state consciousness enveloping him. Experiencing ourself as whole and integrated (not fragmented into the objective) in our waking state has associated Satvic qualities of silence, grounding, etc. which our mind deceives us into believing as enlightenment - the Ultimate state of the Self. But this waking-state consciousness gets swept away by the other states like sleep, dreaming, etc. (*Susupthi, Swapna*), which clearly verifies that it is not the Ultimate state of the Self.

An enlightened person is beyond all states.

An incident in the life of Shirdi Sai Baba, the Great Divine beggar and fakir.

> "In his early years, Baba slept on a wooden plank - four arms in length and a span in breadth, with earthen lamps burning

at the four corners, hanging from the roof, eight feet above the floor. Later, he broke the plank into pieces and threw it away. Once, after Baba described the significance of the plank to Kaka Sahib, Kaka Sahib said, 'If you still love the wooden plank, I will hang one up in the masjid for you to sleep at ease.' To this, Baba replied, 'I wouldn't like to sleep up on a plank and leave Mhalsapati down on the ground.' 'I can provide another plank for Mhalsapati too,' said Kaka Sahib. Baba replied, 'How can he sleep on the plank? It is not easy. Only he who sleeps with eyes wide open can do that. When I go to sleep, I often ask Mhalsapati to sit beside me, place his hand on my heart and watch the chanting of the Lord's name. He can't even do this. He gets drowsy. When his hand feels heavy as stone on my heart, I cry out, 'Oh, Bhagat,' after which he moves and opens his eyes. So how can he, who can't sit or sleep well on the ground, whose posture is not steady and who is a slave to sleep, sleep high up on a plank?'"

This incident appears as a miracle by Baba, but actually it is the natural state of Self and can be seen and recognised as a quality of an enlightened sage. Bhagwan Ramana Maharishi has mentioned in his own words all that has been described so far. (Found in Collected Works of Bhagwan Ramana Maharishi)

> "One becomes unaware of oneself and what one is doing and one's mind gets absorbed in the Self. The subtle state in which even the pulsation subsides is the state of *Samadhi*.
>
> Mind will be cleared of its impurities only by a desireless performance of duties during several births, getting a worthy Master, learning from him and incessantly practicing meditation on the Supreme. The transformation of the mind into the world of inert matter due to the quality of darkness

CHAPTER FIFTEEN: RELUCTANT MASTERS

(*Tamas*) and its restlessness due to the quality of activity (*Rajas*) will cease. Then the mind regains its subtlety and composure. The Bliss of the Self can manifest only in a mind rendered subtle and steady by assiduous meditation. He who experiences that Bliss is liberated even while still alive.

When the mind is divested of the qualities of darkness and activity by constant meditation, the Bliss of the Self will clearly manifest within the subtle mind. Yogis gain omniscience by means of such mind-expanse. He alone who has achieved such subtlety of mind and has gained Realisation of the Self is liberated while still being alive. The same state has been described in the Rama Gita as the *Brahmam* beyond attributes - the one universal undifferentiated Spirit. He who has attained the unbroken eternal state beyond even that, transcending mind and speech, is called '*Videha Mukta*', that is, when even the aforesaid subtle mind is destroyed, the experience of Bliss as such also ceases. He is drowned and dissolved in the fathomless ocean of Bliss and is unaware of anything apart. This is *Videha Mukti*. There is nothing beyond it. It is the end of all.

As one continues to abide as the Self, the experience 'I am the Spirit' grows and becomes natural. The restlessness of the mind and the thought of the world in due course become extinct. Because experience is not possible without the mind, realisation takes place with the subtle mind. Since *Videha Mukti* connotes the entire dissolution of even the subtle mind, this state is beyond experience. It is the transcendental state..."

(The subtle mind, Bhagwan Ramana called *Aham Spurana* is called *Virrithi Gnana* in Vedantic lore.)

ॐ ॐ

SECTION FOUR: RELUCTANT MASTERS

Satsang teachers of Advaitic lore posing as *Gnanis*, impart teachings by mere glances while claiming to be in the state of Ultimate Silence and even award certificates of enlightenment under these means. After using a power-oriented approach to satisfy their personal perverted tendencies, they excuse their acts to be those of Grace. Their statements like, 'I am not the doer. It is this body that is moving and doing', are excuses used to cover up mistakes and the consequences triggered through their body and mind. A few words spoken by Bhagwan Ramana Maharishi address this very nature of pitfall in one's mind.

> "Can the mind which is fixed in its original state possess and ego-sense or have any problem to solve? Do not such thoughts arise due to past tendencies? Not only should the mind be curbed and turned back to its true state but also it should be made to remain unconcerned and indifferent to external happenings. Is it not due to Self - forgetfulness that such thoughts arise and cause more and more misery? Though the discriminating thought, 'I am not the doer, all actions are merely the reactions of the body, senses and mind', is an aid for turning the mind back to its primal state, nevertheless it is still a thought, but one which is necessary for those minds which are addicted to much thinking. On the other hand, can the mind, fixed unswervingly in the divine self and remaining unaffected even while engaged in activities, give in to such thoughts as 'I am the body. I am engaged in work', or again to the discriminating thought, 'I am not the doer, these actions are merely reactions of the body, senses and mind?'"

॥ ॐ ॥

CHAPTER FIFTEEN: RELUCTANT MASTERS

These sorts of fakes lived even in ancient times. Siddha Tirumoolar in his work Thirumanthiram holds them in contempt and teases them by saying a blind man is showing the way to another blind man.

> "The Guru who removes blindness, they seek not,
> The Guru who removes-not blindness, they seek;
> The blind and The blind, in a blind dance, mingled;
> The blind and The blind, in a deep pit, together fell."
>
> Thirumanthiram Verse 1680

The role of a spiritual teacher is pivotal for a seeker and can either make or break his quest. Realisation of Truth is like the flowering of a bud which requires both water and sunlight in symbiosis. When a Master of the heart and an aspirant with longing meet, a seeker is born - called *'Dwija'*, (twice born) - the seeker no more, nor the seeking. Cultural conditioning implants the dual nature of subject and object, mind and body, heart and thought, spiritual and material within us. Studying under teachers insensitive to the pain resulting from inner splits could bring misery, anger, depression, pain, defeat, resentment, struggle, loss of personal power, and the anguish of a meaningless life. Man, already conflicted between daily life and his surroundings, under an improper teacher could grow wearier by their 'un-lived' theories of enlightenment, transformation or mechanical practices. When a seeker senses that freedom at every level is about releasing conflicts, fixations and the constant urge to control life, he realises their teachings are false hopes and empty fantasies. Genuine transformation is meaningful only by creative appropriate expression of unhindered life. Man has been given a unique way to respond to the uncompromising presence of life through ordinary living to unravel the hidden enchantment and magic in day-to-day living. Ordinary life is the Pandora's box. Open it. Living by this treasure chest of fluid intelligence brings a spontaneous response that unifies living into a whole into which all conflict and duality dissolve. Spontaneity is the appropriate response that flourishes from the core and the core is the stable ground where all relationships are ever-related. Man, as is, is a living whole. Being the way he is, by spontaneous action, he can simply assert his immense presence in the larger whole of his environment; an environment that is a reflection and extended quality of who and what he is.

'Crisis' is the real teacher life offers! A true Master brings a milieu of crisis. Do you recall needing to live fully with all of your being? Naked life, stood there - calling! Life calls, but we remain inert, insensitive. We run from the deepest hollows of our mental shells and prefer to hold onto previously established theories and positions. We refuse to peel ourselves off from the known. We latch onto progressive numbness which deadens what was most alive in us. We fantasise about favourable circumstances, exceptional encounters or transformed conditions. We feed these hopes with readymade solutions or leftovers of so-called teachers. We are victims to the doctrinal flea market! Lacking courage to look at how we are, we believe 'safe' ideas will transform life. We wait for a miracle to start our journey, our exploration. But, the real Spirit emerges when we turn to ourself, see us caught under the tyranny of our dreams and stand to face the bitterness of our waking. It shows how we have always demanded everything from others, from groups, and called forth nothing from ourself. Constantly ignoring the call of our inner faculties made them impotent. What fascination do we find in the lure of lethargic teachings that dilute our spirit for the self-evident perspective of the essential? When Nisargathatha Maharaj's Guru told him, 'You are not your body', it created a tremendous crisis in Nisarga. Nisarga remained secluded in a room for three years. We name Bhagwan Ramana Maharishi's death experience at the young age of sixteen as his enlightenment, but after it Bhagwan Ramana remained in complete silence for around two years. Bhagwan lost

CHAPTER FIFTEEN: RELUCTANT MASTERS

his voice due to the complete withdrawal of all identification with the mode of speech. Bhagwan mentions that sometime later, his voice reappeared by itself. Even after breaking his two-year silence, he refrained from speaking, replying only when necessary which continued for around 10-12 years after he had realised himself! He would sit idle immersed in himself.

Speaking of his death experience and the time after, Bhagwan Ramana Maharishi said,

"A big elephant has entered into a small hut."

As a stated fact, enlightenment may be instantaneous but assimilating and settling into this explosive happening takes time. The life sketches of realised persons often mention how they remained in total silence, or encountered madness, or even lived as babies do, etc. (Everything described here is from an onlooker's perspective.)

> "If that beginning less, middle less, end less
> Supreme Expanse, engulfs
> The Truth of non-dual Bliss shall rise.
> The entire clan of us will be redeemed,
> Nothing will be lacking,
> All of our undertakings will prosper.
> Just as the light of sunrise, in the dawn, reaches;
> The mystics emancipated in the dawn of grace, in which
> There is neither abundance nor lack.
> We can play with them.
> If we, be offered heaven and earth
> We won't rejoice,
> Our nature will be like
> Babies, madman, ghouls."
>
> Ninai Vonru, Verse - 7, Sage Tayumanavar

SECTION FOUR: RELUCTANT MASTERS

This is the missing criterion in the lives of so-called teachers proclaiming enlightenment. Taking their momentary experience as the point of ultimate transformation, they overlook the fact that unless the living essence does not flower after an incubation period and ooze from every pore and cell, it remains an intellectual experience! By saying to their followers, 'Relax, you are already eternal awareness,' what are they trying to do? Relaxation is not realisation. Man must awaken from the false assumption that he is already awakened. 'We are the Self.' 'We are always pure awareness.' These are stated facts, but it takes a crisis to shatter man's shadowed side and reveal how deeply he is inert to himself. How he is at the mercy of outside affiliations. There is real heroism in being immersed and moving in one's own true direction, without the external sanction of these teachers. Addiction to predictability or to an established hypothesis blocks one from living in the fertile challenge of uncertainty devoid of associated conditioning. By knowing beforehand, one meets only their projection and becomes nothing more than a suppressed bundle of inner anxiety and hollowness. A true Master, not allowing one to relax, makes one encounter one's self. He evokes the adventurous spirit and has one dive deep into the crisis that is nothing but 'him'. He pushes one to see that he already is in a crisis. The waking-up-to-crisis is the fertile ground where the lotus of unhindered life sprouts and blooms. An internship under a Master unbinds the seeker from mediocre security and prejudice. He grows sensitive to his living whole; to the wide range of possibilities manifesting as the stream of life. If one does endure and stand ground to face the bitter inconsistencies, conflicts and fixations of his psyche, then by the grace of the Master, his conceptual psyche dies. By the death of the conflicted ego-self, comes the birth of a complete, unified presence of the self. The death of conflict, fragmented conditioning and fixation creates a space for the self to be reborn; one that is not limited by narrow perspective or the conflicts and defence of the ego-self. The struggles of everyday life no longer have the same impact and not even a trace of subtle conflict with the world remains. He realises the living essence has fluid unity that is neither identical to, nor apart from, all forms of being, which is one's heart; the core. The core is the whole.

ಒ ಲ

KEY OF THE SIDDHAS

Seekers overlook the simplicity of ancient teachings and opt for quick and easy attitude. The superficial 'quick and easy attitude' doesn't allow seekers to imbibe teachings deep into themselves and their lives. A genuine internship in the ancient path of the Siddhas calls for a seeker to be lovingly dedicated throughout his quest. A seeker's first meeting with a Siddha Master can be a complete life-changing experience - nothing one can ever prepare for. The Master is great. Out of compassion, he accepts the seeker with all his conditioning, drowned in ignorance. But, he won't allow him to remain bound to his conditioning for very long. From the first feeling of acceptance, the seeker feels a natural love and openness flowing toward his Master. And the Master in turn, of great compassion bombards him with challenges, creating situations to uproot acquired rotten conditioning, reactions and limitations that the seeker defines himself with. Before lifting the drowning seeker away from the heaving stormy ocean, the Master firmly makes him go through it by awakening his spirit within, and the seeker transcends by his Master's grace. The Master gradually introduces the seeker to a life of inner riches; crystallised and grounded within himself. Unless and until such a sacred introduction happens and the door opens, we haven't really lived at all. What we call 'Life' is a shallow dip in the sea, a superficial and mechanical way of living. We are, as Siddhas' verses describe, 'walking corpses'. The word '*Vasi*' in the Siddha teachings means 'living', and the teachings urge us to make living 'alive' and 'authentic'.

ఌ ঙ

Sixty-four divine arts such as music, archery, horse riding and so on, known to lead one on the path of Truth, flourished in ancient Tamil Nadu. '*Poo Katuthal*' is the art of weaving flowers into a garland which are offered to temple deities or used during festive worship. A person dedicated to this divine art naturally comes to understand the transitional nature of flowers, seasonal availability and its other finer nuances. Witnessing these natural laws, his understanding would expand and lead him to witness the transitory nature inherent in all other dimensions of life as well. Eventually, within his heart an urge to find that which is not transitory would arise. A simple act even of a bounded realm, whole-heartedly, devotedly and consistently carried out can help one transcend to a higher dimension of life.

By living wholeheartedly in one thing, life will reveal its 'spiral dimension of transcendence!'

"The Buddha's early years were prosperous and of princely lifestyle. It was his only known world from which he derived nourishment and experience. He believed his rich environment was forever, until his crystallised cocoon shattered at the sight of a weak old man, a sick man and a dead body being taken for cremation. The shock of reality uprooted his crystallised ground and transformed it into a burning question; a question that pushed him to embark on a life-changing quest. The fire of Buddha's quest was after all fuelled by his strongly crystallised illusory nature. The solidity of his quest arose from the ground-shattering anguish he suffered on being uprooted. Without compromise and undeceived by false hope, the Buddha arrived to completion - at eternal peace within himself."

Any mode of living, mundane or otherwise, lived consistently with a single wholehearted attitude, invested with all of one's passion, holds potential to transform into one's vital question for Truth. It has the strength to generate the necessary momentum needed to walk the path. The life-sketches of Great Saints tell us the question they asked at the time of their crisis - they asked existential questions based on their life before the quest. Nowadays, people ask borrowed questions like, 'What is *Samadhi*?' 'What is consciousness?', 'What is *Kundalini*?', and 'What is Self?', etc. In the moment we embark on our quest, we know nothing of Truth, then how can we ask questions related to it? Truthful questions are those arising from one's life that may have just been shaken by the compassion of a Master. The Buddha's quest burst forth from an existential crisis. An existential crisis is not a random accident come at you from the outside to block your way. It demands all our attention and we are the entire experience, leaving no fragment of our self untouched. A crisis is that great opportunity to be lived. It is nature offering a doorway to our true colours, true face and true potential. Of course, without doubt, in the moment of an existential crisis we might deliberately avoid the pain of uncertainty while our known approaches and solutions fail. Entangled, we experience the severe anxiety of our non-existence and most often choose not to stay with our misery long enough to embrace or understand it. Out of habit, we try to flee, either by denying, rationalising or manipulating our crisis by some strategy. Unfortunately, apart from our panic, our social setup also supports the idea that misery is unwanted! Only a few can understand that an existential crisis although strikingly painful, is also the most authentic situation that forces you to be the way you actually are, without imposition, masks or acquisitions. One can recognise something as false only by having lived in it without prejudice or reserve. As our pseudo self cannot survive this moment, it turns into what preludes the much needed, 'authentic response'.

Coming to understand something as false by its living experience, leads to Truth!

Ancient Siddhas say, 'Live authentically wherever one stands and however one lives.' After this they ascertain, 'the inherent potential hidden in Authentic Living', by the word *'Vasi'*. In the ancient Siddha system, the greatest challenge in internship is learning by being and not learning by studying.

Narrated below is an occurrence between Ouspensky and George Gurdjieff, the rascal Saint of the last century.

> "Ouspensky, a great scholar, became a student of Gurdjieff. One day, he came to his Master and offered him his scholarly writings. Gurdjieff merely looked at the papers and threw them into a corner of the room. Not comprehending the nature of his Master's harsh action, Ouspensky returned a few months later, bringing corrected writings. Once again, the Master glanced at them and threw them on the table nonchalantly. Several years later, a frustrated Ouspensky asked his Master what was wrong in his writings. Gurdjieff replied, "Your writings are perfectly logical, everything is correct and rational but, I couldn't find you in your writings!"

Ouspensky's writings were from his mind, and not of his direct experience. After a long and deep association with his Master, Ouspensky went on to become a well-known teacher expounding his Master's teachings. By this story, I hope to communicate, to stop for a moment and examine life, as one's life is one's message! Stop and see whether in all the numerous places we dig, is it only skin deep or have we devotedly dug all the way down to the deepest of depths.

Living wholeheartedly urges an inherent spontaneity to reclaim one's true nature.

CHAPTER FIFTEEN: RELUCTANT MASTERS

The stories and incidents in the book are not confined to experiences of only spiritual practitioners, but include those of ordinary people living an ordinary existence with no specific attention to spirituality. I have intentionally shared these to highlight what the Siddhas expound:

There is no difference in the spiritual path and our day-to-day existence. The essence of living transcends both descriptions of life, and instead, prevails over. Insight and understanding of deeper dimensions of the unknown world that unfold for a spiritual practitioner through his *sadhana* are no different from existential revelations and grounding that carry an ordinary man through life.

I would like to share a beautiful story told in ancient Indian Mythology.

> There once lived a peasant and his family in a small village, in India. He lived a simple life, caring for his cows and crops. Each morning at the crack of dawn, before taking his cows grazing, the peasant would walk out of his hut and glance up at the sky with folded hands. He would pray to the Mother to bless him with a peaceful and happy day and then would busy himself with his cows and farm for the rest of the day. At dusk, he would return and once again, standing outside his hut, he would raise his head to the sky and pray, 'Mother, thank you for your blessings for a beautiful day', and enter his hut. Close to the peasant's farm lived a hermit in a small hut. He too was a devotee of the Mother Goddess. The hermit would always be immersed in chanting the Goddess *mantra* or performing *yagnas*, praying for Her *darshan*. One day, the peasant's cows wandered off toward the hermit's hut and started 'mooing'. The hermit, who was busy performing a *yagna,* got irked by the disturbance and angrily chased away the cows. Furious at the peasant for not being more careful,

the hermit began shouting at him, 'You are not aware of the value of the penance I have undertaken for the Mother. You do nothing, how will you ever receive Her blessings?' The innocent and god-fearing peasant was very upset and asked the hermit for forgiveness.

Meanwhile, in the heavenly realm, the celestial beings approached the Mother Goddess and described the hermit's penance. They urged Her to grant him a *darshan* of Her divine form. But, the Mother said, 'Before I go to the hermit, I will first give *darshan* to another more deserving devotee. Curious, the celestial beings asked who the other devotee was. They couldn't contain their surprise when they heard it was the simple peasant. They argued with the Mother saying that the peasant prayed and remembered Her only twice a day, whereas the hermit was chanting Her name all through the day. The Divine Mother smiled, 'I will show you the answer to your question through my divine play.' So, one day, while the peasant was working with his cows in the fields, the sky suddenly darkened with thick grey clouds, lightening struck and the resounding voice of Mother Goddess came booming through, 'O peasant, I will visit your home tomorrow.' The peasant was overjoyed! He awoke early the next day, cooked special food and decorated the house festively way. Since his wife was away at her father's house, he did all of this by himself. And sure enough, the Mother Goddess arrived with her trident and all. She entered his small hut. Seeing Her and having Her *darshan*, the peasant was beside himself with happiness. He welcomed Her to sit on a hammock while he sat himself on the ground beside her, rocking the hammock. After sometime, the peasant invited the Mother to eat the food he had so lovingly prepared. He served Her the food with love and care. When the Mother had finished eating the first serving, touching Her stomach She said, 'My stomach is full.' But the peasant wouldn't hear of it. He urged her, 'Please eat some more. I have cooked so much for you.' He lovingly coaxed her into eating some more. That evening, the Mother asked, 'Dear peasant, what would you like? Ask me for something.' The peasant replied, 'I don't want anything. You have come to my home and eaten the food I have cooked. It has made me very happy. And it would be so nice if you would stay here a few more days.' But the Mother smiled and said, 'I have to leave soon. There is much work I have to take care of in the world.' Once again, the Mother gently asked, 'What would you like? I would like to give you something.' The peasant replied, 'I already have everything I need, by your blessings. But it would give me great joy to share with the other villagers the joyous news of your visit to my hut.'

She smiled and disappeared. The next day, the peasant eagerly and enthusiastically shared his news with all the villagers. The hermit heard the news and was furious. He went to the Mother's statue he worshipped in his hut and asked angrily, 'Why didn't you give me *darshan* first?' Once again, the clouds darkened and lightening struck. From far above came a voice, 'O Hermit, the peasant was more deserving of my *darshan* because his heart was ready and flowing in contentment, which is an ideal home for divinity to preside. His innocence pulled longingly at my heart, calling me in. He doesn't expect anything from me. He is happy cherishing my presence.'"

Back in the old days, man cherished divinity through simple human qualities whereas now, practitioners turn victims to their practice and pursue it blindly or obsessively. The underlying factor in most yogic practices is energy, power. Such potent energy practices followed without understanding their true significance and appropriate attitude can turn into an obsession for acquiring energy and holding onto that power. Eventually, this attitude would reflect in all other dimensions of life, including social activities. Teachers affiliated with institutions and establishments often hold a controlling attitude over disciples, going to the extent of manipulating their lives. Even ashrams are prey to power games. Unless you learn the art of humanising energy practices by nurturing simple human qualities in a meaningful way, the undigested or unassimilated energy will push and urge you toward destructive activities. If this can be called the darker side of Yogic lore, then Advaitic practitioners fall prey to building an easily repulsed psyche. Advaitic practitioners who forcibly follow the *'Neti Neti'* approach (Not this, Not this) by *Kasta Vairagya* (forcible dispassion) will inevitably become victims to their own obsessive attitude. In due course, anything and everything will pose a trigger for irritation and repulsion. The lack of life will be visible on their face. The conditioned psyche of Yogic practitioners reflects a Nemesis; a killjoy approach because of constantly overruling everything around and using a power-oriented mode. And the conditioned psyche of Advaitic practitioners reflects a cynical attitude in relation to their surroundings, along with severe denials of the split in personality they suffer. Any mechanical or forced practice will hang outside the psyche, undigested and un-humanised if it lacks meaning or relevance to the seeker's existential life. By defining the essence of spirituality to be present in day-to-day existence, I do not imply placing all attention on material existence, but on the situational life we find ourselves in which will unfold as the authentic source to the hidden spirit within. The mundane, monotonous and dull is actually the most authentic source - current circumstances. Unaware of this, we keep facing the same kind of obstacles year after year. No sooner does the opportunity arrive, we run and most of the time end

CHAPTER FIFTEEN: RELUCTANT MASTERS

up shifting our geographical location or physical avenues, without actually changing the lock at all. Have we stood firm, wholeheartedly, in this seemingly confined circle to see if it does unfold? It will unfold and divulge itself to be a 'Spiral Ladder'. Life is a spiral ladder, not a confined circle, and the momentum of the energy it spirals by arises from the grounding of where we naturally stand and not as commonly misunderstood to descend from higher ends.

℘ ☙

Nisargadutta Maharaj was a simple Beedi seller, academically illiterate. The writings on Bhagwan Ramana Maharishi show he was dis-interested in daily school studies and instead, chose to spend his childhood days playing and swimming the waters of nearby ponds. A mere physical realm! Is it not ironic that intellectually predominant people are drawn to the teachings of both these saints? Below, I have shared incidents from the lives of two realised persons...

"Nityananda Baba of Ganeshpuri, in his earlier days...

> "One day, a Yogi was walking in a village. He noticed a youth fighting a bull, holding it by its horns. He watched the spirit and energy of the youth. Later, the Yogi called the youth and said, 'You are the one I have been searching for.' The Yogi shared his sacred knowledge of ancient Yogic practices (*Prana Vidya*) with this chosen youth. The Yogi had actually selected thirteen people to share his valued knowledge with. The bull-fighting youth was the only who actually realised the knowledge in just six months after being initiated into intense *Sadhana*. Compared to the other twelve students, six months was an extremely short period to attain realisation of such great knowledge. The Yogi then sent this youth northward

to begin his life as a wanderer, to share knowledge to those inclined. This Yogi is none other than Sivananda Paramahamsa from Vadakarai in Kerala, of the early part of last century and the youth is Nityananda Baba. Although Nityananda Baba never mentioned anything about Sivananda Paramahamsa, the followers of Sivananda Paramahamsa consider and include Nityananda Baba in the lineage of their Guru. They have a rare photograph of Nityananda Baba seated on the lap of his Guru Sivananda Paramahamsa. This I believe to be true on having seen the picture."

Why did Sivananda choose him? Sivananda recognised the agility, energy and grounding of the youth which he knew was precisely needed for the path of *Prana Vidya*, an entirely energy-based path.

ಞ ಲ

An incident about the famous Zen Master, Hui-Neng, (638-713 AD)

"Everyday, he would collect firewood in his native village. Once he heard a Zen Master was reciting a diamond *Sutra* in a monastery in Hupei. Being spiritually-inclined, he set off. He travelled for one month to reach the monastery. There he met the Master who was the fifth Patriarch Head, Hung-Jen. After meeting the Master, he joined the monastery as a cook and was also responsible for cutting and collecting firewood for the kitchen fire. He worked during the day and would meet his Master at night. Time passed. The day came when the sixth Patriarch was to be chosen. The Fifth Patriarch announced, 'All disciples should write a verse that describes their own understanding of the teachings, and give it to me.' No one came forward. Shen shui was one of the

CHAPTER FIFTEEN: RELUCTANT MASTERS

tutors teaching thousand students of the monastery. That night Shen shui wrote a poem but not having the courage to give it directly to the Master, he wrote it on the corridor walls.

> "Our body is the Bodhi Tree,
> Our mind is an illumined mirror,
> With care we wipe them hour-by-hour,
> And let no dust alight."

Next day, the Master read the poem on the wall but was not convinced. Although Shen shui had come close, something was missing. A young monk read the verse on the wall and was reciting it to himself while passing through the kitchen. Hui-Neng, the cook heard the verse and felt something was missing too. Late that night with the help of the boy, Hui-Neng wrote a verse on the corridor wall.

> "There is no Bodhi tree
> Nor stand of a mirror,
> Since all is void,
> How can the dust alight?"

Early next day, the Master read the new verse on the corridor wall and felt immensely satisfied but didn't express it to anyone. He understood Hui-Neng had written it. In front of all the students, the Master erased Hui-Neng's verse from the wall. Secretly, the Master called Hui-Neng, and offered him the Sacred Robe, bowing to him as the insignia of the next in lineage. The Master advised him to leave and go toward the south as jealous and ignorant people would only end up killing him if he stayed here. Saying this, He blessed Hui-Neng with the grace of sharing knowledge to the people in the temple situated in the Kuang province. Hui-Neng's doctrine stated that, 'enlightenment', based on meditation or on core level insights, is the same.

SECTION FOUR: RELUCTANT MASTERS

Hui-Neng was a simple firewood collector; a humble villager. At the monastery, he worked as a cook and wasn't even one of the disciples there. Both these life incidents exemplify how one's existential circumstance and situation can unfold the spiritual realm and bring forth a genuine realisation of Truth.

Accomplishing yourself within your own surrounding is the key to the Source that unlocks the hidden spirit within.

My Master once said,

> 'The Guru is not only within, but also outside as your external circumstances.'

৪০ ෬

RIVER SUTRA

If the edge of a sword meets no resistance, it passes through and cuts nothing.

An egoistic person is quickly hurt, easily takes offence and is likely to interpret things in a way that hurts his sense of dignity. This shows he feels bruised and his self-protective impulse dislikes it.

> "As a teenager, I recall standing on a bridge under which a river flowed. As I stretched out my hands over the bridge railing, I felt a tingling sensation in the palms of my hands. Surprised, I wondered what it was. Although I couldn't come up with any concrete answer, I did know one thing - the river was alive. I checked the waters of a still pond. The sensation wasn't the same. Then, I went up a nearby mountain to a waterfall and checked there. I verified my experience at different points of the falls. I found the tingling strongest

CHAPTER FIFTEEN: RELUCTANT MASTERS

and sharpest and not limited to the palms of my hands over there. I even felt it on my face. Why was the tingling stronger at the falls than the river? And why did the falls feel more alive than the flowing river? The flowing river also has *Prana*, the living force. And the tingling experience was this cohesive wholesome nature mingled with the flowing water. The humble flow of the waterfall enhanced a higher momentum and greatly empowered the living force of *Prana*. This spontaneous insight unfolded and penetrated my core and gradually helped me recognise this very phenomena reflecting in all dimensions of life. The true strength of living comes from humility, not power. Even power derives its strength from absolute humbleness."

Life is an unbound river. People prefer the river of life to flow as the calm waters of a protected canal. They rather be thrust into the mainstream river filled with rapids and free-flowing flexible currents because of being exposed and vulnerable. Here is the resistance! It can even be understood as one's internal condition: the lack of absolute humility. Humility has its own beauty and vulnerability, which carries deep significance.

When there is neither resistance nor egoism, our basic nature, our primal ignorance, is laid upon the altar of life. It no longer belongs to the individual - but belongs to life, which allows a free flow of life; a certain ardour, intensity and integrity. What we think our nature to be is actually our acquired nature, a pseudo gathering of blindly-acquired forces, all in ignorance of our own true nature. What we think we know; all is acquired from here. Many of us live with an existential neurosis born from the web of the acquired nature and try to fill the hollowness within - which nothing can fill. Our efforts and struggles just drag us further into acquired ignorance. And then, when we truly realise the futility of our so-called will, the acquired ignorance falls away. Each one has to eventually confront this primal ignorance born with them. The Primal Ignorance is Mother *Sakthi* and the acquired ignorance is *Maya*. Even, trying to understand truth deepens the well of acquired ignorance. Whatever we do on the path of spirituality would only be through a materialistic approach.

Rather than worshipping the imagined and assumed truth, worshipping the Primal ignorance is true and genuine worship.

> "As with his staff the teacher roused the pupil
> Who in his presence slumbereth, ever unto it,
> The benevolent Lord with Maya awakens,
> The soul that in prolonged egoity slumbereth."
>
> Thirumanthiram Verse 2165

> "To abide in Self within oneself by
> Meditating, ripening and falling in Bliss - Samadhi
> Oh! Mind, you yield Maya
> Like jewels are made of gold,
> If you are free from your stains (impurities)
> I shall attain redemption.
> Who else is as kind to me as you are
> None! None!
> You are equal to the form of Gracious God!
> To my life, you become the body itself."
>
> Verse - 7

> "Amongst those who embodied
> Even if, be they Brahma or any other Gods!
> If they can refuse you or can be without you,
> Hardly possible! Hardly possible!
> What else can be without you
> In the world mundane and beyond?

CHAPTER FIFTEEN: RELUCTANT MASTERS

If understood, to label you 'non-existent' is unjust,
Even I shall adore you as 'the one that exists'!
To end my ignorant state, now you must
Return to the glorious origin from
Where your life started!"

Verse - 8

"You had accompanied with me, many a day
Even if you died now by enquiry
By which you separated from me,
I shall bow down (or salute) your boundary perfectly
By silent (mauna) Guru himself who ruled me
I will become as His grace
Freeing 'I' and 'mine',
Eight Siddhis, Mukthi
Shall be mind upon this world
Through you my sadness will be ended."

Verse - 9

Mandalathin Verses by Sage Tayumanavar

A Siddha is not anti-social, but beyond the social. Even though he rebels against all conditioning, he is well-aware of how it is needed for a true and genuine enquiry for truth to arise. The Siddhas aver that, 'he who becomes aware of the true support, rejects all other supports that earlier lured'. It is true panacea for the cessation of suffering at all levels. Siddhas emphasise the word, '*Saarpu Unardhal*', which means realising the inherent true support. This seems more appropriate than the term '*Advaita*', which is used to indicate the non-dual relation of soul with self. Even though, ultimately the realisation of truth is the same, the Siddhas choose to point the way to truth to begin at the human level - wherever one stands, rather than pointing at truth to be a stated fact, Advaitic style.

> "Soul rises on severing its ties with
> Delusive allurements of maidens and sense objects,
> Approaching the Mother, embodiment of Grace divine,
> Whose clasp he lets go, only to re-unite in oneness with the Father - the Lord of Kachi-Ekamba."
>
> Pattinathar Ekambam Maalai

Soon after birth, at first a child is innately familiar only with its mother and shares an exclusive relationship with her. And the mother introduces the child to the father. Likewise, authentic-living in our Primal ignorance naturally takes us to the Universal Father, the Truth, Siva.

> "The dormant mature dame is stirred to awake,
> Whence He with Her in amity knit - Rise and fly!
> Proclaiming, that you have seen your True Self- rise and fly!"
>
> Tiruvunthiar Verse 14

Below, is a revelation bestowed by the grace of my Sat Guru, glowing with the essence of the above message:

> "As long as one tries to grasp at anything external,
> One would try to grasp internally, too.
> As long as one tries to grasp anything internal,
> One would try the same externally, too.
> Drop Both!
> Live in the remaining that you have...
> And live in that - abiding as you are!"

Our approach to life is a direct reflection of our approach to ourself. Likewise, our approach to ourself, reflects in our approach to the world. By this neurotic movement, we inherit the acquiring nature.

CHAPTER FIFTEEN: RELUCTANT MASTERS

When we are unaware of the nature of truth, how can we be aware of how to reach it?

"Ponder not: think of nothing: see not yourself in the fore-ground;
What you behold; let it be that."

Thiru Arut Payan, Verse 8

In the attitude of spontaneous surrender to Existence, we are in the state of Primal ignorance. Primal ignorance, as a fundamental vibration illumines the non-dual mind, the pure mind. In the pure mind, the original and the mirror-image perception are identical. It is a direct perception of the true nature of relationship between the observer and the object observed. Here, the Hand that holds us ever, unfolds; The Hand we were unaware of...the Hand that devours our individuality and unfolds the infinite dimension.

๛ ☙

THE WALK OF SIDDHAS

Even though Siddha Masters are hard to find in society, they are ever-present, emanating their distinguishable yet disguised presence. They are known for their reluctance to speak and express as teachers only because their very nature goes against the self-proclamation of being a teacher. They do not separate themselves from their teaching.

A Siddha Master doesn't verbalise a teaching. It speaks through him.

Even a single *darshan* of a Siddha Master could be an unconventional life-shaping event; a beginning to true living. Today, we are missing easy access to true Masters only because of our prejudice of how a Master should look and behave. Dropping such censorship would free us of the fallacy holding us apart from the grace of arriving and surrendering at the feet of the *Sat Guru*. Many Siddha Masters appear eccentric, devoured by madness - a picture of extreme inapproachability. Strongly conditioned minds find it hard to approach such a Master. The Divine Masters remain under the guise of inapproachability or inaccessibility not as escapism from the world, but are actually mirroring the conditioning-gripped society around. When one is truly ready to approach them in all trust and openness, the Master serves as the mirror reflecting the conditioning one is attached to. Initially, this shock brings out a deep fear and threat toward his believed identity. This rare experience feels like the carpet being pulled out from under with no ground to stand on. The Master skilfully exposes our ever-trembling ego.

He exposes the root cause that triggers you to escape realistic situations, and hide safely behind a life of illusion and habitual acquiring.

This root encounter leaves one in an unknown space. Then, as balance gradually reappears within one's being, once again the Master creates a milieu of uncommon circumstances that further break our conditioning and shake the feeble balance. At this point, one may feel he has entered a completely irrational world, but from the irrationality of our Siddha Master unfolds a deep understanding. One sees how feeble and false his ground has been. After this, one feels pushed to fall into him'self' or into a surrendering communion with his Guru, which is not separate from your 'Self'.

A life of being with a Siddha Master is a journey of mirroring, breaking and eventually transcending of conditioning, bringing one to fall and settle in one's natural state.

CHAPTER FIFTEEN: RELUCTANT MASTERS

The spirit of a Siddha is indescribable, the state of his activities incomprehensible and the depth of his simplicity indefinable by our complex mind. He knows the power hidden in contentment and nurtures it; he knows the valour hidden in compassion.

Pampatti Siddha Sings

"In the clash of caste, we will kindle the fire
In the open market, we will plant our staff
On the cross road of the street, we will play and dance,
In the undesirable house, we will make friendships,
Strolling, loitering, we will sleep,
Felicitous women we will enjoy.
All the five primal Brahma are ignorant.
O Snake, Dance, saying this."
    Pampatti Siddhar, Verse - 3, Songs of Pampatti Siddhar

This indescribable divine Siddha Master is spontaneously living his understanding without a thought to possible consequence and is in a state of no resistance between understanding and action. He moves in abandonment, spontaneity, happiness, and peace. He has the fearlessness and humility to live his understanding - come what may. To him, every ripple on the boundless ocean of life has its tale to tell! Life is not static but constantly expanding, transforming, evolving, unleashing as individual forms and expressions of itself. Each moment unfolds significance, a great sensitivity and a full expression of life. Siddhas live one with nature, inseparable from each and all. A communication was forged between nature, plants, animals, birds and them. They spoke. Ancient Siddhas have revealed the healing properties of thousands of herbs and the multidimensional nature of pulse in a human being, based on the characteristic movement of animals and the cosmic nature.

ಸಿ ಲ

SECTION FOUR: RELUCTANT MASTERS

MEETING WITH THEM

Meeting with a Siddha Master is unpredictable and preceded by an element of mystery. I have shared two personal meetings with my teachers to illustrate how unique each experience is and no matter how I may have readied myself, how contrary the actual meeting happened to be.

Poi Sollan Ayya - Tantric Teacher

Living in my native town, there was a time when I repeatedly heard the name of Poi Sollan from spiritual followers. He was known to frequent the shady-yard, a place where second-hand goods were sold. He would sit by a small teashop or sometimes be found mending old clothes. He was described as peculiar and non-compromising. Some said he often chased away visitors shouting uncommon utterances showing little or no consideration. Keeping in mind all that I had heard, I went to the shady-yard. I didn't find him. A year later, I heard he was living at Gorakkar cave at Elephant Hill; a place where several sadhus lived. I decided to visit.

It was almost afternoon by the time I arrived. I stood facing the steps leading up to the cave. At the entrance, sat an old villager or herdsman. I contemplated asking him the whereabouts of Poi Sollan but thinking, 'what would a poor old herdsman know of a great Siddha Tantric,' I ignored him and entered the cave. Three sadhus, clad in orange robes and foreheads decorated with religious symbols, greeted me. Expectation glittered in their eyes. Close by, around a corner sat two people grinding herbs. The Swamis appeared to be native healers and had me figured as their new client. I asked for Poi Sollan to which

CHAPTER FIFTEEN: RELUCTANT MASTERS

they showed both shock and disappointment. One of them commented, 'Where are you coming from and what do you need from that useless old man?' Taken aback by his manner of reference, I asked, 'Why do you call him so?' Another swami answered, 'Yes, he is useless. He is a friend of our Master but of no use to us. He is too old to even grind herbs. We even have to feed him as and when we cook for ourselves.' The third swami suddenly asked, 'But what is your purpose of meeting him?' Referring to the person who had guided me here, I expressed my wish to know about the Siddha path. They laughed. 'Who told you this about him? Our Master is the Yogi and we are his disciples. People come for our *darshan*, to cure health problems and resolve other difficulties in life.' Irritated by his proud claims, I kept quiet. Sensing this one of them said, 'Didn't you notice him on your way in? He usually lays down on the rock to the left of the steps.'

I was stunned. 'Was that Poi Sollan?' Politely thanking them, I took their leave. I was relieved at escaping the ignorant vultures but Poi Sollan's appearance nagged me. 'Was he really the Siddha Tantric Master people were so afraid of?'

Held by two controversial views, I stood before him. He wore only a *dhoti* and a dirty old towel rested over his left shoulder. A stick lay on the rock beside him, on his right. Seeing me, he politely said, 'Please come and sit on this rock, you have come a long way in this heat.' All my fears left me as I went and sat on a small rock beside him. I told him my name and the name of the person who had guided me to him. He immediately responded saying, 'Yes, but it was necessary for you to hear two different types of recommendations before you actually met me.' I understood what he meant by the 'second' recommendation, but only later did I understand the reason he hid behind the business-minded Swamis was to guard the secret ways of Tantra. And I learnt he had chosen to spend his final days at the cave which was his friend's *samadhi* shrine. Both had been spiritual colleagues of younger days and somewhere down the line had separated for a period.

Seeing Poi Sollan Ayya, one would imagine him to be nothing more than an illiterate villager or a simple herdsman. His glowing expertise in reading the mysteries of Nature and skill at changing or altering the array of invisible elements and powers hidden within Her was veiled by his simple appearance.

ಙ ಲ

My meeting with Peria Swami was quite contrary to my meeting with Poi Sollan Ayya. If I describe the meeting with Poi Sollan Ayya as a battle of contradictions then Peria Swami made certain I knew!

Peria Swami - the Alchemy Siddha

I speak of the time when I did a '*patha yatra*' (pilgrimage on foot) to Palani. Palani is the holy hill where Siddha Bogar's *Samadhi* Shrine and the Navapashana statue of Lord Murugan, created by Siddha Bogar are found. After having the *darshan* of both, Lord Murugan and the *Samadhi* of Siddha Bogar, I chose to continue my stay there. I went to a place around half a kilometre away from Palani where Sivananda Paramahamsa, the founder of the Siddha Samaj had attained *Videha Mukthi*. After I sat in the mysterious silence there, I returned to the *Mandapam*, (a shed like structure of stone

CHAPTER FIFTEEN: RELUCTANT MASTERS

pillars) where beggars and sadhus spent their nights. I lay down there for the night. Unable to sleep, I tossed and turned for thirty minutes. Maybe it was the new surroundings. Just as I sat up, I noticed an old man smiling at me. I smiled back. He wore an orange *dhoti* and an orange towel wrapped around his head. All of a sudden, he asked, 'You had *darshan* of my great grandfather?' (*Paattanaar* - in Tamil). Still looking at him I pondered his weird question, '*Darshan* of great grand father?' He pointed towards the hill. I understood. In that sense, I had not yet seen Siddha Bogar so I replied, 'No.' 'When the drums are beaten you will see him,' was his reply. Once again I was at a loss and had no idea what he meant. Having turned his face the other way, I didn't ask him anything more. Five minutes passed without any exchange of words. I decided to offer him a cup of tea. Just as I stood up and began walking down the steps, I saw him walking too.

We walked toward the teashop, leaving the sleeping people behind. I asked, 'Can I offer you tea?' 'Do you know Vana Durga?', was his question in response. 'She is there, we can go.' Vana Durga is the name of 'Goddess Durga living in a forest' and is situated at the bottom of Palani hill. We arrived after a fifteen minute walk. The road was isolated and the only sound was the blowing of wind. He sat by the temple compound wall. I sat close-by. Coming from his body was the distinct smell of zinc. Then I saw his eyes. His pupils were surrounded by a bluish ring. It struck me. Only a high Siddha Yogi or a Siddha of inner alchemy can have such eyes. My observation told me that he was in the process of *Dasa Diksha* (the ten kinds of initiations involved with physical transformation.) I looked at his body. I was stunned. There were no wrinkles and his skin was soft like that of a baby.

Noticing my curiosity, he burst into a laugh, 'My guru offered me this,' he said. 'Bogar?' I asked. 'Sage Vishwamithra,' he said. Unable to keep calm I asked, 'What is *Vasi*?' During this period of my life I was passionately seeking the secret Yogic practice of the Siddhas, called *Vasi* Yoga. He replied, 'It is Siva residing as Life vapour in each and everything.' Keen to know more, I prompted, 'Can you initiate me?' 'Why do you need to know? Do you even realise what it is that you are asking?' I shook my head in response. He said, 'No need of practicing it as Yoga. First sense the life principle divinely residing in everything and everybody.' He pulled out two tiny bottles from a small old bag. The moment he opened them, a strong smell of something like horse urine filled the air. He mixed them in specific ratios and handed me a little portion to drink. At first, I hesitated, but, when with a Siddha one needn't doubt! He watched my eyes. In that instant, his face changed to that of an eagle. His ears grew a little bigger and nose appeared lengthier and sharper. The smell of zinc coming from his body grew strong. I grew dizzy. I accepted the potion and drank. 'Oh God!' It was like swallowing burning charcoals. I felt my entire body on fire and hairs stood on end. I grew highly sensitive. I saw smoke emerging from each and every pore of my body. I began coughing incessantly. I began jumping about unable to tolerate the burning pain. My entire body was being pierced by needles of fire. He laughed, 'Run run, go to the temple area and drink raw milk. I ran. I drank some milk and felt a little better. I could gather my thoughts. 'What had he given me? It seemed to be a distilled solution of a sort. But why had his face changed to that of an eagle? Was he a black magician or a Left-hand Tantric alchemist'? Years ago, my medicinal teacher had said, 'Never accept anything from a *Vaathi* (Alchemist). They will test their alchemical

CHAPTER FIFTEEN: RELUCTANT MASTERS

preparations on you.' He might have been a *Rasa* Siddha; an alchemist. I sensed a strong hesitation within me. My mind was masqueraded by unstoppable thoughts related to the so-called security of life. The smell of horse urine and zinc filled the air. I panicked. Was he somewhere close again? I realised the smell was coming from the pores of my own skin. Since this is my path, this is a life or death opportunity granted to me, I thought. This was Siddha Bogar's blessing. I resolved to approach him this time without prejudice.

I returned. His face was normal but his tone was teasing. He said mischievously, 'If you be with me you will often run, as you just did!'

༄ ༅

"Remain Summa - Oh the ghost within,
As I told the Sutra
The place where it happens - Oh the ghost within,
That will burn you beyond."

-Agapai Siddhar songs, Verse 3

The path of *Gnana* is the path of Primal Wisdom and *Gnana* Siddhas don't insist on any philosophy or practice, to realise Truth. Some are just wandering Siddhas and some are *Avadhootas*, sitting idle, without asserting their presence at all.

SUMMA IRU: PILGRIMAGE TO NOWHERE

"Bereft of illusions, bereft of ignorance, bereft of intellect;
Without embracing fish-eyed damsels and their attachments,
Themselves as themselves, remaining in 'simply be';
Thus are they,
The sacred beings in Siva robes."

Thirumanthiram 1678, by Thirumoolar

For the wandering and idle Siddhas, the underlying attitude remains *Summa Iru*. *Summa Iru* literally means 'just be' or 'simply be' - 'apparent non-activity'. *Summa Iru* is not a noun but a verb with several implied attitudes and principles and stands against all conditioning - personal, social, religious and philosophical. The Siddhas are *Sahaja Manushas*, Spontaneous Persons, and don't believe in living for any purpose other than spreading the message of Existence. For Them, the bliss of *Samadhi* and the objective distractions are equal. To Him, being is life in time, as existence in eternity.

SECTION FOUR: RELUCTANT MASTERS

Pampatti Siddhar sings:

> "Four Vedas, six Sastras, several treatises
> On modus Operandies,
> Epics, Tantric literature espousing arts,
> Varieties of general other books -
> Oh! Snake, dance!
> Declaring all these as useless."
>
> — Pampatti Siddhar, Verse 98

> "Rites are just Moss - Oh the ghost within,
> Knowledge — a hollow stable,
> The God is but an illusion — Oh the ghost within,
> All is like that!"
>
> Agapai Siddhar, Verse 72

The above songs sing the spirit of the Siddhas - soaring high against all conditioning.

Says Bhagwan Ramana Maharishi ...

> 'Summa Iru is non-action. Non-action is unceasing eternal activity. His stillness is like the apparent stillness of a fast-spinning top (gyroscope). Its very speed cannot be followed by the eye so it appears to be still. Yet it is spinning.'

The apparent inaction of a Siddha is not inertness! The incessant activity emerging through him cannot be grasped by the mind. A more common definition for *Summa Iru* is, 'to tightly hold on to your-self' which feels incorrect, because *Summa Iru* is actually, non-confronting in nature. By non-confronting or by dropping all confronting tendencies, one naturally abides in himself. A river always moves ahead, flows to its next, without confrontation. One cannot judge which way the waters of a river are about to turn.

CHAPTER FIFTEEN: RELUCTANT MASTERS

Siddha Pattinathar sings:

> "Wandering like a ghost, lying like a corpse,
> Eating up all the alms like a dog, labouring like a fox,
> Treating good maidens as mothers,
> Greeting everybody with humility,
> Will live like babies -
> Those who have realized the Truth."
>
> General songs - Verse 35, by Siddha Pattinathar

The above songs show us the eccentric attitudes of wandering Siddhas. No human method, strategy or technique can bring man to 'doing nothing', or *Summa Iru*!

Living in 'simply be' is a humble allowing; a great openness!

'Allowing' is ever-present and eternally happening at our core, the heart. Allowing is the primordial relationship with life. Life orients through 'allowing'; 'simply being' in what is completely and creatively present in the beginning-less and endless flow of life. Life has no history. Allowing is being the way one's presence is completely, freely and truly is. This allowing is *'Summa Iru'*. Allowing is neither acquiring nor refusing, but contemplating. A Siddha is open to the emerging whole being by abiding in yielding presence.

> They speak of states two, 'I' and 'He',
> But there is a state, where 'I' and 'He' are undifferentiated,
> Those who are in Supreme non-activity state,
> Will not the difference cognise,
> Abiding in Self, and He and Self as one uniting,
> Is the state of 'Sutha', Absolute pure."
>
> Thirumanthiram, Verse - 2348, Siddha Thirumoolar

Doing nothing, *summa iru* is an acceptance of our limitation!

Everything changes, is transitory and confined by a boundary. The boundary of our body is what gives it shape. Our feet stand upon earth, facing a dead end while our head is towards endless sky. Our body is a chamber where the endless and the end, both play and dance or where, both heaven and earth meet. Standing our ground on earth with our heads turned to sky - is being 'upright'. Every limitation carries the seed for its release. Each limitation bears potential and a significant message to deliver. One who allows himself to 'simply be' in his limitation, is released from it.

Summa Iru is abiding in one's limitation!

By accepting limitation, one naturally abides as his core, the unlimited heart, from where eternal Life shapes its play of limitation. The limited and the limitless, both are continuing participants in the arena of Life. There is no duality where the Siddhas 'simply be'.

Holy words spoken by Jesus Christ:

> "For there is nothing covered that shall not be revealed,
> Neither hid, that shall not be known.
> Therefore what so ever, you have spoken in darkness
> Shall be heard in the light;
> And that which you have spoken
> In the ear in the closets
> Shall be proclaimed upon the house-tops."

୨୦ ଓଃ

SUMMA IRU - Authentic Surrender

Bhagwan Ramana Maharishi once told the story of a realised wanderer who appeared irrational and more than insane to onlookers.

The story of 'UPPU KOTTHAN'.

> "Once upon a time, an idle person by the name of 'Uppu Kotthan' lived in a small village by the seashore. He had elephantiasis in his right leg, which made him limp. His life was devoid of any social

CHAPTER FIFTEEN: RELUCTANT MASTERS

activity. He remained idle and useless. The villagers wondered why he wasted his life in vain. One day, they encouraged him to earn a living for himself. They gave him money and advised him to procure salt from the seashore and sell it in the plains, and procure rice from the plains and come sell it by the seashore. Uppu Kotthan went to the plains to procure salt where it was expensive and sold it by the seashore where it was cheap! With the remaining money, he procured rice from the seashore area and sold it in the plains! After a few such strange transactions, he lost all the money given by the villagers. The villagers were at a complete loss of words and abandoned any further idea of helping Uppu Kotthan.

Uppu Kotthan once again went back to his ways and spent his days pushing a rock up a nearby hill with the help of a stick and from the top of the hill letting it roll back down. This would bring him great joy and laughter. He would spend his nights eating and resting at a nearby cremation ground. He didn't need to beg for food. For his daily meal, he would collect rice from the mouths of the corpses brought for cremation. (In Hindu funeral rites, the dead persons would be cremated after being fed with rice offering). He would cook the collected rice and have it for his meal. One night while cooking rice, several subtle beings, who served Goddess Kali, appeared, attempting to chase him away. They danced vigorously and made threatening sounds to scare him, but their efforts were in vain. Uppu Kotthan was immersed in cooking the rice. Finally, Mother Goddess Kali herself appeared before him. Unmoved by Her appearance, Uppu Kotthan continued. Feeling ignored, Mother Kali was enraged and filled with wrath. In a thundering voice she said, 'I, Bhadhra Kali, has come'.

(Bhadhra Kali is the most wrathful form of Mother Kali. The word *Bhadhra* means wrathful or ferocious but in Tamil the word '*Bhadhra*', used colloquially, also means 'ten and a half'.)

Even these words didn't make him fear. Instead he retorted, 'Then I am Pathin Ondrai Kali.' (*Pathin ondrai* means eleven and a half).

By his fearless response, She recognised him to be no ordinary being. Expressing Her wish to bless him, she asked what he wanted. He asked to live forever. She said this blessing wasn't Her's to grant and that he must ask for something else. Uppu Kotthan asked death to come to him in that very moment. She could not grant that either. Hearing Her refusal, Uppu Kotthan said, 'Why have you appeared before me then? You can leave.' She urged him to ask for something She could bless him with. So, Uppu Kottan asked Her to shift the disease afflicting his right leg to his left leg!
It was granted..."

What does this story mean?

One day, Kapali Sastri while walking with Bhagwan Ramana Maharishi on the Arunachala mountain asked in all sincerity if Bhagwan Ramana Maharishi would tell him about what state Bhagwan was in. To this Bhagwan replied, 'Even if the Trimurtis appear before me, give me *darshan* and ask me to choose a boon, I would tell them, "Be pleased, let me have no more *darshan*."'

(*Trimurti Darshan* is the *darshan* of Lord Brahma, Lord Vishnu and Lord Siva)

"Behold the fowls of the air;
For they sow not, neither do
They reap, nor gather into barns,
Yet your heavenly Father feedeth them.
Are ye not much better than they."

Jesus Christ

CHAPTER FIFTEEN: RELUCTANT MASTERS

LETTING BE

The Reluctant Siddhas believe in complete submission to the act of living. Their main teaching is 'Don't exert your will in existence'. Remaining *'summa'* is the pathless way of the spirit; it is the open mind and lightning spirit that moves spontaneously in any direction, through any given situation, according to the *Dharma* - the inherent order of Existence. Once we begin to believe in factual knowledge, spontaneity ceases to be. Yet, neither can we deliberately adopt a line of inaction, for that would at once turn into an action!

> "You! Gorakkar - as a disciple, asked many questions humbly.
> You asked what is the need for God to create and sustain?
> I ask you, what is the need for mind to acquire and wear out?
> Just dive deep into this enquiry and the answer is hidden in it!
> Where there is no experience at all -
> That nothingness is the Grand Release, the Mukthi!
> What you need for it, is 'devoted feeling', the Bhakthi!"
>   -Collected Verse on 'the phenomena of making Gold',
>   By Agasthiyar Suvarna Jala Thirattu

'Remain *summa*' does not mean literally doing nothing, but letting everything do what it really does for its nature to be satisfied! This is - living without assertion. The daring 'letting be' holds the secret to mastering circumstances without asserting oneself for or against them. It is the attitude of yielding to an oncoming force in a way that it is unable to affect you. 'Remaining *summa*' requires a daring letting-go, sitting and wandering loose to life.

Summa Iru is letting-be!

Letting-be is not keeping a distinguished idea of how one is 'letting oneself be' and how one is 'letting others be'. No, there need be no difference. In a 'Daring letting-be', everything 'is' a living whole; without separation; yet with nothing identical - a grand paradox.

> "Oh! Mother! It is amazing
> Isn't it? Isn't it?
> Making me Grand expanse
> So that to realise myself,
> You made me 'Summa' there
> Apart from being in bliss there,
> What else is there to speak?"
>
> Kallalin, Verse - 25, Sage Tayumanavar

It is the *mantra* – *'Summa Iru'*; do not make any change in it. Always bear whatsoever falls as your lot – be it pleasure or pain. When somebody or something troubles us, we try to change it. This can be avoided. Instead, try and bear it calmly as it comes - *'summa iru'*. Many people are given to chant the *mantra* of the divine name of Lord Rama or Lord Sankara. All these *mantras* lead to *'summa iru'*. *Bhajans*, Yoga, etc. all lead to the same – *'summa iru'*. Real happiness lies in *'summa iru'*, no matter the circumstance. Be it good, bad, pleasurable or painful, be content with it; do not avoid nor change it; in this lies all happiness.

The Siddhas ever-stay in the state of 'Daring letting-be'. What is meant by *'summa iru'*, now? He quietly drifts along without any resistance toward things we label dirty or bad, hot or cold, rain or storm, fasting, eating and so on. Neither is he overly pleased on experiencing the opposite of each. His divinity shines as he does not cause change in his surrounding nor in any affairs of the world. He lives in simple continuity, facing everything that comes from the outside toward him, with no attempt to interfere in its progressive flow. And while amidst the welcome or unwelcome circumstance, neither does he attempt to change himself from within to ward them off or protect himself in any way. There is a wholesome allowing and a daring letting-be from within to without and likewise from without to within. He faces things as they come, transparent to differences or separation. This is the state of *'summa iru'*. He who remains in the state of *'summa iru'* always experiences the state of God – the state of Infinite Bliss. He can be likened to a blade of grass enduring all weather conditions, yet alive and rooted to the earth in glowing crisp green freshness! We try to have things the way we want and each of us are used to this standpoint right from birth. The behaviour of a Siddha is the exact opposite. And because of Their contrary behaviour, we tend to label them insane, even so, They remain in the state of *'summa iru'*, unperturbed.

> Knows not Itself, knows not others to be,
> If thrives, would annul; has no origin-in Its Presence
> The five functionings, by the word of bliss
> Listening even little, then possible!
> Olivil Odukkam, Verse-24, By Sage Kannudaiya Vallal

ಲ ଷ

LIKE THE FIGURES!

There are only ten figures in this world - one to nine and zero. That is all. You may write a sum of ten or even twenty figures, yet the sum is only about placing these ten figures in different places. All the affairs of this world move based on the figures of one to nine and zero; zero being the last. Similarly, the affairs of the world are managed amongst 84 lac living forms. Whether it is God or anybody else, He only has this fixed set of 84 lac living forms to play with - that is all. Like in the play of figures, you can either run about from one to nine or arrive at zero. Once you arrive at zero – there is nothingness in the world, the world play is over. Whether you run about from one to nine or, arrive at zero depends on you! To arrive at zero is to return to the Original State and accomplish the only one attitude - the attitude of *Summa Iru*.

In truth, *Summa Iru*, the attitude of letting be, is neither action nor non-action.

ஓ ௌ

QUALITY IS ALWAYS 'IN LESS'

"The Brahmins who wished to listen to Vedanta,
They didn't give up their desire, even after listening to it.
Vedanta is the place where desire ends
Those who truly hear Vedanta are desire less."
              Thirumanthiram, Verse 229, by Siddha Thirumoolar

According to the reluctant Siddhas, yielding to existence requires dropping all acquired inessentials. Many verses describe the changing nature of illusion and the world, emphasising the need to renounce the unnecessary as the first step. Renunciation doesn't mean literal or forcible begging. It implies understanding the mechanical functionality of inessential things in relation to oneself and hacking away at them to unravel a finer quality in one's way of living. It is an attitude, not a physical act. It is not about giving up, but allowing things to go away. "This too shall pass", is the motto of nature. It is the difference between need and desire. True renunciation conserves energy in a meaningful assimilable form to live authentically in one's own nature. When everything is in constant change, renunciation is only the acceptance of it.

Security and clinging will only be mocked at by Life. Seeing things 'as they are' preludes acceptance of 'going away'. A Siddha is a drifting flow in that ever-changing quantum field of energy. To realise one's unconditional nature, de-conditioning of inessentials is needed. Once we realise what we know is different from what we are, renunciation happens naturally and living manifests a quality. Spirit is: Creativity without Destruction, Production without Possession, Action without Self-assertion and Development without Domination...

> "Women become prisons for those who seek them;
> The learned are imprisoned by their learning;
> Those in penance are imprisoned because of their penance;
> The self-aware who strain to reach Him are in prisons too.
> All these don't know the nature of the Lord."
> Thirumoolar Thirumanthiram Verse 2073

It is important that the attitude of a wandering Siddha is not to be used as a technique to manipulate the laws of Karma nor to undermine the world's response to one's current or past actions. In fact, the majority of people in both the East and the West misunderstand the theory of Karma and its meaning. The superficial yet popular view of Karma is a fatalistic viewpoint which is not how the Siddhas, who are sensitive to how the universe responds to itself, understand Karma.

> "He is Dharma, birthless, kinless,
> Resides in the wild, lives by alms,
> He, seeing anybody who renounced,
> Sunders their bonds of birth.
> - you have seen a Divine Madman."
> Thirumanthiram, Verse 1616, by Siddha Thirumoolar

SECTION FOUR: RELUCTANT MASTERS

> "One God, pervades all ten directions,
> None of any direction, where He is not,
> Refuge his flower feet; you can cross the roaring karmic sea,
> And safely reaching the shore, beyond."
>
>   Thirumanthiram, Verse 1451, by Siddha Thirumoolar

Types of Karma are named differently in different cultures. *Kriyaman Karma* is generated as the result of a decision. Making a decision based on spiritual principles and aligning an action with a compatible stream of energy, present in the cosmos, at a particular moment can make one's actions take on the quality of that energy. By this, one becomes a Karmic surfer; catching waves of energy that enable him to get safely and happily to shore. By working with, instead of against the flow of nature's great energy, misfortunes are greatly reduced and disasters avoided.

> "All manifested Karmic actions - Oh the ghost within!
> Look!! Are only void,
> That which was before un-manifested - Oh the ghost within!
> Will emerge - the infinite!"
>
>   -Agapai Siddhar Verse 88

> "The place where the self ceases to be - Oh the ghost within!
> There you see the abode of Siva,
> For those who lose body consciousness - Oh the ghost within!
> There is no lacking."
>
>   -Agapai Siddhar

CHAPTER FIFTEEN: RELUCTANT MASTERS

LIVING NOW TO NEXT

> "To realize oneself - Oh the ghost within,
> Follow the pathless path.
> Otherwise realizing others—Oh the ghost within
> Is, the knowledge about the devil."
>   Songs of Agapai Siddhar - Verse 78, by Agapai Siddhar

Life moves from now to next, just like a river moves to its forefront. Why does man miss?

Man's fragmented consciousness mechanically sticks together by way of association, between the nature of matter and its function. It hangs in this condition when it is 'unawake'. While asleep or dreaming, it does not respond fully nor can it see clearly, which is how habit or blind impulse take over. When we act 'mechanically' we brush the surface of things and connect only by a fraction of our entirety. Even something beautiful doesn't reach our core. Of sheer habit, we pass an offhand comment and move onto something else. We mechanically voice our likes and dislikes rather than actually feeling their quality. Our superficial response to life's happenings leaves us unsatisfied and hollow, because for an action or response to be complete, it must rise from the totality of our being. True action is action without acting. There is no depth in our activity if it rises from the mind like words and concepts. It often appears as though our depth rises only from memories, while a depth of an altogether different nature dwells in the pure response arising from the point of no-dimension; the heart, charged with primordial creativity. These depths have no foothold in time and may be described as the spirit of infinite space - having vitality, infinite possibilities and a freshness that belongs to life.

Motivated actions from the past are artificial.

A Siddha is one who has reached beyond doing anything. This 'doing nothing' is spontaneous activity. Instead of a sense of intentional progression, it acts from the direct working of natural laws, *Prakruthi*; as a consort of a Siddha. This is Absolute Action; completely natural. Change happens before a Siddha without hindrance; things are accomplished without assertion.

> "If becoming is to cease - Oh the ghost within!
> Let there be no mental imagery.
> Abide at the feet of the Sat Guru - Oh the ghost within!
> You shall not taste death."
>
> — Agapai Siddhar Verse 20

This core is one's being, one's spirit.
Spirit is that nature within us which responds constructively to everything that exists.

Sensitivity, residing with wholeness, makes every moment perfect and independent of past or future. A Siddha remains *summa*, doing nothing and through Him all acts manifest making Him a self-portrait of Lord Siva, the *Kriyaman* - the upholder of all action. Response arising from the whole being is best reflected through Chuang Tzu's ancient Taoist story of the fighting cock.

> "In ancient China there once lived Chi Hsing Tzu, renowned for his ability to train roosters to fight in sport. Being a specialised trainer, he worked for King Hsuan. Once, Chi Hsing Tzu was training a truly fine bird and the king was rather eager and impatient for the bird to be readied for combat. 'Not yet,' said Chi Hsing Tzu. 'He (the rooster) is brimming with agitation and is easy and willing to pick a fight with any other bird. He is arrogant and proud of his strength.' The king waited for another

ten days before enquiring again. The trainer answered, 'O king, he is not yet ready. The bird still flies into a fiery rage on even hearing the crow of another.' The king had no choice but to wait for another ten days. 'No Lord, not yet', said Chi Hsing Tzu. 'He still wears a ferocious look and fluffs out his feathers.' After another ten long days, finally the trainer, Chi Hsing Tzu went to the king and said, 'Yes, Lord, the bird is ready. He doesn't even blink on hearing another bird crow. He stands stock-still like a log of wood. He is a fulfilled and accomplished fighter now. Other birds will take one look at him and run.'"

The word *Dhyanam*, or meditation means (Dhi + yana) - the way up, beyond intellect. It is when the body, mind and spirit are properly attuned to natural rhythm; similar to tuning a musical instrument to play high resonance music from seven notes. Glimpses of Truth manifest beyond the level of intellect through such attuning. *Dhyanam* is a dimensional transformation. It is the silencing of the centre of 'me'. With this silence emerges a new energy-awareness, which sees and acts in the world in a non-dual way; without dividing life. This is the pre-reflective state, where there is no subject and object. When *Dhyanam* crystallises, it transcends the conditioned mind. When the meditator is engulfed by the ever-staying ground or the Self, experiencing ends. In the flowering state, awareness of unity flowers into compassion and the illusory walls separating one life from another dissolve into oneness. There is no longer subject and object but a communion with the wholeness of life; an 'a-logical' whole. The unfolding essence of *Dhyanam* was showered forth under the Divine sayings of my Sat Guru, which I share below...

"Thinking not of anything in its concreteness,
Nor seeking to interpret symbols, as if deciphering objects material.

Neither putting yourself as one who sees,
Regard steadily the loving wisdom that sees you.
Entering within, lie hidden...
What you cannot see, do not drive towards
In whatever way grace absorbs you,
Wholly, yield yourself,
In purity remain, grace entwined,
Repose, under this refreshing shade,
In this, enjoying supreme felicity,
...is humble simplicity."

The beauty of a flower does not derive its virtue and significance from anything external. Likewise, a true response comes from the heart, the Self; a response that arises without impediment of reflective thought or division of subject and object. In such a pre-reflective state, in its own point of origin and for its own significance, each thing is present. Each occurring event becomes a key that turns consciousness and unlocks another mysterious facet residing there. Then the energy called Life wells up as if from a fountain, from its unknown source and flows into forms and patterns giving full expression to its latent significance and releasing its potential.

The force of this release gives life, intensity and spirit!

Fundamentally speaking, energy is simply energy and life is simply its moving presence. It is we who objectify emerging actions with association or imagery. It is we who fragment it into power energy, spiritual energy, sexual energy, compassionate energy and so on and condition ourselves. When we feel a massive energy, we often associate it by outwardly blaming others but psychically experience an inability. This energy is anger. Or, when a psychological need for love combines with a physical need for catharsis, we call it sexual energy. When we feel psychically deprived and crave for physical attention such as love and care, we call it our need for compassion. We are always projecting the fundamental energy of life and its different patterns into various associations and affiliations. But when our mind ceases to be the identifier of choice, and once we drop setting ideals that define what should be instead of what actually is, there will be no struggle coming from our concentration of energy on assumed objectives to acquire or control.

> "Study for what? - Oh the ghost within!
> Activity for what?
> All rules and principles - Oh the ghost within!
> Have been annulled".
> - Agapai Siddhar Verse 77

The Siddhas' songs about the wisdom of Self describe *chakras* to signify the fragmented nature of human energy. They name it '*Upathys*'; the confining states that colour human perception. In truth, there are no *chakras*! There is neither categorisation nor different levels of energy. Everything is a single field of energy and energy is in its flow; what would happen if one lives in it, as it is? My Siddha teacher once said, 'If you repeat *Vasi - Vasi* continuously, it will resound as Siva, Siva...' When we abide in ever-flowing energy, by its moving presence from one moment to its next, we feel the throbbing effervescence - the source of its movement.

Life is in its moving presence leaping out from its ever-stay existence - That, Siddhas salute as Siva.

When a person lives delighted and content, life is an end in itself. Here I recall a story:

"A pandit, deeply bothered about the meaning of life approached a hermit living nearby in a hut. The hermit took him to a stream and filled a pot with water.

Hermit: (Pointing to the stream) What is that?
Pandit: A stream.
Hermit: (Pointing to the pot) What is this?
Pandit: A pot full of stream water.

Hermit:	Why don't you call it a stream?
Pandit:	The water does not flow in the pot, so it is not a stream.
Hermit:	How can it be a stream?
Pandit:	When you let it go.
Hermit:	As long as you search for the meaning of life you will feel the meaningless within you. As the pandit made the gesture of letting go, he understood what the hermit was driving at. Life is a flowing stream and the meaning of life is only a pot full of water."

ಸ ಆ

NOTHING TO SAY

"Their holy heart trembles not,
Neither comes death, nor suffering, nor night, nor day,
Nor fruits of karma to experience;
Those who, attachment dropped subsided with themselves."
   Thirumanthiram, Verse 1624, by Siddha Thirumoolar

The Avadhoota Siddhas, after enlightenment, don't move anywhere, nor do they interact with the world assuming authority or position. They sit in one place, living in primordial awareness (a state prior to the consciousness of duality). They repose in the primal dimension of *Vettaveli*, space infinite, where the 'I' consciousness fades into nothingness and the fragmentary subject and object relationship subsides.

"They don't want liberation - Oh the ghost within!
They don't want enlightenment.
They don't want initiation - Oh the ghost within!
Who are Chit itself."
   Agapai Siddhar songs, Verse 82, By Agapai Siddhar
   ('Chit' – awareness prior to reflective consciousness)

CHAPTER FIFTEEN: RELUCTANT MASTERS

> "Where are the temples? Where are the sacred ponds?
> You loathsome people, who worship temples and ponds;
> Temples and ponds are in one's mind,
> There is neither creation nor destruction,
> Never, never, never!!!"
>
> Songs of Siva Vakkiyar, Verse 83, by Siddha Siva Vakkiyar

First, be at peace with the way things are. In the natural state of things we are already at One. Everything is fundamentally One, it is we who interpret differently. For instance, the element of sound. The doorbell 'rings', the ocean 'roars', a snake 'hisses', a car 'honks', a 'clap' of thunder, a 'cat purrs', the phone 'rings', etc. Truth is One. But if we don't interpret we fear we cannot know. The feeling of unknowing is more intimate than the sense of knowing. To be beyond both - the sense of 'knowing' and 'unknowing' is most intimate, as Truth is Unknowable. Living in the flow of life is to live in 'continuous unknowing'. Mind cannot direct the unknown and so has to live in it; its only possibility. 'Learning' keeps us from being truly intimate and splits us. We no more feel at One. Perplexed by what will be next, we constantly build a new image of ourself. We have allowed little space in ourself for 'unknowing'.

'Unknowing' experiences each moment afresh, without pre-occupied content to urge it on.

Life manifests not from the birth of this body, but from the core of the uncaused cause.

Our mind can never grasp this. On one hand, life is unborn and undying and on the other hand, it is being born and is dying every moment in itself. It is a grand paradox. We, as scientists, say the universe is both expanding and contracting. We also say there is a black hole. We can call our movements of activity and rest or birth and death as expansions and contractions, similar to that of the universe. But, if we fall and vanish into the black hole, is it relevant to say, we are being blown in and out?

Yes, it is a grand suction, an eternal immutable void - the abyss. It is the realm of the *Avadhoota*.

The essence of us is the heart of life. When we find our essence, we begin to be present in the present. By humbly being present, we are at once grounded and centred to our core, and move with unencumbered ease - that is life. Life is a great circle and loosening the identifier and the identification is the way to participate in it. This daring loosening allows us to flow; to become the whole circle. To hold on at any point on this circle is to forget our original unborn nature as there is no place we begin and nowhere we end. Embracing the Self in unobstructed fullness, yielding, returns eternity. Silently, the universe gently falls transparent and open, with no boundaries, being a mirror for everything now and transparent of everything.

In the spacious heart, *Chit-Akasa*, as fragrance emanates from a flower, Self yields Presence.

This makes the mirror-play that, I am, too. In the symbiotic, synchronised, finely orchestrated, grand simultaneity, the present embraces and is embraced by all past and all future. Our very presence is reflected everywhere and in everything, and everywhere and everything resonates in us. Even with each moment drifting to its next, everything manifests in its Grand Now. Think about this... even though in each moment there is a multitude of cellular deaths and cellular births within our body.... Does our face turn into anothers?

> "Falling leaves. Paddy fields sway in the wind. Neem trees burn a joyful green in the summer heat. Pine trees breathe by the cold. The red light of the Sun. The pale illumination of the moon. White cranes flying by dark black clouds. Calm on the face of a dead body. A baby's smile. His innocent gestures. A calf playfully runs towards its mother. A stone - self-secluding, oblivious to the compulsive need to become an idol. Beauty of ever-rest, completion, spoken from the graveyard. Nodding of friends. Tender tears of a mother..."

CHAPTER FIFTEEN: RELUCTANT MASTERS

Springing from itself and falling back on Itself, Creation, Sustenance and Destruction ends, there is no self at all.

Life's moving presence arises, each moment from its million origins; from its absolute ever-stay existence. Life has no preferences. The boundaries of race, country, religion, creed; the boundaries of time and space are irrelevant to life and living. Life is simple 'isness'.

We live once and that is forever.

"No atom moves without Its motion,
This is the declaration of the Sages,
Perceive it thus:
What is knowing, and what is unknowing?
Who are the Knowers and the Knowers-not, Who?
Who are the Silent ones and the babblers like myself?
From where arises, the illusory mind?
Apart from IT is there anything?
Oh! Life of Life! That sustains everything,
In existence, here and here after,
Your plenitude that pervades All."

Thayumanavar Verse - 89

ஸ்ரீ

reluctant masters

CHAPTER FIFTEEN: RELUCTANT MASTERS

SONGS OF THE ACCOMPLISHED

Kudhambai Chittar songs...

Kudhambai Chittar is one of the ancient Siddhas. When I was in the Nambhi Mountain ranges I visited the cave where he carried out tapas (penance). All his songs mention him as Kudhambai, an ancient Tamil word with many meanings.

The root word Kudhambai comes from the word Kudham

- earthen earring
- one which is boiling up
- one which bubbles up
- one which is furious/agitated

If we take the meaning to be 'agitated', he is referring to the agitated mind. He also refers to the agitated mind by a feminine gender as in 'maid' or 'lass', which is also indicated by the word 'Kudhambai'. So the reader is free to assume any of the meanings. Writing a commentary for songs, sutras, is nothing but our interpretation that confines the original. And as the Siddha's songs are multifarious, it is not appropriate to confine it by interpretation. A multifarious nature of song is depicted below.

> "For those who remain in the mountain, dining the juice of mango,
> Where is the need for coconut milk - Oh lass Kudambai?
> Where is the need for coconut milk?"

Cryptic meaning:

In a coconut, water is stagnant which symbolises the 'static' nature; ideational experience. The mango fruit has no water but a full-bodied outflow of juice. A person living in Truth is embodying the nature of flowing Life: living moment to moment in ever-fresh awareness.

Figurative meaning:

The shape of a coconut can be a symbol of a woman's breast. A mango, at a horizontal angle, represents a bowl. The milk from the breast symbolises passion that generates further craving, and the mango symbolises the bowl of nectar - the One who lives in the natural state, Sahaja Sthithi.

We could continue to interpret, but that deviates us from the original spirit of the song. Just read the song and allow it to reach you however it wants. While you read, if it makes you calm, stay there. If it makes you alive in spirit, flow with it. If it makes you angry, be anger - it is also a human way of adoring their songs.

> "For those who Realised, the Truth is plain expanse;
> Where is the need for Royal grants - Oh lass Kudambai?
> Where is the need for Royal grants?
>
> For those remaining as real Gnanis, who realised the Truth,
> Where is the need for Elixir - Oh lass Kudambai?
> Where is the need for Elixir?
>
> For those who repose with vacant eye,
> Where is the need for spurious desires - Oh lass Kudambai?
> Where is the need for spurious desires?
>
> For those who have seen the uncorrupted path,
> Where is the need for confusion - Oh lass Kudambai?
> Where is the need for confusion?
>
> For those who have seen the top and bottom of 'IT',
> Where is the need for disputation - Oh lass Kudambai?
> Where is the need for disputation?

CHAPTER FIFTEEN: RELUCTANT MASTERS

For those who remain in contemplation, bereft of sleep,
Where is the need for Mudra - Oh lass Kudambai?
Where is the need for Mudra?

For those who stand in mystical ground,
Where is the need for Mantra - Oh lass Kudambai?
Where is the need for Mantra?

For those who are in real penance,
Where is the need for sacrificial fire - Oh lass Kudambai?
Where is the need for sacrificial fire?

For those who reach the core inhering awareness,
Where is the need for withering - Oh lass Kudambai?
Where is the need for withering?

For those real Gnani who mastered the trinity of Tamil,
Where is the need for blabbering - Oh lass Kudambai?
Where is the need for blabbering?

For those reaching beyond the peak, who have seen Supreme Expanse,
Where is the need for earthly cravings - Oh lass Kudambai?
Where is the need for earthly cravings?

For those who have seen Ethereal Light by searing without burns,
Where is the need to end passions - Oh lass Kudambai?
Where is the need to end passions?

For those who go in ways unique, crossing without dying,
Where is the need for solitude - Oh lass Kudambai?
Where is the need for solitude?

SECTION FOUR: RELUCTANT MASTERS

For those liberated, who are dancing in Space,
Where is the need for magic - Oh lass Kudambai?
Where is the need for magic?

For those poised in awareness, who brim in bliss,
Where is the need for knowledge - Oh lass Kudambai?
Where is the need for knowledge?

For those who see daily the picturised drama,
Where is the need for documentation - Oh lass Kudambai?
Where is the need for documentation?

For those who as Gnani, emerge from triangle in oneself,
Where is the need for six-pointed triangle - Oh lass Kudambai?
Where is the need for six-pointed triangle? (Yantra)

For the Head who dancing all eight direction,
Where is the need for imitation - Oh lass Kudambai?
Where is the need for imitation?

For the real Gnani who attained liberation and abides as Self,
Where is the need for diet rules - Oh lass Kudambai?
Where is the need for diet rules?

For those who cast aside sorrow,
Where is the need for palanquin - Oh lass Kudambai?
Where is the need for palanquin?

For the real Gnanis who master Astanga Yoga,
Where is the need for props - Oh lass Kudambai?
Where is the need for props?

CHAPTER FIFTEEN: RELUCTANT MASTERS

For those real Gnanis in whom subsided all urges,
Where is the need for Yoga - Oh lass Kudambai?
Where is the need for Yoga?

For those being in mountain, who conquered objectifying identity,
Where is the need for hearing compliments - Oh lass Kudambai?
Where is the need for hearing compliments?

For the real Gnanis who wander like the dead,
Where is the need for cymbals - Oh lass Kudambai?
Where is the need for cymbals?

For those who poised in IT, which is Seeing,
Where is the need for rejoice - Oh lass Kudambai?
Where is the need for rejoice?

For those who realised of the 'core', conquering death,
Where is the need for further undertakings - Oh lass Kudambai?
Where is the need for further undertakings?

There where is [1]onion, [2]pepper and [3]dry ginger,
Where is the need for eatables- Oh lass Kudambai?
Where is the need for eatables?

1,2,3-these cryptic words symbolise the trinity of philosophers stone or elixir.

For those who remain in the mountain, dining the juice of mango,
Where is the need for coconut milk - Oh lass Kudambai?
Where is the need for coconut milk?

SECTION FOUR: RELUCTANT MASTERS

For those who wander around town in day time,
Where is the need for covering - Oh lass Kudambai?
Where is the need for covering?

For those who don't have a sloping roof and house of their own,
Where is the need for gospel chanting - Oh lass Kudambai?
Where is the need for gospel chanting?

For those who reached the Supreme by realising oneself,
Where is the need for residual desires - Oh lass Kudambai?
Where is the need for residual desires?

For those who remain as the way to God,
Where is the need for direction - Oh lass Kudambai?
Where is the need for direction?

ಙ ಆ

ANNEXURE 1

A tribute to my Guru Lineage

Each Siddha teacher has his own style, but now a days most of them speak of the yogic way - attaining the truth that is somewhere far away. But, Thiruvadi (the holy-feet tradition), which is my Guru lineage, is different. My Guru always said, "...primal intelligence is already within and that is what fortifies the growth of the embryo and life after birth. We emphasise God as dynamic (Chit), not only static..."

THE DYNAMICS OF US

Spider

Spiders have been found even two-and-a-half miles up in the air, and 1,000 miles out to sea. Certain spiders can travel through the air from one place to another even though they do not have wings, using a behaviour called 'ballooning'. From an exposed point, they raise their abdomens to the sky, extrude strands of silk, and float away. Ballooning helps them to flee from predators or rivals, or carries them toward new regions and abundant resources. Darwin himself found the rapidity of the spiders' flight to be "quite unaccountable" and its cause to be "inexplicable." Research shows that spiders sense the Earth's electric field, and use it to launch themselves into the air. Forty thousand thunderstorms crackle around the world even on sunny days and cloudless skies turning the Earth's atmosphere into a giant electrical circuit. The upper reaches of the atmosphere have a positive charge, and the planet's surface has a negative one. Ballooning spiders operate within this planetary electric field. The silk that leaves their bodies, typically picks up a negative charge, which repels the similar negative charges on the surfaces on which the spiders sit, creating enough force to lift them into the air. Spiders increase those forces by climbing onto twigs, leaves, or blades of grass. Plants, being earthed, have the same negative charge as the ground that they grow upon, but they protrude into the positively charged air. This creates substantial electric fields between the air around them and the tips of their leaves and branches—and the spiders ballooning from those tips. The idea of flight by electrostatic repulsion uses various electric-field strengths from the environment to affect the physics of takeoff, flight, and landing.

Golden Plover

According to the common ways of evolution migratory birds fly to a better climate, moving a little further north or south each year according to the changes in climate. The Golden Plover, a small sized shore bird, breaks that rule. About the size of a dove, it is not a swimmer. It lives up in the arctic in Alaska where it lays its eggs. Once the eggs hatch it leaves the young ones and migrates directly to Hawaii for the winter. Alaska to Hawaii is an 88 hour non-stop

ANNEXURE 1

flight because there is no land in between. How does the Golden Plover fly three days and four nights nonstop?

It begins to eat until it gains about 70 grams of burnable energy. But there is still a problem. This bird burns energy at exactly 1 gm per hour which gives them 70 hours worth of fuel and the flight is a total of 88 hours, in which case it would drop into the ocean to it's death. The survival intelligence of this bird makes them fly in a formation and alternates leaders which breaks the air waves and makes it easy. It's not uncommon for birds of that size to loose 50% of their total body weight as fat being burned up along their migration routes. It's an incredible feat. It is similar to a 100 pound human losing 50 pounds in a 5 day period as they travel across the world which they cant actually do. Another interesting thing is that the parent birds fly to Hawaii after their eggs hatch leaving their young ones to eat and grow and gain their 70 grams of fat buildup. But the young ones have never been to Hawaii before, so how do they navigate and know where to go? Even when they miss the route due to side winds that blow them off course, they still are able to arrive at the exact same location every year accurate to an area the size of a room, after crossing thousands of miles.

At the core of every living form are a host of movements that connect it to the Cosmos and ensure its survival. The universal life-force fuels every living form with individual life energy through these existential movements. Sustenance in the world depends upon the proper function of the EMs. Every living form has a unique set of EMs which allow it to receive universal life force and exhibit survival and evolutionary behaviours that define its place in the natural world. Scientists continue to discover more and more unique behaviours exhibited by plant, animal, insects, and birds but all of it is aimed toward propagation and survival of its species. Humans in that sense are designed a little differently. According to the Siddhas, Man is a microcosm, capable of every behaviour a macrocosm exhibits. The path of the Siddhas is about realising this. We can attune to our distinctive cosmic connect and grow closer to the source, through existential movements because, the primal life force of the Universe is dynamic.

Humans are the only species that can do more than just survive. Humans can influence the basic behavioural patterns by acquiring new habits. Even though humans depend upon the existential movements of breathing, eating, reproducing, protecting our young for individual as well as evolutionary survival, we by our lifestyle and new habits collect impurities that corrupts them. Acquired conditioning more often than not veils the human potential, which is what spiritual traditions help us tap into and discover. The spiritual path comes into play only when a human being feels the need for more than just survival-related existence. The Siddhas begin with the body to do so.

As the acquired conditioning gradually drops, it unveils the natural potential of the human body and eventually leads deeper and beyond, to the universal source until the source itself can freely manifest itself within the human frame. This path is called Vasi in the Siddha Tradition. Siddha-hood or immortality and the universal creative spirit carry unlimited possibilities and potential which are not available at the basic survival cycle level. In the Minimalistic Movement practice we first begin to perceive our connection with our own body. Our dulled sensitivity is awakened so that you can experience your place in Nature and connect to the whole because of which we live meaningfully with a clear understanding of our purpose. If u go out of station for work but your boss doesn't tell you the exact purpose of your visit, how successful do you think your visit will be? If a golden plover didn't gain the 70 grams of fat would he reach Hawaii? If each living form fulfils its design to connect to the whole, it not only sustains, but flourishes to fullest

ANNEXURE 1

potential. A golden plover is defined by its journey, and we by our dharma? Humans seem to be more complex and have more individualistic expressions and possibilities. Getting in touch with it and living it is the personal journey.

Palpandian
Holy Hill

ಶೋ ಚ್ಞ

Palpandian now involves in guiding and teaching the Primal Movement based on the Thiruvadi lineage, where he facilitates our connect to existence and teaches how to re-root ourselves consciously. More about this can be found at www.thiruvadi.org

GLOSSARY

A

Adharam	Base
Aham	I
Agama	Literature of Tantra, Dravidians
Akasa	Space, Sky
Amritha	Ambrosia, Nectar
Anubhava	Experience
Andam	Cosmos
Anahatam	Cardiac plexus in heart region
Agnai	Pineal plexus
Apana	Downward moving air element
Arul	Grace
Avadhoota	Literally a 'non – messenger'
Agni	Fire
Amla (nellikai)	Gooseberry, a sour fruit
Ardhanareeswara	The form of half Shiva & half Sakthi combined (equal combination of both masculine & feminine aspect)
Asana	Posture
Asura	Literally means Demon; symbol of Ignorance
Avathar	Divine Incarnation
Asuddha	Impure
Ahamkara	Individuating Principle, The power of identification

B

Bakthi	Devotion
Brahma	The ruling deity of Hypogastric Plexus, the Creator
Bindu	Literally it means Point, Centripetal force
Buddhi	Intellect
Bhuta	Element
Bala varga	One of the lineage of ancient Siddhas, founder as Lord Murugan
Brahmarandhra	Entrance, aperture to the Ultimate
Brahman	The Absolute, The Ultimate

C

Chandra	Moon
Chandra kalai	Path of Moon; frontal line of energy pathway in human body (in this book)
Chit	Pure consciousness
Chittar	One who abides as pure consciousness
Chakra/chakram	Plexus; energy centres
Chinmudra	The forefinger rests on the thumb; other fingers are separate & open

D

Dharma	Inherent order of existence
Dosham	Humor
Dhyanam	Meditation; the whole perception beyond intellect
Dwadhasantham	Literally the twelfth place; the place where Ultimate Yogic experience occurs

G

Ganapathi	A male deity ruling basal energy center
Gathi	Gait
Gnana/Gnanam	Wisdom/realisation
Guru	Master
Gnanendriya	Senses of perception

H

Hridaya	Heart

I

Idam	This
Ida Nadi	A major energy channel running on the left side of the body through which the nature of passion predominantly works.
Indriya	Sense powers; senses

J

Japa	Repetition of a holy name; Mantra
Jothi	Light
Jiva	Individual soul

K

Kan	Eye
Kala/Kaala	Time
Kumbha Kalasha	Pot used in sacrificial ceremony
Kalai	Fragmentary part; channel
Kalari	Ancient South Indian Martial Art System

Kapham	One of the three humors majorly dominated by water element
Karma	Law of action & reaction; binding force of action
Kaal	Literally leg; Prana in yogic terms
Karpagam	Wish fulfilling
Kundalini	The spiritual energy; also the energy not fully realised within the body
Kumbagam	Breath retention
Kriya	Action
Kaya Kalpam	Procedure in Siddha system for physical rejuvenation & longevity
Kovil	Temple
Kandam	Throat

L

Laxmi	Female deity ruling solar plexus energy center

M

Manas	Cosmic mind
Mana	Individual mind
Mahat	Primal intelligence
Mantharam/Mantra	Sacred Sounds
Moolavarga	One of the lineages of ancient Siddha founder as Thirumoolar
Maya	Illusion; cosmic delusion
Maya suzhi	Spot in the frontal position of forehead
Moksha	Liberation

Mukthi	Realisation (of truth); Salvation
Mudra	Symbolic gesture; particular gesture to channelise energy in yogic practice
Muladhar/Mooladharam	Pelvic plexus; basal chakra; first energy center
Maheswara	Male deity ruling the energy center in throat area; carotid plexus
Maheswari	Female deity ruling the energy center in throat area; carotid plexus
Moolagni	The fire in the base; Kundalini heat
Manonmani	Female deity ruling pineal plexus; energy center in the fore head
Muni	Ascetic
Muyalakan	A demon; symbol of ignorance
Maharishi	Great Seer

N

Nadi	Energy channel; pulse
Nada	Primal sound
Natarajar	Siva in dancing form
Niradharam	Without base
Nadanusandhana	Absorption in the inner sounds

O

Ojas	The part of ambrosia that upholds the seven basic tissues of the body & rejuvenates them
Om/Omkar	The cosmic vibration; sound or primal vibration at the time of Creation; also the Universal mantra

P

Paduka	Sandals of a Holy person
Panch Bhuthas	Five elements; sense particulars
Pitham/Pitta	One of the three humors; majorly dominated by the fire element
Poorvam	Here/beginning
Prakruthi	Cosmic substance/Primal substance
Purusha	Primal/cosmic spirit
Prana	Life force
Pingala Nadi	Main energy channel running on right side of the body through which the nature of 'will' predominantly works
Pindam	Body
Poorakam/Puraka	Inhalation; assimilation
Pranayama	Expansion of prana by breathing practice
Poorna/Purna	Fullness
Pooja	Ritual worship

R

Rishi Patni	Spiritual Wife
Rudra	Male deity ruling Heart center/plexus
Rudri	Female deity ruling Heart center/plexus
Rajasa/Rajas	Dynamic principle/attribute of nature
Rasa	Nourishing devoted mood
Rechaka/Resaka	Exhalation/depletion

S

Sadasiva	Male deity ruling pineal plexus in eyebrow center
Sadhaka	Spiritual aspirant

Sadhana	Spiritual practice
Saraswathi	Female deity ruling hypogastric plexus
Sahasradalam	Field of thousand petaled lotus; area on the top of the head
Samadhi	Merging with source(Sam + adhi)
Samadhi shrine	(i)Tomb of sage to be worshipped (ii)The place where the sage attained realisation & one can feel His presence
Sat	Being; existence
Samskara	Mental impressions
Satva	The harmony (or) balancing nature of 3 attributes; illuminating attribute of nature
Sahasrarm	Axis of the thousand petaled lotus above Suzhi Munai or Agnai Chakra
Sakthi	Goddess/Female deity/Universal power of consciousness
Siva	Male Deity; God; Pure consciousness
Sivam	The Source; The Ultimate
Sastra	An authoritative treatise on any subject
Sri chakra	Symbolic composition/representation of the universal power (Sakthi)
Swadhistanam	The second energy center; hypogastric plexus
Summa Iru	Just be; denoting non activity
Siddha	Person who attained perfection
Suddha	Pure; unpolluted
Sahaja manush	Spontaneous man or person
Siddhi	perfection; psychic powers
Sthula	Gross

GLOSSARY

Sushumna/Sushamza	Central channel anterior to the spinal cord
Suzhi munai	The center of vortex on the end of central channel (true agnai chakra)
Suksma	subtle
Sutra	Axiom
Surya	Sun
Surya Kalai	Path of Sun as the posterior line in the human body
Surya saram	Solar breath; right nostril breath
Sanjeevi	Ever living
Suddhi	Purification
Swara Yoga	A branch of ancient yogic system dealing with the science of the breath cycle

T

Tamil	Language spoken by the people living in the state of Tamil Nadu in India
Tamasa	The restraining quality of the three attributes in nature
Tanmatra	Subtle elements
Tattvas	Principle of cosmic evolution
Tantra	The spiritual path that gives importance to the human faculty of passion/emotions/feelings; also 'weaving nature'
Tapas	Self discipline in austerity; intense penance
Tejas	Lustre or brilliance
Trimurti	The Holy Trinity: Lord Siva/Lord Vishnu & Lord Brahma

U

Upanishad	Ancient pedantic scripture of India
Upasana	Worship of personal deity with a specific procedure
Uma	Consort of Siva
Utharam	Beyond/above
Udukkai	A mini drum
Upadesha	Personal spiritual instruction

V

Vaasi (yoga)	Primal pulsation; primordial esoteric breathing practice unique to Siddha tradition; (not classical pranayam)
Valam	(in Sanskrit pradakshina); a clockwise circumambulation of a holy place or holy person
Vasal	Gate
Visuddhi	Energy center in throat area; carotid plexus
Varma	Vital Spot
Vallabai	Female deity ruling the first energy center in pelvic area
Vedas	Ancient scriptures in Sanskrit language
Vishnu	Male deity ruling solar plexus energy center
Vedanta	Culmination of Vedic philosophy
Vatha/Vatham	One of the three humors majorly dominated by Air element

Y

Yantra	(Geometrical) symbol representing Sakthi
Yoga	Literally it means 'Union'; A spiritual path that gives exclusive importance to the human faculty of 'will'

ೞ ಢ

APPENDIX

Names of Samadhi Shrines I have visited or heard of from reliable sources

Meenakshi Amman Temple	Sri Vidya as the Goddess & Siva as Ellam Valla Siddhar, Madurai
Mayandi Swamigal	Thiru Koodal Malai
Somappa Swamigal	Thiru Koodal Malai
Kugai Kovil	Then paran Kundram
Nadana Gopala Nuyogi Swamigal	Kaatha Kinaru
Gorakkar Samadhi	Adhi Gorrakanath Temple, Thiruppuvanam
Mahalingam Malai	The tapas realm of the ancient Siddhas (Chaturagiri Mountain), Vathra Gruppu.
Valla Naatu Siddhar	Valla Naadu
Vishwamithra Ashram	Vijayapuri
Nambi Malai	Thaipaadham, Thiru kurung Kudi
Kudambai Siddhar Tapovanam	Nambimalai

APPENDIX

Velambika Samadhi (woman Siddhar)	Bottom of Mahendra Giri Mountain
Bogar Peedam	Mahendra Giri Mountain
Bogar Samadhi Shrine	Palani
Eswara pattar Samadhi Shrine	Idumban Malai
Thiru Uddhara Kosa Mangai Temple	Ancient Tantric spot, Uddhara Kasa Mangai
Satti Swamigal Samadhi Shrine	Uddhara Kasa Mangai
Chellapa Swamigal	Ekka Kudi
Patanjali Peedam	Rameshwaram
Kolli Malai	Ancient mysterious mountain of the ancient Siddhas, Kolli Malai
Kaalanginathar Peedam	Kanchamalai
Mangai Mahali (Varahi) Temple	Uddhara Kosa Mangai
Saint Ramalingam, Vallalar Sathya Gnani Sabai	Vadalur
Natarajar Temple	Chidambaram
Ramanujar Shrine	Sri Rangam
Sada Siva Brahmendrar Samadhi Shrine	Nerur
Ramana Ashramam	Thiru annamali
Mathru Budheshwarar Temple	Ramana Ashramam (Sri chakra mehru continuing presence)
Yogi Ramsurat Kumar Ashramam	Thiru annamalai
Seshadri Ashram	Thiru annamalai
Adi Mudi Siddhar	Thiru annamalai

Virupaksha cave &	Skandaashramam, on Thiru annamalai
	Gugai NamaSivar shrine
Esanya Desikar Math	Thiru annamalai
Ammani Amma Samadhi Shrine (woman Siddhar)	Thiru annamalai
Gaudhamar Maharishi Shrine	Thiru annamalai
Poondi Mahan Shrine	Poondi
Paravadha Malai	
Velliangi Malai	
Pattinathar Samadhi Shrine	Thiruvotriyar
Kamaakshi Amman Temple	Kanchipuram
Saradha Ambal Temple	Shrikeri
Sri Sailam	Andhra Pradesh
Sri Ragavendra Temple	Mantralayam
Aggalkote Maharaj	Aggalkote
Gnaneshwar Shrine	Alandi
Shirdi Sai Baba	Shirdi
Upasani Maharaj	Sarkuri
Gajanam Maharaj	Nasik
Lord Venkateshwara	Thirupatti
Alagar Kovil	Madurai
Narasimha peetam, Ramadevar Siddhar	
Agasthiyar Temple	Papanasam
Agasthiyar Kudil	Karaiyar Dam
Khwaja Mohaidheen	Ajmer
Tattha Peedam	Girnar

Sivanandar Paramhamsa Samadhi shrine	Vadakara, Kerala
Bagavadhi Amman Temple	Chottani karai
Mohambigai Temple	Kallur
Renugambal Temple (Chinnamastha Goddess)	Padaiveedu
Kumari Amman (Goddess Valai)	Kanya Kumari
Pancha Lingam	Thiru chendur
Er Vadi Darga	Ervadi
Beer Mohammed	Thakkalai
Mouni Swami Samadhi Shrine	Nambi malai
Muthu Vaduganathar Temple	Singampunari
Kaamagya	Orissa
Taajudhi Baba	
Baba John	Nagpur
Naga Dheertham	Nagamalai
Gopal Swami Samadhi Shrine	Ramnad
Kulandaiya Nandhar Samadhi Shrine	Madurai
Reddiya Patti Swami	Reddiyapatti
Mouna Guru Swami Shrine	Kasavanampatti
Tayumnavar Swami Shrine	Ramnad
Mayamma Samadhi Shrine	Salem
Kodi Swami Shrine	
Ananda Mai Ma	Rishikesh
Ramakrishna Parmahamsar	Dakshineshwar Temple
Saadhu Appadhovai	Thirukonamalai, Sri Lanka
Yogar Swami Shrine	Sri Lanka
Chellapa Swamigal Shrine	Sri Lanka

Kadaiyil Swami, Natarajar Shrine	Sri Lanka
Ancient Murugan Temple	Katthir Kaamam, Sri Lanka
Muruganar Manthiram	Ramnad
Sadhu Om Samadhi Shrine	Thiru annamalai
Ramana Manthiram	Madurai
Sundara Manthiram	Thiruchidi
Eral Arunachala Swami	Eral
Annamalai Swami	Thiru annamalai
Vido Ba Swami Samadhi Shrine	Bolur
Dakshina Murthi Swami	Thiruvaarur
Muthu Swami Dhikchithar Samadhi Shrine	Ettaiyapuram
Thiyagara Swamigal, Nada Brahmam	Thiruvaiyaru
Thirumoolar Peedam	Thiruvaaduthurai
Guru Namasivayar Samadhi Shrine	Arudaiyur Kovil
Chidambaram Swamigal (merged in temple shrine)	Thiruporur
Sundaresa Sarma Samadhi Shrine	Veera cholam
Dhatha peet	Gangapur
Naganath Temple	Nayinar Kovil

೮೦ ೦೩

Ingram Content Group UK Ltd.
Milton Keynes UK
UKHW010720130623
423368UK00001B/15